BACK-ALLEY
BANKING

BACK-ALLEY BANKING

Private Entrepreneurs in China

Kellee S. Tsai

Cornell University Press

ITHACA AND LONDON

First published 2002 by Cornell University Press

Printed in the United States of America

Library of Congress Cataloging-in-Publication Data
Tsai, Kellee S.
    Back-alley banking : private entrepreneurs in China / Kellee S. Tsai.
        p.   cm.
Includes bibliographical references and index.
    ISBN 0-8014-3928-0 (cloth : alk. paper)
    1. Finance—China.   2. Financial institutions—China.   3. Informal
sector (Economics)—China.   4. Banks and banking—China.   I. Title.
    HG187.C6   T726   2002
    330—dc21   2002000007

Cornell University Press strives to use environmentally responsible
suppliers and materials to the fullest extent possible in the publishing
of its books. Such materials include vegetable-based, low-VOC inks
and acid-free papers that are recycled, totally chlorine-free, or partly
composed of nonwood fibers. For further information, visit
our website at www.cornellpress.cornell.edu.

Cloth printing   10 9 8 7 6 5 4 3 2 1

For my mother

The Brownian motion of social life—the emergence of destabilizing opportunity out of stabilizing methods—provides the occasion for influences that may shape long-term context change. These influences, working in concert or in opposition, account for a remarkable possibility. Contexts may change in quality as well as content. They vary in the force with which they imprison the people who move within them.

—Roberto Unger, *Politics: The Central Texts,* 1997

Contents

Preface

Any traveler in China today sees a rowdy, rapidly growing private sector. What she won't see is how that growth has been financed. Since the late 1970s, tens of millions of private entrepreneurs have started new businesses without access to formal sources of credit. The story of how they achieved this improbable feat is fundamentally political and has implications for how we think about economic growth in developing and transitional economies. Rather than waiting for officials in Beijing to sanction private financial institutions or establish reliable property rights for commerce, China's entrepreneurs have mobilized political and social resources at the grassroots level to finance themselves.

This book is about the murky and largely illegal world of informal finance. It draws on nearly two years of fieldwork over the course of 1994 to 2001. The research had three components: (1) administering an original survey to microentrepreneurs in Fujian, Zhejiang, and Henan; (2) conducting interviews with government officials, bank managers, local bureaucrats, and academics; and (3) gathering documents relating to finance, private enterprise, and local economic conditions. The survey process, conducted over an eighteen-month period in 1996 and 1997, was especially challenging. When I showed up in various towns and villages with a stack of word-processed questionnaires, private entrepreneurs were skeptical that someone would actually be interested in learning about their experiences with no regulatory strings attached.

"Did the Industrial and Commercial Management Bureau send you here?" the street vendor in Anxi, Fujian, asked suspiciously.

"No, I'm just collecting information for a research project."

"Well then, I don't have to answer your questions, do I?"

"If you aren't too busy I could really use your help for my research."

The storeowner glanced at the bundle of surveys. "What are you going to do with those forms?"

"I'm using them to interview private entrepreneurs."

"And then what?"

The suspicions and fears of my informants were understandable. Microentrepreneurs in China expend tremendous energy in dealing with the staff of the state. On a typical day a vegetable vendor may be approached, and perhaps harassed, by cadres from the Industrial and Commercial Management Bureau, Sanitation Bureau, Public Security Bureau, local tax department, and other bureaucrats charged with monitoring and taxing those engaged in the most vibrant part of China's economy, the private sector. Minding one's own business is not a practical option for staying in business. It seemed odd that I requested only their time, not cash or political compliance.

After administering 374 surveys and conducting 186 official interviews, I had answered my basic question many times over. In the absence of access to conventional sources of capital, private entrepreneurs have devised an amazing array of informal financing mechanisms, ranging from interest-free interpersonal lending and rotating credit associations to more institutionalized financial intermediaries such as private "money houses" and credit cooperatives. Most of these credit facilities are creatively organized, community-based, and convenient for small business owners. Most are also explicitly banned by the People's Bank of China. The ability of such nongovernmental financial institutions to survive and adapt reveals fundamental limits on the capacity of the party-state to regulate the supply of credit in the economy. While informal finance has certainly played a productive role in fueling private sector development, at times it has also compromised stability at the local level. Informal finance is not only essential to the private sector but politically sensitive and, in many cases, deeply personal. My greatest debt therefore goes to the hundreds of private entrepreneurs and informants who are listed anonymously in Appendixes B and C. I have tried to present their experiences and perspectives with minimal normative and methodological distortion.

The surveys, formal interviews, and document-gathering processes were facilitated by Qu Hongliang at the Fujian Academy of Social Sciences (1994, 1996–97), He Daming at the Henan Academy of Social Sciences (1996–97), institutional affiliation at the Chinese University of Hong Kong's University Service Centre (1994, 1996–97), and Hong Kong University's Centre for Asian Studies (1997). My research and writing were supported by fellowships from the following sources: Columbia University's Department of Political Science (1993–99), the Ford Foundation Workshop on Research and Research Methods in the Developing World (1994–95), the Committee on Scholarly Communication with China of the American Council for Learned Societies (ACLS) (1996–97), the Fulbright-Hays Doctoral Dissertation Research Abroad program (1996–97), and the Harvard Academy for International and Area Studies (1997–99). I thank all of them for their generosity.

My two years at the Harvard Academy for International and Area Studies provided an intellectually stimulating environment for writing the earliest version of this book. As a Kukin Fellow, I received valuable feedback from participants in the Comparative and International Political Economy Workshop, cofacilitated by Alberta Alesina, Peter Hall, Jeffry Friedan, Lisa Martin, and Steve Vogel; the Performance of Democracies Workshop, cofacilitated by Jorge Dominguez, Grzegorz Ekiert, Robert Putnam, and Steve Vogel; the Fairbank Center East Asian Colloquium, coordinated by Merle Goldman; the China Business Project Breakfast, organized by Ezra Vogel; and the Harvard Academy itself, led by Samuel Huntington. I am grateful to the workshop organizers and participants.

Many other people offered constructive and critical commentary on various sections of the manuscript. For reading my work in progress, I thank Robert Bates, Mark Blyth, Davis Bookhart, Alexander Cooley, Sara Friedman, David Kang, Steven Liebo, Hue-Tam Ho Tai, Laurel Kendall, Jean Oi, James Ron, Steve Solnick, Bridget Welsh, Wu Jieh-min, Li Zhang, and members of our "rotating writing and reading association" in Cambridge, Massachusetts (1997–98)—Benjamin Read, Elizabeth Remick, Adam Segal, Eric Thun, and Lily Tsai. At Columbia, Professors Thomas Bernstein, Myron Cohen, Andrew Nathan, Richard Nelson, and Madeleine Zelin also provided thoughtful suggestions. My mentors, Andrew Nathan and Thomas Bernstein, were exceptionally persistent and patient.

I have also benefited from conversations and correspondence with many people, including Louis Augustin-Jean, Richard Baum, Thomas Berger, Joseph Bosco, Isabel Crook, Michael Crook, Cui Zhiyuan, Richard Doner, Du Xiaoshan, Nancy Hearst, Hsu Sze-chien, Jean Hung, Devesh Kapur, Stephen McGurk, Liu Wenpu, Roderick MacFarquar, Michael Montesano, Albert Park, Florence Padovani, Elizabeth Perry, Dorothy Solinger, Tao Yi-feng, Ren Changqing, Jay Rosengard, Tony Saich, Kaja Sehrt, Patricia Thornton, Ezra Vogel, Wang Xiaoyi, Andrew Watson, and Wing Thye Woo.

The final phases of writing were done while I was employed as an assistant professor in the Department of Political Science at Emory University (1999–2000) and Johns Hopkins (2000–01). Roger Haydon was instrumental in this process, providing timely feedback with good humor, as were the excellent comments of Hill Gates and an anonymous reader, William Connolly's guidance, and Laura Locker's careful assistance in indexing.

The *China Quarterly* has kindly allowed me to use some of the material originally published as "Banquet Banking: Gender and Rotating Savings and Credit Associations in South China," *China Quarterly*, no. 161 (March 2000): 143–70.

On a more personal note, my family deserves gratitude for tolerating my work habits. I thank Davis Bookhart, who introduced me to my first team of research assistants in Fuzhou and saw me through the research, writing, and rewriting process. My sister Linda made sure that New York continued to be home long after I had left. And finally, I am grateful to my parents, especially my mother, Katherine Tsai, who inspired my interest in the topic, never lost confidence in the value of the project, and always goes far beyond the call of motherhood to help out in every way imaginable. She is a truly remarkable woman.

K. S. T.

Baltimore, Maryland

Abbreviations

ABOC	Agricultural Bank of China
ADB	Agricultural Development Bank
AFP	Agence France-Presse
AIDIS	All-India Debt and Investment Survey
AX	Anxi County, Fujian Province
BAAC	Bank of Agriculture and Agricultural Cooperatives (Thailand)
BIMAS	Bimbigan Massal (Mass guidance)
BRAC	Bangladesh Rural Advancement Committee
BRI	Bank Raykyat Indonesia
CASS	Chinese Academy of Social Sciences
CBT	Cooperative Bank of Taiwan
CCB	China Construction Bank
CCP	Chinese Communist Party
CGAP	Consultative Group to Assist the Poorest
CITIC	China International Trust and Investment Company
CL	Changle County/City
CMA	(People-run) Capital Mutual Assistance Association
CPPCC	Chinese People's Political Consultative Conference
CUHK	Chinese University of Hong Kong
FAO	Foreign Affairs Office
FASS	Fujian Academy of Social Sciences
FBIS-CHI	Foreign Broadcast Information Service—China
FDI	Foreign Direct Investment
FINCA	Foundation for International Community Assistance

FJ	Fujian Province
FJNJ	*Fujian tongji nianjian* (Fujian statistical yearbook)
FPC	*Fupin* (Helping the Poor) Cooperative
FZ	Fuzhou, Fujian Province
FZNJ	*Fuzhou tongji nianjian* (Fuzhou statistical yearbook)
GB	Grameen Bank
GDP	Gross Domestic Product
GNP	Gross National Product
GVAO	Gross Value of Agricultural Output
GVIAO	Gross Value of Industrial and Agricultural Output
GVIO	Gross Value of Industrial Output
HA	Huian County, Fujian Province
HASS	Henan Academy of Social Sciences
HN	Henan Province
HNNJ	*Henan tongji nianjian* (Henan statistical yearbook)
HNRB	*Henan ribao* (Henan daily)
ICB	Industrial and Commercial Bank
ICCIC	International Committee for the Promotion of Chinese Industrial Co-operatives
ICMB	Industrial and Commercial Management Bureau
ILA	Individual Laborers' Association
IMF	International Monetary Fund
IO	International Organization
ITIC	International Trust and Investment Company
JJ	Jinjiang County/City, Fujian Province
JRNJ	*Jinrong tongji nianjian* (official translation: Almanac of China's finance and banking)
JV	Joint Venture
KF	Kaifeng City, Henan Province
KMT	Kuomintang
K-REP	Kenya Rural Enterprise Program
KTV	Karaoke TV
LY	Luoyang City, Henan Province
MAS	Ma'had Abhath As-Syasat Al-Iqtisadiyeh Al Filistini (Palestine Economic Policy Research Institute)
MFI	Microfinance Institution
MOA	Ministry of Agriculture
MOF	Ministry of Finance
NBFI	Nonbanking financial institution
NGO	Nongovernmental organization
NIC	Newly industrialized country
NPC	National People's Congress

PBOC	People's Bank of China
PEA	Private Entrepreneurs' Association
PLA	People's Liberation Army
PRC	People's Republic of China
PRCS	Pakistan Rural Credit Survey
QZ	Quanzhou Municipality/City, Fujian Province
RCA	Rotating Credit Association
RCC	Rural Credit Cooperative
RCF	Rural Cooperative Foundation
RDI	Rural Development Institute (in CASS)
RMB	*Renminbi* (Chinese currency)
RMRB	*Renmin ribao* (People's daily)
ROSCA	Rotating Savings and Credit Association
SCMP	*South China Morning Post*
SEZ	Special Economic Zone
SOE	State-owned Enterprise
TCCA	Tenth Credit Cooperative Association
TIC	Trust and Investment Company
TVE	Township and Village Enterprise
UCB	Urban Cooperative (Commercial) Bank (United City Bank)
UCC	Urban Credit Cooperative
UNDP	United Nations Development Programme
USAID	United States Agency for International Development
USIC	United Society of Industry and Commerce
WF	Women's Federation
WZ	Wenzhou City, Zhejiang Province
WZNJ	*Wenzhou tongji nianjian* (Wenzhou statistical yearbook)
ZJ	Zhejiang Province
ZZ	Zhengzhou City/Municipality, Henan Province

Note on Conversion of Key Measures and Romanization

The conversion of key measures is as follows:

1 *mu* of land = 0.0667 hectares or 1/6 acre
1 *jin* = 0.5 kilograms or 1.123 pounds
U.S.$1.00 = 8.278 *renminbi* (RMB) or *yuan* (as of 1998)

The *pinyin* system of Romanization is used throughout the text except in cases where the Wade-Giles term is more familiar.

BACK-ALLEY BANKING

1

The Power of Informal Institutions

> We must severely attack all actions in the financial arena that are
> illegal or in violation of regulations. We must guarantee that
> financial laws, regulations, and rules are implemented thoroughly.
> We must emphasize the prohibitions against banks using high
> interest rates to monopolize deposits, illegal fund-raising in
> society, and haphazard financial activities.
>
> —*Renmin ribao* (People's Daily), February 1, 1999

As financial turmoil swept through Asia in the late 1990s, Beijing
stoically announced that China would not devalue its currency. It would act
as a responsible member of the international economy and weather the
storm. Sure enough, the *renminbi* retained its value, and macroeconomic
indicators reveal that the Chinese economy emerged relatively unscathed
from the regional financial crisis.

Over the last two decades of the twentieth century, however, symptoms
of domestic financial malaise were in fact accumulating at the local level.
A vast underworld of informal financial intermediaries emerged in the
wake of economic liberalization. Moreover, official efforts to clamp down
on illegal financial practices and institutions had the perverse effect of triggering public expressions of discontent.[1] Consider the following incidents:

- November 1998, Zhengzhou, Henan: Over two thousand people stage
  a demonstration in the provincial capital after their savings are lost in
  a failed investment firm.

---

1. In July 1998 the State Council issued formal "Provisions on the Cancellation of Illegal
Financial Institutions and Activities," which stipulated (rather repetitively) that illegal financial institutions should be banned. See "Procedures for Banning Illegal Financial Institutions
and Illegal Financial Business Activities," *Xinhua News Agency*, July 22, 1998, reported in
FBIS-CHI-98-209.

- September 1999, suburbs of Changsha, Hunan: Some fifty demonstrations involving five thousand farmers are staged to protest the closure of two thousand branches of rural credit and savings foundations.
- November 1999, Chongqing: Three hundred protesters waving large portraits of Chairman Mao demonstrate against corruption after the collapse of a local investment firm.

This modest sampling of local crises reveals the dark, destabilizing side of informal finance in contemporary China. This is the side that makes conservatives in Beijing worry that the first two decades of economic reform proceeded too fast, that makes the party-state feel out of control. Private financial transactions can sabotage state efforts at controlling inflation, foster speculative capital investments, and, at the feared extreme, undermine the political legitimacy of the regime.

At the same time, it is apparent that informal finance has also played a productive developmental role in the economy. The private sector has clearly been the most vibrant part of China's economy since the initiation of economic reform in 1978. More than thirty million private businesses were established in the next two decades, but official state banks chiefly extend credit to state and collective enterprises, not private ones. As of the end of 2000, *less than 1 percent* of loans from the entire national banking system had gone to the private sector.[2] Business owners take their exclusion from formal sources of credit for granted.

When I surveyed private entrepreneurs, the question "Have you ever borrowed money from a bank?" typically elicited animated, if not condescending, responses. For example:

"Are you crazy? Private entrepreneurs can't get loans from banks!"

"I'm not literate, I have no collateral, and I'm not even registered as an urban resident in this city. Would *you* lend me money?"

And a favorite from a restaurant owner who laughed in my face:

"A state bank wouldn't give me a loan if Chairman Mao himself rose from the dead and told them to give me one!"

Such responses demand an answer to the question: How could an entire economic sector develop and flourish without access to the state-dominated banking system? If banks are not lending to private entrepreneurs, then how has China's "economic miracle" been financed?

The short answer: informal, and often illegal, finance. Private entrepreneurs rely on a cornucopia of informal financing practices. These range from casual interpersonal borrowing and trade credit among wholesalers

---

2. Calculated from Table 19.3 of the *Zhongguo tongji nianjian 2000* (China Statistical Yearbook).

and retailers to more institutionalized mechanisms such as rotating credit associations, grassroots credit cooperatives, and even full-service yet unsanctioned private banks. The sheer variety of informal financing options used by entrepreneurs is impressive and worthy of documentation for an empirical understanding of private-sector finance in reform-era China. Indeed, a study of such a central component of China's political economy is much needed. Western scholars have focused on the more salient dimensions of the economic reform process, and Chinese publications barely acknowledge informal finance. It is like the unattractive grease in the wheels of the transitional economy—necessary for movement, but no one really wants to call attention to it. Yet behind the precarious balance sheets of state banks and national statistics showing private-sector growth, everyday people are operating at the margins of legality. Millions of individuals have begged, borrowed, and stolen to create new businesses, new lives, and new challenges for the regime. Drawing on twenty-three months of fieldwork between 1994 and 2001, this book sheds light on how the deftly disguised world of informal finance has contributed to China's private-sector development since the late 1970s.

This book also shows that the dynamics of informal finance have implications for our understanding of China's contemporary political economy and, more broadly, the way we think about economic and institutional development. Informal finance is embedded in a larger untold story about private-sector growth in the absence of a developed system of property rights. Not only are China's business owners excluded from state banks, but their economic exchanges are only weakly protected by the rule of law, and in many cases their private financial transactions are technically illegal. These operational realities challenge conventional notions about the necessary conditions for economic growth. Economists associated with the influential property rights tradition of Douglass North, for example, might wonder why anyone would want to participate in China's transitional economy.[3] Scholars take for granted that the prosperity generated by Western capitalism rests on a clearly defined body of laws regulating the ownership, use, and transfer of assets. When consistently enforced, according to this view, property rights reduce the uncertainty and transaction costs of market exchanges, and provide economic actors with the information

3. James M. Buchanan, *Property as a Guarantor of Liberty* (Aldershot: Edward Elgar, 1993); Harold Demsetz, "Towards a Theory of Property Rights," *American Economic Review* 57, 2 (1967): 347–59; Douglass North and Robert P. Thomas, *The Rise of the Western World: A New Economic History* (New York: Cambridge University Press, 1976); Douglass North and Barry R. Weingast, "Constitutions and Commitment: The Evolution of Institutions Governing Public Choice in Seventeenth-Century England," *Journal of Economic History* 49, 4 (1989): 803–32; and Douglass North, *Institutions, Institutional Change, and Economic Performance* (New York: Cambridge University Press, 1990).

and incentives to maximize efficiency.[4] Consequently, some explain the persistence of Third World underdevelopment by its lack of formal property rights. Hernando de Soto, for example, argues that if the poor were legally permitted to accumulate, exhibit, and trade their informal wealth, they would be much richer.[5] In China, however, there *has* been a dramatic expansion of private economic activity. Financial entrepreneurs, private businesses, and discriminating consumers are accumulating, exhibiting, and trading their assets, both formal and informal. That this is occurring despite the nebulous nature of private property rights presents a challenge to conventional theories of capitalist growth.

The property rights perspective provides incomplete insight into China's transitional economy because its assumptions of economic rationality oversimplify the political and social context of real-life interactions. Instead of focusing on lack of transparency in property rights, this book explains how and why the private sector has flourished in certain parts of the country under apparently uncertain and risky circumstances. I do not dismiss the utility of developed property rights; I do suggest, however, that their causal logic should be redefined and tailored to China's actual conditions.[6] Within what has been called the ambiguous and vaguely defined character of property rights in China, political and economic actors have been able to devise mutually comprehensible agreements regarding the use and control of various assets.[7] Sometimes these agreements are explicitly contractual and become legally binding, as in the case of thirty-year leases for land-user rights. At other times, economic agreements represent bargained outcomes between local officials; preferential tax treatment for local collective enterprises is a common example. And in many forms of informal finance, the institutional arrangements reflect self-enforcing innovations by ordinary people who are unlikely to seek legal enforcement of their activities

4. Ronald H. Coase, "The Nature of the Firm," *Economica*, November 1937, 386–405; Coase, "Social Costs," *Journal of Law and Economics* 3 (October 1960): 1–44; Yoram Barzel, *Economic Analysis of Property Rights* (Cambridge: Cambridge University Press, 1989).

5. Hernando de Soto, *The Mysteries of Capital: Why Capitalism Triumphs in the West and Fails Everywhere Else* (New York: Basic Books, 2000). Cf. Mancur Olson, *Power and Prosperity: Outgrowing Communist and Capitalist Dictatorships* (New York: Basic Books, 2000).

6. A volume that does just that is Jean C. Oi and Andrew G. Walder, eds., *Property Rights and Economic Reform in China* (Stanford, Calif.: Stanford University Press, 1999). Cf. Hu Xiaobo, *Problems in China's Transitional Economy: Property Rights and Transitional Models*, East Asian Institute Occasional Paper no. 6 (Singapore: World Scientific/Singapore University Press, 1998).

7. David D. Li, "A Theory of Ambiguous Property Rights in Transition Economies: The Case of the Chinese Non-State Sector," *Journal of Comparative Economics* 23, 1 (1996): 1–19; Victor Nee and Sijin Su, "Local Corporatism and Informal Privatization in China's Market Transition," in Thomas Lyons and Victor Nee, eds., *The Economic Transformation of South China: Reform and Development in the Post-Mao Era* (Ithaca: Cornell University East Asia Program, 1994); Martin Weitzman and Chenggang Xu, "Chinese Township-Village Enterprises as Vaguely Defined Cooperatives," *Journal of Comparative Economics* 18 (1994): 121–45.

because they are illegal in the first place. Ultimately, there is a vast gray area between ideal-typical property rights–observing economies and impoverished countries with imperfect legal systems, and much of East and Southeast Asia's growth falls into that category. Informal finance is a vital yet typically neglected part of the story.

In order to specify the actual workings of informal finance in China, this book is structured around three thematic questions: (1). *The popularity of informal finance despite its illegality*: Given that the central government forbids private financial institutions, how have entrepreneurs managed to create unofficial alternatives to state banks? (2). *Local variation in informal finance*: Given that private entrepreneurs all over China share the structural condition of restricted access to formal bank credit, why do some localities harbor a colorful range of informal financial intermediaries, while other localities have barely any at all? (3). *Variation in private entrepreneurs' use of informal finance*: Why do entrepreneurs with similar capital constraints, operating in the same area, employ vastly different types of financing strategies? The following chapters provide rich empirical answers to these questions, but the questions themselves have important analytical implications.

First, the disjuncture between official state regulations and the popularity of informal finance suggests that the financial capacity of the state in China is not as strong as one might expect, given its authoritarian mode of governance. Informal finance is thriving, and official funds are leaking out of the state banking system despite the potentially extreme penal consequences.

Second, the variation in the local supply of private finance challenges the notion that similar macro-level economic constraints will yield similar solutions. Even though the private sector as a whole shares limited access to the formal financial system, the actual expression of informal finance varies widely across localities. Instead of institutional isomorphism, there is remarkable institutional diversity.[8] Some localities have a limited range of informal financial institutions, while others have a myriad of private credit facilities. I attribute this variation to local governments' orientation toward private businesses and, hence, their degree of tolerance for the unusual institutional camouflage that private financial intermediaries often have to wear.

---

8. One branch of organizational theory expects institutions to become more similar to one another as a result of competitive and adaptive pressures. See Marco Orrù, Nicole Woolsey Biggart, and Gary H. Hamilton, "Organizational Isomorphism in East Asia," in Walter W. Powell and Paul J. DiMaggio, eds., *The New Institutionalism in Organizational Analysis* (Chicago: University of Chicago Press, 1991), 361–62. This argument is also made in Paul J. DiMaggio and Walter W. Powell, "The Iron Cage Revisited: Institutional Isomorphism and Collective Rationality in Organizational Fields," *American Sociological Review* 48 (April 1983): 147–60.

Third, the variation in entrepreneurs' choice of financing practices derives from the micro-logic of institutional choice and market segmentation at the grassroots level. Two business owners operating at the same scale, in the same locality, may use completely different types of informal finance because they draw on different social networks and political resources. Although some forms of informal finance rely primarily on economic selection criteria and enforcement mechanisms (e.g., business performance and the use of collateral and interest rates), most informal credit arrangements also involve a combination of social pressure, goodwill, and trust among the participants. In other words, the noneconomic characteristics of entrepreneurs matter in the world of informal finance.

In exploring these three issues, this book demonstrates that informal micro-level interactions have macro-level consequences—and, relatedly, considers why the state has repeatedly attempted to eliminate something that is actually essential to the economy. Institutional development is not merely a top-down process, neatly reproducing the official mandates of the center. Political and economic realities at the local level distort the implementation of national policies.[9] The assumed market logic of financial transactions is actually mediated by a political and social logic. The creation and use of private finance are not purely market-driven, even when they occur beyond the scope of the state.

The Political Production of Informal Finance

The overarching question of this book concerns the paradox of institutional creation in a politically and financially repressive environment. How are entrepreneurs even able to create unofficial alternatives to state banks when the central government explicitly forbids private financial institutions? The People's Republic of China (PRC) remains an authoritarian, Communist party-state that monopolizes not only the legitimate use of force in the Weberian sense but also the legitimate distribution of capital in the economy. Powerful nationalistic and ideological reasons were articulated during the Mao era for public ownership and allocation of capital. Before the socialist state withered away, it had to defend its borders from "imperialist invaders" and expunge the "capitalist bourgeoisie" from within. Although this ideological imperative has now faded, concerns for maintaining macroeconomic (and therefore political) stability have

9. Joel S. Migdal, Atul Kohli, and Vivienne Shue, eds., *State Power and Social Forces: Domination and Transformation in the Third World* (New York: Cambridge University Press, 1994); Kevin O'Brien and Lianjiang Li, "Selective Policy Implementation in Rural China," *Comparative Politics* 31, 2 (1999): 167–86.

rendered monetary control no less pressing. The party-state still dominates the financial system and still deploys ideological rhetoric at times to justify this domination. Yet finance capitalists systematically eliminated by the Communist revolution—either through domestic persecution or by being driven abroad to Hong Kong, Taiwan, and other parts of Southeast Asia— have reappeared. After a four-decade hiatus the back-alley loan sharks, pawnbrokers, and professional financiers are back in business; further- more, additional players are offering new and creative financial services. How is this possible?

Neoclassical economists might suggest that the emergence of informal finance is a natural product of market mechanisms. The elementary laws of supply and demand expect alternative sources of finance to appear as long as the official supply of credit falls short of actual market demand for credit. Because official state banks are institutionally biased toward extending soft loans to state-owned enterprises, they are unable to meet the financing needs of private businesses. Thus, most economists would not be surprised to find that profit-motivated entrepreneurs have risen to tap a structurally available market. As one factory manager turned loanshark put it, "The state factory doesn't really need me, but the local entrepre- neurs do. Lending money is a better use of my talents, time—and money." Informal finance, or what economists call the "curb market," is a universal phenomenon. Even advanced industrialized countries harbor substantial pockets of curb market activity to serve those excluded from the formal financial system for reasons of credit history, gender, ethnicity, and legal status. This economic explanation makes intuitive sense, and its theoreti- cal parsimony helps explain the existence of informal finance during China's reform era. It remains unclear, however, how curb market opera- tors are able to flourish under the glare of the party-state. In other words, the intellectual progeny of Adam Smith can account quite well for the demand for additional finance in the economy, but their determinist logic fails to explain the ability of ordinary economic actors to supply private- sector finance. Why did the state not crush China's flourishing informal markets?

Politics is the largest chunk of the puzzle missing from the free-market economic paradigm, because capital markets are not in fact free in China, or in most other parts of the world for that matter. Karl Polanyi and many other scholars have observed the irony that the most liberalized economies entail extensive intervention by a regulatory state.[10] The United States and Britain represent archetypal historical examples of this phenomenon. A

10. Karl Polanyi, *The Great Transformation: The Political and Economic Origins of Our Time* (Boston: Beacon Press, 1944). Cf. Steven K. Vogel, *Freer Markets, More Rules: Regulatory Reform in Advanced Industrial Countries* (Ithaca: Cornell University Press, 1996).

liberalized financial system requires the highly visible hand of the state to hold the invisible hand of the market. The mature capitalist state preserves a competitive market environment and ensures the reliability of profit-oriented transactions by serving as the ultimate third-party enforcer of contractual exchanges, deploying punitive recourse when property rights are violated. The party-state in China has not reached the point of holding the legal door open for private financial institutions or permitting regulated competition within the financial sector—and, I would argue, one should not assume that it will inevitably converge upon the U.S. or British model of the liberal regulatory state.[11] Nonetheless, over the course of reform, the party-state has established increasingly specialized agencies to govern financial institutions. Liberalization and monetization of the economy have been accompanied by heightened efforts to standardize the management of state-sanctioned financial intermediaries, commercialize their lending procedures, and reform or close down noncompliant operations. In this sense, China's reform era could be depicted as a period of regulatory state-building, which suggests restricting the space for informal financial transactions and moving toward a more corporate and politically neutral commercial banking system.[12]

Political realities complicate this theoretical ideal type of the regulatory state, however. In particular, even though the banking system has gone through commercializing reforms, state banks continue to engage in "policy lending" to state-owned enterprises (SOEs) in industries targeted by the center as development priorities. In contrast to commercial loans, policy loans are extended on the basis not of creditworthiness but rather, of political considerations. When asked about the large portion of policy loans in their lending portfolios, state bank managers instinctually respond, "It is our patriotic duty to support pillar industries." When pressed about the definition of "pillar industries," however, most credit officers will concede that authorities pressure banks to subsidize politically important enterprises. Because these interventionist policies have occurred in tandem with rapid growth rates, some political scientists have cited China as yet another example of a successful developmental state in East

---

11. Although China's membership in the World Trade Organization includes a commitment to full liberalization of foreign bank franchises over a transitional five-year period, the extent of interest-rate liberalization and the relative autonomy of domestic banks to deal in foreign currencies remain to be seen.

12. The rationale for this argument is that new forms of economic interaction have inspired regulatory interventions by the state. Victor Nee, "Peasant Entrepreneurship and the Politics of Regulation in China," in Victor Nee and David Stark, eds., *Remaking the Economic Institutions of Socialism: China and Eastern Europe* (Stanford, Calif.: Stanford University Press, 1989). Cf. Vivienne Shue, "State Sprawl: The Regulatory State and Social Life in a Small Chinese City," in Deborah Davis, Richard Kraus, Barry Naughton, and Elizabeth Perry, eds., *Urban Spaces and Contemporary China* (New York: Cambridge University Press, 1995).

Asia, joining the ranks of South Korea, Taiwan, Singapore, and Hong Kong.[13]

The basic notion of the developmental state implies that the authoritarian center in Beijing ("the state") has demonstrated relative autonomy from "society." In China's case, society may be broadly construed as comprising all particularistic interests falling outside the innermost core of the central state's leadership and bureaucracy.[14] This would arguably include a panoply of organized interests that actually receive public sponsorship, such as mass associations, social organizations, and even parts of local governments.[15] According to state-centric perspectives, a key expression of the state's relative autonomy from society is its ability to formulate developmental policies that promote the overarching interests of the national economy, not just those of an important locality or interest group.[16] And an integral component of industrial policy in developmental states is the allocation of credit toward *nationally defined* strategic economic sectors, not the ones that lobby the hardest.[17] As Alexander Gerschenkron contended, in late industrializing countries the state may need to take on

13. See Gordon White, ed., *Developmental States in East Asia* (New York: St. Martin's Press, 1988). Cf. Marc Blecher, "Developmental State, Entrepreneurial State: The Political Economy of Socialist Reform in Xinju Municipality and Guanghan County," in Gordon White, ed., *The Chinese State in the Era of Economic Reform* (Armonk, N.Y.: M. E. Sharpe, 1991); and Ming Xia, *The Dual Developmental State* (Brookfield, Vt.: Ashgate, 2000).

14. In this context, "society" refers to organized interests that deviate from a relatively autonomous state—not only civil society, which connotes social groups, processes, and movements that are nongovernmental in character. For a thoughtful debate that distinguishes between civil society and the Habermasian notion of the public sphere, see the special symposium, "'Public Sphere'/'Civil Society' in China?" *Modern China*, 1993.

15. This is typical of state corporatist systems. As applied to China, see Yijiang Ding, "Corporatism and Civil Society in China: An Overview of the Debate in Recent Years," *China Information* 12, 4 (1998): 44–67; Jonathan Unger and Anita Chan, "Corporatism in China: A Developmental State in an East Asian Context," in Barrett McCormick and Jonathan Unger, eds., *China after Socialism: In the Footsteps of Eastern Europe or East Asia?* (Armonk, N.Y.: M. E. Sharpe, 1996), 95–126; Kenneth W. Foster, "Associations in the Embrace of an Authoritarian State: State Domination of Society?" *Studies in Comparative International Development* 35, 4 (2001); Vivienne Shue, "State Power and Social Organization in China," in Migdal, Kohli, and Shue, *State Power and Social Forces*, 65–88; and Gordon White, Jude Howell, and Shang Xiaoyuan, *In Search of Civil Society: Market Reform and Social Change in Contemporary China* (Oxford: Clarendon, 1996). On "social organizations" (*shehui tuanti*), see Tony Saich, "Negotiating the State: The Development of Social Organizations in China," *China Quarterly* 161 (March 2000): 124–41.

16. For the now classic articulation of this approach, see Theda Skocpol, "Bringing the State Back In: Strategies of Analysis in Current Research," in Peter Evans, Dietrich Reuschemeyer, and Theda Skocpol, eds., *Bringing the State Back In* (New York: Cambridge University Press, 1985), 3–37.

17. A vast literature has emerged since Chalmers Johnson's *MITI and the Japanese Miracle: The Growth of Industrial Policy, 1925–1975* (Stanford, Calif.: Stanford University Press, 1982). For a thoughtful evaluation of the developmental state research agenda, see Meredith Woo-Cumings, ed., *The Developmental State* (Ithaca: Cornell University Press, 1999).

the role of the financial entrepreneur by making potentially risky investments that ordinary economic actors would eschew for lack of resources
or entrepreneurial verve.[18] Hence, the German state developed a universal
banking system to finance heavy industrialization during the late nine-
teenth century, and the Japanese state created banks to develop a military-
industrial complex during the Meiji period.[19] During China's reform era
the party-state has similarly established or resuscitated its share of industry-
specific banks in an effort to catch up with more advanced industrialized
countries. From this point of view, the socialist state of the Mao era has
become more a capitalist developmental state.[20]

The comparative insights of statist perspectives help explain the party-
state's regulatory and developmental roles in China's transitional economy.
In particular, they reinforce the state's presiding role in the formal financial system—coming one step closer to filling the political gap left by the
neoclassical framework. But the original question remains unanswered.
China's party-state appears to be sufficiently autonomous from society to
reshape the banking system.[21] Yet the vast majority of private financing
mechanisms reside beyond the scope of permissible economic activity.
Private entrepreneurs are violating official laws and regulations to finance
their businesses. They are banking creatively behind the legal lens of the
state.

Furthermore, that entrepreneurs are actually banking behind different
bureaucratic parts of the state in different localities leads to the second
question of the book: Why does tremendous variation exist in the scope
and scale of informal finance throughout the country? Some areas have
a wide variety of private financing mechanisms, which compete with one
another and even with some formal financial institutions. Other areas, by
contrast, are nearly devoid of private financial mechanisms. Again, economists would speculate that informal finance is flourishing in localities
where the private sector is a central part of the economy, whereas places

18. Alexander Gerschenkron, *Economic Backwardness in Historical Perspective* (Cambridge,
Mass.: Harvard University Press, 1962).

19. Additional modes of financial intermediation in capitalist economies are discussed in
John Zysman, *Governments, Markets, and Growth: Financial Systems and the Politics of Industrial
Change* (Oxford: Martin Robertson, 1983).

20. Gordon White, *Riding the Tiger: The Politics of Economic Reform in Post-Mao China* (London:
Macmillan, 1994).

21. Kaja Sehrt, "Banks versus Budgets: Credit Allocation in the People's Republic of China,
1984–1997" (Ph.D. diss., University of Michigan, 1998). Yasheng Huang makes the broader
argument that the center retains considerable authority over the localities as evidenced by
the implementation of macroeconomic stabilization measures that are not necessarily in the
interest of the fastest growing provinces. Yasheng Huang, *Inflation and Investment Controls
in China: The Political Economy of Central-Local Relations during the Reform Era* (New York:
Cambridge University Press, 1996).

with a smaller private sector would not be expected to have much of a curb market because the demand for credit would be correspondingly limited. But the evidence suggests otherwise: localities with comparable economic structures and, presumably, comparable levels of demand for private finance exhibit dramatic variation in curb market activity.

A more nuanced application of the state-centric framework might question the uniformity of the central state's financial capacity in various localities. If entrepreneurs are evading financial regulations to varying degrees, then perhaps the growing regulatory state in Beijing does not exercise financial authority consistently in all parts of the country.[22] As a matter of fact, "the state" has not allocated credit to private enterprises in the systematic manner that one would expect in a "developmental state." Although China's central party-state performs key regulatory and developmental functions, the uneven occurrence of informal finance suggests that central banking regulations are not being enforced consistently across localities.

Breaking Down the Conventional State-Society Dichotomy

Rather than viewing the endurance of informal finance as a mere function of market demand, one must consider the political circumstances supporting its emergence and survival. Specifically, one must disaggregate the party-state's administrative capacity in order to explain variation in informal finance across China's different regions. Although the People's Republic of China is technically a unitary rather than a federal system, the party-state actually consists of multiple levels of government and Communist Party branches at the national, provincial, city or county, and township levels. At the same time, the "state" (or "government") also consists of functional bureaucracies duplicated at each of those administrative levels. Recognizing the organizational reality of these cross-cutting governmental structures is the first step in explaining China's empirical paradoxes.[23]

Indeed, the most insightful studies of China's reform-era political

22. I would not go so far as to suggest, however, that geographical and administrative fragmentation poses a serious risk of Soviet-style collapse. Concern about this risk is expressed in Wang Shaoguang and Hu Angang, *Report on the State of the Nation: Strengthening the Leading Role of the Central Government during the Transition to the Market Economy* (New Haven: Yale University Press, 1993), also published as *Zhongguo guojia nengli baogao* (Hong Kong: Oxford University Press, 1994). The authors toned down this position, however, in *The Political Economy of Uneven Development: The Case of China* (Armonk, N.Y.: M. E. Sharpe, 1999), 202.

23. Kenneth Lieberthal, "The 'Fragmented Authoritarianism' Model and Its Limitations," in Kenneth Lieberthal and David M. Lampton, eds., *Bureaucracy, Politics, and Decisionmaking* (Berkeley: University of California Press, 1992), 1–30.

economy have been those that systematically disaggregated the multiple and often competing levels and branches of government. They have looked beyond the battles of elite politics in Beijing to the politics of economic development at the subnational level.[24] Different provinces, counties or cities, townships, and even villages have pursued policies that led to outcomes not originally anticipated by the center. The decollectivization of agriculture, rural industrialization based on Township and Village Enterprises (TVEs), the influx of foreign investment, and the de facto privatization of state and collective enterprises have all contributed to China's macroeconomic growth (and, at times, instability)—and the key message is that these developmental processes may be attributed to the selective interpretation, if not outright violation, of central policies by local governments.[25]

Meanwhile, the corporate attempt by particular state bureaucracies to carry out their duties has also been credited with contributing to national growth.[26] Given that most if not all of the vertically organized governmental agencies face budgetary constraints, it is in their economic interest to pursue policies that enhance their material resources. Even bureaucracies in noneconomic sectors such as research institutes and the People's Liberation Army have engaged in explicitly for-profit business ventures.[27] Therefore, China could be considered an "entrepreneurial state" because bureaucratic branches of the state are increasingly involved in running for-profit businesses.[28] Although the increasing involvement of local governments and individual bureaucracies in local commerce has certainly occurred in tandem with economic growth, I would argue that one cannot automatically equate their economic pursuits with positive developmental

24. Joseph Fewsmith, *Dilemmas of Reform in China: Political Conflict and Economic Debate* (Armonk, N.Y.: M. E. Sharpe, 1994); Susan Shirk, *The Political Logic of Economic Reform in China* (Berkeley: University of California Press, 1993); and Jonathan Unger, ed., *The Nature of Chinese Politics, from Mao to Jiang* (Armonk, N.Y.: M. E. Sharpe, 2002) focus on elite politics.

25. Marc J. Blecher and Vivienne Shue, *Tethered Deer: Government and Economy in a Chinese County* (Stanford, Calif.: Stanford University Press, 1996); Peter T. Y. Cheung, Jae Ho Chung, and Zhimin Lin, eds., *Provincial Strategies of Economic Reform in Post-Mao China: Leadership, Politics, and Implementation* (Armonk, N.Y.: M. E. Sharpe, 1998); Jean C. Oi, "Fiscal Reform and the Economic Foundations of Local State Corporatism in China," *World Politics* 45, 1 (1992): 99–126; Jean C. Oi, *Rural China Takes Off: Institutional Foundations of Economic Reform* (Berkeley: University of California Press, 1999); Kristen Parris, "Local Initiative and National Reform: The Wenzhou Model of Development," *China Quarterly* 134 (June 1993): 242–63; Ezra F. Vogel, *One Step Ahead in China: Guangdong under Reform* (Cambridge: Harvard University Press, 1989); and Lynn T. White III, *Unstately Power*, vol. 1, *Local Causes of China's Economic Reforms* (Armonk, N.Y.: M. E. Sharpe, 1998).

26. Blecher, "Developmental State," 265–91; and Jane Duckett, *The Entrepreneurial State in China: Real Estate and Commerce Departments in Reform Era Tianjin* (London: Routledge, 1998).

27. James Mulvenon, *Soldiers of Fortune: The Rise and Fall of the Chinese Military-Business Complex, 1978–98* (Armonk, N.Y.: M. E. Sharpe, 2001).

28. Blecher, "Developmental State"; Duckett, *Entrepreneurial State*.

outcomes. Commercial and extractive activities that are justified as contributing to budgetary (and extrabudgetary) revenue may in fact be more like predatory rent-seeking. Indeed, the rise in rural unrest over excessive fees and levies and anticorruption campaigns points to the less appealing side of economic liberalization.[29]

In short, by viewing "the state" in its administrative and bureaucratic subcomponents, earlier studies of China's reform-era political economy have exposed a contextually contingent matrix of incentives which has inspired a mix of developmental, entrepreneurial, and predatory behavior at the subnational level. Building on these insights, this book digs below the analytic lens of a purely state-centric approach to expose the intentionally shrouded workings of informal finance. For an understanding of how informal finance has contributed to China's economic growth—and also to sporadic episodes of instability—it is necessary to examine the multiple layers of institutional interests, both complementary and competing.

Furthermore, just as breaking down the state is important for revealing the variety of vertical and horizontal governmental actors, transcending the definitional boundaries of the "society" half of the conventional state-society divide is also essential for unveiling informal finance. Analyses of state-society relations typically exclude actors whose interests are not sufficiently concentrated or organized to be a recognizable component of society in the way that most political scientists conceptualize it. Moonlighters, peddlers, and loan sharks would all fall into this extrasocietal category. The problem with excluding these apparently marginal actors, however, is that they may simply go ahead and evade banking regulations at the ground level, even if they do not formally lobby the party-state for financial liberalization.[30] Curb market operators generally maintain a low profile to avoid unpleasant political attention. As a result, the elusiveness of their activities also presents challenges for conventional research methodologies. To my knowledge, the state does not possess a list of all the private banks or finance companies in China. They are illegal, so they cannot be officially registered as for-profit financial intermediaries. They operate beyond conventional notions of state and society. Therefore, in

---

29. Thomas P. Bernstein, "Farmer Discontent and Regime Responses," in Merle Goldman and Roderick MacFarquar, eds., *The Paradox of Post-Mao Reforms* (Cambridge: Harvard Contemporary China Series, Harvard University Press, 1999), 197–219; Thomas P. Bernstein and Xiaobo Lü, *Taxation without Representation in Contemporary China* (New York: Cambridge University Press, forthcoming); Xiaobo Lü, "Booty Socialism, Bureau-preneurs, and the State in Transition: Organizational Corruption in China," *Comparative Politics* 32, 3 (2000): 273–94.

30. In the context of agricultural decollectivization and evasion of population control policies, Kate Xiao Zhou has referred to similar grassroots phenomena as the "unorganized power of the peasants" in *How the Farmers Changed China: Power of the People* (Boulder, Colo.: Westview Press, 1996). Cf. Daniel Kelliher, *Peasant Power in China: The Era of Rural Reform, 1979–1988* (New Haven: Yale University Press, 1992).

addition to conducting a survey of private entrepreneurs, the second component of my fieldwork entailed interviews with managers of state and nonstate financial institutions, officials from various agencies, and academics with the relevant expertise.

Learning from Grassroots Actors

I found that the entrepreneurs themselves offered the most valuable insights into the puzzling persistence of illegal financial activity and the political economic differences among localities. Recall, for example, the restaurant shop owner who exclaimed that she could not get a loan from a state bank even if the embalmed Chairman Mao made the request on her behalf. Her comment identified one of the most basic challenges facing financial reformers in Beijing. Even the paramount leader of China could not single-handedly command commercialization of the banking system. The Ministry of Finance has tried. The State Council has tried by separating the central bank, the People's Bank of China, from the Ministry of Finance. And then the People's Bank of China itself has tried. State banks literally cannot afford to carry any more nonperforming loans; meanwhile, everyone knows that private enterprises face capital constraints. Even the *People's Daily* has critically noted the inefficiency of this situation numerous times. Yet state banks continue granting soft loans to state enterprises rather than to profit-making operations. Why?

Survey data, official statistics, and the voices of business owners, bank managers, financial entrepreneurs, and cadres demonstrate how the local political economy fundamentally mediates the way in which national policies and regulations are implemented at the grassroots level. The scope and scale of informal finance relies on what I call the *local logics of economic possibility*. Specifically, the orientation of the local government toward the private sector plays a key role in explaining the contours of informal finance in any particular locality. To simplify a bit, some local governments have been very supportive of private-sector development since the earliest years of reform; they have gone out of their way to provide more favorable conditions for private businesses. In other localities, however, the local governments are less supportive of the private sector, focusing their energies instead on the state and, especially, collective sectors. Still other local governments are best described as having an ambivalent attitude toward private businesses; they are neither explicitly supportive nor unsupportive. I argue that these differing orientations toward the private sector in turn translate into varying degrees of implicit support for informal financial activity in any given locality. Local governments may choose to ignore the regulatory infractions of curb market insti-

Stoney Mao flanked by two goddesses at a TVE. Huian, Fujian, June 1994.

tutions, actively collaborate with local financial entrepreneurs, or make it very inconvenient for them to operate.

But why would local governments have such different approaches to dealing with the private sector? I suggest that the developmental orientation of subnational governments is primarily a path-dependent function of the economic structural legacies that localities inherited from the Mao era.[31] The importance of prior developmental experiences in shaping the economic reform process has been observed also in the context of the transitional economies in Eastern Europe and the former Soviet Union.[32] In China, some areas were intentionally deprived of investment capital, for geostrategic or other political reasons, during the first three decades of Communist rule. The regime was reluctant to build industrial capacity in the southern coastal provinces, for example, because of their relative proximity to Taiwan and thus their potential for destruction should full-scale warfare break out between the Chinese Nationalists in Taiwan and the PRC.

31. On how Mao-era legacies have influenced reform-era property rights arrangements in rural industry, see Susan H. Whiting, *Power and Wealth in Rural China: The Political Economy of Institutional Change* (New York: Cambridge University Press, 2001).

32. David Stark and László Bruszt, *Post-Socialist Pathways: Transforming Politics and Property Rights in East Central Europe* (New York: Cambridge University Press, 1998).

Ironically, the relative poverty and isolation of such places put them in a better position later to engage in private income-generating activity. Even before the formal commencement of economic reform in 1978, governments in these areas quietly allowed decollectivization of land and a return to household-based production.

The case of Wenzhou in Zhejiang Province (Chapter 4) offers a vivid example of this dynamic. Wenzhou was once considered a remote, backwater district with few developmental prospects, given its limited arable land and dense population. Within the first decade of reform, however, Wenzhou had a bustling private sector and an equally active curb market. By the mid-1980s, informal financial activity had reached its peak: private money houses were charging interest by the hour; rotating credit associations had degenerated into Ponzi schemes; loan sharks were kidnapping relatives of debtors; pawnshops were brimming with fraudulent real estate titles; and state banks had experienced a massive outflow of savings deposits. Local economists estimated that 80 to 95 percent of the capital flows in Wenzhou were tied up in informal finance at the time. Although things have calmed down since then, the local government continues to be an ardent supporter of private enterprise and creative financing practices.

In contrast to the neglected localities, districts specifically targeted for industrial development were better off during the Mao era but slower in developing their nonstate sectors, because they now face the burden of reforming Soviet-vintage SOEs with large payrolls and outdated machinery. Governments in these areas exhibit ambivalence about private-sector development. They would like to see private-sector growth, but because of more pressing economic challenges they cannot devote limited resources to private businesses at the expense of the other sectors. The industrial cities in the north-central province of Henan (see Chapter 5), factionalized by competing developmental needs, are therefore ambivalent about the range of permissible financial institutions in their territories. Consequently, curb market institutions in the traditional heartland of China are encouraged to clothe their operations in ideologically palatable disguises, but they often bear the brunt of political campaigns against corruption and illicit financial activities.

The economic conditions of localities where the government tends to be unsupportive of private businesses lie at the extremes: they have been generally either extremely impoverished or highly collectivized with significant concentrations of rural industry under the leadership of strong commune and brigade institutions. In the latter situation, local officials have preferred to maintain close ties with (or de facto ownership stakes in) collective enterprises. In other words, collective rather than private economic activity has been the preferred engine of growth because the township and village governments, formerly communes and brigades, were accustomed to playing a central role in the local economy. In such cases, larger collective enterprises enjoy preferential access to existing financial institutions, while small-scale operators are left to their own devices to raise investment and working capital. Chapter 3 presents cases in Fujian Province which exhibit this tendency. Rotating credit associations, a mutual assistance–based form of informal savings and lending that can be found around the world, have become quite popular among female vendors in these localities.

Unlike local governments in highly collectivized areas, those in extremely destitute areas are not necessarily biased toward collective over private-sector development, but their physical locations may be so ecologically disadvantaged or isolated that outmigration appears to be the most expedient escape from protracted poverty. Such localities can be found even in provinces, such as Fujian (Chapter 3), which are now relatively more prosperous.

Although it is useful to classify localities in political economic terms, in reality both the structural condition and the developmental orientation of localities have changed since 1978. Local economies have not been frozen into discrete developmental categories or insulated from broader changes in China's political economy. They have evolved over time. By the late 1990s, for example, some localities that had been known for their dominant collective sectors were beginning to privatize their TVEs.[33] Furthermore, major shifts in the national political and economic environment have clearly had refractory effects at the local level. History-making events such as the Tiananmen Square crisis in 1989 and the Fifteenth Party Congress in 1997, which announced deeper restructuring of the state sector after Deng Xiaoping's death, redefined the macro context of interaction between national and local governments and the relative balance of power among central bureaucracies. Nonetheless, the point remains that the implementation of central policy is subject to interpretation at the grassroots level.

Although legacies from the Mao era have certainly shaped the developmental trajectories of localities, their actual paths have been dynamic and experimental rather than overdetermined. My concluding chapter elaborates on the local logics of economic possibility—in contrast to the top-down logic of the developmental state or the new institutional economic logic of minimizing economic uncertainty through well-defined property rights. Ultimately, individual staff of the state decide whether and how to enforce specific regulations, collect fees and taxes, and issue licenses.[34] Poli-

---

33. Oi, *Rural China Takes Off*; Whiting, *Power and Wealth in Rural China*.
34. Michael Lipsky, *Street-Level Bureaucracy* (New York: Russell Sage Foundation, 1983); Cf. James Ron, "Savage Restraint: Israeli, Palestine, and the Dialectics of Legal Repression," *Social Problems* 47, 4 (2000): 445–72.

Curbside capitalist, Kaifeng. Henan, July 1996.

cies are not implemented uniformly because individual agencies and bureaucrats are not implementing them uniformly. And more important, an integral part of their decision-making calculus in policy implementation stems from their interaction with local economic actors. Entrepreneurs can offer material, employment, and social incentives to their state-appointed regulators. Even as economic structure affects the immediate political incentives facing local officials and their rank-and-file cadres, it is equally apparent that private entrepreneurs themselves exercise agency in devising their financing strategies. By definition, entrepreneurs are not passive products of structural constraints; they are innovative actors who draw on preexisting resources to create new products for the market and new lives for themselves. This leads to the third puzzling issue.

Breaking Down the Private Sector

In addition to dramatic variation among localities in the scope and scale of informal finance, I found that business owners differ widely in their choice of financing mechanisms. This is the third puzzle: some private entrepreneurs rely primarily on personal savings or peer group rotating credit associations; others use the more highly institutionalized sources of curb market credit. Economists might attribute this diversity to the availability of certain financing mechanisms in any given locality. As rational choice theorists would put it, the local supply of informal finance constrains the choice set for private business owners. The limitation of this perspective is that entrepreneurs within the same locality exhibit wide variation in their financing behavior. Rationalists would expect similarly situated actors to make roughly similar economic choices, yet two storeowners, selling the same kind of merchandise and operating on the same street, may employ completely different financing strategies.

The solution to this third puzzle, I argue, lies in recognizing that private entrepreneurs have varying social and political identities. These mediate their access to noneconomic resources and networks, which in turn affects their economic strategies. In other words, private entrepreneurs as a group do not share equal access to the curb market even within a single locality because, economic similarities notwithstanding, they are not in fact similarly situated in other significant realms. As this book demonstrates, entrepreneurs' economic behavior also operates according to a social and political logic. Just as explaining the variation in the supply of informal finance invokes the political considerations of local officials, explaining individual use of financing mechanisms transcends bottom-line economic issues. Women in the coastal south who dominate rotating credit associations, migrant peddlers in an industrial center who rely on native-place networks for short-term credit needs, and former Communist Party officials who run private finance companies are all private entrepreneurs, but it would be simplistic to view them as sharing similar identities, resources, and interests. I found that business owners' financing practices vary with their gender, residential origin (local or migrant), length of time in business, and strength of local political ties. Local male business owners with strong political ties, for example, are more likely to tap the more highly institutionalized financing mechanisms than are migrant women who operate businesses at a similar scale in the same locality. Different entrepreneurs tap different forms of informal finance because they rely on different interpersonal dynamics to create the level of certainty and "credible commitment" that formal financial institutions and sophisticated property rights would theoretically provide. Informal credit markets are segmented even at the grassroots level. Access to social and political capital mediates access to finance capital. The so-called capitalist class is not a unified whole.

The importance of disaggregating both the state and the private sector, is that breaking down these broader conceptual categories exposes micro-level interactions between political and economic actors which are typically obscured by conventional economic or state-centric approaches. Entre-preneurs and bureaucrats are not single-mindedly motivated by, respectively, profit-making and policy implementation. They face a multi-dimensional array of constraints and opportunities, incentive structures that vary by locality. For these reasons, entrepreneurs and state actors must be seen in both their local political economic contexts and their individ-ual networks. Informal institutions at these lower levels of analysis consti-tute the unarticulated rules of a game that its players take for granted on a day-to-day basis—and that political scientists tend to ignore.

At the same time, however, this shift in focus to the contextual contin-gency and social embeddedness of the key players should not be taken to a deterministic extreme.[35] The apparent rules of the game are not static but are continuously renegotiated as state and nonstate actors interact. The norms that guide human interaction cannot be divorced from their daily reproduction.[36] Every time a state clerk registers a private enterprise as a col-lective one, or a restaurant owner treats a tax collector to a lavish banquet, certain norms are being chosen over others. These everyday transactions are more than practical acts of survival or symbolic acts of resistance.[37] They subvert the formal, state-defined rules of the game. They create alternative scripts, incentives, and even institutions. They generate new possibilities. In the aggregate, that is how private-sector development in China has been financed in the absence of official sources of credit. That is why the party-state does not monopolize the supply of capital in the economy. Ordinary acts and informal institutions can produce macro-level outcomes.

Beyond Control: Potential Lessons for the Party-State

In addition to demystifying the empirical puzzles, my theoretical claims have broader policy implications for the party-state's ongoing attempts to reassert its authority over the financial system and alleviate the capital con-straints of private entrepreneurs through official channels. Both regulatory and redistributive efforts have met with limited success. In light of the operational reality of local hierarchies among business owners and their complex interaction with various staff of the state, the relative ineffective-ness of such policy interventions becomes more understandable. Political leaders in Beijing (and other capitals during the Imperial period) have

35. Mark Granovetter, "Economic Action and Social Structure: The Problem of Embeddedness," *American Journal of Sociology* 91 (November 1985): 481–510.

36. Pierre Bourdieu, *Outline of a Theory of Practice* (Cambridge: Cambridge University Press, 1977).

37. James C. Scott, *Weapons of the Weak: Everyday Forms of Peasant Resistance* (New Haven: Yale University Press, 1985).

Family at work. Beijing, August 2001.

always recognized the challenges of standardizing governance in a country of China's size and diversity. Nonetheless, the statist tendency to assume both faithful policy implementation by subnational bureaucrats and citizen compliance remains. What are the effects of such flawed assumptions?

Approximately every other year since the initiation of economic reform, financial rectification campaigns have been conducted to reform mismanaged banks and close down unsanctioned financial institutions. Such campaigns, coupled with anticorruption campaigns, grew in intensity during the Asian financial crisis of the late 1990s. The center's heightened concern about financial system health was not surprising, but the effects of increased supervision and disciplinary action often surprised officials: public investigations of dubious financial practices triggered runs on banks, and when private finance companies were shut down, their customers took to the streets in protest. In order to understand and perhaps anticipate how regulatory scrutiny could have the unintended effect of sparking local financial crises, one must return to the basic yet critical point that local political and economic context matters. Official attempts at formalizing informal finance (or eliminating it altogether) disrupt the preexisting equilibria of local political and economic forces and introduce a potentially destabilizing element of uncertainty in the short run. When everyday consumers of private financial services realized that the implicit bargains struck between local governmental agencies and financial entrepreneurs were threatened by external intervention from above, they panicked—and lost confidence in state banks as well.

Thinking in market-oriented terms, national banking officials assume that entrepreneurs turn to the curb market because the formal financial system does not meet their credit needs. The logical solution, therefore, is to enhance the access of business owners to official lending institutions. Since forcing banks to engage in commercially viable lending has proved to be so difficult, funds have been allocated quota-style for small and medium private enterprises. Ironically, this means that certain types of "commercial" loans have become yet another component of the "policy" loans mandated by the state. The local reality of segmented credit markets, however, suggests that merely earmarking small business loans through a specific state agency or financial institution may leave out a substantial portion of the creditworthy population. In fact, such credit facilities may not even reach the intended group.

The paradoxical effects of state intervention in the informal financial sector are not unique to China; international development practitioners in microfinance have observed similar problems with state-directed credit programs in other contexts (Chapter 6). Examples abound of funds intended for agricultural credit being diverted for nonagricultural uses and subsidized microfinance loans landing in the pockets of local elites. This is not to say that the state cannot play a productive regulatory and redistributive role; rather, it is dangerous to assume that well-intentioned policies will have their intended effects. Legislative fiat should not be equated with legislative compliance.

State policies travel quite a distance between their genesis in air-conditioned drafting chambers and implementation at the ground level. This book makes a similar journey through each of the distorting dimensions of the process. To situate the emergence of informal finance in the context of China's broader developmental dilemmas, Chapter 2 identifies political and economic reasons for the structural exclusion of private entrepreneurs from the formal financial system and lays out my research methodology. Chapters 3 through 5 turn to the specific curb market experiences of various localities in Fujian, Zhejiang, and Henan Provinces and show how the seemingly straightforward economic issue of private-sector finance involves a network of complex interactions between political and economic actors. Case studies of localities, financial institutions, and entrepreneurs reveal that collaboration between the local government and the private sector can usually be traced to individual relationships. But it would be misleading to conclude that informal finance is merely a personalistic expression of corruption. Curb market activity depends on more than random acts of back-scratching among friends and family; the production of informal finance operates more like an underground factory fueled by a permissive configuration of local political and business interests. Of course, although common patterns of production technologies may be observed across localities with similar social and political economic structures, the process is not perfectly mechanical or predictable. Delays occur, accidents happen, and every once in a while the underground factory is exposed by higher-level regulators for what it is—illegal—and key divisions are shut down. But where the local government has compelling political reasons to look the other way, the underground factory finds a way to reconfigure itself and continue its business.

The stubborn persistence of informal interactions and informal finance is how China's economic miracle has been financed. Not the establishment of state-run commercial banks. Not the establishment of transparent property rights. In quiet and creative collaboration with local officials, private entrepreneurs have cultivated more accessible, if not always reliable, sources of credit for themselves.

2

The Political Economy of Informal Finance in China

Have you ever borrowed money from a state bank?

"You must be kidding." She laughed, exposing a gold-capped tooth. "Banks don't lend to petty entrepreneurs like me."

Then how did you raise the capital to start this business?

She paused. "Savings."

You saved that much money from working in a state-owned factory?

The owner lowered her voice, "Well, actually I borrowed most of the money from a private credit association."

Is that like a private bank?

"Not exactly. Private banks are illegal. We meet once a month in the back of that clothing store across the alley."

—Fieldnotes from Fujian Province, 1996

Since November 1987, pawnbroking, which had withered on the Chinese mainland over the past three decades, has come back to life in one place after another.... It should be noted that today's pawnshops in the country are not entirely what they used to be. Pawnshops in old China took in personal effects at very low prices when the owners were poverty-stricken. However, such businesses today represent a medium for normal commodity circulation.... The newborn pawnbroking aims to serve the people and social production.

—Beijing Institute of International Finance,
Ministry of Finance, 1993

Examining the contextual background of the evolution of informal finance in China, a look at the research strategy for this book, and a summary of the main findings demonstrate that the overall use of infor-

mal finance does not vary provincially or regionally. The much more striking differences *within* provinces suggest that the state does not exercise consistent levels of financial capacity even in a particular province. This finding
defies the expectations of conventional economic and statist frameworks
and paves the way for a more detailed look at the dynamics of informal
finance in each of my specific field sites.

Informal Finance in Imperial China

The few trends in informal credit that have held over from the prerev-
olutionary era include the oldest credit institutions on record in China: the
pawnshops that were operated by Buddhist monasteries.[1] Dating back to
the middle of the Six Dynasties (317–589 A.D.), the pawnshops relied on
donated funds and extended credit to both wealthy and impoverished
peasants. Although pawnbroking by monasteries faded with the decline of
Buddhism in the Ming (1368–1644) and Qing (1644–1911) periods, civil-
ians adopted pawnshops as accepted businesses serving all tiers of society.
With the rise of traditional and modern banks in the eighteenth century,
however, the role of pawnbrokers as the primary source of credit dimin-
ished accordingly. Native banks (*qianzhuang*) first appeared in Ningbo and
Shanghai and served as local, independent merchant banks for individual
traders—unlike the larger, semigovernmental banks of Shanxi, which
handled interregional remittances.[2] Petty traders, however, were not qualified to access the more elitist *qianzhuang*; hence, they dealt primarily with
the money-changing shops (*qianpu*) for the purpose of exchanging their
everyday copper currency into silver for larger transactions. In some cases,
traders were able to negotiate loans with the *qianpu* at lower interest rates
than those offered by pawnshops.[3]

In addition to pawnshops, Buddhist monasteries started running cooperative loan societies, called *she*, during the Tang Dynasty (618–907 A.D.).
These societies were originally established to finance religious activities,
but they also extended credit to members for funeral and travel expenses.
Outside of monasteries, there is also evidence that poor peasants in the
southern province of Hunan participated in mutual financing associations
(*huzhuhui*) during the Tang period. The operating procedures of these *hui*

1. Lien-sheng Yang, *Money and Credit in China: A Short History* (Cambridge: Harvard University Press, 1952), 71.
2. For a comparison of the Shanxi banks with the *qianzhuang*, see Susan Mann Jones,
"Finance in Ningpo: The 'Ch'ien Chuang,' 1750–1880," in W. E. Willmott, ed. *Economic Organization in Chinese Society* (Stanford, Calif.: Stanford University Press, 1972), 47–77.
3. Peng Xinwei, *A Monetary History of China*, trans. Edward H. Kaplan (Bellingham, Wash.:
Center for East Asian Studies, 1993), 814–26.

were similar to those of a modern-day rotating savings and credit association (ROSCA). Members would contribute a fixed sum to the collective pot each month and draw lots to determine who would collect the total amount to purchase a cow or some other farm asset. By the end of a *hui* cycle, one by one, each member would have purchased a badly needed asset.[4]

Historians and anthropologists writing at the turn of the century documented in greater detail the use of rotating credit associations with different names and operational terms. It is worth delineating the forms of *hui* from this period (late Qing and Republican era), since essentially the same types can be observed nearly a century later in China and elsewhere.[5] The basic *hui* specifies a fixed monthly or semiannual contribution to the pot by all members, typically a group of friends or neighbors, and then the pot is rotated on an interest-free basis so that each participant ultimately receives back the same nominal amount.[6] This is called a rotating association (*lunhui*), since the order in which members collect the pot is determined at the first meeting. Another popular form is called a dice-shaking association (*yaohui*) because the highest roller of two dice at each meeting would receive the pot. In both the *lunhui* and *yaohui* the organizer or head (*huitou*) of the association was responsible for preparing a feast at each meeting, and then the pot collector would pay for it.[7] In *yaohui* the lot drawing would occur after the feast.[8] A third type of *hui* documented in southern China (Guangdong, Fujian) and Taiwan is called a bidding association (*biaohui*): the order of pot recipients is determined by secret bidding, whereby the member who bids the highest interest rate receives the pot.[9]

4. Ibid., 75–76.

5. An excellent analysis of the different types of *hui* is Thierry Pairault, "Approches tontinieres (deuxième partie): Formes et mecanismes tontiniers" *Etudes chinoises* 9, 2 (1990). (Tontine approaches, part 2: Typology and operation of tontines).

6. Of course, depending on the length of the *hui* and local inflation, later members might actually receive less money in real terms than they originally contributed.

7. In the variant described by D. H. Kulp, however, the organizer always pays for the feast: *Country Life in South China: Phoenix Village, Kwantung, China* (New York: Teachers College, Columbia University, 1925), 1:190–96.

8. Sidney D. Gamble, *Ting Hsien: A North China Rural Community* (New York: International Secretariat Institute of Pacific Relations, 1954), 267–70.

9. This is the dominant form in present-day Fujian: Interview No. 30 (see Appendix B for a numbered list of the interviewees and their institutional affiliations; to protect their confidentiality, actual names are not provided.) For example, if the leader of a group borrows 100 units of currency in the first month of the arrangement, that person might pay 20 percent interest to the pool, amortized over the term of the *hui*, but receive a net amount of $100 - 100 * i\,(n-1)$ in the first month, where i is the interest rate and n represents the total number of members. Assuming constant interest rates and straight-line amortization of interest, the net monthly amount received for the remaining members would be calculated as follows: $P\,(n-1) - [i * P\,(n-1)]/(t-m)$, where P = payment of each member; n = number of members;

By the late Imperial period, a wider range of institutional options was available to those in need of credit. Still, petty capitalists generally relied on less formalized sources of finance. In addition to interpersonal lending and rotating credit associations, as Hill Gates explains, they raised capital through "the transfer of brideprice and dowry, pawnshops, money lending, gambling, protection rackets run by gangs, and other mechanisms large and small."[10] In rural northern China, however, it appears that most rural credit was used for consumption or payment of taxes and rent, not production. According to one study, neither borrowers nor lenders differentiated between production and consumption uses of loans. Moreover, it is believed that *hui* were typically used to finance ceremonial needs like weddings and funerals rather than profit-driven ones like starting a business or purchasing land.[11] Those who participated in a *hui* viewed themselves as helping the organizer out of patrilineal, kinship duty. Most *hui*s seem to have been organized around male relatives. As Fei Hsiao-Tung observed in his study of Kaixiangong village in the lower Yangzi Delta, "Given a proper purpose, the organizer will approach his relatives: father's brother, brother, sister's husband, mother's brother, wife's father, etc. These have an obligation to join the society. Even when they are unable to subscribe, they will find some of their relatives to take their place."[12]

The male-centric orientation of *hui* participation in pre-Revolutionary China is consistent with the patriarchal norms governing social and economic interaction of the period; however, *hui* are now more popular among women than men (Chapter 3).

Formal and Informal Finance in Mao's China

Since the Communist revolution, the state of informal finance in China has received minimal attention, largely because private banking was banned during the Mao era. In the early years of the PRC the new banking system was modeled after the Soviet monobank system and used as a tool to encourage the socialization of commerce, communization of agriculture, and elimination of private enterprise.[13] By the mid-1950s all but two

---

i = annual interest rate; t = total number of months of the *hui* cycle; and m = the month of the *hui*. The last person who borrows would not have to pay interest and might actually earn or lose interest in real terms, depending on inflation.

10. Hill Gates, *China's Motor: A Thousand Years of Petty Capitalism* (Ithaca: Cornell University Press, 1996), 32.

11. Hsiao-Tung Fei, *Peasant Life in China: A Field Study of Country Life in the Yangtze Valley* (New York: Oxford University Press, 1946), 264 (citing R. H. Tawney, *Land and Labour in China* [London: George Allen and Unwin, 1932], 62), 267.

12. Fei, *Peasant Life in China*, 267.

13. The Soviet monobank system essentially consisted of one main state bank and several

banks from the Republican era had been confiscated (or closed) and converted into joint state-private banks or merged with branches of the People's Bank of China.[14] Notwithstanding occasional institutional changes in the formal financial sector during the Great Leap Forward and the Cultural Revolution, the national banking system was meant to manage the official supply and distribution of credit in the economy. In fact, the state banking system did not serve as a regular source of credit even for state-owned enterprises, since the fixed and working capital needs of SOEs were financed primarily through local government budgetary expenditures. During the 1960s, bank loans were supposed to supply only 20 percent of the SOEs' working capital requirements (as determined by a quota system).[15] But the distinction between fiscal allocations and bank credits was often blurred, since personnel appointments in the local banks were controlled by local Party committees. Operationally, this meant that local banks ended up, says William Byrd, acting as "little more than 'treasuries' for local governments," a problem that has persisted through the reform era.[16] In any case, the combined monopoly of local governments and banks over official credit resulted in a situation where individuals were effectively denied access to formal bank credit.

Given that most of the Chinese population was employed in either collectivized agriculture or state work units throughout most of the Mao era, it is probably safe to infer that most households did not turn to informal financing mechanisms for production-related reasons. Rather, the responses of my interviewees indicate that when farmers participated in informal schemes such as rotating credit associations, they generally used the collectively raised capital for ceremonial purposes such as weddings and funerals. In urban areas, rotating credit associations called *duihui* were sometimes organized within work units as a form of social insurance in case of emergencies and for financing expensive consumer products. Various interviewees recalled that during the Cultural Revolution a bicycle cost

supporting specialized financial institutions. See O. Kuschpeta, *The Banking and Credit System of the USSR* (Boston: Nijhoff Social Sciences Division, 1978); Adam Zwass, trans. Michel C. Vale, *Money, Banking, and Credit in the Soviet Union and Eastern Europe* (London: Macmillan, 1979); and William Byrd, *China's Financial System: The Changing Role of Banks* (Boulder, Colo.: Westview Press, 1983), 41.

14. The two banks that survived the confiscation process were the Bank of China and the Bank of Communications. Both became subject to PBOC governance, however. For more detail, see Cecil R. Dipchand, Zhang Yichun, and Ma Mingjia, *The Chinese Financial System* (Westport, Conn.: Greenwood Press, 1994), 1–18.

15. This was called the "separate sources" (*fenkou*) system. Katharine Huang Hsiao, *Money and Monetary Policy in Communist China* (New York: Columbia University Press, 1971), 48 and 76 (for table showing the changes in percentage shares between the state budget and the banking system in providing working capital to SOEs).

16. Byrd, *China's Financial System*, 37.

about 100 *yuan,* which was equivalent to the average worker's annual wage. By contributing one to five *yuan* each month to the work unit's collective pot, each participant could in turn purchase a bike, watch, or other coveted item. None of the people I interviewed could recall distinct gender differences in *hui* participation within the urban work unit, though some suggested that women in rural areas were more likely than men to participate.

Revolutionary Changes in the Post-Mao Era?

As part of the economic reforms initiated at the Third Plenum of the Eleventh Central Committee of the Chinese Communist Party (CCP) in December 1978, the People's Bank of China (PBOC) was elevated to ministerial status and in 1984, officially designated as China's central bank. Related financial system reforms included the establishment of the Industrial and Commercial Bank (ICB) to take over the PBOC's commercial banking functions (1984), the reestablishment of the Agricultural Bank of China (ABOC) (1979), the revitalization of the People's Construction Bank of China (1979), and the establishment of the China Investment Bank (1981) to handle foreign transactions. In addition, a host of officially designated commercial banks and nonbanking financial institutions (NBFIs) were established to serve specific developmental objectives and market niches. Throughout the 1980s and early 1990s, a de facto functional division of labor emerged between the specialized banks and NBFIs such as credit cooperatives and trust and investment companies whereby specialized banks extended credit primarily to SOEs, while the NBFIs were more active in financing the non-state sector.[17] Table 2.1 shows that the percentage of lending by officially sanctioned financial institutions to private businesses remained extremely small throughout the 1990s. Table 2.2 shows that Urban Credit Cooperatives accounted for over three-fourths of official credit to the private sector in 1996, the last year they were permitted to operate before their forced conversion into Urban Commercial Banks.

Despite the central bank's repeated efforts to encourage commercial-based lending standards on the part of state banks, they have continued to face local political pressures to extend to state-owned enterprises loans that do not exhibit high prospects of being repaid. Meanwhile, official interest rates have been held artificially low in an effort to curb the inflationary tendencies in the rapidly growing economy. By 1993 the banking system

17. For a discussion of China's financial reforms between 1979 and 1991, see Xiaoping Xu, *China's Financial System under Transition* (New York: St. Martin's Press, 1998).

Table 2.1 Official Lending to Private Entrepreneurs, 1990–2001

Year	State Banks[a] (%)	All Official Financial Institutions[b] (%)	Total Official Lending to Private Sector (100 mil RMB)
1990	0.09	0.23	40.2
1991	0.08	0.23	49.2
1992	0.09	0.26	67.6
1993	0.10	0.33	108.6
1994	0.13	0.38	155.9
1995	0.09	0.39	196.2
1996	0.11	0.46	279.8
1997	0.27	0.52	386.7
1998	0.30	0.54	471.6
1999	0.41	0.62	579.1
2000	0.55	0.66	654.6
2001[c]	0.59	0.77	791.1

Sources: *JRNJ*, various years; and *China Monthly Statistics*, no. 5 (Beijing: Chinese Statistical Information and Consultancy Service Centre, June 2001).
[a] Includes people's banks, policy banks, state-owned and other commercial banks, and city commercial banks.
[b] Includes all "State Banks" plus urban/rural credit cooperatives, postal savings institutions, financial trust and investment companies, and financing and leasing companies.
[c] As of March 2001.

Table 2.2 Breakdown of Official Lending to Private Sector, 1996

Type of Lender	Amount (100 mil RMB)	% of Total
State Banks	53.8	19.2
Other Banks[a]	13.4	4.8
Urban Credit Cooperatives	212.6	76.0
Total	279.8	100.0

Source: *JRNJ, 1997*, 465.
[a] Includes Everbright Bank, Huaxia Banking Corp., China Investment Bank, China Minsheng Banking Corp., Guangdong Development Bank, Shenzhen Development Bank, China Merchants Bank, Shanghai Pudong Development Bank, Fujian Industrial Bank, Bangbu Housing Bank, and Yantai Housing Bank.

was experiencing net outflows of capital into the black interbank market, real estate ventures, the recently established stock market, and other speculative investments. As a result, the loan loss reserves of the specialized banks declined to well below the 4 percent standard set by the international Basle Committee on Banking Supervision. Although it was not widely publicized in the Chinese or Western press, the financial system was in crisis.[18] A series of reforms between 1993 and 1995 attempted to put an end to interbank lending and phase out policy-based lending from specialized banks so that they would operate as genuine commercial banks, while designated "policy banks" would take over credit allocation based on political and developmental objectives. Following these reforms, the structure of the formal financial system was as shown in Figure 2.1.

Although the institutional structure of the formal financial system became increasingly complex and diversified over the first two decades of reform, as of 2001 state banks were not yet acting as truly profit-oriented commercial banks. In other words, when a state bank was trying to decide whether or not to extend a loan to an enterprise, it did not take into account such standard measures of creditworthiness as the profitability of the enterprise, credit history (whether it had a preexisting debt burden), professionalism of management, efficiency of operations, and, most fundamentally, the ability of the borrower to repay the loan. By the end of 1997 over 20 percent of the state banks' portfolios consisted of bad assets of loans more than three months overdue, and uncollectible debts accounted for an additional 6 to 7 percent.[19] Because of the tendency of the provincial-level PBOCs to succumb to local political pressures for subsidizing SOEs, they were replaced by nine regional PBOCs in 1999.[20] According to Vice Premier Wen Jiabao, the objective of this financial centralization was "to protect the banking system from interference by local governments, to penalize people who have violated financial laws and regulations, and to improve the efficiency of banks."[21] A secondary goal of the reform was to increase the availability of credit to small and medium-sized enterprises.[22]

Although official statistics report that bank lending to the non-state

18. For more detail on the 1993 financial crisis and ensuing reforms, see Minxin Pei, "The Political Economy of Banking Reforms in China, 1993–1997," *Journal of Contemporary China* 7, 18 (1998): 321–50.

19. These figures were provided by Dai Xianglong, governor of the PBOC. See Chu Chia-Chien, "Dai Xianglong: China to Establish New Financial System in Three Years," *Wen Wei Po*, November 2, 1998, B16, reported in FBIS-CHI-98-306. Standard & Poor estimated that China had US$200 billion in nonperforming loans, accounting for 25 percent of total loans outstanding in 1997: Shawn X. Xu, "PBOC Holds Key to Averting Crisis," *South China Morning Post (SCMP)*, May 14, 1998. The actual percentage of nonperforming loans is difficult to assess because of lax definitional standards. See Nicholas R. Lardy, *China's Unfinished Economic Revolution* (Washington, D.C.: Brookings Institution, 1998), 115–26.

20. This was inspired in part by the U.S. Federal Reserve System: "Zhu's Protege Must Put Together Mainland's Answer to the Fed," *SCMP*, May 14, 1998. The branches are located in Tianjin, Shenyang, Shanghai, Nanjing, Wuhan, Jinan, Guangzhou, Chengdu, and Xi'an.

21. "Major Reform in People's Bank of China," *Xinhua News Agency*, November 15, 1998, reported in FBIS-CHI-98-319.

22. Chu Chia-Chien, "Dai Xianglong."

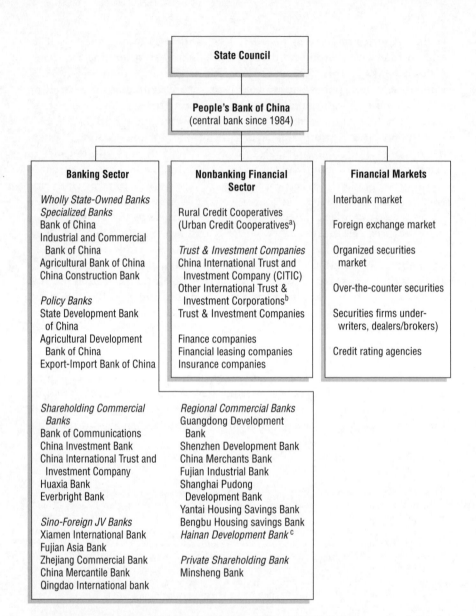

State Council

People's Bank of China
(central bank since 1984)

Banking Sector	**Nonbanking Financial Sector**	**Financial Markets**
Wholly State-Owned Banks		Interbank market
Specialized Banks	Rural Credit Cooperatives	
Bank of China	(Urban Credit Cooperatives[a])	Foreign exchange market
Industrial and Commercial Bank of China		Organized securities market
Agricultural Bank of China	*Trust & Investment Companies*	
China Construction Bank	China International Trust and Investment Company (CITIC)	Over-the-counter securities
	Other International Trust & Investment Corporations[b]	
Policy Banks	Trust & Investment Companies	Securities firms under-writers, dealers/brokers)
State Development Bank of China		
Agricultural Development Bank of China	Finance companies	Credit rating agencies
Export-Import Bank of China	Financial leasing companies	
	Insurance companies	

Shareholding Commercial Banks
Bank of Communications
China Investment Bank
China International Trust and Investment Company
Huaxia Bank
Everbright Bank

Sino-Foreign JV Banks
Xiamen International Bank
Fujian Asia Bank
Zhejiang Commercial Bank
China Mercantile Bank
Qingdao International bank

Regional Commercial Banks
Guangdong Development Bank
Shenzhen Development Bank
China Merchants Bank
Fujian Industrial Bank
Shanghai Pudong Development Bank
Yantai Housing Savings Bank
Bengbu Housing savings Bank
Hainan Development Bank [c]

Private Shareholding Bank
Minsheng Bank

Sources: Lardy, *China's Unfinished Economic Revolution* (1998), 59–76; *JRNJ 1997*.
[a] In 1995, Urban Credit Cooperatives began to be converted into Urban Commercial Banks. Experimental efforts to reform Rural Credit Cooperatives started in 1998.
[b] The People's Bank of China closed down the Guangdong International Trust and Investment Company in October 1998 because it defaulted on a US $1.2 billion debt payment. Plans to "rectify" other ITICs were announced shortly thereafter.
[c] The People's Bank of China closed down Hainan Development Bank in June 1998.

Figure 2.1 Structure of China's Formal Financial System

sector remains minuscule, the private economy has in fact received a some-what higher proportion of bank credit, thanks to ongoing leakage of funds from the formal financial system. Even the vice governor of the central bank, Liu Mingkang, admits, "Certain problems have indeed taken place in China's financial sector. Some banks have indeed engaged in off-the-books operations, kept small private coffers, and paid high interest to attract deposits, causing pernicious competition and operations. Certain loans have even been extended without having loan contracts signed."[23]

Why Bank Doors Are Closed to Private Enterprises

Of five basic reasons why the state banking system does not extend more credit to private businesses, the first three are political; the last two relate to the system's lack of institutional experience in and incentives for lending to the private sector.

The first and perhaps most important reason that SOEs continue to receive the preponderance of bank credit results from political pressures to maintain social stability by minimizing unemployment. In certain local-ities dominated by SOEs, many are not performing as efficiently as their collective or private counterparts.[24] Since a large percentage of the work force depends on state employment, however, local governments pressure the state banks in their jurisdictions to extend loans to subsidize the SOEs rather than letting them downsize or simply go bankrupt. This is the case in parts of Henan (Chapter Five). Although the Fifteenth National Party Congress in October 1997 announced ambitious measures to reform, liquidate, or sell all but the largest one thousand SOEs, wholesale pri-vatization of small and medium-sized SOEs has proceeded more slowly than initially implied because of the destabilizing effects of mass unemployment.[25]

23. Sun Zhi with Wang Zhenning, "Central Bank Official on Restoring Financial Order," *Ta Kung Pao*, October 12, 1998, 2, reported in FBIS-CHI-98-289.

24. A succinct statement of this view is Lardy, *China's Unfinished Economic Revolution*, 21–58. See also "China's State Enterprise Reform Is a Heavy Responsibility," *Jingji cankao bao*, Decem-ber 16, 1997, cited in FBIS-CHI-98-035. A somewhat more optimistic perspective is Edward S. Steinfeld, *Forging Reform in China: The Fate of State-Owned Industry* (New York: Cambridge Uni-versity Press, 1998).

25. Wang Xiangwei, "Beijing Signals Rethinking on Reform Plans," *SCMP*, July 11, 1998; Nicholas Lardy, "China Chooses Growth Today, Reckoning Tomorrow," *Asian Wall Street Journal*, September 30, 1998. An anonymous editorial said, "At present, the tendency of 'selling enterprises' has become more rampant in some localities. This format has misguided state enterprise restructuring, confused people's minds, hampered enterprises' healthy devel-opment, and disrupted the reemployment of suspended staff and workers of state enterprises. It has even sparked serious social problems in some localities": "We Should Stop the Tendency of 'Selling Enterprises,' " *Xinhua News Agency*, August 4, 1998, reported in FBIS-CHI-98-225.

The second reason state banks lend primarily to SOEs relates to both centrally and provincially defined industrial priorities. For example, a certain locality may decide that it is important to develop an auto industry or to invest in high-tech industries.[26] The pressure to develop these targeted industries is passed on to banks, which are instructed to extend loans to specific enterprises. These are called policy loans. This kind of lending is not illegal or corrupt; rather, it is a function of which industries the central and provincial governments choose to promote over others. The practice was quite common in Korea during the 1960s and 1970s when the steel, auto, and shipbuilding industries gained preferential access to credit because the Korean government thought it strategically important for Korea to build up a heavy industrial base; similar targeting has also occurred in Japan. In China the central PBOC restructured the banking system along regional lines in 1999 and claimed that the commercial banks would no longer extend policy loans. Nonetheless, one strategy that private enterprises (especially those operating in sectors that match the industrial priorities of local governments) have used to secure bank credit is to register as "collective enterprises" (*jiti qiye*).

Third, during the early years of reform there was widespread prejudice against people who pursued private profit and seemed to be getting richer than everyone else. Would reform continue, or would there be some sort of political backlash against the new capitalists? Throughout the 1980s political campaigns against "bourgeois liberalization" and "spiritual pollution" held up private entrepreneurs as examples of the ill effects of capitalist infiltration. As a result, state banks did not feel comfortable about extending loans to private enterprises. In fact, many banks were suspicious of private entrepreneurs and worried that they might get in trouble for doing business with them. The stereotype of the earliest group of private entrepreneurs was that they were the dregs of society like criminals who were not able to get proper jobs in state enterprises and offices (which in some cases was true).[27] Because of the initial negative ideological stereotype associated with the pursuit of private profit, some de facto private businesses disguised their ownership structure by registering as "people-run enterprises" (*minying qiye*). In contrast to "privately operated enterprises" (*siying qiye*), which refers to larger-scale private businesses with more than eight employees, the term "people-run" (*minying*) carries a less nakedly capitalistic connotation.

In addition to the political pressures on banks to lend to the state and collective sectors, the fourth reason for the state banks' sluggish transition

26. See Eric Thun, "Changing Lanes in China: Industrial Development in a Transitional Economy, 1999" (Ph.D. diss., Harvard University, 1999); and Adam Segal, *Digital Dragon: High Technology Enterprises in China* (Ithaca: Cornell University Press, forthcoming).

27. Interview No. 87.

toward market-based standards of credit extension was the fact that banks simply lacked experience in lending to private enterprises. As one bank director explained, in the early years of reform "we did not even know how to go about processing an individual request for a loan. All our previous loans were affiliated with state units, so it would have been a real hassle to change the application form or make an exception."[28] Credit officers in post-1949 China were trained as bureaucrats, not commercial bankers, so minimal precedence existed for extending loans on a profit-oriented rather than political basis. Moreover, until recently the educational system was not geared toward the kind of technical training required for evaluating creditworthiness.

Fifth, the banking system itself remains institutionally biased toward lending to state units. Loan officers may expect forgiveness for making bad loans to state entities because, after all, they are essentially different parts of the same "state"—a rationalization that could not be used for bad loans to private businesses. As the bank director quoted above went on to point out, "It's safer to make a loan to a state unit than an individual stranger." Financially, private borrowers may indeed pose a higher credit risk than public clients because the former may lack conventional forms of collateral such as land, which is technically owned by the state. While charging higher interest rates to higher-risk clients is a standard practice among commercial banks in liberalized financial environments, the persistence of interest rate ceilings in China restrains the ability of state banks to structure loans in a commercially viable manner. In short, credit officers lack institutional incentives for extending private-sector loans.

The Other Side: Informal Finance in Contemporary China

It is not surprising, therefore, that entrepreneurs have created a wide array of nongovernmental financing mechanisms and institutions. Many of these financing practices are not officially sanctioned; indeed, some are explicitly illegal. While casual lending among friends and relatives is generally seen and condoned by banking officials as an innocuous form of mutual assistance (*huzhu xingshi*), such practices as rotating credit associations and short-term trade credit reside within the gray area of quasi-legality in China.[29] Other financing practices—such as private money houses and high-interest brokering—are unquestionably forbidden by the

28. Interview No. 17.
29. By "gray area of quasi-legality," I mean that some financing practices may be sanctioned by some bureaucracies but not others; similarly, different administrative levels of the government (central, provincial, municipal, county, township, village) may have conflicting regulations governing substantively similar practices.

central bank. In contemporary Chinese writings on the nonbanking financial sector, great care is taken to distinguish between "private" (*siren, siying*) and "popular, folk, of the people" (*minjian*) credit activities. Popular finance (*minjian jinrong*) is seen as comprising small-scale, informal undertakings that connote a spirit of mutual aid and local tradition. On the other hand, "private" is typically used to denote for-profit, noncommunal financial activities that are generally illegal because they involve interest payments.

Notwithstanding these politically significant differences in nomenclature and legality, most of the financing mechanisms employed by private entrepreneurs in China may be classified as residing within the informal financial sector that economists call the curb market, or sometimes "unorganized finance."[30] But that term is misleading, since many of the financing arrangements it includes are in fact well organized and institutionalized. Hence, I use the terms "informal finance" and "curb market" to denote the full range of financing practices and institutions that lie beyond the state banking system (see Table 2.3).

The vast majority of private entrepreneurs rely on the curb market, though the actual scale and volume of each of these financing mechanisms is difficult to assess, since they occur outside of the official banking system. A conservative estimate would be that during the first two decades of reform, curb market activities accounted for at least one-quarter of all financial transactions.[31] To put it in perspective, the informal financial sector as a percentage of the Chinese economy is similar to the scale of informal finance in Taiwan, Thailand, and Korea during their respective

30. See Alek A. Rozental, "Unorganized Financial Markets and Developmental Strategy," *Journal of Developing Areas* 1, 4 (1967): 453–60.

31. One study, based on rural surveys conducted in Jilin and Jiangsu, estimated that informal sources accounted for one-third to two-thirds of all rural credit during the 1980s: Gershon Feder, Lawrence J. Lau, Justin Y. Lin, and Luo Xiaopeng, "Agricultural Credit and Farm Performance in China," *Journal of Comparative Economics* 13, 4 (1989): 508–26. A more recent estimate was that in 1994 one-quarter of all commercial financial transactions in China occurred beyond the state banking system, totaling over 200 billion *yuan* (US$24.6 billion): Shi Jianping, "Jinrong lifa yu yinhang tizhi gaige" (Financial legislation and reform of the banking system), in *Zhongguo jingji daqushi 1996* (Major trends in China's economy 1996) (Hong Kong: Shangwu yinshuguan, 1996), 160–63 (that 200 billion *yuan* figure may include financial flows in state-sanctioned nonbanking financial institutions like urban and rural credit cooperatives). A more conservative estimate of the volume of informal lending in 1995 was 30 billion *yuan* (US$3.7 billion): Zhu Delin and Hu Meiou, *Zhongguo de huiheise jinrong—shichang fengyun yu lixing sikao* (China's grey black finance—market trends and reflections on improvements) (Shanghai: Lixin huiji chubanshe, 1997), 44. Yet another study reported 20 percent of the total Chinese population participating in informal finance and a minimum of 70 billion *yuan* (US$8.6 billion) circulating in the form of high-interest loans annually: Huang Weiting, *Zhongguo de yinxing jingji* (China's hidden economy) (Beijing: Zhongguo shangye chubanshe, 1996), 252, which points out that the main participants in informal finance are farmers and microentrepreneurs.

Table 2.3 Overview of Curb Market Activities in China

Legal	Quasi-Legal	Illegal
interpersonal lending	rural cooperative foundations (illegal since 1999)	professional brokers and money lenders (loan sharks)
trade credit	shareholding cooperative enterprises	private money houses
rotating credit associations (in some areas)	red hat/hang-on enterprises	rotating credit associations (in some areas)
pawnshops (in some areas)	financial societies/capital mutual assistance associations	pyramidal investment schemes (scams)
	pawnshops (in some areas)	

Note: None of the practices/institutions in the second and third columns are sanctioned by the People's Bank of China. Those in the first column are "legal" only if they do not entail the use of interest rates. "Quasi-legal" practices are those that are registered by a bureaucracy outside of the financial hierarchy.

postwar decades of rapid economic growth (see Chapter Six). In private-sector finance, however, the significance of informal finance relative to official sources is much higher. If we consider that the non-state sector has accounted for the preponderance of China's economic growth and that state banks are not available to most private businesses (including the illicit diversion of official bank credit from state units to the curb market), then it is conceivable that informal sources have accounted for up to three-quarters of private-sector credit in those two decades.

Despite the imprecise nature of these estimates, officials in Beijing are clearly concerned about the bottom-line monetary scale of informal finance in China. Moreover, from a regulatory perspective, they are also attuned to the organizational attributes of private entrepreneurs' financing mechanisms. Highly institutionalized forms of private finance, for example, are more readily identifiable for official punishment than less institutionalized ones. Therefore, for heuristic purposes, private entrepreneurs' financing practices may be classified along a categorical continuum of "low," "medium," and "high." Financing practices with low degrees of institutionalization would include casual interpersonal borrowing and lending. At the other extreme, financing practices with high degrees of institutionalization follow standardized procedures that are employed in an organizational context. Financing practices with medium degrees of institutionalization may be contractual but lack a physical organization, and the relationships among the participants tend to be more personalized.[32]

32. The way I operationalize and define "institutionalization" resonates with Zuckers "ethnomethodological approach to institutionalization." She writes, "Acts are not simply institutionalized or not institutionalized. The meaning of an act may be perceived as more or less

For the range of informal financing mechanisms according to degree of institutionalization, see Table 2.4.

Although the primary focus of this book is on financial *institutions*, the interpersonal relationships on which noninstitutionalized financing practices depend may enable them to evolve into institutions. A politically insulated loan shark, for instance, might decide after a few years of successful moonlighting to open a pawnshop or money house. The boundary between somewhat institutionalized and clearly institutionalized financing arrangements is not always sharp, but the basic distinction is worthwhile for the purposes of understanding why some informal practices become more institutionalized than others and under what circumstances private financial institutions in fact emerge. Furthermore, some localities exhibit the full range of curb market mechanisms, while others have only a moderate or negligible level of informal financial activity. Therefore, for heuristic purposes I have classified localities according to whether they had a low, medium, or high range of financial institutional diversity.

Organizing the Research

I organized my research around two empirical questions: First, what explains the variation among localities in the range of informal finance? Second, what explains the differences among private entrepreneurs in their use of informal finance? On the basis of the first objective I chose eighteen research sites distributed across different levels of development (urban, peri-urban, and rural areas) in different regions: Henan in central northern China and Fujian and Zhejiang in the coastal south (Table 2.5). Then I administered surveys to business owners in each site to answer the second question.

My proposed hypothesis for the first issue was that the orientation of local governments toward the private sector had a defining impact on the contours of financial institutional supply at the local level. Given that I did not know a priori the attitude of local government towards the private sector, or the extent of informal financial activity in various localities, I selected sites that would ensure variation in two competing independent variables posited by the economic-based and state-centric explanations:

---

exterior and objective, depending on the situation in which the act is performed and/or depending on the position and role occupied by the actor. For example, acts which are dependent on a particular unique actor are low on institutionalization as in personal influence. In contrast, acts which are performed by an actor occupying a specified position or role are high on institutionalization": Lynne G. Zucker, "Institutionalization and Cultural Persistence," *American Sociological Review* 42, 5 (1977): 729.

Table 2.4 Summary of Private Entrepreneurs' Financing Practices and Institutions

Name	Description	Degree of Institutionalization
Interpersonal lending (*minjian jiedai*)	lending among friends, relatives, neighbors, and work colleagues	low (interest-free) low–medium
Trade credit (*hangye xinyong*)	short-term merchandise credit extended by wholesalers to retailers, typically interest-free	medium
Brokers, money lenders, middlemen (*yinbei*)	financial brokering among savers and borrowers at high interest rates	medium
Red hat/hang-on enterprises (*dai hongmaozi, guahu qiye*)	raising capital from banks and state-owned enterprises by posing as a collective enterprise	high
Shareholding cooperative enterprises (*gufen hezuo qiye*)	pooling of operations and capital among enterprises via the issuance of shares	high

Credit associations (*hui*)
  1. Basic (*chenghui, hehui, juhui*)
    a) Rotating (*lunhui*)
 	
    b) Bidding (*biaohui*)
 	
  2. Escalating (*taihui, paihui*)
	
	1. lending and savings among a set group of peers
	  a) order of loans determined by pre-set rotating schedule
	  b) order of loans determined by bidding system
	2. pyramidal investment scheme (scam)
		medium–high

Underground private money houses (*dixia qianzhuang*)	provision of savings and credit services under the guise of a nonfinancial operation	medium
Private money houses (*qianzhuang*)	provision of savings and credit services	high
People-run enterprises capital mutual assistance society (*minying qiye zijin huzhushe*)	provision of financial services to private entrepreneurs	high
Peri-urban cooperative savings foundations (*jiaoqu hezuo chu jijinhui*)	provision of financial services to private entrepreneurs	high
Rural cooperative foundations (*nongcun hezuo jijinhui*)	village-operated savings and lending institutions	high
Pawnshops (*dangpu, diandang*)	collateralized discount lending	high

Table 2.5 Distribution of Research Sites by Region and Level of Development

	Urban	Peri-Urban	Rural[a]
North Central (Henan)	Zhengzhou (HN) Luoyang (HN)	Yanshi (HN) Kaifeng (HN)	Yellow River villages (4): Nanzhao; Yucheng
Coastal South (Fujian and Zhejiang)	Fuzhou (FJ) Quanzhou (FJ)	Changle (FJ) Huian (FJ) Jinjiang (FJ) Wenzhou (ZJ)	Mountainous villages outside of Changle (4): Haixing; Chongwu, Anxi

Note: Province abbreviations in parentheses: FJ, Fujian; HN, Henan; ZJ, Zhejiang.
[a] Although I studied four villages along the Yellow River and four in the mountains flanking Changle, I implemented the survey in only two villages in each case.

respectively, the level of private commercial activity and the degree of state capacity in implementing central policies.

The logic of the economic explanation is that a wider range of financial institutions would be expected to develop in localities where there is a higher demand for credit on the part of private entrepreneurs. Therefore, I used official employment statistics to evaluate the relative scope of the private sector in each site.[33] Table 2.6 lists the figures. As pointed out by Ole Odgaard, official statistics on China's non-state sector have serious shortcomings.[34] Discrepancies between figures listed in the provincial statistical yearbooks and those internal numbers compiled by the Industrial and Commercial Management Bureau (ICMB) were striking; specifically, the ICMB cited much higher numbers of people employed in the private sector. This is curious, given that small businesses (*getihu*) tend to *under-report* their number of full-time employees, since the *getihu* registration status limits the number of employees to eight. One explanation for the discrepancy is that state-owned enterprises, to continue receiving subsidies,

33. Other possible measures for evaluating the degree of "private commercial activity": (1) the contribution of the private sector to the local economy's GDP or GVIAO; (2) the amount of taxes collected from private businesses; (3) the absolute number of registered private businesses; (4) the number of officially designated private markets in a given locality. The first is probably the best for the purpose; I did not use it, however, because statistics were not available to me for all the localities under consideration. The second would be a less valid measure because it might conflate the extractive capacity of the local state (a separate issue) with the actual size of the private sector. The third and fourth are similar in conception to the measure that I ultimately used, private-sector employment, but I chose to focus on the number of people involved in private business.

34. Ole Odgaard, "Inadequate and Inaccurate Chinese Statistics: The Case of Private Rural Enterprises," *China Information* 5 (Winter 1990): 29–38. Chinese economists are also well aware that the current classificatory system for differentiating economic organizations is ambiguous and misleading. See, e.g., Li Chengrui, "Current Statistical Issues for Economic Sector Classification and Ownership Composition," *Jingji yanjiu* (Economic research) (July 20, 1997): 63–67.

Table 2.6 Sectoral Distribution of Employment by Research Site, 1996

Research Site	State (%)	Collective (%)	Other/ Private (%)	Degree of Private Commercial Activity
Jinjiang City/County (FJ)	24.6 (14.9)[a]	9.0	66.5	more
Wenzhou City (ZJ)	40.3 (22.8)	(28.5)[a]	(48.6)[a]	more
Quanzhou District (FJ)	48.5 (25.7)	16.3	35.2	more
Changle County/City (FJ)	49.4	27.7	22.9	more
Quanzhou City (FJ)	52.9	19.0	28.2	more
Fuzhou District (FJ)	59.0 (57.2)	18.7	22.3	less
Yanshi City (HN)	62.5	27.8	9.7	less
Fuzhou City (FJ)	62.7 (60.7)	18.3	19.0	less
Zhengzhou City (HN)	69.1 (49.2)	21.8	9.2	more[b]
Anxi County (FJ)	62.4	9.0	28.6	less
Huian County (FJ)	62.8 (44.6)	26.8	10.4	less
Luoyang City (HN)	72.4 (45.6)	24.8	2.8	more[b]
Kaifeng District (HN)	79.3 (44.0)	19.7	1.0	more[b]
Kaifeng City (HN)	87.3	12.6	0.1	less

Source: 1997 Provincial Statistical Yearbooks (*tongji nianjian*) from Fujian (FJ), Henan (HN), and Zhejiang (ZJ).
[a] Table excludes the 4 villages in Henan and Fujian, in which surveys were administered.
[b] Percentages in parentheses were calculated by the author based on the number of people employed in the private sector according to the local ICMB. (FZ = 1995.)
[c] This classification based on ICMB figures is probably a better reflection of the actual scale of private-sector employment than general provincial statistics would suggest.

may count employees who have effectively left to work in the private sector full time. In any case, for the purpose of evaluating the actual scale of full-time employment in each sector (state, collective, private), I recalculated the percentages based on the ICMB's private-sector numbers; these figures are presented in parentheses and noted with an asterisk in the table. In classifying each locality according to the size of its private sector (far right column), I also took into consideration the relative size of the collective sector, since private enterprises sometimes register themselves as collectives to secure preferential treatment.

In contrast to the economic expectation that greater private commercial activity would bring about a wider variety of informal financial institutions, the state-centric explanation would focus on the central government's exercise of different degrees of "financial capacity" over different provinces through the formal financial system. More specifically, the state-centric view would expect greater financial institutional diversity in areas where the state has exercised relatively less financial capacity, and fewer types of curb market mechanisms in areas where the state has exercised greater financial capacity. This difference in capacity is reflected in the wide variation of provincial loan-to-deposit (L/D) ratios. For example, where the state banks lend as much as they are collect in savings deposits, the L/D ratio is

Table 2.7 Comparison of Loan-to-Deposit Ratios of State Banks: Henan, Fujian, and Zhejiang, 1988–1999

Year	Henan Province	Fujian Province	Zhejiang Province
1988	1.48	1.23	1.26
1989	1.42	1.18	1.19
1990	1.36	1.07	1.05
1991	1.28	0.96	0.97
1992	1.25	0.88	0.93
1993	1.20	0.95	0.92
1994	1.16	0.90	0.90
1995	1.12	0.83	0.81
1996	1.09	0.78	0.75
1997	1.13	0.75	0.77
1998	1.14	0.79	0.73
1999	1.12	0.79	0.74

Sources: Ratios from 1988–93 were calculated by Lardy, *China's Unfinished Economic Revolution*, 226, Table A.2. Ratios from 1994–99 were calculated by the author based on data from *JRNJ 1997*, 191, 199, 210; *JRNJ 1998*, 194, 202, 213; *JRNJ 1999*, 126, 133, 141; and *JRNJ 2000*, 153, 160, 168.
Note: The national average loan-to-deposit ratio is 1.0.

1.0. Less than 1.0 would indicate that the province as a whole was not lending out as much as it was receiving in deposits; greater than 1.0, that the province was receiving a greater share of funds for on-lending than the provincial financial institutions were mobilizing in deposits. The discrepancy in L/D ratios demonstrates that the center is exercising *financial* (as opposed to *fiscal*) capacity over certain provinces and reallocating bank funds to other provinces. Provinces that are net suppliers of capital may thus be seen as having less financial capacity vis-à-vis the center than provinces that are net recipients of bank capital. Table 2.7 shows how the ratios varied by province from 1988 to 1999.

In the specific provinces under consideration, it is evident that L/D ratios have declined over the course of the 1990s. On the whole, however, the state has demonstrated greater financial capacity in mobilizing deposits from Fujian and Zhejiang (coastal south) than in Henan (northern central China). The latter continues to be a net recipient of bank credits, while Fujian and Zhejiang have been net suppliers of state capital since 1991. In other words, despite the coastal south's earlier start on economic reform, the center has exercised greater financial capacity over state banks in those provinces.[35]

35. "Financial capacity" should not be conflated with the "fiscal capacity" of the center. The southern coastal provinces have been in a favorable negotiating position with regard to fiscal revenue retention relative to poorer provinces.

Table 2.8 Research Sites Organized by Economic and Statist Explanatory Variables

Economic Hypothesis → Statist Hypothesis ↓	Areas with less commercial activity	Areas with more commercial activity
Areas with greater state capacity	Yanshi (Henan) Nanzhao (Henan) villages along the Yellow River (4 in Henan)	Luoyang (Henan) Zhengzhou (Henan) Kaifeng (Henan)
Areas with less state capacity	Fuzhou (Fujian) Anxi (Fujian) Moutainous villages outside Changle (4)	Wenzhou (Zhejiang) Quanzhou (Fujian) Jinjiang (Fujian) Changle (Fujian) Huian (Fujian)

Table 2.8 shows the distribution of the research sites across the economic and statist explanatory categories. (Note that the municipalities of Beijing and Shanghai were intentionally excluded, given their unique political and economic positions within reform-era China.)

As I had hoped, the research sites also demonstrated variation across the values of my proposed independent variable: the local government's orientation toward the private sector. If local governments that are more supportive of the private economy are also more likely to sanction non-governmental financial institutions—even technically illegal ones, according to the People's Bank of China—one would expect greater financial institutional diversity in areas where the state has a supportive attitude toward the private sector; less where the state is less supportive of private-sector development; medium levels of diversity where the state has an ambivalent attitude toward the private sector. I used the following indicators to evaluate qualitatively the extent to which the local government (city, county, township) had been "supportive" of the private economy: (1) The presence of an active ICMB, the agency responsible for registering and monitoring the activities of private entrepreneurs; (2) the presence of an active Individual Laborers' Association (ILA–*geti laodongzhe xiehui*), the mass organization representing the interests of microentrepreneurs; (3) lower de facto rates of taxation (measured by the surveyed entrepreneurs' self-reported taxes and fees paid as a proportion of gross monthly income); (4) supportive internal policy documents regarding the regulation and development of the private sector; (5) supportive public rhetoric (in the local press and public campaigns) regarding the private sector and related reform issues; and (6) interviews with cadres and officials from various bureaucracies indicating a high priority on private-sector development.

Those indicators provide a basic means to assess the local government's stance at any given point in time. The argument could be made, however, that it would be more challenging to formulate a general evaluation of a locality's position on the private sector over time because considerable variation in the national policy environment, as well as in the nuances of local politics, is discernible throughout the 1978 to 2001 period.[36] At the national level, the agricultural reforms initiated in late 1978 ultimately enabled individual rural households to engage in production for private profit after fulfilling state quotas.[37] But not until 1984 were liberalizing reforms extended to urban areas, and then the process remained uneven and cyclical throughout the 1980s. After the political crisis of 1989, Deng's southern tour in 1992 signaled that economic reform would indeed continue. And Jiang Zemin's "July 1" speech celebrating the CCP's eightieth anniversary in 2001 represented another controversial turning point when he suggested that private entrepreneurs be permitted to join in party. To a certain extent the vicissitudes of reform and retrenchment emanating from Beijing can be seen in similar dynamics at the subnational level. Nonetheless, convincing arguments have also been made that the course of economic reform has been more of a "bottom-up" process. Numerous studies have shown that economic innovations often originate at the local level and are only later sanctioned by a reactive central government.[38] I agree with the latter position regarding the influence of localities in charting the course of their local economic development since the beginning of reform. To be sure, localities have demonstrated their share of political uncertainty, factionalism, and regulatory flip-flopping. But over time, examination of the six measures listed are adequate for an observer to form an impression about whether a particular locality's attitude has been supportive, ambivalent, or nonsupportive toward the private sector. Thus, the empirical chapters incorporate local political complexities without losing sight of the overall developmental orientation of the local government during the reform era.

In my fieldwork, I attempted to collect the same information from each

36. See the debate summarized in Richard Baum, *Burying Mao: Chinese Politics in the Age of Deng Xiaoping* (Princeton: Princeton University Press, 1994), 5–23; cf. Kenneth Lieberthal, *Governing China: From Revolution to Reform* (New York: Norton, 1995), 137–44; and Joseph Fewsmith, *China since Tiananmen: The Politics of Transition* (New York: Cambridge University Press, 2001).

37. Note that considerable regional variation could be seen in the process of decollectivization and implementation of the Household Responsibility System.

38. Carol Hamrin, *China and the Challenge of the Future: Changing Political Patterns* (Boulder, Colo.: Westview Press, 1990); Daniel Kelliher, *Peasant Power in China: The Era of Rural Reform, 1979–88* (New Haven: Yale University Press, 1992); Kristin Parris, "Local Initiative and National Reform: The Wenzhou Model of Development," *China Quarterly* 134 (June 1993): 242–63; Ya-ling Liu, "Reform from Below: The Private Economy and Local Politics in the Rural Industrialization of Wenzhou," *China Quarterly* 130 (June 1992): 293–316; and Kate Xiao Zhou, *How the Farmers Changed China* (Boulder, Colo.: Westview Press, 1996).

research site in a systematic and theoretically informed manner.[39] The strategy entailed three components: (1) surveying microentrepreneurs (*getihu*) and selected private entrepreneurs (*siying qiyejia*) ($n = 374$); (2) interviewing managers of state banks, credit cooperatives and informal financial institutions, governmental officials, bureaucrats in the ICMB and the ILA, Women's Federation (*fulian*) cadres, scholars, and development practitioners ($n = 186$); and (3) gathering documents relating to economic and financial system reform, taxation, social stratification, internal migration, and gender issues.[40]

Because many small-scale private entrepreneurs are not officially registered with the ICMB—the agency charged with regulating private businesses—I did not rely on its rosters to select survey participants. Instead, upon arriving at each site I first enlisted the assistance of a local scholar or resident to identify the central retailing and wholesaling markets and, as well, more peripheral areas for private commerce such as back roads, sidewalks, alleyways, and night markets in order to include private businesses not formally registered with the ICMB. I noted the approximate distribution of private vendors in various commercial trades (e.g., food service, clothing, electronics) and their relative differences in scale, and later compared that to official documentation of the local private sector. To get a sense of the grassroots market context, I also paid attention to evidence of segmentation by product (e.g., specialized markets that sold only one type of good) and the socioeconomic characteristics of vendors (e.g, market ghettos of migrants from a particular province or former employees of a particular state factory).

After engaging in informal conversations with local residents and vendors about their general impression of the local markets, my research assistant and I would start approaching individual vendors to enlist their participation in the survey. Potential respondents were informed that the survey was intended only for academic purposes and guaranteed confidentiality. On average, nearly 60 percent of the vendors we approached were willing to participate in the survey.[41] It is important to note that the sampling was not "systematic" in the technical sense of the word. We did not, for example, approach every so many vendors, nor did we engage in

39. In social science, this is known as the method of "structured, focused comparison" in collecting data across case studies: Alexander L. George and Timothy J. McKeown, "Case Studies and Theories of Organizational Decision Making," *Advances in Information Processing in Organizations* 2 (1985): 21–58.

40. The formal interviews date back to the summer of 1994, before I commenced the survey portion of the research.

41. The response rate was calculated as follows: (number of entrepreneurs willing to participate in the survey)/(number of entrepreneurs approached to participate).

Vendors freezing outdoors. Tangshan, Hebei, January 2000.

"snowball sampling"—relying on referrals for the next interview—which would have introduced even stronger bias into the aggregate data. (Appendix A discusses limitations and potential biases in the survey data and how these shortcomings were addressed.)

With only a handful of exceptions, the survey questions were administered orally, and either my assistant or I recorded the responses.[42] I also asked follow-up questions and encouraged the business owner to elaborate on the details of the business, past experiences, and almost anything else that facilitated a more natural exchange of conversation. The length of time required to complete a single survey ranged from half an hour to several hours.[43] Under typical conditions the process was interrupted only two or three times by everyday business activities and took about forty-five minutes. I also paid informal follow-up visits to entrepreneurs who had had particularly interesting experiences.

42. Of 374 surveys (see Appendix C), fewer than ten were completed by the entrepreneurs themselves, well-educated persons who felt that it would be faster for them to check off the responses themselves.

43. Some surveys were coupled with a tour of the production facilities or factory and meeting family members, capped off with a banquet.

The interviews with officials, bankers, and academics were less standardized than the surveys because of their differing areas of expertise.[44]
Nonetheless, the same kinds of questions were asked of interviewees within
the same profession (e.g., bank managers were all asked finance-related
questions). Nearly all the interviews were arranged by official hosts at
the provincial, municipal, county, or township level, though some were
set up less formally, through friends and acquaintances. (Meetings with
financial entrepreneurs engaged in quasi-legal or explicitly illegal operations such as "loan sharking" were generally arranged through informal
means.)[45] Taken together, the interviews with officials were intended to
supplement the survey findings with Chinese elite perceptions of past and
contemporary political, economic, financial, and social issues and, more
specifically, to evaluate the local governmental attitude toward the private
sector. Chinese-language publications (policy documents, scholarly books
and articles, newspapers, statistical compilations) provided a broader
empirical context within which I could frame my primary research and
engage in "triangulation" to reconcile or clarify contradictory or ambiguous findings.

Summary of Research Findings

As explained, the core of my argument is that the orientation of the local
government toward the private sector accounts for the degree of institutional diversity in informal finance. Table 2.9 shows that only two of my
eighteen sites did not conform to the hypothesized outcome: Jinjiang and
Luoyang, indicated in italicized text.[46] In all the remaining localities the

44. Throughout the book I use the term "survey" or "surveyed" to refer to the formal
surveys of business owners, while the term "interview" is reserved for meetings with non-
entrepreneurs and professional moneylenders (a.k.a. "financial entrepreneurs") that did not
complete surveys. By the same token, those "surveyed" are referred to as "respondents"; those
"interviewed," as "informants" or "interviewees." The distinction between "respondents" and
"interviewees" is also made in William L. Parish and Martin King Whyte, *Village and Family in
Contemporary China* (Chicago: University of Chicago Press, 1978).

45. However, some of my interviews with financial entrepreneurs running illicit financial
institutions were arranged by governmental officials and employees, suggesting local governmental knowledge and complicity in sanctioning their operations. Some officials were
actually proud that the institutions had been able to devise ingeniously legal disguises for
engaging in the business of finance.

46. The local government in Jinjiang County has been explicitly supportive of private-sector
development throughout the reform era, yet local entrepreneurs have not devised a wide
range of financing mechanisms—perhaps because the private sector is so dominant in Jinjiang that private businesses have been better able to access credit from state-sanctioned financial institutions than have those in other areas. In the second anomalous case, Luoyang City,
the government is interested in fostering private enterprise, but the private sector remains
relatively small, and local entrepreneurs continue to rely on a limited repertoire of interpersonal lending and trade credit.

Table 2.9 Summary of Hypotheses and Cases Concerning the Institutional Supply of Informal Finance

Attitude of Local Government toward Private Sector	Empirical Cases	Prediction (diversity of institutional supply)	Actual Outcome
Supportive	Fuzhou (FJ)	high (>6 types)	high
	Changle (FJ)		high
	Jinjiang (FJ)		*medium*
	Quanzhou (FJ)		high
	Wenzhou (ZJ)		high
Ambivalent	Kaifeng (HN)	medium (4–6 types)	medium
	Luoyang (HN)		*low*
	Yanshi (HN)		medium
	Zhengzhou (HN)		medium
Not supportive	Anxi (FJ)	low (0–3 types)	low
	Haixing (FJ)		low
	Huian (FJ)		low
	Nanzhao (HN)		low
	4 Villages (FJ, HN)		low

expected and actual outcomes were consistent; that is, the orientation of the local government toward the private sector corresponded with the resulting diversity of informal financial institutions.

A quick glance back at Table 2.8 shows that although both the economic and state-centric arguments appear to perform relatively well on the surface, their explanatory strength falls short in several key cases. With the exceptions of four sites in Henan (Yanshi, Kaifeng City, Luoyang, and Zhengzhou), localities with a more developed private sector indeed had a broader menu of informal financial institutions, as the economic hypothesis expected. This may be explained in part by the unsurprising relationship between the orientation of local governments toward the private sector and the size of the private sector itself. But Chapter 5 on Henan will demonstrate how the four aberrant cases actually lend strong support to my contention that local governmental policies toward private businesses are central in mediating the proliferation or restriction of informal finance. In each of the outlying cases, specific decisions and policies can be identified which reflect deeper developmental and political priorities of local governments. Even in areas where a substantial portion of the population is employed in the state sector, local officials may implicitly permit the innovative provision of private credit.

A state-centric approach to analyzing the politics of informal finance would expect local variation in private credit activity to reflect regional or provincial biases in the central state's developmental strategies, but the state-centric lens is too broad to explain the gap between central policies and empirical reality in subprovincial localities. Ultimately, local political and economic actors work around the constraints of central state policies by molding them to suit locally defined interests.

Do regional and provincial differences matter? The short answer is yes, but not in a manner that accounts for the observed local variation in the institutional supply and demand of private finance. Nonetheless, it is worth pointing out that notable regional differences exist in economic endowments, historical political position relative to the central government, and reform-era trajectories.

First, within the first decade of reform it became apparent that some rural areas were industrializing along more socialistic, collective forms of corporate organization. Areas whose rural industrialization derived primarily from collective Township and Village Enterprises became known as following the "Sunan model" because of the proliferation of TVEs in Jiangsu. The Sunan model of development seemed to be particularly popular in areas where Mao's collectivist, communal policies had taken a stronger hold. In contrast, areas with weaker institutional traditions of Maoist collectivism were industrializing along more private forms of corporate organization; this became known as the "Wenzhou model" because private entrepreneurship reemerged particularly early in the coastal district of Wenzhou in Zhejiang Province.[47] The provinces covered in this study—Henan, Fujian, and Zhejiang—also inherited significantly different economic legacies from the first several decades of PRC rule, which has in turn shaped their reform-era development. Specifically, unlike the southern coastal provinces, Henan received substantial heavy industrial investment during the Mao period. As one of the core provinces in the PRC's First Five-Year Plan and Mao's Third Front strategy for industrial development, Henan became a home for Stalinist-scale production of steel, coal, and military supplies and equipment.[48] Fujian and Zhejiang, on the other hand, were systematically prevented from developing substantial industrial bases because they were physically more accessible to potential invaders.

---

47. For an excellent discussion of the different developmental models, see Jieh-min Wu, "Local Property Rights Regime in Socialist Reform: A Case Study of China's Informal Privatization" (Ph.D. diss., Columbia University, 1998).

48. In 1965 the State Planning Commission issued an economic program for military preparedness in which the central government would devote its resources to building a strategic industrial base in China's hinterland, or what became known as the "third tier" or "third front." It included Sichuan, Yunnan, Guizhou, Shaanxi, Qinghai, Ningxia, and western parts of Shanxi, Henan, Hubei, and Hunan. The so-called first tier included the coastal areas, Xinjiang, and Inner Mongolia; the second comprised the areas between the first and the third tiers. The "third tier construction" (*sanxian jianshe*) is generally considered to have been an inefficient use of resources, since the state emphasized heavy industry and military industry and neglected light industry and agriculture. Moreover, the projects were not well planned or coordinated. See Barry Naughton, "The Third Front: Defense Industrialization in the Chinese Interior," *China Quarterly* 115 (September 1988): 351–86.

This means that although Henan's infrastructure and transportation facilities were relatively well developed on the eve of reform, it then faced the burden of reforming large state-owned enterprises, employing twenty thousand to sixty thousand people each. In addition to absorbing the surplus labor released from agricultural reform, Henan's economy has faced the challenge of dealing with unemployed workers in urban industrial areas since the mid-1990s.[49]

Second and relatedly, northern inland and southern coastal provinces have had vastly different political experiences in the course of Chinese history.[50] In the immediate post-Republican era the base of CCP power was ultimately consolidated in the north, while campaigns to wipe out Nationalist elements—dubbed "anti-Communists," "rightists," and "counterrevolutionaries"—continued vigorously in the coastal south for many years after the PRC was formally established.[51] This is not to say that northern provinces were spared in anti-rightist campaigns and other nationwide political movements but, rather, that Guangdong, Fujian, and Zhejiang— given their propinquity to non-Communist countries—tended to be treated with greater political suspicion, whereas Beijing perceived its neighboring northern provinces in less threatening terms.

Third (and as a consequence of the first two differences), experimental zones for economic reform and "open cities" for foreign investment were first permitted in the southern coastal provinces of Guangdong, Fujian, and, later on, Zhejiang. In other words, the coastal south had an earlier start on various reform measures, including preferential tax treatment for collective and foreign-invested enterprises, the formation of export-processing zones, and even the establishment of financial institutions to support these new transactions. For example, the first Chinese-foreign joint venture bank, Xiamen International Bank, was established in 1985.[52] Joint venture banks were not sanctioned in the central and northern provinces until the late 1990s.

Fourth, the central government has exercised different degrees of

49. When I was in Henan during the summer of 1996, unemployed workers and workers who were owed back wages gathered almost daily outside the city or provincial government offices. In 1998, violent incidents involving disgruntled workers increased dramatically. See, e.g., *China News Digest*, January 15, 1998 (laid-off railroad worker from Henan blows himself up in Beijing); *SCMP*, April 17, 1998 (rivalry between licensed and unlicensed coal miners leads to explosion killing fifty-five people in Pingdingshan, Henan).

50. For overviews of long-standing regional differences in Chinese history, see John King Fairbank, *China: A New History* (Cambridge: Harvard University Press, 1992); and Jonathan D. Spence, *The Search for Modern China* (New York: Norton, 1990).

51. See A. Doak Barnett, *Communist China: The Early Years, 1949–1955* (New York: Praeger, 1964); Ezra F. Vogel, *Canton under Communism: Programs and Politics in a Provincial Capital, 1949–1968* (Cambridge: Harvard University Press, 1969).

52. Kazuhiko Shimizu, "Breaching the Great Wall," *Institutional Investor* (June 1998), 95.

"financial capacity" over different provinces through the formal financial system, reflected in the loan-to-deposit ratios discussed above.

It is important to specify which of these regional differences have relevant empirical implications in local credit markets.[53] The main question is whether the state-influenced, provincial-level differences between Fujian and Zhejiang on the one hand and Henan on the other explain the observed variation in financial institutional diversity in the informal financial sector and private entrepreneurs' capital-raising strategies. If so, then the statist hypothesis would gain credence, since provincial differences could be traced back to specific central state policies; if not, then it is necessary to examine other potential explanations.

Among the broad regional variations in the formal financial system, southern coastal provinces had an earlier start in developing regional banks and other state-sanctioned institutions oriented toward attracting foreign investment. In terms of financial institutional diversity in the informal financial sector, a similar time lag exists. During the initial 1978–84 reform phase, for example, it is evident that certain areas in the coastal south had already developed (or revived) a substantial range of innovative financial institutions geared toward serving the local private sector, whereas provinces in northern and central China had not produced much more than rural cooperative foundations (RCFs), which were limited to rural areas. This difference may of course be attributed to the fact that the private sector also developed earlier in the coastal south. By the time I was conducting my field research, however, the gap in private-sector development between Fujian and Henan had narrowed somewhat. Furthermore, intraprovincial variation in private-sector development and financial institutional diversity was equally, if not more, striking than broad provincial or regional differences. Fujian (Chapter Three) has its share of localities with severely limited financing options. By the same token, the range of informal financial institutions in certain parts of Henan (Chapter Five) is by no means backward or stunted relative to those in southern coastal sites. To be sure, the private financial institutions in Henan take on somewhat different corporate forms, given the constraints of local policy, but diversity nonetheless exists. As shown in Table 2.9, areas with a high degree of financial institutional diversity are indeed located in the coastal south. Yet localities with a low degree of financial institutional diversity may be found in both the north and the south.

The existence of intraregional variation in the degree of financial institutional diversity calls into question the explanatory strength of the statist argument, which would expect greater diversity in areas where the state has experienced relatively less financial capacity. Conversely, fewer types of

53. See Wu, "Local Property Rights Regime in Socialist Reform."

financial institutions would be expected in areas where the state has experienced greater financial capacity. In short, the statist approach can account for the difference between areas with high versus medium levels of financial institutional diversity, but the finding that both types of provinces also contain localities with minimal financial institutional diversity complicates the story. An explanation cast at a lower level of generality than the state-centric lens is needed to account for such intraregional differences. As such, this book complements the analysis of central policies and regional differences in state capacity by examining the orientation of specific *local* governments toward the private sector.

The attitude of the local government toward the private sector may explain the variation in the institutional supply of informal finance in different localities, but the demand-side issue of what determines entrepreneurs' choice of financing mechanisms involves looking at the individual characteristics of business owners themselves. Overall, 70 percent of the entrepreneurs I surveyed reported participating in some form of informal finance. Of the respondents with curb market experience, 80 percent reported using less institutionalized forms of financing, 37 percent reported using informal credit mechanisms with medium degrees of institutionalization (e.g., rotating credit associations), and 11 percent reported accessing credit from more highly institutionalized curb market sources. These percentages total more than 100 percent because 20 percent used low *and* medium forms; 5.7 percent used medium *and* highly institutionalized forms; and 2.6 percent participated in the full spectrum of informal financing mechanisms. Despite this overlap, it is worth distinguishing among entrepreneurs who tend to rely on highly versus less institutionalized financing strategies in order to clarify the appeal and operational logic of each type of informal finance. Why some entrepreneurs rely primarily on loan sharks, for example, while others use more institutionalized financial intermediaries has theoretical and practical implications for understanding market segmentation at the local level. The specific research question is, what accounts for the variation in institutional choice within particular localities? The economic hypothesis would be that private business owners with higher incomes are more likely to use more institutionalized sources of credit than are lower-income entrepreneurs—the implication being that those entrepreneurs with greater economic resources at their disposal would be better equipped to meet the somewhat more standardized or stringent membership requirements of more institutionalized credit operations. In contrast, the state-centric hypothesis would take the broader view that entrepreneurs in localities where the state has experienced relatively less financial capacity would use more institutionalized financing practices.

The argument set forth here is that private entrepreneurs in a particu-

Table 2.10 Results of One-Tailed Bivariate Correlations

FININST by	R	N	Implication
Strength of political ties (POLTIES)	.1570***	264	highly significant relationship between strong political ties and highly institutionalized financing mechanisms
Residential origin (HOME)	−.0872**	372	locals significantly more likely to use more institutionalized financing mechanisms
Years in business (BUSTIME)	.2177***	263	more experienced businesses significantly more likely to use more institutionalized financing mechanisms
Gender (GENDER)	.1235**	264	men more likely to use more institutionalized financing mechanisms
Gross annual income (INCOME)	.0991*	372	higher-income entrepreneurs somewhat more likely to use more institutionalized financing mechanisms
Province (REGION)	.1179**	374	entrepreneurs in the south more likely to use more institutionalized financing mechanisms

Note: See Appendix A on the measurement of these variables (in caps).
*** Significant at or below the 1% level.
** Significant at or below the 5% level.
* Significant at or below the 10% level.

lar locality may be expected to choose different financing mechanisms, depending on their individual characteristics. Indeed, the survey data show that entrepreneurs vary in financing strategies depending on their length of time in business, strength of political ties, residential origin, and gender. These attributes give them access to different sorts of networks, which in turn mediate the types of financing arrangements available to them. The bivariate correlations in Table 2.10 show that private entrepreneurs are more likely to choose highly institutionalized financing arrangements if they have strong political ties, better-established businesses, higher incomes, and a local operation. In addition, women and entrepreneurs in the north are less likely than men and those in the south to employ highly institutionalized financing arrangements. Note, however, that the economic hypothesis associating entrepreneurs' income level with more institutionalized forms of credit performs at a weaker level of significance than the other indicators, which suggests that lower-income entrepreneurs are not necessarily excluded from more organized forms of financial intermediation. Besides income level, other social and political attributes of entrepreneurs influence their use of curb market finance.

Although the bivariate correlations demonstrate that all the variables in Table 2.10 have statistically significant relationships with FININST—the variable representing the degree of financial institutionalization—none of them have a strong linear relationship with FININST. The Pearson product correlation coeffficient (r) used in bivariate correlations ranges from +1 to −1 such that an r of zero would indicate the absence of systematic *linear* association, and the extremes of positive or negative 1 would demonstrate perfectly linear relationships. In short, these results suggest that the relationship between FININST and each of the variables is statistically significant but not in a linear fashion. Individually, none of the variables can account for a direct shift in private entrepreneurs' choice of financial institutions from low (1) to medium (2), or medium (2) to high (3). The nonlinearity of the correlations suggests that the unit-level qualities of private entrepreneurs operate in a contextually dependent manner. In other words, the ways in which the specific attributes of private entrepreneurs influence their financing strategies hinge on the political and economic environment of each locality.

Descriptive statistics comparing the institutionalization of financing mechanisms employed by private entrepreneurs in the north (Henan) and south (Fujian, Zhejiang) show that the primary category of financing arrangements exhibiting regional variation is in those classified as having a medium degree of institutionalization: that is, rotating credit associations. Specifically, rotating credit associations or *hui* are more popular in the south than in the north: 28 percent of surveyed entrepreneurs in the south had participated or were participating in some form of *hui*, versus only 8 percent in the north.

Although some observers might be tempted to attribute the relative paucity of *hui* in contemporary Henan to "cultural" differences, the cultural argument does not hold up, because people in Henan and other north-central provinces did participate in *hui* during the pre-reform era; as noted, the earliest documentation of *hui* goes back to Buddhist monasteries in the north during the Tang Dynasty. In the early twentieth century too, historians and anthropologists observed the use of *hui* in various north-central provinces for economic as well as social and ceremonial purposes. Although private finance was not legally permitted during the Mao era, informal savings and credit societies were often established within the institutional boundaries of the *danwei* to provide workers with a source of emergency funds, or as a means to finance expensive consumer items. As an elderly clothing stand owner in Henan explained, "Back in the days of Mao, we only earned about 45 *yuan* a month as railway workers, but things like bikes and watches cost over 100 *yuan*, so it made sense for each of us to contribute a small amount of money to a collective pool and then draw from it as needs would arise."[54] Other vendors and

54. Survey No. 261. In this respondent's railway *danwei, the huzhuhui* (mutual assistance association) was popular. Each *hui* consisted of seven or eight people who each contributed 20 *yuan* per month. He explained that at the time food was cheap, since it was subsidized,

interviewees who had participated in *hui* in their *danwei* echoed similar sentiments.[55]

Given that the practice of *hui* in Henan is as recent as the Cultural Revolution, it is curious that private entrepreneurs have not adopted rotating credit associations as a convenient form of credit. When the dichotomy between the communal nature of the *danwei* and individualistic basis of private enterprise is considered, however, the relative absence of *hui* among private entrepreneurs in Henan is less surprising. In the coastal south, *hui* are most prevalent among women in the developing rural and peri-urban areas—not former *danwei* workers.[56] Most of the surveyed entrepreneurs in Henan were urbanites who were either moonlighting while employed, had been formerly employed by state units, or were laid-off staff and workers from state units. As such, it is plausible that former *danwei* workers lacked a *guanxi* network composed of a significant number of others also needing credit. The *guanxi* networks of villagers, on the other hand, were replete with people in need of credit.[57]

When I asked vendors in Henan why *huzhuhui* were not as popular in the *danwei* anymore, most explained that it was because people had more money than before.[58] Be that as it may, the fact remains that private entrepreneurs constantly face liquidity constraints since so many of their assets are tied up in inventory. Moreover, the survey results show that entrepreneurs in Henan are more likely than their southern counterparts to rely on more formal financial institutions for savings and are equally likely as to engage in informal borrowing (albeit not in the form of *hui*). Therefore, although the foregoing explanation for regional differences in *hui* participation remains speculative, it does not fundamentally affect the logic of the broader argument.

Over two-thirds of all interviewees both north and south had engaged in some form of informal finance. Furthermore, the entrepreneurs surveyed in the north were no more likely than their southern counterparts to access

---

but consumer products were scarce and expensive. When asked what he used the money for, he said, "Of course I remember, I bought a bike for 150 *yuan*."

55. In the north, these include Interview Nos. 45, 92, 94; and Survey Nos. 195, 199, 202, 217, 239, 245, 261, 262, 291.

56. Of course, there are fewer former *danwei* workers in Fujian than in Henan.

57. See, e.g., Yunxiang Yan, *The Flow of Gifts: Reciprocity and Social Networks in a Chinese Village* (Stanford, Calif.: Stanford University Press, 1996), 143, 237. Another possible explanation is that the surveyed micro-entrepreneurs in Henan represent those who had experienced the Communist socialization of the *danwei* but had chosen an income-generating alternative path that is markedly individualistic in essence. These are people who relied on the state but dared to go against the communal grain to further their own standard of living. I suspect that this rejection (whether conscious or not) of group-oriented activity may explain in part why *getihu* do not organize *hui* for raising capital.

58. The clothing store vendor added, "As long as Mao doesn't return from the grave, people will continue to make money."

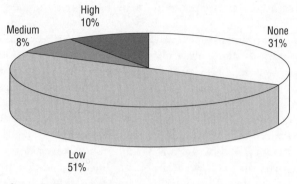

Source: Tsai surveys (1996–97)

Figure 2.2 Distribution of Private Entrepreneurs' Financing Practices: North

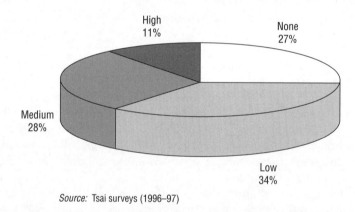

Source: Tsai surveys (1996–97)

Figure 2.3 Distribution of Private Entrepreneurs' Financing Practices: South

highly institutionalized sources of credit (10 percent of respondents in the north and 11 percent in the south) or to avoid borrowing all together (31 percent in the north and 27 percent in the south). This indicates that overall levels of participation in informal credit arrangements do not vary by province (see Figures 2.2 and 2.3).

As shown in Table 2.11, 62 percent of the surveyed private entrepreneurs in the north and south had lent money to others; 59 percent of the surveyed microentrepreneurs in the north and nearly 44 percent in the south had borrowed from friends, relatives, neighbors, or colleagues.

Regional differences in the amount, length, and interest rates of the interpersonal loans are apparent. Table 2.11 shows that lenders in the

Table 2.11 Descriptive Statistics: Regional Comparison of Informal Lending

Region	% Have Lending Experience	Average Amount of Loan (RMB)	Average Term of Loan (months)	Average Interest Rate (monthly)	% Satisfied w/Lending Experience
North	62.0	27,118	11.2	0.83%	77.0
South	62.5	10,792	4.5	2.80%	76.4

Source: Tsai surveys, 1996–97.

Table 2.12 Descriptive Statistics: Regional Comparison of Informal Borrowing

Region	% Having Borrowing Experience	Average Amount of Loan (RMB)	Average Term of Loan (months)	Average Interest Rate (monthly)	% Satisfied w/Borrowing Experience
North	59.0	18,863	10.5	0.32%	74.5
South	43.6	43,003	6.1	1.14%	83.8

Source: Tsai surveys, 1996–97.

north reported extending loans that were on average 151 percent larger than those in the south (27,118 versus 10,792 RMB per loan) and longer in duration (11.2 versus 4.5 months), yet *lower* in interest rates (0.83 percent per month versus 2.8 percent per month). On the borrowing side (Table 2.12), the regional differences in loan size are reversed: northerners extend larger loans but report borrowing smaller amounts; southerners extend smaller loans but borrow much larger amounts. This apparent discrepancy may derive from a variety of factors. For one, given the potential sensitivity of discussing the monetary details of informal lending habits, my respondents may have underestimated the loan amounts; if such bias exists, however, it would be consistent across region. Another possibility is that the surveyed entrepreneurs who reported lending money to others may not have been borrowing money from the same population of surveyed entrepreneurs, and vice versa. In other words, the borrowers in the south who reported average loan sizes of 43,003 *yuan* may not have been borrowing money from those entrepreneurs who reported lending an average of 10,792 *yuan*. As many interviewees pointed out, "I wouldn't be borrowing money from people if I had enough cash on hand to lend to others." Indeed, entrepreneurs who had *both* lending and borrowing experience made up only 43 and 36 percent of the respondents in the north and south, respectively.

Regardless of average loan size, however, it is evident that interpersonal lending among entrepreneurs in the south tends to be for shorter terms and at higher interest rates than in the north. This reflects in part the extent to which interpersonal relations among entrepreneurs in the southern coastal provinces are somewhat more commercialized. Although charging friends and relatives interest on loans is far from standardized practice in China, private entrepreneurs who need working capital on a day-to-day basis and understand the interest-generating potential of bank savings deposits are increasingly willing to charge interest on interpersonal loans. Their reactions to the question of whether or not they charged (or were charged) interest on informal loans were distinctly polarized. Most (the 93 and 72 percent of those who engaged in interest-free lending or borrowing, respectively) seemed surprised by the question: "You can't charge friends and relatives interest when they need money. That would be embarrassing." The interest-charging and interest-paying respondents (7 and 28 percent of those surveyed, respectively) answered the question like any other one, pausing briefly to recall the terms of the loan. A number of entrepreneurs and bankers noted that the practice of charging interest on interpersonal loans tends to increase when the Central Bank slashes interest rates on savings deposits. The rationale for this phenomenon is that opportunistic savers will withdraw their money from state banks to earn more money by extending high-interest loans to cash-constrained entrepreneurs. The Central Bank, of course, condemns such behavior as illegal loan-sharking.[59]

As for entrepreneurs' perceptions about participating in informal finance more generally, over three-quarters of the surveyed vendors who had lent money to other individuals expressed satisfaction with the experience. "I don't mind helping other entrepreneurs out," many interviewees said. But interpersonal borrowing and lending is not as innocuous or unproblematic as it may seem. Many interviewees qualified that response with a comment about the social pressure to lend to friends or relatives: "It isn't really an issue of being 'satisfied' or 'unsatisfied' with the lending experience," several vendors pointed out. "Even if you don't really want to lend money, when someone you know well asks for a loan, you can't refuse." Some vendors were explicitly "dissatisfied" with lending money under social duress: "I do it because I have to. It would be embarrassing to turn someone down when they know I have money, but that doesn't mean that I feel good about it. I'm in business, so I need to stay liquid." More often than not, though, those who expressed dissatisfaction with informal lending had experienced late repayments and defaults. Even though the length of the loan is not always specified between the individual lender and borrower,

---

59. For example, after the Central Bank cut the savings deposit rates in May 1996, newspapers reported capital flight from banks, accompanied by an increase in underground loan-sharking. The interest rates in the informal financial sector were reported to be 30 to 100 percent higher than the official bank rate: "Jingyi shehui jizi rezhong xin taitou" (Be vigilant about the rise in capital-raising in society), *Baokan wenzhai* (digest of newspapers and magazines), June 10, 1996, from *Renmin ribao* (People's daily), June 3, 1996.

resentment starts to build in when the lender sees the borrower accumulating assets or purchasing luxury goods (apart from those associated with a wedding) while the loan is still outstanding. "How a debtor would have the gall to flaunt a fancy new motorcycle in front of me before repaying a three-year-old loan is incomprehensible to me," a convenience store owner complained. "I helped out a friend and then he doesn't even have the courtesy to repay me." It is an even greater source of distress when the borrower or *hui* organizer simply disappears from town without communication.

Private entrepreneurs lack access to formal sources of credit because the state banking system remains hostage to the socialist legacy of SOEs that require continued subsidization. Despite the efforts of the central government to reduce the policy-oriented lending of state banks, local governments continue to face local political pressures to prevent mass unemployment and to direct bank credit toward strategic industries.

The inability of small-scale entrepreneurs to borrow from official banks is not limited to reform-era China. Small businesses have resorted to informal financing mechanisms throughout Chinese history; even during the Mao era, when private enterprise was severely curbed, individuals turned to grassroots credit arrangements to finance their consumption—if not production—needs. The scattered pockets of informal finance in Mao's China, however, pale in comparison with the relentless growth of financial institutions serving the private sector since the late 1970s. In order to understand why this growth has been so uneven at the local level, both scholars and policymakers instinctually look to the center for evidence of state-directed distortions in the economy.

Broad regional differences in developmental conditions may indeed be traced back to specific state policies that devoted greater capital investment to northern inland areas in the Mao era and permitted greater economic experimentation in the coastal south during the post-Mao period. Nonetheless, the finding that even heavily industrialized places such as Henan have an impressive range of curb market institutions suggests that the reemergence of informal finance is not merely a function of state-directed developmental policies. Indeed, the considerable *intraregional variation* in private-sector development, the degree of financial institutional diversity in the informal sector, and private entrepreneurs' choice of financing mechanisms challenge the explanatory efficacy of top-down approaches and call for a richer contextual analysis of local political economic conditions.

3

Gendered Worlds of Finance in Fujian

The thirty members of Mr. Chang's society were asked to meet at his house on the 18th of the seventh month. As they were coming at his request . . . to help him with his need for funds, Mr. Chang provided a feast for his friends. A feast was served at all subsequent meetings of the [credit] society, but after the first meeting each member paid his share of the expense.

—Sidney D. Gamble, "A Chinese Mutual Savings Society," 1944

Men generally don't participate in rotating credit associations because they think that it's too bothersome to deal with such complex procedures for small sums of money. Women have more time on their hands to organize such associations. . . . The monthly meetings also give them a chance to socialize with one another.

—Male interviewee, Fujian, Fieldnotes, 1996

Developmental diversity makes the southern coastal province of Fujian an economic microcosm of China in the reform era. At one extreme, the dramatic effects of economic liberalization and foreign (Taiwanese) direct investment can be seen all along the eastern coast in the form of high rises and ongoing construction projects, culminating with the Special Economic Zone of Xiamen. At the other extreme, stretches of rural villages in the mountainous interior of the province remain impoverished.[1]

1. This is the case even though overall rates of poverty in the province have decreased since the beginning of economic reform. See Thomas P. Lyons, *China's War on Poverty: A Case Study of Fujian Province, 1985–1990* (Hong Kong: Chinese University of Hong Kong, 1992). Nonetheless, as of 1997 12 counties and 209 townships in Fujian were still officially classified as "impoverished counties" (*pinkun xian*). The provincial government aimed to raise the living standards of the estimated 507,000 impoverished people by the end of 1997: Fujian Window website, ⟨http://www.china-window.com/Fujianw/jianjie/2010/w/20104k.html⟩ [in Chinese], November 1998.

Between these extremes lie scores of cities and rural counties that are copying the successes of their more prosperous neighbors by investing in the non-state sector and waging campaigns to attract capital from abroad.[2] Adding to the complexity of these structural differences, Fujian is among the most culturally diverse provinces in China. In light of such economic and demographic contrasts, a strong methodological argument can be made that Fujian should be studied in intraprovincial comparative terms rather than as a single case study representing China's coastal south.[3] Generalizing about Fujian is almost as challenging as generalizing about China as a whole.

The reality of intraprovincial variation in private-sector development helps to explain different degrees of financial institutional diversity in the several Fujian localities where I interviewed entrepreneurs and officials. Specifically, local governmental stance toward private enterprise has had an impact on the contours of the informal financial sector. Some localities in Fujian have been clearly supportive of private-sector development (Fuzhou, Changle, Quanzhou, Jinjiang); others have been less supportive or placed a higher priority on promoting the collective sector (Haixing, Huian, Anxi). The resulting array of curb market institutions in each local-ity is a reflection of the local government's developmental priorities more than of the logic of the market. In other words, the local presence of private commerce does not mean that informal financial institutions will auto-matically arise, as the economic hypothesis would expect.

A more discrete grassroots phenomenon on the demand side of the equation has been the dominance of women in rotating credit associations during the reform era. My research revealed that the relative popularity of these associations among women in Fujian varies according to the struc-ture of the local economy and demographic trends. This finding is consis-tent with the logic of the broader argument that social and political factors fundamentally mediate the means through which small-scale entrepre-neurs finance their businesses. Even in an environment of capital scarcity, the identities and resources of entrepreneurs differ significantly enough that credit markets are segmented at the local level.

Fujian's Economy and Financial Environment

First, it is worth reiterating that many of the localities in Fujian have expe-rienced above-national-average rates of growth in industrial output and per

2. See Thomas P. Lyons, *The Economic Geography of Fujian: A Sourcebook* (Ithaca: East Asia Program, Cornell University, 1995).

3. Cf. Thomas P. Lyons, "Fujian: Challenge to the East Asian Development Model?" *American Asian Review* 16, 1 (1998): 35–98.

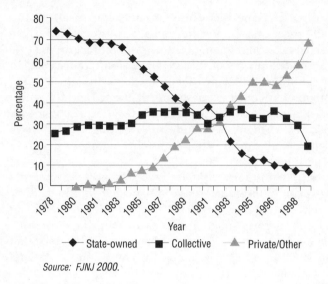

Source: FJNJ 2000.

Figure 3.1 Share of Industrial Production by Ownership Type in Fujian, 1978–1999

capita GNP (20 to 50 percent annually).[4] This growth is generally traceable to the proliferation of township and village enterprises (TVEs) and private enterprises, investments by overseas Chinese, and exports of light industrial products and textiles. Its aggregate effects are evident in provincial statistics that demonstrate the rising share of the non-state sector in industrial output, as well as a structural shift toward increasing production in the tertiary (services) sector (see Figures 3.1 and 3.2).

Most local economists attribute the relative economic success of southern coastal provinces in the reform period to their underdevelopment during the Mao era, when capital investment by the center was concentrated in the northern inland provinces because the coastal south, with its proximity to Taiwan, was considered geostrategically sensitive. Consequently, the advent of reform in the late 1970s unleashed decades of suppressed entrepreneurial activity, so the argument goes. Another important

4. Note, however, that even within a wealthier southern coastal province such as Fujian, substantial intraprovincial variation exists in standard of living. See Zhao Hui and Wei Yu, "Zhanwang weilai, renzhong daoyuan: Fujian juxing jiti gongsi" (Making greatest possible efforts to eliminate poverty: Fujian Juxing corporate group), *Fazhan yanjiu* (Development research) 8 (1996): 6–11; and Zhou Ji and Liu Bingwen, "Shilun Fujian pingkun diqu de kedai fazhan" (On the continuity of poverty-stricken areas' development in Fujian Province), *Fazhan yanjiu* 2 (1996): 32–33. A case study of Anxi as a successful example of poverty alleviation in the 1980s is Thomas P. Lyons, *Poverty and Growth in a South China County: Anxi, Fujian, 1949–1992* (Ithaca: East Asia Program, Cornell University, 1994).

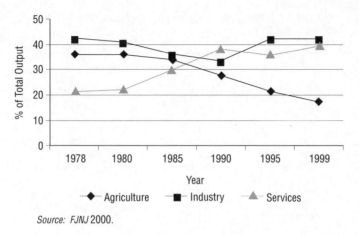

Source: *FJNJ* 2000.

Figure 3.2 Contribution to Production Value by Sector in Fujian, 1978–1999

factor that accounts for regional growth differentials between the coastal south and the interior during the reform era is the fact that the central government's Open Door Policy designated certain coastal areas as special economic zones (SEZs) for economic reform.[5] Established in 1980, the first four were Shenzhen, Zhuhai and Shantou in Guangdong, and Xiamen in Fujian. The dramatic growth in foreign capital in the province is shown in Table 3.1. By 1995, foreign direct investment (FDI) accounted for nearly half of the province's investment in fixed assets; and 80 percent of the total FDI came from Hong Kong and Taiwan investors.[6] The existence of special economic districts enhanced the sense of governments in those and neighboring areas that deviations from the socialist economic norm might be tolerated, especially when leaders from Beijing visited the SEZs and praised their progress. For example, Zhao Ziyang's visit to Fujian at the beginning of 1988 was followed by reform measures that increased the number of open counties and districts in southern Fujian, and shortly thereafter the

5. Overviews include George T. Crane, *The Political Economy of China's Special Economic Zones* (Armonk, N.Y.: M. E. Sharpe, 1998); Chong-dong Pak, *China's Special Economic Zones and Their Impact on its Economic Development* (Westport, Conn.: Praeger, 1997); and Xuiping Sun, *New Progress in China's Special Economic Zones* (Beijing: Foreign Languages Press, 1997).

6. Official statistics only indirectly reflect the fact that Hong Kong served as a conduit for much of the trade between Taiwan and Fujian. Official figures reveal that Hong Kong's share of imports from Fujian increased by 42.9 percent during 1980–85, but in 1985–91, when direct trade with Taiwan became less problematic, it declined to 14.2 percent. During the same years, Fujian's imports from Taiwan grew by over 34 percent annually (some three times the volume of the earlier period). See Robert F. Ash and Y. Y. Kueh, "Economic Integration within Greater China: Trade and Investment Flows between China, Hong Kong, and Taiwan," *China Quarterly* 136 (December 1993): 711–45.

Table 3.1 Foreign Direct Investment (FDI) in Fujian, 1979–1999 (in millions of US$)

Year	FDI Contracted	FDI Actually Used
1979	1.05	0.83
1980	4.64	3.63
1981	19.06	1.50
1982	16.12	1.21
1983	21.20	14.38
1984	200.97	48.28
1985	376.81	117.82
1986	64.56	61.49
1987	117.53	51.39
1988	462.60	130.17
1989	902.58	328.80
1990	1,161.83	290.02
1991	1,448.71	644.49
1992	6,351.01	1,416.33
1993	11,336.17	2,867.45
1994	7,179.46	3,712.00
1995	8,906.47	4,038.81
1996	6,535.72	4,078.76
1997	4,537.51	4,196.66
1998	5,001.50	4,212.11
1999	4,899.96	4,024.03

Source: FJNJ 2000, 293.

province became an official experimental reform area with an export-led growth strategy.[7] Annual visits by high-ranking leaders after Deng's 1992 southern tour also served to reinforce the green-light effects on economic liberalization that his well-known trip had signaled.[8]

Given this more permissive, market-friendly political orientation, Fujian province harbors an above average range of nonbanking financial institutions (NBFIs) relative to the rest of the country. As of 1995, officially registered NBFIs in Fujian included trust and investment companies (1,034 branches), rural credit cooperatives (948 branches), urban credit cooper-

7. *Fujian ribao* (Fujian daily), January 29, 1988, cited in Shawn Shieh, "Provincial Leadership and the Implementation of Foreign Economic Reforms in Fujian Province," in Peter T. Y. Cheung, Jae Ho Chung, and Zhimin Lin, eds. *Provincial Strategies of Economic Reform in Post-Mao China* (Armonk, N.Y.: M. E. Sharpe, 1998), 316. For a broader discussion of Fujian's economic reform experience during 1979–89, see Shawn Shieh, "The Entrepreneurial State: Local Governments, Property Rights, and China's Transition from State Socialism, 1978–90" (Ph.D. diss., Columbia University, 1996).

8. Li Peng visited in 1993 and 1995, followed by Jiang Zemin in 1994, Yang Shangkun in 1996, Qiao Shi in 1997, and Li Ruihuan in 1998. As is customary in the Chinese press, these high-level trips were reported both nationally and locally. See FBIS-CHI-94-124, 95-029, 97-099, 96-019, 97-349, 98-320.

Table 3.2 Distribution of Short-Term Bank Credit in Fujian, 1993–1996

Type of Loan	1993	1994	1995	1996
SOE industrial	32.6%	31.6%	30.9%	30.7%
SOE commercial	29.0%	29.6%	29.8%	28.6%
SOE construction	2.9%	2.8%	2.9%	3.9%
Agricultural	6.5%	5.9%	5.9%	5.8%
Township and village enterprises (TVEs)	8.1%	8.2%	7.9%	7.9%
Private enterprise	1.1%	1.2%	1.5%	1.6%
"Three Capital Enterprises"[a]	10.7%	9.3%	9.7%	10.4%
Other	9.1%	11.4%	11.3%	11.0%
Total loans (in bil RMB)	55.41	69.89	86.15	106.0

Source: *FJNJ 1997*, 33. (The "short-term loans" category did not appear in the provincial yearbook until 1993. After 1996, *FJNJ* eliminated SOE construction, TVEs, private enterprise, and other short-term loans from this table.)

[a] The Chinese term is *sanziqiye*; it refers to three kinds of partially or wholly foreign-owned enterprises: Sino-foreign JVs, Sino-foreign contractual JVs, and wholly foreign-owned enterprises. The three forms were approved under the July 1, 1979 "Law of the People's Republic of China on Joint Ventures and Wholly Foreign-owned Enterprises."

atives (115 branches), insurance companies (105 branches), postal savings offices (471 branches), and pawnshops (21 branches).[9] In addition, the Fujian Industrial Bank, a joint-stock commercial bank established in 1988, had 225 branches as of 1998.[10] The province also boasts twenty-one joint-ventured or wholly foreign-owned banks with offices in Xiamen, Fuzhou, and Quanzhou. With the exception of pawnshops and postal savings facilities, however, these financial institutions are geared toward serving foreign and large industrial concerns rather than smaller businesses. Moreover, as can be seen in Table 3.2, private enterprises in general continue to receive an extremely small portion of official short-term bank credit. As of 1996, individual and private enterprises received only 1.6 percent of all short-term bank loans—higher than the national average of 0.5 percent that year but still far from commensurate with the private sector's contribution to industrial output in Fujian: at least 15 percent in 1996, and possibly as high as 70 percent if private businesses disguised as collectives and businesses in the "other" category are included.

Although private entrepreneurs account for a small portion of bank lending, larger private businesses have devised a number of strategies for accessing bank capital (see Chapter Four). In brief, they include register-

9. *JRNJ 1997*, 198. Note that in 1997 the Urban Credit Cooperatives began to be converted into standard commercial banks called Urban Cooperative Banks.

10. Most are in Fujian, but the bank has branches also in Shanghai and Shenzhen and a representative office in Beijing. "Fujian Industrial Bank Reports Rapid Asset Growth," *Xinhua News Agency*, September 1, 1998, reported in FBIS-CHI-98-244.

ing as a "collective" enterprise, registering as a "joint venture" by enlisting the use of a foreigner's name (but not ownership capital), and borrowing at a higher level of interest from SOEs that have access to bank capital. Smaller businesses, however, are less likely to rely on such strategies since the scale of their operations may not warrant large sums of capital on a regular basis or justify the potential risk entailed in employing such deceptive techniques. The willingness of micro-entrepreneurs to take extreme measures in accessing credit varies from locality to locality and may be seen as a function of the willingness of local officials to ignore (or even condone) such practices.

Fuzhou Municipality: Welcoming Foreign and Private Capital

As the provincial capital of Fujian, Fuzhou is a commercial center for the northern part of the province. From the beginning of reform it attracted substantial inflows of capital and labor in the form, respectively, of Taiwanese investment and migrant workers from poorer provinces such as Anhui, Jiangsu, Sichuan, and Henan.[11] The city was designated an "open city" in 1984.[12] Since then, according to official statistics, the local economy has maintained double-digit rates of growth in industrial output, value of exports, and FDI receipts (see Figures 3.3 and 3.4). Moreover, the municipal government has become increasingly active in facilitating construction and infrastructure projects that are intended to make the city more attractive for foreign investment. As I conducted my research, Fuzhou's urban landscape was being transformed from a city of narrow roads, two-story wooden plank houses, and squat concrete buildings to one that displayed its recent acquisition of wealth in the form of commercial high rises, Western fast food chains, white-tiled residential complexes with blue-tinted windows, wide paved roads and highways, and other ongoing construction projects.

11. As of 1995, official statistics estimate that the floating population in Fuzhou exceeded 600,000 people at its peak, of which only 260,000 were officially registered. *Fuzhou nianjian 1996* (FZNJ–Fuzhou yearbook) (Beijing: Zhongguo tongji chubanshe, 1997), 176. As of year-end 1995, Fuzhou municipality had a population of 5.6 million with nearly 1.4 million people living in the city proper.

12. After the State Council approved Fuzhou as one of the open coastal cities, the Mawei Economic and Technological Development Zone was established in January 1985. Following Deng's southern tour an additional four specialized zones were established within the Mawei district, including the Science and Technological Zone of Agriculture, the Fuzhou Bonded Area, the Fuzhou Science and Technology Zone. The Rongqiao Economic and Technological Development Zone in Fuqing was also established.

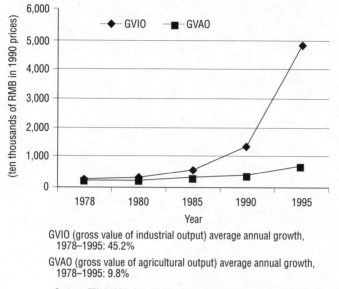

GVIO (gross value of industrial output) average annual growth,
1978–1995: 45.2%

GVAO (gross value of agricultural output) average annual growth,
1978–1995: 9.8%

Source: FZNJ 1996, 270–71. Note that after 1995 the Fuzhou Statistical
Yearbook stopped reporting GVIO and GVAO in 1990 prices.

Figure 3.3 Growth of Industrial and Agricultural Output in Fuzhou, 1978–1995

The local government has also encouraged the development of private retail and wholesale markets throughout the city, which has attracted micro-entrepreneurs from neighboring rural and peri-urban areas. Since mid-1993 the Fuzhou City Industrial and Commercial Management Bureau (ICMB) has established a number of specialized wholesale markets (*zhuanye pifa shichang*), including those focusing on steel products, construction materials, auto parts, dried foodstuffs, fresh fruits and vegetables, seafood, and grain. The five district-level ICMBs—in Gulou, Taijiang, Cangshan, Mawei, and Jin'an districts—have also designated specialized market areas for wholesale and retail trade. By the end of 1997 there were 377 commodities trade markets throughout Fuzhou.[13] Although the physical establishment of ICMB-approved marketplaces can be disruptive for the unregistered businesses that they displace (at least temporarily), once they are up and running, discrete market sites offer micro-entrepreneurs a certain degree of insulation from the often arbitrary extraction of taxes and assorted fees to which free-standing vendors are subjected. In a typical

13. Fujian Window, ⟨http://www.china.org.cn/Fujian_w/city/Fuzhou/fzgl/ea-5.htm⟩, March 1, 1999.

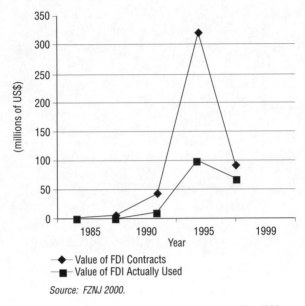

<figure>
—◆— Value of FDI Contracts
—■— Value of FDI Actually Used

Source: *FZNJ 2000.*
</figure>

Figure 3.4 Foreign Direct Investment in Fuzhou, 1985–1999

retail vegetable and produce market in Fuzhou, for example, each stall is charged a set monthly rent for the space, which includes the ICMB and security fees. An itinerant fruit vendor operating across the street, however, may end up paying five times more, since the staff of various agencies may pass through and impose their own fees without taking into account the aggregate "tax" burden on the vendor. The paradoxical coexistence of a developmental yet predatory local state is discussed further in later chapters. For now, suffice it to say that the establishment of official markets by the ICMB and city government is by no means unproblematic, but on balance the markets represent the first step in providing more standardized (rather than personalistic) interaction between private entrepreneurs and the local staff of the state.

Although the local government was active in nurturing an attractive investment environment and strengthening the regulation of private entrepreneurs—particularly during the latter part of the 1990s—it has been somewhat less proactive in promoting the availability of official credit for private businesses. This is not to say that it is impossible for private entrepreneurs to access bank credit; rather, the officially sanctioned financial institutions lack both the experience and institutional mandate to cater to small businesses. In practice, micro-entrepreneurs face a variety of bureaucratic obstacles in the loan application process. These obstacles may be alleviated somewhat if the loan applicant has a strong social relationship with a bank insider, but unless that insider is a loan officer or upper-level management, the process can be quite cumbersome.

Consider, for example, one farmer's application for a loan from the Agricultural Bank of China to raise ducks. In 1996 Mr. Zhang was a fifty-one-year-old illiterate farmer.[14] He had worked the land full time with his wife and two sons until 1991, when he decided to enter the duck business. By 1993 he was able to rent a premium selling space in the meat and livestock section of the central wholesaling market in Taijiang for a one-time (annual) rental fee of 8,000 *yuan* (US$966), plus assorted fees and taxes. He enjoys the fact that he works at the stand for only half a day, 6:00 A.M. to noon, and then goes home to tend to the ducks. Mr. Zhang does not find his business sufficiently profitable, however, and the path to scaling up the duck business has not been easy. When he first started raising ducks, he needed money to build a fence around his dilapidated house, as well as a temperature-controlled room to facilitate the egg incubation process. He approached a number of friends for loans, including one who had worked in a low-level position in the local branch of the ABOC for several years. That friend offered to introduce Mr. Zhang to the appropriate loan officer, put in a good word for him, and help him complete the loan application forms. Mr. Zhang applied for a one-year loan of 10,000 *yuan*. The loan officer wanted to see for himself how many ducks he had already raised and the conditions under which they were being raised. Since the loan officer was unimpressed by his first couple of visits, Mr. Zhang borrowed about 20,000 *yuan* from friends and relatives to build the necessary setup and purchase an electric incubator. Of course, the whole point of borrowing was to establish his productive capacity in the first place. But he was not confident that the official loan would come through. After eight months of paperwork, review meetings, and site inspections, the ABOC finally extended him an eight-month loan of 8,000 yuan. Since repaying the ABOC loan, Mr. Zhang has borrowed an additional 30,000 *yuan* from friends and relatives. In retrospect, he does not think that the ABOC was worth the time and uncertainty that it entailed.

Although it is conventional wisdom among microfinance practitioners that official banks do not work with small businesses (*getihu*) because of the transaction costs associated with extending multitudes of small loans, it is worth pointing out that the capital requirements of *getihu* can be quite substantial. Mr. Zhang initially underestimated the cost of raising ducks, but he ended up borrowing a total of 58,000 *yuan* (US$7,006) over a two-year period.

---

14. Survey No. 99. To protect the identity of the respondents, all names given are pseudonyms.

Another farmer turned business owner, Mr. Wan, knew from the outset that he needed a substantial cash outlay to purchase equipment, yet he was discouraged from attempting to access bank credit.[15] In 1986 Mr. Wan was a junior-high-school-educated farmer who planted barely enough food to feed his family of four. Since farmers all around him seemed to be leaving their land and pursuing petty business ventures, Mr. Wan decided to try his hand at selling a variety of everyday products but found that there were too many people peddling the same knickknacks. In 1994 he made a bolder move by switching his business strategy and tapping a new market—arcade entertainment. He reasoned that spoiled urban children had disposable income that they would be happy to spend on inexpensive games. He envisioned renting out a store space in the center of town and displaying a dozen or so colorful game machines. Perhaps parents would drop off their children at his mini-arcade while they ran errands, and older children would gather at his place after school. The problem was that each arcade game machine would cost 4,000 to 5,000 *yuan*, an astronomical sum to a man whose monthly income at the time hovered around 300 *yuan*. He considered approaching the Industrial and Commercial Bank for a start-up loan, but his brother-in-law told him that a state bank would never consider lending money for slot machines, which could be regarded as a soft form of gambling.[16] Mr. Wan finally borrowed a total of 40,000 *yuan* (US$4,832) at 24 percent annual interest (much higher than the bank rate) from various relatives.

By mid-1996, fifty-two-year-old Mr. Wan had rented a modest-sized room in a reasonably trafficked part of town and hired three employees. His arcade of fifteen game machines was open fifteen hours a day, seven days a week. He explained that at 3 *mao* per game, his customers usually spend anywhere from 10 to 40 *yuan* at a time, since the games are short and the kids like to spend hours in front of the machines. Yet despite the popularity of his arcade, Mr. Wan is concerned that he will not be able to repay all his debts. His monthly gross income averages around 4,000 *yuan*, but after subtracting his interest payments (800 *yuan*) and operating expenses (rent 500 *yuan*; electricity, 600 *yuan*; ICMB fee, 50 *yuan*; taxes, 200 *yuan*; and wages, 1,500 *yuan*), he nets only about 350 *yuan*.

Given the experiences like those of Mr. Zhang, the duck vendor, most small-scale entrepreneurs in Fuzhou do not put themselves through the tedious process of applying for official bank credit. Instead, they borrow from friends and relatives, as Mr. Wan did, and draw on other informal

15. Survey No. 49.
16. Video arcades with slot machines or other gambling-related games have in fact been subject to raids during antigambling campaigns. See, e.g., "Fujian Cracks Down on Prostitution, Gambling," *Zhongguo Xinwenshe*, October 31, 1995, reported in FBIS-CHI-95-211.

sources such as neighborhood loan sharks, underground money shops, pawnbrokers, and rotating credit associations. These sources generally charge higher interest rates than state banks (about 1.2 percent a month in 1996), but the rates depend on both the amount of the loan and the relationship between the borrower and the lender. For example, friends and relatives tend not to charge any interest on loans less than 1,000 *yuan.* But if the loan is over 10,000 *yuan,* then respondents said that they felt obligated to offer lenders at least the bank's savings deposit rate to compensate them for the effective loss in interest income. As many vendors pointed out, "Everyone needs money these days, so you wouldn't want to take advantage of a friend or relative's generosity by borrowing money so you can make money, and then returning it without interest. That would seem ungrateful and you would lose face." On the other hand, going through a loan shark or money lender bypasses the potential social awkwardness of deciding on an appropriate interest rate, because by definition, loan sharks are people who charge high rates of interest. One seafood vendor who has borrowed more than 100,000 *yuan* from them explained that it is easier to rely on them as a regular source of working capital (even at 11 percent interest per month) because he does not like to trouble friends and relatives every time he needs to make a major seafood purchase.[17]

As for participation in rotating credit associations (*hui*), the days of interest-free forms of *hui* are long gone. In the traditional "rotating association" (*lunhui*) the collective pot would be rotated among the members until everyone had had a turn. Given that this would mean some members would have to wait several months for their turn, contemporary associations generally charge higher rates of interest to those who receive the collective pot early in the rotating cycle, while those who wait until the later months end up as net recipients of interest payments from the other members who had already collected. The interest-charging variant, called a "bidding association" or *biaohui*, is the dominant form in present-day Fujian. Even though rotating credit associations give the appearance of being rather informal, association members take the rules quite seriously and typically record the specific operating procedures on paper in a contractual form to which all members are required to sign their names.

The rules of a bidding rotating credit association in Fuzhou were provided by a biscuit and dried fruits vendor. It is common practice for the organizer to receive the collective pot in the first month. After that, the basic idea is that each month, members secretly write down their "bids," the amount of money they are willing to pay in interest to the others.

17. Survey No. 101.

Whoever bids the highest amount (i.e., is willing to pay the highest amount in interest) gets to collect the collective pot for that month. The written rules translate as follows:

> The start date of this bidding association is April 20, 1995. The amount of each member's contribution is 2,000 RMB. Including the leader of the association [*huitou*], we have thirty-seven members. Our meetings are set on the 20th of odd months and the 5th and 20th of even months. In total we will gather eighteen times in a one-year period. Meetings that do not start at 2:00 P.M. will be invalid. The lowest allowable contribution [or interest bid] is 350 RMB. The person who wins the bid should come with his or her guarantor to pick up the money. In the case of unforeseen circumstances and she or he cannot deliver the contribution within three days, his or her guarantor will be responsible for it and be required to pay the money on his or her behalf. The members of the association are expected to hand in their contributions within two days after someone wins a bid. The winner of the bid will receive the money on the third day after the bid.[18]

The rest of the rules sheet includes the names of all the members and their guarantors, and a financial record of the meetings that have already transpired.

In Fuzhou, participation in *hui* seemed to be concentrated among particular sectors of migrant entrepreneurs. Many locals (*bendiren*) were not even familiar with the practice, relying instead on more straightforward borrowing from friends and relatives, but large concentrations of people participating in *hui* could be found in markets dominated by migrants from other parts of Fujian. Clothing vendors from Lianjiang County, for instance, tended to organize *hui* among themselves in the peri-urban district of Hongshan Township, as did leather goods wholesalers from Changle and dried foods wholesalers from Fuqing in the Taijiang wholesale market complex. As in other parts of Fujian, women dominated *hui* participation, reflecting the sexual division of labor in family-owned businesses whereby the husband travels around to replenish the inventory while the wife manages the store and its finances.[19] Because so many microentrepreneurs, especially women, are bound to their stores for most of day, *hui* organizers often go directly to the stores to collect monthly payments.[20] As a result, some *hui* members never meet each other.[21]

18. Addendum to Survey No. 121.
19. Among farming families, however, the roles may be reversed: the husband may stay home and work the land while the wife goes to the market to sell their crops (Survey No. 141).
20. According to the 141 valid survey responses of micro-entrepreneurs in Fuzhou, the average store is open for twelve hours a day.
21. Seventeen percent of surveyed *hui* participants in Fuzhou indicated that they did not know all the members of their *hui*.

Business owners often appreciate the convenience of having the *hui* organizer make "office calls." Ms. Bing, for example, was in 1996 a twenty-six-year-old elementary-school-educated owner of a packaged snacks business that she runs with her husband.[22] The couple left Fuqing to start business in Fuzhou's Taijiang wholesaling market in 1995. The modest appearance of their five-by-eight-foot stand in the dimly lit flea market–style complex belies the monetary scale of their wholesaling operation. Their monthly operating expenses are 28,360 *yuan* (US$3,426), and inventory purchases require an additional 20,000 to 30,000 *yuan*.[23] The couple frequently faces working-capital constraints. They once borrowed 10,000 *yuan* from the local Industrial and Commercial Bank but decided never to do so again because of the complex procedures entailed and the 10,000 *yuan* limit. Ms. Bing said that she prefers to borrow from friends, loan sharks, and underground banks that lend up to 30,000 *yuan* at a time. In addition, she participates in rotating credit associations of fifty to sixty members making individual contributions of 1,000 *yuan*, which means that when it is her turn to receive the collective pot, it ranges from 50,000 to 60,000 *yuan* (US$6,040 to 7,248). What Ms. Bing likes best about the *hui* is that she does not even have to attend the monthly and semimonthly meetings. The organizer goes directly to her stall in the market to collect her contributions. And even though that means she does not know all of the members of the association, she is not worried about the possibility of other people defaulting, because the organizer is a good friend of hers.

In summary, Fuzhou municipality's active promotion of foreign investment and private-sector development is reflected in the relatively wide range of officially sanctioned nonbanking financial institutions (e.g., credit cooperatives). From the perspective of micro-entrepreneurs, however, the problem is that the NBFIs are not geared to serving small private businesses. Microentrepreneurs have turned instead to a variety of informal financing mechanisms, including interpersonal lending, borrowing from loan sharks, rotating credit associations, and underground money shops. Significantly, local officials acknowledge the existence of these informal financial institutions in Fuzhou but have not interfered in their operations, since the institutions serve an important sector of the local economy.

Changle County/City: Private Enterprise and Private Finance

Changle falls under the administrative jurisdiction of Fuzhou and maintained a low profile as a cluster of poor fishing villages until the early

22. Survey No. 120.
23. Ibid.: The monthly 28,360 *yuan* in expenses includes rent (15,000), electricity (60), ICMB fee (800), taxes (4,500), and storage facilities (8,000).

Table 3.3 Contribution to Economic Output by Sector: Changle, Fujian, 1990–1999

Sector	1990	1995	1999
Agriculture	35.1%	25.4%	19.5%
Industry	47.8%	47.8%	52.9%
Services	17.1%	26.8%	27.6%
Total	100.0%	100.0%	100.0%

Source: FJNJ 1996, 299; FJNJ 2000, 338.

1990s.[24] Provincial officials attribute the administrative upgrading of Changle's status from "county" to "city" in 1995 to its increase in population and relative wealth. Within the first fifteen years of reform, Changle's GNP had increased 8.2 times; its Gross Value of Industrial Output (GVIO) had increased 58.3 times; and the ratio of agricultural output to industrial output had shifted from 7:3 to 2:8.[25] Table 3.3 shows that the share of the tertiary sector also grew in Changle's economy between 1990 and 1999.

As in other urbanizing districts along Fujian's coastline, the economic growth was particularly marked in the proliferation of TVEs and foreign-invested enterprises after 1992. Between 1990 and 1995 the average annual growth rate in the value of output by SOEs was 23.5 percent; the average increase in TVE production was 46.3 percent; and the value of foreign exports increased an average of 38.7 percent annually.[26] The new rural industries included textile factories, shoe factories, beverage bottling plants, a pharmaceutical research institute, construction businesses, electrical equipment factories, and a host of additional light and heavy industrial operations. In addition, private and collective enterprises took advantage of Changle's coastal resources by focusing on fishery-related businesses. The case of Sea Star Village offers a glimpse into the dynamics of a typical TVE in one of Changle's administrative villages.[27]

Sea Star Village (*haixingcun*) has a population of 1,900 consisting of four hundred households. Since it is surrounded (and divided) by water, the local economy centers on fishing, seafood processing, and other water-related production. According to the village chief, before "liberation" in 1949, families lived on boats because land was too scarce for agricultural production. Now there are other economic opportunities. The village runs a shipbuilding factory, a ship repair enterprise, a fishball-processing factory, and a seafood refrigeration and export enterprise. The latter is run

24. The administrative center of Changle is forty kilometers south of Fuzhou.
25. *Changle* (Fuzhou: Haifeng Publishing House, 1994), 11.
26. *FZNJ 1996*, 199–201; and *Fujian nianjian 1996* (FJNJ–Fujian yearbook), 299.
27. Survey No. 145 and Interview No. 79.

by Director Xia, the fifty-six-year-old village chief and party head of Sea Star Village. Director Xia, who has a junior-high education, recounted that in 1984 Fuzhou City gave Sea Star permission to engage in fish processing and build a factory with an initial one million *yuan* investment from government coffers. The TVE is involved in all three stages of the frozen seafood business: it dispatches boats to Micronesia, freezes the catch (fish and shrimp), and exports the frozen seafood to Japan (and, to a lesser extent, the United States). Although the TVE specializes in refrigeration, it also sends live fish and vegetables to Japan. "We tailor production to market demands," Xia explained proudly, for example, exporting headless and de-intestined shrimp and canned shrimp meat to the United States. Financially speaking, the enterprise pays 7 percent of its gross earnings in taxes to the Changle City government. In the 1994–95 fiscal year, that worked out to 80 million *yuan*, since it exported so much fish to Japan. The TVE was honored with a "bright star enterprise" (*mingxing qiye*) designation and, more impressively, a visit by then the chairman of the National People's Congress, Qiao Shi.

Operationally, the TVE employs 154 workers, of which 15 are permanent administrative and accounting staff (mostly men aged eighteen to thirty years old), and 135 are nonpermanent female workers. When the need arises (as when the boats return from Micronesia), the enterprise uses the village's loudspeaker to recruit temporary workers for simple production tasks such as sorting shrimp by size and trimming them. Director Xia said that prior to reform, women in Sea Star stayed at home and made fishballs; now the TVE makes use of their "surplus labor." He added that the enterprise has a policy of taking on all the available workers the village before accepting any from outside.

When asked about the existence of *getihu* in Sea Star village, Xia said that there were not many before 1984 but that boats are now sold to groups of individuals for fishing. For example, a boat might be sold at three million *yuan* to thirty-six people who use it collectively (a typical boat holds about eighteen people). Sometimes the ABOC is willing to extend loans for such purposes. Although fishermen can now earn over 50,000 *yuan* annually, it is still considered a difficult and burdensome profession. Those with education are no longer willing to fish for a living but move on to Changle for more lucrative business possibilities. Director Xia added that the current generation of youth has at least a junior-high-school education and that ten people in the village have graduated from vocational colleges.

In addition to the visible growth of Changle's collective sector, the opening of the Fuzhou Changle International Airport in 1997, displacing the military airport in Fuzhou as the destination of all commercial flights to and from northern Fujian, further attests to the rising political and economic status of Changle.[28] Local officials are quick to point out that people in Changle have always been prone to travel abroad. Official statistics estimate that more than 300,000 natives of Changle have emigrated legally to forty countries around the world, and about one-third of them to Taiwan.[29] Given that Changle's population is approximately 660,000 (it was 656,780 in 1995), this means that nearly one-third of Changle's total population worldwide resides abroad, though it is difficult to estimate the proportion of migrants who have left more recently but maintain a strong native-place identity. While local cadres admit that illegal emigration (*toudu*) from Changle was a problem in the past, the official line is that very few people use underground channels to leave the country illegally.[30] Nonetheless, the fact that provincial authorities have conducted ongoing campaigns to crack down on human smuggling suggests that the problem persists.[31]

In contrast to government officials, local entrepreneurs are very forward in acknowledging that Changle represents the primary port of exit for illegal migration from Fujian, including the now notorious *Golden Venture* freighter that transported 286 aspiring immigrants to the United States in 1993.[32] An American sociologist estimates that 95 percent of all illegal Chinese immigrants to the United States in the 1990s left from Changle.[33] And the residential origin of those departing from Changle appears to consist primarily of three counties around Fuzhou—Changle, Fuqing, and Tingjiang.[34] Given the scale of emigration from Changle, it is apparent that

28. Before the opening of the Changle International Airport, flights to and from Fuzhou used the small Yixu airport, which was originally built for military purposes. During the Taiwan Straits crisis in 1996, civilian flights to Fuzhou were often delayed. Since then, the Fuzhou airport has reverted to military use.

29. Interview No. 76. The migration to Taiwan has largely been through illegal means. See, e.g., "Illegal Immigrants from Mainland China Repatriated," *Taiwan Central News Agency*, February 14, 1999, reported in FBIS-CHI-1999-0214.

30. In casual one-on-one conversations, however, local cadres concede that illegal migration continues.

31. The Fujian Provincial CCP Committee, Fujian People's Government, and Public Security Bureau have conducted numerous investigations to capture such smugglers. Between 1993 and 1997 the Fuzhou Frontier Guard Unit caught nearly 1,000 organizers and transporters, including some fifty from abroad. Between 1993 and 1996 about 4,500 illegal migrants were caught, and more than 16,000 were repatriated from abroad. See Jiang Baozhang, "Fujian zhandou toudu xianxiang" (Fujian combats illegal migration), *Renmin ribao* (People's daily), May 24, 1997, 5.

32. The boat ran into the Rockaway Peninsula in Queens, N.Y., and ten people died in jumping ship: Seth Faison, "Hunt Goes On for Smugglers in Fatal Trip," *New York Times*, July 18, 1993, 27. Of the original 286 would-be U.S. immigrants, 118 have been returned to Changle: *South China Morning Post*, January 30, 1994, 12.

33. Ko-lin Chin, *Chinatown Gangs: Extortion, Enterprise, and Ethnicity* (New York: Oxford University Press, 1996). Cf. Peter Kwong, *Forbidden Workers: Illegal Chinese Immigrants and American Labor* (New York: New Press, 1997).

34. Seth Faison, "With Eye on Dollar, Chinese Are Blind to Danger," *New York Times*, October 21, 1995, 2.

overseas remittances from relatives in the United States and other parts of the world have fueled much of Changle's growth in the last decade. Ties with its recent migrants remain deep. One local official claimed that in 1995 alone the city received over US$300 million from Changle people working abroad.[35] On an average day, local banks report one hundred to two hundred cash wire transactions into personal savings accounts from foreign banks. Smuggling migrants has become an integral part of Changle's local economy, and this is reflected in the scale and volume of *hui*: 73 percent of the interviewees participating in *hui* said that they were doing it to pay off "snake heads" (*shetou*), who specialize in arranging transportation and other logistics involved in illegal migration. It can cost up to US$50,000 to send a relative abroad, though the going rate seems to be around $30,000 to $40,000. Unlike Fuzhou, where *hui* participants contribute from 100 to 1,000 *yuan* each month, in Changle the monthly *hui* contribution may be as high as 10,000 *yuan*. Such mammoth payment streams are maintained by participating in multiple *hui* at the same time and juggling monthly cash payments in a manner evocative of consumer credit run amok in the United States.

Although no statistical profile of illegal migrants is available, my interviewees unanimously claim that over 90 percent of the foreign-bound migrants are male: "Many men don't survive the trip, which can last up to six months, so women certainly wouldn't be able to handle spending all that time on a boat. . . . The conditions are so stressful that sometimes violence breaks out." Women in Changle are generally left behind to finance the transportation of husbands, sons, and other male relatives by organizing large-scale *hui* and to deal with the risks associated with such large cash transactions.[36]

The case of Ms. Chen, in 1996 a fifty-three-year-old illiterate vegetable vendor, is revealing.[37] Ms. Chen was a *hui* organizer (*huitou*) until she lost her life savings in 1991 when the other members (also women) defaulted on the payments and disappeared. She had organized the *hui* in order to send her immediate male relatives abroad. Ultimately, her son made it to the United States by boat in 1993 when he was twenty-one years old; she

---

35. Interview No. 64.

36. At least four teenage girls made the *Golden Venture* trip in 1993; U.S. immigration officials inadvertently released them to the gang that had smuggled them in and gang-raped them during the trip: "Chinese Girls Released to Gang," *Newsday*, June 21, 1993, 6. In May 1998 a powerboat carrying twenty-three Chinese men from Changle ended up in New Jersey. They had originally been part of a group of fifty aboard the *Oriental I*, a coastal freighter, which had departed from Venzeula and picked up the men in Suriname; the rest wound up in the Bahamas. See Keven McCoy, "First Inside Look at Smuggling Ring," *New York Daily News*, July 2, 1998, 38; Robert D. McFadden, "22 Illegal Immigrants Seized after a Jersey Shore Landing," *New York Times*, June 1, 1998, 1.

37. Survey No. 165.

paid 21,000–22,000 *yuan* to a snake head. As of 1996, her son was working somewhere in the U.S. "countryside" and sending her US$4,000–5,000 a year.

Her son-in-law tried to go by boat twice. In 1992 the first boat almost sank but was rescued by the Japanese Coast Guard and sent back to Changle. Four months later, however, he made it. When I asked where he arrived in the United States, she responded, "Well, he had to ride in the back of a truck for four hours to reach New York." As of 1996 he was living in New York, working on houses (painting, fixing bathrooms, etc.), and sending home US$500 a month. Ms. Chen also told us about a friend's son who was caught by the U.S. Coast Guard, taken to court, found guilty of attempting to immigrate illegally, and sent back. They all cried about it. Now most people go by plane and are charged US$36,000. (Note that the first time her son left, Ms. Chen had to pay "only" US$1,000, since he did not reach his destination. Usually, full payment is due upon arrival.)

As women are busy juggling *hui* to send their male relatives abroad, and snake heads are devising new air and water itineraries for their human cargo, the rest of the local economy could pass for almost any other rapidly developing district along Fujian's coastline. Roads are either dusty or muddy from ongoing construction; new white-tiled buildings seem anomalous next to the old squat wooden structures; factories dot the mountainsides, and commercial market areas are beginning to look somewhat standardized. Meanwhile, dance halls and karaoke dens (KTV)—badges of pop cultural modernity in East Asia—have sprung up all over town. Given that an increasing portion of Changle's young male population is abroad or in transit, it seems ironic that the karaoke "singing and dance halls" (*gewuting*), also known for offering female companions to their guests, are doing so well. Apparently, enough men remain in Changle to sustain the local entertainment industry, even to the point of attracting migrant women from poorer areas to staff the businesses.[38] Of the multiple economic realities that exist in Changle, one of them is that older women are working to send men abroad, while younger women are prostituting themselves to the men that remain behind.

My late-night interview with a teacher-turned-KTV manager was informative. Although Mr. Ge had been the manager of a dance club for over one year when we met in 1996, people still called him "Teacher Ge" because he had been the choral instructor in a local high school for nearly thirty

---

38. There have been periodic attempts to crack down on prostitution in Fujian's "open cities," including Fuzhou, Xiamen, Zhangzhou, Quanzhou, and Putian, but smaller up-and-coming places such as Changle have not been subject to that kind of publicized discipline. Judging by newspaper reports and the patterns of other political campaigns, the crackdowns appear to be quota-driven. See, e.g., "Fujian Cracks Down on Prostitution, Gambling."

years.[39] The rest of his family is also well educated: his wife is the head of the math department in his old school; his daughter is a Xiamen University graduate who now works in Hong Kong; and his son is a doctor. Since Mr. Ge had a background in music, the local government recruited him for the managerial position at a collectively owned KTV dance club. When asked about the performance of the club under his tenure, Mr. Ge spoke openly about its popularity among cadres and successful entrepreneurs. "Everyone works hard to earn money in Changle," he explained, "so the club gives them a chance to relax and have fun." Although wealthy women entrepreneurs sometimes bring a group of clients to the club and treat them to tea service at a table off the dance floor or public KTV area, the vast majority of his customers are men who seek the company of professional "public relations misses" (*gonggong xiaojie*) or "young female sitting companions" (*zuotai xiao jie*) for an evening of drinking, singing, and dancing. Private KTV rooms are also available.

Mr. Ge said that about twenty young women live on the club's premises permanently and generally earn 2,000–3,000 *yuan* per month. He does not limit their earnings, though he also did not divulge the financial relationship that he has with the women. On an average evening the escorts earn about 100 *yuan*, working from 12:30 to 4:30 P.M. and then from 7:00 P.M. to midnight. The place officially closes at 12:30 A.M., but the cadre accompanying me said that people often stay there well into the morning. Mr. Ge estimates that 90 percent of the escorts are from outside of Fujian, including young women from Jiangxi, Hubei, Jiangsu, and Henan.

In addition to rotating credit associations, loan sharks, and snake heads, Changle also harbors such institutionalized sources of private finance as "people's livelihood enterprise economy service bureaus" (*minsheng qiye jingji fuwubu*) and "people's livelihood enterprise economy limited liability companies" (*minsheng qiye jingji youxian gongsi*). Despite the ambiguity of these names, local officials and private entrepreneurs both understand that these businesses serve as financial intermediaries for brokering the large sums of money involved in private enterprise and human smuggling. As of 1996, local officials remained complicit in allowing the de facto private financial institutions to operate; however, their activities have attracted the attention of banking officials at the provincial and central levels, which means that the institutions may be "rectified" from above.[40]

---

39. Interview No. 77 (I have modified identifying personal details to preserve anonymity).
40. *JRNJ 1997*, 197.

Mountain Villages: Poverty and Depopulation

While the city center (formerly the county seat) of Changle is bustling with construction and commercial activity, the mountainous areas on its western flank remain impoverished. Mountains that lie in the way of highway projects are blown up on a regular basis, producing explosive rumbling sounds that can be heard even in the city center. And the more inaccessible mountainous areas have experienced dramatic depopulation over the last few years. We visited four remote villages in the mountains bordering Changle—Shiyan, Shiping, Gaohu, and Yanyang.[41] All four were sparsely populated. Just as Changle residents view Fuzhou as the nearest urban center for purchasing supplies and pursuing potential employment, the mountain-based villagers consider Changle their urban center—one that warrants monthly visits by any remaining able-bodied adults. The difference in linkage between Changle and Fuzhou on the one hand and mountain villages and Changle on the other is the fact that transportation is now readily available between Fuzhou and Changle, whereas few vehicles are able to navigate the steep and rocky mountain trails separating the villages from Changle City. In addition, whereas many Changle residents aspire to emigrate to the United States, mountain villagers only hope that they or their children will be able to move to Changle City at some point—and empty houses and untilled land provide eerie evidence that many have indeed succeeded in relocating. In mid-1996, for example, only 200 people were left in Shiyan Village where only two years earlier there had been over 500 residents. Similarly, only 1,800 of Shiping Village's 6,000 inhabitants were left; only 27 of 90 families were still living in Yanyang Village; and Gaohu Village was virtually abandoned. Even the offices of the village "government" (they still called it the brigade) were empty. Mainly, it is the elderly and children who have been left behind in these villages. When we asked working-age people why they stayed in the mountains, they responded that they did not have a sufficient level of education to work in Changle City, or that they had remained behind to look after relatives.

Not surprisingly, the local economy in these villages is stagnant. Villagers generally grow only enough for their own subsistence, and the one household we found that sold food and livestock locally admitted that the income was not stable. In fact, most families rely on bartering with other households for relative diversity in their diets. To the extent that cash enters the economy at all, it is through young relatives who go down to the city and make a little money. In Shiyan it was clear how the cumulative trickles of cash had been spent: all the buildings in the village were dilapidated except for a freshly painted temple.

41. My research assistant in Changle grew up in that particular mountain range, so we were able to rent a four-wheel pickup truck and direct the driver to get us close to various villages.

Quanzhou Municipality: Capitalist Competition for Outside Investment

For many centuries, Quanzhou (known in medieval Western literature as Zaiton) was one of the most vibrant trading ports in South China. As migrants were departing from Zaiton for Taiwan and Southeast Asia during the Yuan and Song Dynasties (960–1341), Marco Polo and other foreign traders were passing through Zaiton at the end of the Silk Road and collecting Chinese goods to export to India, Arabia, and Central Asia.[42] Some traders settled in Zaiton, and Quanzhou remains to date the most populated municipality in Fujian with a population of about 6.3 million.[43] According to local officials, during the Mao era the commercial impulses of Quanzhou's people were curbed but never fully suppressed. Even before the formal commencement of reform in 1978, local entrepreneurs were starting to establish de facto privately owned retail businesses and factories. And the local governments were complicit in this process by allowing private entrepreneurs to register as "collectives" and permitting smaller-scale businesses to operate without a formal registration status. The Industrial and Commercial Management Bureau was reestablished in 1978, and the mass organization representing the interests of private entrepreneurs, the Individual Laborers' Association (ILA, *geti laodongzhe xiehui*), was revived in mid-1982[44]—which was early relative to the rest of the country, given that it was by no means clear that reform would eventually be extended to urban areas. Even before the central government signaled greater tolerance for the non-state sector and established the regulatory infrastructure to govern non-state operations, TVEs and private businesses had been developing rapidly. Figures 3.5, 3.6, and 3.7 graph the number of registered private businesses, the number of people employed in the private sector, and a comparison of the growth in total reported capitalization, production value, and profit among Quanzhou's private enterprises from 1981 to 1995. Growth has been steady except for fluctuations during the late 1980s and early 1990s. More interesting, the State Council's February 1985 designation of the triangular area of Xiamen, Zhangzhou, and Quanzhou as an "open economic district" in Fujian's coastal southeast

---

42. Quanzhou also boasts the oldest mosque in eastern China, built in 1009 by the local Muslim population.

43. The municipality's population as of year-end 1995 was 6,259,200, with 521,130 (8.3 percent) residing in the city proper: *FJNJ 1996*, 440.

44. After the PRC's establishment, Quanzhou held its first Small Business Representative Conference in June 1951, followed by a second one in 1954. It remained inactive until after 1964, but was not formally recovened until July 1982. In 1984 the ILA established branches in the other counties under Quanzhou's administration, including Nanan, Huian, Yongchun, Dehua, Jinjiang, and Anxi: Tang Shan, "Huihuang de lishi, guangcai de shiye" (Brilliant history, Glorious profession) in *Shizai guangcailu*, 351.

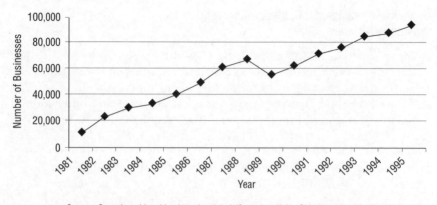

Source: Quanzhoushi geti laodongzhe xiehui (Quanzhou ILA), *Shizai guangcai lu* (A radiant path of ten years), 1996, 560–62.

Figure 3.5 Registered Private Businesses in Quanzhou, 1981–1995

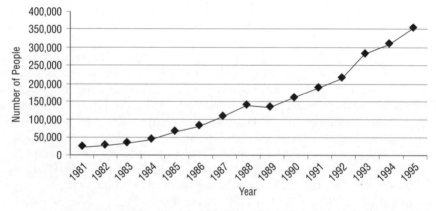

Source: Quanzhoushi geti laodongzhe xiehui (Quanzhou ILA), *Shizai guangcai lu* (A radiant path of ten years), 1996, 558–59.

Figure 3.6 People Employed in the Private Sector in Quanzhou, 1981–1995

did *not* produce any notable change in the progression of growth in Quanzhou's private sector. The more permissive investment environment after 1985 (and especially after 1992) did, however, enhance the official level of exports and influx of foreign capital.

The growth in Quanzhou's collective, private, and foreign (primarily Taiwanese) investment has resulted in a structural shift away from agricul-

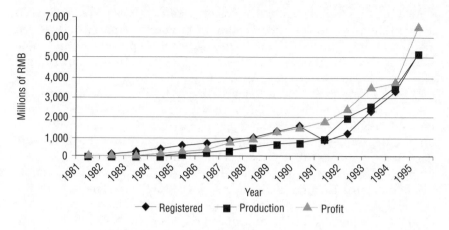

Source: Quanzhoushi geti laodongzhe xiehui (Quanzhou ILA), *Shizai guangcai lu* (A radiant path of ten years), 1996, 558–59.

Figure 3.7 Capitalization, Production Value, and Profit of Private Enterprises in Quanzhou, 1981–1995

tural production toward light industry and services. This shift is remarkable, given that well over 90 percent of the population was classified as rural at the outset of reform. The economic production in certain localities has become quite specialized: for example, Shishi Township is known for its clothing factories, Chendai Township for manufacturing shoes, Cizao Township for its ceramics, Dongshi Township for its weaving, Qingyang Township for its food processing, and Luncang Township for its plumbing equipment. Light industrial operations can also be found in Quanzhou's city proper—called Licheng District since 1985—where new construction projects have razed many old sections of town in which small businesses used to operate alongside historical sites.[45] Nonetheless, impressive stretches of everyday retail markets remain, and Quanzhou continues to attract its share of entrepreneurial migrants from rural areas and other provinces. An estimated 50,000 migrants are crowded into the seven-square-kilometer city proper's permanent population of 200,000.[46]

45. On the tension between preserving the historical character of Quanzhou and constructing a more modern-looking city, see Michael Leaf et al., *Planning for Urban Redevelopment in Quanzhou, Fujian, China*, Asian Urban Research Network Working Paper No. 5 (Vancouver: Centre for Human Settlements, School of Community and Regional Planning, University of British Columbia, 1995); it notes that an official moratorium was issued on further construction around the oldest part of town (by the Kaiyuan temple, which dates back to 1009), but it was obvious that construction projects had proceeded nonetheless between my visits in the summer of 1994, fall of 1996, and spring of 1997.

46. Ibid., 5 and n. 11, 28.

My interview with a couple that has traveled extensively in search of an appropriate place to run their restaurant business is typical. In 1996 Mr. Fan was a thirty-three-year-old elementary-school-educated owner of a simple indoor restaurant not far from the first Pizza Hut in Quanzhou.[47] He and his wife, from rural Anhui originally, at the outset of reform decided to leave their land to relatives and enter the restaurant business. They did not have enough money to rent the space or to purchase the necessary dining furniture and cooking implements for an established restaurant, so they settled for running an outdoor fast food stand attached to the back of a three-wheeled bicycle cart. They found the market for prepared food sluggish in Anhui (at least in their locality), so in 1984 the couple decided to move to Zhengzhou, the provincial capital of Henan. Although business picked up a little there, the winters were too cold for serving food outdoors. Beijing was similarly problematic for them between 1990 and 1991. After trying various places in Hubei, interspersed with visits home, they heard through relatives that the private economy in Quanzhou was doing well. Since 1993 Mr. Fan, his wife, and his younger brother have been running a restaurant together in Quanzhou, starting with a smaller-scale operation for one year before expanding to their current location. "We are finally making some money in Quanzhou," he explained. "That's all we wanted to do in all the other places." Nonetheless, Mr. Fan did not regard the business situation as ideal, since competition was increasing from year to year and they were working seventeen hours a day (6:00 A.M. to 11:00 P.M.). Eventually, he hopes that they will be able to save enough money to return home and live with their ten-year-old son in Anhui.

Amid migrant vendors like Mr. Fan, toiling to create better lives for themselves, the establishment of higher-end commercial, industrial, and high-technology districts in Quanzhou is under way. For instance, in 1994 the Licheng District Central Committee and local government initiated an industrial development strategy roughly translated as, "establish pillar [industries], increase [economies of] scale, create famous brands, and strive for first place." The "pillar industries" include petrochemicals, textiles, ceramics, foodstuffs, real estate, and tourism. This strategy also advocates governmental support for product innovation, independent scientific and technological research, and various electronics-related industries.[48]

47. Survey No. 324.
48. Another publicized strategy in the mid-1990s was to build seven types of markets to serve as the district's economic bases. Dubbed the "Seven Big" plan, the priority sectors were marketable grain, fruit, vegetables, aquatic products, raising birds, growing flowers and plants, and tourism.

On balance, however, the municipal government is more focused on modernizing the city's infrastructure to inspire investor confidence in Quanzhou as a strategic trading port that offers ready access to the existing and untapped industrial capacity of the municipality's counties.[49] Four economic belts were identified in 1996 and instructed to promote industries that suited their "own distinct characteristics."[50] Part of the rationale for imposing this economic division of labor between the city proper and the adjacent rural and peri-urban counties is that the local government hopes to capitalize, quite literally, on the fact that millions of overseas Chinese trace their roots back to the Quanzhou area, including a substantial portion of Taiwanese who speak the same *min'nan* dialect as people do in southern Fujian.[51] In this respect, Quanzhou must compete with Xiamen and Fuzhou: Xiamen shares the cultural and linguistic connection with Taiwan and has a special economic status; meanwhile, as the provincial capital, Fuzhou appears to potential foreign investors as the other logical entry point for investing in Fujian.[52] Yet as any Quanzhou resident will point out, Quanzhou arguably has a much richer trading history than either Xiamen or Fuzhou.[53] Notwithstanding issues of intraprovincial competition and envy, practical developmental considerations also underlie

49. Licheng District itself is not opposed to infrastructural construction, but as the preceding examples show, it has broader objectives as well. District-level infrastructure initiatives included naming 1994 as the "Road Construction Year" and calling 1995 the "Cities and Towns Construction Year": *FJNJ 1994*, 285; *FJNJ 1995*, 326.

It is also worth mentioning that private businesses have become increasingly involved in infrastructural financing. The Mingliu Company in Quanzhou, for example, invested 250 million *yuan* to build a 1,530-meter bridge across the Jinjiang River: "China: Privately Run PRC Companies Eye Infrastructure," *Xinhua News Agency*, March 15, 1998, reported in FBIS-CHI-98-074.

50. "Fujian's Quanzhou City Maps Out New Development Strategy," *Xinhua News Agency*, March 26, 1996, reported in FBIS-CHI-96-067.

51. One source estimates that eight million Taiwanese trace their roots to Quanzhou: "Qiaoxiang quanzhou jubian" (Tremendous changes in Quanzhou, home to overseas Chinese), in *Fujian fenjin de sishi nian* (Forty years of struggle and progress in Fujian) (Fuzhou: Fujiansheng tongji ju, 1989), 207. Another source claims that 44.8 percent of the nine million ethnic Han Chinese living in Taiwan are descendants of Quanzhou. *FJNJ 1985*, 470. This latter figure is also cited on the Fujian Province web site: ⟨http://www.china-window.com/Fujian_w/city/quanzhou/c-index-1.html⟩, February 1999 (in Chinese).

52. Xiamen and Fuzhou have also held more commerce and investment-related fairs and conferences. In December 1998, Quanzhou finally hosted the high-profile China National Tourism and Trade Fair. Sponsored by the National Tourism Administration and the Fujian Provincial Government, the annual fair showcases investment-worthy businesses in tourism and trade: "China: Quanzhou to Host China National Tourism Trade Fair," *Xinhua News Agency*, April 30, 1998, reported in FBIS-CHI-98-120.

53. The PRC government ranks Quanzhou as the third most historic city in the country, after Beijing and Xi'an. A local saying about Quanzhou's historical value is, "See underground antiquities in Xi'an, but see relics on the ground in Quanzhou" (*dixia kan Xi'an, dishang kan*

Driving for a living, Quanzhou, Fujian, November 1996.

Quanzhou's increasingly assertive efforts to project itself as a desirable destination for foreign investment—the reality of ongoing capital scarcity in the local economy.

During the 1980s, small and medium-sized enterprises flourished throughout the municipality. The financing of these non-state businesses derived from personal savings, borrowing from friends, trade credit, rotat-

Quanzhou): *Quanzhou: lishi wenhua mingcheng* (Quanzhou: A historical and cultural city) (Fujian: Haifeng chubanshe, 1995), 7. Besides the remains of Marco Polo's ship, the Quanzhou Museum of Maritime Communications History also houses the research-oriented Maritime Silk Route Studies Center funded by UNESCO.

ing credit associations, and a variety of nonbanking financial institutions such as pawnshops and rural cooperative foundations. By the mid-1980s, some of the more successful entrepreneurs had turned to professional moneylending: that is, brokering between savers seeking high interest returns and borrowers who were willing to pay even higher interest for ready access to credit. Some of these moneylenders even quietly established private banks to conduct their financial business in a more efficient manner. Amid this expansion in private enterprise and the emergence of an unofficial financial infrastructure supporting its growth, the local government played a facilitating role. Registered *getihu* who had more than eight employees were not chastised for violating official laws but encouraged to register as collective enterprises. By the same token, private financial institutions were instructed to sell shares to the local public in order to qualify as credit "cooperatives."[54] But such interventions were largely cosmetic. As long as people were pursuing income-generating activities that in turn added to local coffers, there was no immediate reason for the local government to crack down on financial practices that seemed to be part of the growth process.[55]

In the early 1990s, however, the city proper experienced a scare caused by this implicit "policy" of ignoring the color of the financial cats. As rotating credit associations, in particular the "bidding" variant (*biaohui*), became very popular among micro-entrepreneurs in Quanzhou, the scale grew so large that some associations began to collapse; members defaulted on payments, and *hui* leaders absconded with the collective money. The official reading of the crisis seems to be that what started out as a healthy form of mutual assistance at the grassroots level mutated into a perverse form of speculation, fueled by capitalist greed. In mid-1994, therefore, the city government launched a campaign to wipe out the practice of *hui*.[56] So many people became insolvent due to the *hui* that the city government actually

---

54. In an official public report of Quanzhou's financial situation in 1985, there is actually a reference to the fact that the municipal government had encouraged "private financial enterprises" (*siying jinrong qiye*) to "redeem their shares." See *Fujian diqu jingji* (Fujian's local economies) (Fuzhou: Fujian renmin chubanshe, 1986), 533.

55. More recently, however, the Quanzhou ICMB and the Foreign Trade and Economic Relations Commission have taken a more interventionist role in monitoring foreign-funded enterprises and even closed down nearly three hundred of them in 1997 for not complying with auditing or registration requirements. See "Fujian City Closes 300 Foreign-Funded Enterprises," *Zhongguo xinwenshe*, March 4, 1997, reported in FBIS-CHI-97-063.

Periodic crackdowns on illegal commercial activities are also occurring. For example, Public Security cadres busted a small factory that was producing some 30,000 bootleg CDs daily, a high output it sustained by hiring rural migrants from Guangdong, Jiangxi, and Hunan. They arrested eleven people and seized over 80,000 finished and semifinished disks: "China: Pirated Disc Production Line Closed in Fujian," *Xinhua News Agency*, September 29, 1998, reported in FBIS-CHI-98-271.

56. Interview Nos. 7, 18, 142, 143.

established an ad hoc committee to identify and prosecute well-known *hui* organizers and raise money to compensate victims of collapsed *hui*. But most people simply lost their money.

One example is Ms. Dong, an unfortunate *hui* participant who had enough money to tie up in several shares (*fen*) of a bidding association but never had a chance to collect her share of the collective pot.[57] After completing second grade at the age of ten, Ms. Dong started working as a farmer. She explained that as the oldest of five siblings, she was used to having multiple responsibilities. Aged forty-one in 1996, she held a regular market space in one of the retail vegetable markets in Licheng District. Ms. Dong lives with her husband and two teenage children in a three-story house equipped with modern appliances and consumer electronics such as a color television, CD player, washing machine, and even a motorcycle. It took her over fifteen years of peddling vegetables to achieve a reasonably comfortable lifestyle, however, and her hours remain long: every morning she wakes up at three or four o'clock to purchase vegetables from a distant wholesale distributor, and then she oversees her market stall until seven in the evening. Her husband, a retired soldier, helps out with washing, trimming, and arranging the vegetables, but she handles all the major business decisions because she has had more experience.

In 1993 it was also her decision to start participating in *biaohui*. Ms. Dong was introduced to a bidding association through one of her younger sisters, who in turn had been introduced to it through her husband's older sister. None of them knew the organizer firsthand, but they did not really worry about it, since most of their friends and acquaintances were also participating in *biaohui* at the time. As it turned out, they should have been concerned. The organizer was a thirty-five-year-old unemployed man who had no way of repaying the participants aside from raising it from other *biaohui*. As his payment streams grew increasingly complex, he had to default on several *hui*, and Ms. Dong ultimately lost about 150,000 *yuan*, which she was hoping to put toward building a new house when her son married. After the *hui* members reported the organizer to the city government, he committed suicide.

Local officials claim that most people are afraid to participate in *hui* after witnessing the destruction they can bring. Nonetheless, over half of the Quanzhou entrepreneurs surveyed in 1996 were still participating in *hui* (and 90 percent of those were women); participants said that the risk of default did not deter them from continuing to engage in *hui* because they trusted the other members and basically felt that they had no other financing options.[58] A former *hui* participant I will call Ms. Li, for instance, lost

---

57. Survey No. 322.

58. A similar phenomenon occurred in Taiwan. When there were large-scale *hui* failures during 1983–85, *hui* participation declined significantly but it had just about recovered to

substantial sums of money to *hui*.[59] Unlike Ms. Dong, however, she is much more resentful about her *hui* experiences, since the monetary losses caused friction in her family life and adversely affected her confidence to be in business.

After working in a state factory for fifteen years, Ms. Li decided to enter the private sector in 1993. Her daughter was old enough to look after herself at the age of twelve, and all their friends seemed to be getting rich by opening their own businesses. The problem with her plan, Ms. Li said in retrospect, was her naiveté and lack of education. She had attended only four years of elementary school during the early years of the Cultural Revolution and had no idea how to run a business. The dusty products in her display case indeed defy thematic classification; cassette tapes are sold alongside packets of soap and shampoo, calculators, and rusty key chains. The most profitable item in the store appears to be the public phone, which brings in 300–400 *yuan* each month. Ms. Li keeps the shop open fourteen hours a day (7:00 A.M. to 10:00 P.M.) and earns an after-tax monthly profit of 400–500 *yuan*.

The store owner spoke bitterly of her attempt to help friends by borrowing money at 30 percent annual interest on their behalf and losing over 10,000 *yuan*. Adding to this loss, after her sister-in-law introduced her to the practice of *hui*, Ms. Li lost an additional 12,000 *yuan* to four different *hui* that collapsed in 1993 (at the peak of her involvement she was participating in seven different *hui*). When Quanzhou established a *biaohui* relief office, *hui* victims were told that the city government would cover 50 percent of their losses, but ultimately the government compensated Ms. Li for only 10 percent. To pay off her remaining debts, they had to sell her husband's motorcycle. These days, her husband continues to blame her and call her stupid for losing so much money.

Jinjiang County/City: From Household Factories to World Markets

Until 1985 the area encompassed by "Quanzhou municipality" in southeastern Fujian was actually a separate "district" called Jinjiang District. The implicit administrative downgrading of Jinjiang was due not to its economic performance, which has been remarkable, but, rather, to Quanzhou's designation as an open coastal city. That Quanzhou was the site of the munic-

---

1977 levels by 1991 (20–30 percent of all households). See Alec R. Levenson and Timothy Besley, "The Anatomy of an Informal Financial Market: Rosca Participation in Taiwan," *Journal of Development Economics* 51, 1 (1996): 45–68.

59. Survey No. 321.

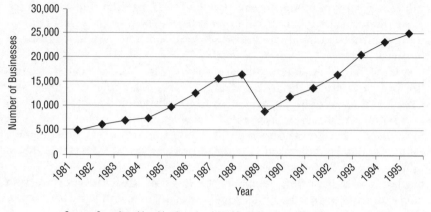

Source: Quanzhoushi geti laodongzhe xiehui (Quanzhou ILA), *Shizai guangcai lu* (A radiant path of ten years), 1996, 563.

Figure 3.8 Registered Private Businesses in Jinjiang, 1981–1995

ipal government served to reinforce the logic of renaming the municipality to reflect the liberalizing trends that would be expected to spread from the coast toward the more rural inland counties. Of the six counties in greater Quanzhou, the non-state sector in Jinjiang developed earliest. By 1981, Jinjiang already had 4,361 registered private enterprises—more than twice the number in Quanzhou city proper (2,287 enterprises) and nearly half of all private enterprises in Quanzhou municipality (9,651).[60] As can be seen in Figures 3.8, 3.9, and 3.10, the number of private enterprises, the number of people employed in the private sector, and the capitalization of private enterprises in Jinjiang all increased annually over the 1981 to 1995 period with the exception of 1988 and 1989, years marked by double-digit inflation and political uncertainty.

In addition to relatively large numbers of officially registered private enterprises, Jinjiang has a disproportionately high number of Taiwanese-invested cooperative enterprises relative to its population.[61] In terms of sheer numbers, one-fourth of all private and foreign-invested cooperative enterprises in Quanzhou municipality are in Jinjiang, and as of 1995 these enterprises accounted for 63.7 percent of all foreign investment flows into Jinjiang.[62] Other expressions of foreign "investment" in the city have taken

60. *Shizai guangcai lu*, 563.
61. As of 1995, Jinjiang's population was 970,700, or 15.4 percent of the total population in Quanzhou Municipality (6.3 million): *FJNJ 1996*, 440.
62. *Shizai guangcai lu*, 21.

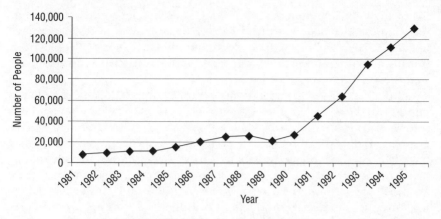

Source: Quanzhoushi geti laodongzhe xiehui (Quanzhou ILA), *Shizai guangcai lu* (A radiant path of ten years), 1996, 563.

Figure 3.9 People Employed in the Private Sector in Jinjiang, 1981–1995

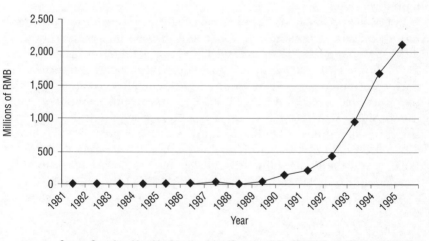

Source: Quanzhoushi geti laodongzhe xiehui (Quanzhou ILA), *Shizai guangcai lu* (A radiant path of ten years), 1996, 563.

Figure 3.10 Total Annual Registered Capitalization of Private Enterprises in Jinjiang, 1981–1995

the form of outright donations of production tools and equipment by overseas Chinese, the value of which totaled HK$110 million in 1996, accounting for 55 percent of all such donations in Quanzhou.[63] People from Jinjiang are known for maintaining particularly strong clan and kinship ties with their native place.

Although the aggregate economic performance of Jinjiang is certainly impressive, the typical profile of its enterprises is not. The development trajectory of its economy has become known as the "Jinjiang model," which is similar to the "Wenzhou model" of development except that Jinjiang has long benefited from the availability of overseas Chinese investment. In brief, the overwhelming majority of Jinjiang's private sector businesses are small-scale (87 percent were *getihu* in 1995) and engaged in labor-intensive, light industrial production. In Chendai Township, for example, the sector consists primarily of family-run factories (with the Chen surname) engaged in either producing sneakers or processing the materials required for sneaker production.[64] And the working conditions of most of the smaller factories that we visited appeared cramped and unsafe; for example, workers were using blowtorches without goggles in rooms piled with flammable materials, and narrow halls between production rooms were lined with production refuse.[65] Larger factories appeared somewhat more orderly.

Interestingly, some of the more successful factories started out much more modestly. For example, in 1981 eleven *getihu* who were all producing different components of sneakers decided to pool their savings and open a joint-household (*lianhu*) factory that could produce an entire sneaker.[66] Each contributed a couple of hundred *yuan*, and after a year of operation they were able to distribute over 2,000 *yuan* to each of the founders. After the second year, Ms. Chu, one of the partners, bought out the remaining shares and continued to build the business. By the mid-1990s the factory was geared entirely to exporting "famous brand" sneakers to Romania, Poland, and the Philippines. The sneaker models on display in the glass showcases included such labels as "abibas," "*MIKE*," and "beebok."

Although Ms. Chu never attended school full time—she took classes at

63. Ibid., 20–21.

64. Other industries include garment manufacturing and commerce or service industries. Chih-Jou Jay Chen, "Local Institutions and the Transformation of Property Rights in Southern Fujian," in Jean C. Oi and Andrew G. Walder, eds., *Property Rights and Economic Reform in China* (Stanford, Calif.: Stanford University Press, 1999), 59.

65. Shortly before my field visit in 1997, a shoe factory in Jinjiang burned down, killing thirty-two workers who were trapped by iron-barred doors and windows and seriously injuring two others: "China: Shoe Factory Inferno Claims 32 Souls," *Zhongguo xinwenshe*, September 22, 1997, reported in FBIS-CHI-97-265. The same factory had actually burned to the ground four years earlier.

66. Survey No. 314.

a night school for about three years when she was a teenager—she says that her lack of education did not hold her back, since she had employees who could handle the accounting, billing, and general correspondence. And now that her four children are in their twenties, she can rely on them for administrative help. During the earlier years she traveled extensively, alone, to keep up with the latest market trends in sneakers. She would attend trade fairs and wholesale markets in Beijing, Dongbei, Shandong, Chengdu, Guangzhou, Shenzhen, and Kunming, and bring back samples for her factory "to learn from" and reproduce. Now she relies mainly on catalogues to suggest new production lines.

As of 1996 the factory employed 160 people, many of whom were migrant workers. She explained that so many local families have businesses of their own that most factories in Jinjiang have to hire workers from poorer areas.[67] In this sense, Ms. Chu reasoned, Jinjiang is a net producer of sneakers *and* jobs. Because she has witnessed firsthand the infrastructural transformation of her township, she does not mind paying an average of 15,000 *yuan* per month in assorted fees and taxes: "Everything is run locally—hospitals, schools, sanitation—so the government needs to get the money from somewhere." Ms. Chu also has a solid working relationship with the local Agricultural Bank of China, from which she regularly receives four-month loans in the range of 150,000 *yuan*.

Because of the sustained growth and relative importance of Jinjiang's economy, in mid-1996 it was upgraded from a "county" to a "city."[68] Government officials in Jinjiang felt that the upgrading was long overdue, as they had played active roles in courting potential foreign investors, even to the point of traveling abroad to advertise the economic importance of Jinjiang.[69] Moreover, the local economy had been flourishing quietly for years in a relatively independent manner. Jinjiang had been relatively poor and completely rural at the outset of reform. By 1986, fourteen of the original eighteen industrial SOEs had already implemented the factory manager responsibility system, whereby factory managers exercised effective control over production decisions, and two had been rented out.[70] By the mid-1990s the rest of the province had heard about the success of its *privately owned* rural enterprises. Whereas private businesses in other parts

67. In official statistics comparing the percentage of the population employed in the private sector within Quanzhou Municipality, the average for all six counties is 5.6 percent. The percentage in Jinjiang is listed as 213.5 percent, meaning that there are more people working in its private sector than its total registered population. *Shizai guangcai lu*, 563.

68. Jinjiang Airport was also opened at the end of 1996. Direct flights between Jinjiang and Hong Kong started at the end of 1998: "Charter Flight Connects Jinjiang with Hong Kong," *Xinhua News Agency*, January 21, 1999, reported in FBIS-CHI-99-021.

69. See, e.g., Chen Junjun, "Xiao qiye, da shijie" (Small enterprises, big world), in *Shizai guangcai lu*, 44–46.

70. *FJNJ 1987*, 628.

of Fujian have felt compelled to register themselves falsely as collective enterprises, Jinjiang has a relatively low proportion of "red hat" registrations.[71] The local government has maintained a distinctly noninterventionist stance toward private entrepreneurs, and local rural cooperative foundations (RCFs) and rural credit cooperatives (RCCs) are unapologetic about the fact that most of their borrowers are private businesses.

Huian County: Private Peddling on the Margins

Huian County also falls under the administrative jurisdiction of the Quanzhou Municipality. Until recently, Huian's economy depended primarily on fishing, agriculture, and a smattering of stone-carving factories. Its reform-era experience has been typical in some ways of the model of rural industrialization that has transformed the standard of living for formerly impoverished counties in various parts of China.[72] TVEs developed under the guidance of local governments have instrumentally directed credit toward local collective enterprises and accorded them favorable tax treatment. As of 1995, TVEs accounted for 90 percent of the county's industrial output, and the overwhelming majority of the workforce was employed in the state and collective sectors.[73] The developmental trajectory of Huian deviates from the so-called "Sunan model of development," however, in the sense that Huian has also attempted to capitalize on its cultural and historical ties with people in Taiwan.[74] As in Jinjiang, many villages have received substantial infusions of Taiwanese investment in the form of export-oriented enterprises and real estate projects. Meanwhile, the construction of new roads and bridges has increased the accessibility of Huian to the nearest urban center, Quanzhou.

Despite the continuing dominance of the state sector and the recent development of the collective sector, Huian's small-scale private enterprises have also developed rapidly. The graphs in Figures 3.11, 3.12, and 3.13

71. The political acceptability of private enterprise in Jinjiang is also highlighted in Chih-jou Jay Chen, "Property Rights Transformation in Rural China: Local Institutions and Economic Organizations" (Ph.D. diss., Duke University, 1997), 52–61.

72. The average rural income increased nearly sevenfold (from 394 to 2,723 *yuan*) between 1985 and 1995: *FJNJ 1986*, 627; *FJNJ 1995*, 329.

73. In 1995, TVEs accounted for 6.7 billion *yuan* of the total 7.4 billion *yuan* in GVIO: *FJNJ 1996*, 328. Although employment statistics are not available in the provincial yearbooks on the share of employment in the state and collective sectors, *Shizai guangcai lu*, 563, reports that the private sector accounted for only 2.4 percent of employment in 1995.

74. The local government estimates that Huian is the ancestral home to approximately 900,000 Taiwanese. "Huianxian renmin zhengfu and Huianxian duiwai wenhua jiaoliu xiehui" (Huian County people's government and the Association of Huian County Cultural Exchange with Abroad), in *Zhongguo Huian* (China's Huian) (Huian: Haihu sheying yishu chubanshe, 1993), 7.

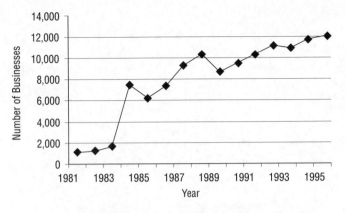

Source: Quanzhoushi geti laodongzhe xiehui (Quanzhou ILA), *Shizai guangcai lu* (A radiant path of ten years), 1996, 563.

Figure 3.11 Registered Private Businesses in Huian County, 1981–1995

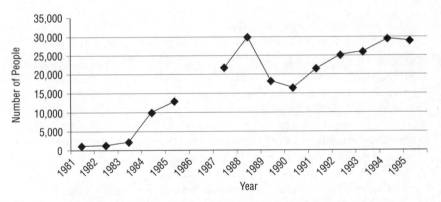

Source: Quanzhoushi geti laodongzhe xiehui (Quanzhou ILA), *Shizai guangcai lu* (A radiant path of ten years), 1996, 563.

Figure 3.12 People Employed in the Private Sector in Huian, 1981–1995

show that the official record of the growth has been rather erratic, however. Some of the dramatic statistical fluctuations from year to year may be attributed to changes in governmental efforts to register and document the private sector. The particularly large 1983–84 increase in the number of registered businesses, the number of people employed in the private sector,

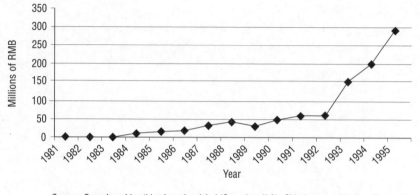

Source: Quanzhoushi geti laodongzhe xiehui (Quanzhou ILA), *Shizai guangcai lu* (A radiant path of ten years), 1996, 563.

Figure 3.13 Total Registered Capitalization of Private Businesses in Huian County, 1981–1995

and the registered capitalization of the private sector are probably due to the fact that the ILA was not established in Huian County until 1984. The constriction of the private sector in 1989 and subsequent renewed expansion in 1992 are more directly related to the shifts in political orientation toward reform at the national level.

Although the private sector in Huian has certainly grown over the course of reform, the state and, especially, collective sectors continue to play a dominant role in the local economy. The best-performing SOEs and TVEs are engaged in producing stone carvings, national brand beer (*Huiquan pijiu*), bicycles, machine-processed sugar, household glass, and leather shoes. Throughout the reform era the county has recognized their ongoing need for investment and working capital and therefore actively encouraged the growth of RCCs and RCFs to finance their operations. Given that these financial institutions are devoted to mobilizing savings deposits from villagers and lending to collective and state enterprises, private businesses in Huian rely primarily on interpersonal lending and "mutual assistance associations" (*huzhuhui*), which are basically rotating credit associations. Nearly 90 percent of the *getihu* that I surveyed in Huian County had participated in *hui*, and nearly 70 percent of the *hui* participants were women. Even though in recent years, as in Quanzhou's city proper, there have been increasing incidents of *hui* organizers running off with the collective pot, *hui* remains a popular capital-raising strategy among private vendors.

Some micro-entrepreneurs express bitterness over the years of hard work and setbacks. Ms. Xie, for example, decided to sell shoes instead of retiring.[75] A sixty-year-old owner of a small shoe stand in the county seat of

75. Survey No. 347.

Huian, Ms. Xie never went to school but was lucky enough to be assigned a job in a state-owned food and beverage store, where she worked for thirty years. Meanwhile, her husband worked as a baker in another SOE. In the mid-1980s both of them lost their state jobs: she was forced into early retirement, and her husband's SOE went bankrupt. Shortly thereafter, their *danwei* housing was torn down, and they were forced to rent new living quarters. Given that their only income was her 220 *yuan* a month retirement pension and that her husband had no intention of finding work, Ms. Xie decided to go into business. Hearing through friends that shoes were easy to sell, she joined a mutual assistance association to raise the 10,000 *yuan* needed to rent and fix up a small storefront, apply for a business license, and purchase inventory from Jinjiang, Quanzhou, and Guangdong shoe wholesalers.

Ms. Xie had been running the shoe store with one of her sons for nine years as of 1996. Although her family's standard of living certainly increased in the reform era (e.g., among household appliances they own a color TV, a telephone, and a refrigerator), she explained that the business had been a series of ongoing frustrations. First, the hours are long; the store is open from 7:00 A.M. until 9:00 P.M., and she stays there the entire time because it is cheaper for her to watch the store than to hire someone at 500 *yuan* a month. Second, the number of fees levied on private businesses has increased over the years. In addition to the standard ICMB fee and sales tax, her business also has to pay a sanitation fee, a local tax, an ILA fee, and other assorted charges. Third, participating in rotating credit associations is not as safe as it used to be. When they became popular again in Huian in the mid-1970s, people did not have to worry about the security of their money, but now the possibility is greater that one member will abscond with the collective money. Ms. Xie has lost about 5,000 *yuan* from participating in *hui*, but she said that many of her relatives have lost more than that. The dishonest organizer of the last one that she participated in is now "sitting fat at home," since the members did not think that it was worth the effort to report her to the police. "No one can be trusted anymore," Ms. Xie concluded.

The gendered participation in *hui* reflects in part the sexual division of labor. In Huian as in Changle, men are prone to migrate to wealthier areas in search of employment or to take extended fishing trips, while women of marriageable age (late-twenties and older) are left to tend the fields, raise the children, and maintain the household.[76] The Huian County

---

76. Meng Xianfan, "'Nangong nügeng' yu Zhongguo nongcun nüxing de fazhan" ("Men at work, women on the farm" and Chinese rural women's development), *Funü yanjiu* (Research on women) 4 (1995): 48–51.

Women's Federation estimates that women account for 70 percent of the local industrial labor force, 80 percent of agricultural labor, and over 90 percent of small-scale entrepreneurs.[77] The skewed ratio of working women to absent men is apparent to the naked eye: throughout the county, women can be seen working on construction sites, tilling the fields, selling vegetables and seafood in outdoor markets, and operating three-wheel pedicabs.

Typical of this phenomenon are people such as Ms. San, a thirty-two-year-old illiterate driver of a three-wheel motorcycle cab in Chongwu Township, Huian.[78] Her husband is away from home for two to three years at a time, since he works on boats that transport migrant workers to Taiwan and other countries. He sends back about 350 *yuan* a month when he has the chance. Given his extended absences, however, Ms. San considers herself the head of the household. Once her son and daughter were old enough to be left with her in-laws full time, it was her decision to stop peddling dried shrimp and invest in a 6,000-*yuan* motorcycle cab. The business is physically demanding because she spends about ten hours each day driving through the semipaved roads of Chongwu, but it is reasonably profitable (she grosses an average of 1,000 *yuan* a month), and she enjoys the work more than squatting behind a large basket of shrimp in the local market and waiting for customers to come to her. When asked if she was concerned about her personal safety as a female cab driver, she responded that it was not a problem because she tends to choose female customers. Ms. San has participated in *hui*, but when she needed to come up with 10,000 *yuan* for her brother-in-law's funeral, she went through a loan shark (who charged 36 percent annual interest) because she had already taken her turn in the *hui* to purchase her motorcycle.

While this demographic trend is typical of many rural areas in China, local traditions distinguish "Huian women" (*Huiannü*, or *anminpu*) from women in other parts of Fujian. Aside from being known for their diligence—which is the case for women in the *minnan* region of Fujian in general—Huian women engage in a host of customs that have attracted the attention of Chinese and Western anthropologists.[79] First, a woman from the coastal villages of Chongwu Township wears a bright floral scarf on a wide headband that extends the height and width of the head, accom-

77. Interview No. 22, 24.
78. Survey No. 340.
79. The people of Huian are classified as Han Chinese. See the periodicals *Chongwu wenxue* (Chongwu literature), *Chongwu yanjiu* (Research on Chongwu), and *Huidongren yanjiu* (Research on people in eastern Huian) (Fuzhou: Fujian jiaoyu chubanshe, 1993). For more detail, see Sara Friedman, "Reluctant Brides and Prosperity's Daughters: Marriage, Labor, and Cultural Change in southeastern China's Hui'an County" (Ph.D. diss., Cornell University, 2000).

panied by a wide-brimmed yellow bamboo hat with a pointed top, a short jacket that barely reaches the navel, and loose ankle-length pants with a wide embroidered or silver belt. Second, newlyweds traditionally practiced "delayed-transferred marriage" (*changzhu niangjia*), whereby a young wife continued to live with her natal family, paying monthly conjugal visits in the middle of the night to her husband, until she gave birth to her first child.[80] It appears that this particular custom has given way, for the most part, to more conventional living arrangements for newlyweds such as living alone as a couple, or moving in with in-laws on the male side (patrilocal residence). Third, Huian women continue to organize "sister societies" among themselves as a means to cope with unhappy marriages, tyrannical mothers-in-law, and pressures to bear sons.[81] Also documented are several cases of "sister suicides," when two to eight women commit suicide together by jumping into the sea from the rocky crags that line the coast.

Anxi County: Climbing out of Poverty through Collective Ventures

Located in the southwestern part of Fujian, Anxi is largely mountainous.[82] It was also the least developed county in Fujian throughout most of PRC history; when the national government launched its antipoverty campaign in 1985, Anxi was officially designated one of fourteen impoverished counties in the province.[83] Consequently, the local government has taken an active role in meeting national and provincial antipoverty goals by promoting educational and technical training, infrastructural projects, investment by overseas Chinese and Taiwanese,[84] specialized agricultural households, and collective, sector-led rural industrial development.[85] The last strategy has been the most effective. By 1995, TVEs accounted for over 90 percent of the Gross Value of Industrial and Agricultural Output

80. Interview Nos. 22, 45, 142, 143.

81. One anthropologist also found that some women pray to sets of tiny dolls every night and put the dolls under their pillows with the hope that their grievances may be alleviated while they are sleeping: Interview No. 45.

82. Its land is classified as medium mountains (24.6 percent), low mountains (38.4 percent), high hills (22.2 percent), and low hills (14.8 percent): *FJNJ 1987*, 633.

83. At the outset of reform, the average annual rural income was only 50 to 60 *yuan*: *FJNJ 1986*, 628.

84. Official statistics estimate that Anxi has about 550,000 overseas Chinese compatriots in Hong Kong, Macao, and Southeast Asia (especially Singapore, Indonesia, and Malaysia). In addition, Anxi claims that about 1.8 million people in Taiwan can trace their ancestral homes to Anxi: *FJNJ 1997*, 633.

85. For a detailed analysis of Anxi's poverty alleviation efforts, see Lyons, *Poverty and Growth in a South China County*.

(GVIAO).[86] Although Anxi's development strategy has been to increase the production of its traditional products—which include sixty different types of tea, rattan furniture and baskets, mushrooms, and various fruits—increasing efforts are also being made to expand into more technology-intensive projects such as hydroelectric plants.

The financing of the collective sector derives primarily from the Agricultural Bank of China, Rural Credit Cooperatives, and Rural Cooperative Foundations. According to the 1995 PRC Commercial Banking Law, the specialized state banks (including the ABOC) are supposed to shift to commercial-based lending and divest their portfolios of "policy loans," meaning loans that are extended on the basis of politically defined developmental goals rather than commercial viability.[87] The law was intended to reform the four specialized banks into truly "commercial" banks, while "development banks" such as the Agricultural Development Bank (ADB) would be created to extend policy loans. Anxi was the last county in Fujian to establish an ADB; as of late 1996, the ABOC was still extending policy loans for rural industry, tea production, animal husbandry, and other priority areas.[88] The RCCs operate on a more commercial basis than ABOCs. They are managed by a "united society" (*lianshe*) of RCCs, which is in turn managed by the People's Bank. Nonetheless, the RCCs are also subject to local political pressures. Although the People's Bank does not recognize the RCFs as legitimate financial institutions (and were eliminated in 1999), they too have played an important role in Anxi's rural development. As one official put it, "RCFs fill in the gaps that ABOCs and RCCs leave at the grassroots level."[89] Since RCFs were run by township governments and village committees, their lending activity also reflected local priorities.

Unlike the other counties discussed above, Anxi has a Poverty Alleviation Office, which is responsible for extending low-interest loans to impoverished rural households. In practice, however, the subsidized loans do not necessarily go to the most destitute but, rather, to households that have already demonstrated their capacity to be productive.[90] The Women's Federation (WF) also assists in identifying promising loan recipients, reflecting the fact that the Chinese government's approach to poverty alleviation seeks quantifiable, short-term results to fulfill the quotas set by higher administrative levels. In addition, the designation and publicity of

86. In 1995, TVEs accounted for 3.4 of the 3.8 billion *yuan* in Anxi's GVIAO: *FJNJ 1996*, 329.

87. Eighth National People's Congress, *Zhonghua renmin gongheguo shangye yinhangfa* (PRC commercial banking law) (Beijing: Falü chubanshe, 1995).

88. In November 1996 I was told that Anxi's ADB would open in May 1997: Interview No. 145.

89. Interview No. 146.

90. Interview Nos. 138, 143.

"model households" offer outside inspectors and visitors tangible proof of the effectiveness of the local government's success at increasing the peasants' productive capacity and standard of living. The mayor of Anxi and the director of the Women's Federation accompanied me to one such model household in Hutou Township.

In 1991, Ms. Chu was a participant in the "double learnings, double competition" program run by the Women's Federation to increase women's literacy and technical skills.[91] Since she performed particularly well, the WF decided to extend her a 500-*yuan* poverty-alleviation loan to buy feed so that she could raise more ducks. Ms. Chu's small duck farm proved to be a good investment. When her husband saw how well it was doing, he quit his fledgling one-person clothing business and joined her full time. The WF continued to extend the business low-interest loans of 5,000 to 10,000 *yuan*. As of 1996, the couple was busy raising ducks, chickens, and pigs; and had just invested 30,000 *yuan* in building concrete farrowing cubicles, complete with heated dens so that they could continue to raise piglets through the winter.

Relative to the other counties in Quanzhou, the private sector is the least developed in Anxi. As of 1995, only 1.8 percent of the population was employed in the private sector, and the average scale of private business in terms of number of employees and capitalization remains very small (see Figures 3.14, 3.15, and 3.16).[92]

The Anxi ICMB reports that 70 percent of individual businesses (*getihu*) are registered under male names.[93] In reality, 70 to 80 percent of small businesses are actually run by women. As in Fuzhou and Quanzhou, the sexual division of labor is that women manage the store while men deal with registering the businesses, purchasing supplies, and marketing the products.[94] Unlike those two sites, however, *hui* are not popular among microentrepreneurs in Anxi; only 14 percent of the surveyed entrepreneurs had participated in *hui*; 71 percent of the small-scale vendors surveyed relied instead on informal borrowing from friends, relatives, and neighbors.

Summary Comparison of Sites in Fujian

Table 3.4 provides a summary of the sectoral distribution of employment, orientation of the local government toward the private sector, and the

91. Interview Nos. 141, 149.
92. As of 1995, the average private business comprised only 2.1 people and was capitalized at 16,030 *yuan* (US$1,955).
93. Interview No. 147. Over 95 percent of larger private businesses (*siying qiye*) are registered under male names.
94. Interview No. 154.

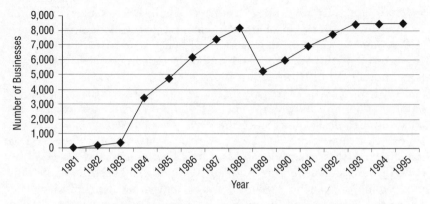

Source: Quanzhoushi geti laodongzhe xiehui (Quanzhou ILA), *Shizai guangcai lu* (A radiant path of ten years), 1996, 563.

Figure 3.14 Registered Private Businesses in Anxi County, 1981–1995

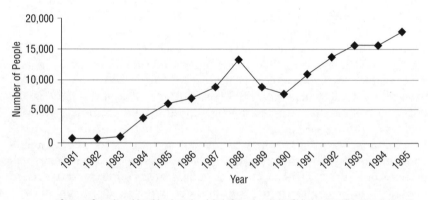

Source: Quanzhoushi geti laodongzhe xiehui (Quanzhou ILA), *Shizai guangcai lu* (A radiant path of ten years), 1996, 563.

Figure 3.15 People Employed in the Private Sector in Anxi County, 1981–1995

degree of financial institutional diversity in the informal financial sector of Fujian.

As suggested by the table, the economic argument that areas where the private sector is dominant would be more likely to have high degrees of financial institutional diversity is only partially supported by the empirical evidence. Only Huian and Anxi appear to illustrate the economic logic that places with proportionally fewer private entrepreneurs would also have a

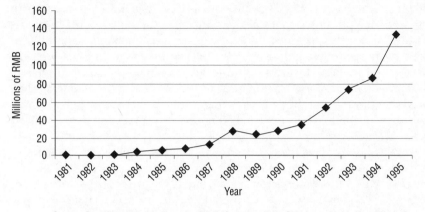

Source: Quanzhoushi geti laodongzhe xiehui (Quanzhou ILA), *Shizai guangcai lu* (A radiant path of ten years), 1996, 563.

Figure 3.16 Total Annual Registered Capitalization of Private Businesses in Anxi County, 1981–1995

Table 3.4 Summary Comparison of Sites in Fujian

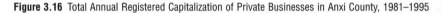

Research Site	% of Workforce Employed in Private Sector	Orientation of Local Government toward Private Sector	Degree of Institutional Diversity
Fuzhou Municipality	22.3	supportive	high
Changle County/City	22.9	supportive	high
Mountainous villages outside Changle	100[a]	not supportive	low
Quanzhou Municipality	5.6	supportive	high
Jinjiang County/City	213.5[b]	supportive	medium
Huian County	2.4	not supportive	low
Anxi County	1.8	not supportive	low

[a] Villagers that remain behind are all engaged in small-scale private farming.
[b] This calculation reflects the total number of people employed in Jinjiang's private businesses divided by Jinjiang's registered population; the percentage is over 100% because Jinjiang is a net recipient of migrant workers who are reported to the ICMB by their employers as "private-sector employees."

less-developed informal financial sector. Given that only 5.6 percent of the workforce in Quanzhou municipality is employed in the private sector, an economic perspective would predict a low degree of financial institutional diversity, yet the opposite turns out to be the case. Inconsistencies between the predicted and actual outcomes are also evident in Jinjiang and the mountain villages outside of Changle; while Fuzhou and Changle offer indeterminate evidence for the economic hypothesis. In contrast, my argument that local governmental orientation toward the private sector is a better predictor of financial institutional diversity is more consistent with the evidence presented in Table 3.4. Jinjiang is the only case that appears anomalous for this argument; the local government is highly supportive of the private sector, yet only a modest range of informal financial intermediaries are available to private businesses. The reason that local governmental orientation toward the private sector does not yield a perfect prediction in the case of Jinjiang is that the non-state sector plays a dominant role in the local economy, making formal sources of credit relatively more accessible to private entrepreneurs.

Three reasons may be identified for the limited explanatory strength of the economic logic. First, reliance on official statistics to estimate the relative scale of the private sector in each site is problematic. Quanzhou, for example, is widely known for having a large private sector, but municipal-level statistics fail to capture this fact because many private businesses are registered as collective enterprises or not registered at all. Second, the indicator of workforce percentage employed in the private sector does not capture broader economic conditions that may factor into the state of informal finance in any given locality. Everyone remaining in the mountain villages outside of Changle may be engaged in private farming, but the areas are so impoverished that cash is not used as the primary medium of exchange. Third, the economic perspective does not take into account the mediating effect of local governmental practices regarding private-sector development. Even though statistics show that less than a quarter of the workforce in Fuzhou and Changle are engaged in private commerce, the governments in both areas have been active in establishing official market areas for private businesses and exhibited relative tolerance for informal financial activities.

Just as the supply of informal financial institutions is dictated by more than a purely economic logic, private entrepreneurs' choice of financing arrangements is similarly mediated by noneconomic factors. That is to say, in the absence of perfectly competitive, nondiscriminatory credit markets, the social and political attributes of individual business owners fundamentally influence the financing options that they will engage in. Curb markets are "segmented," economically speaking, and in the case of rotating credit associations, gender has become a defining indicator of participation.

The Gendered Revival of Rotating Credit Associations

In the course of field research I found that women micro-entrepreneurs were more likely than their male counterparts to participate in rotating credit associations.[95] Specifically, of the 90 surveyed micro-entrepreneurs who participated in some form of *hui*, 64 percent (or 58 respondents) were women.[96] In areas where a higher proportion of micro-entrepreneurs participated in *hui*, the percentage of women was even higher. Moreover, I found a strong correlation between areas where women are known for taking a particularly active role in economic production and the popularity of *hui*; that is, *hui* were more popular in southern Fujian.

Within Fujian, stereotypes abound regarding the tradition of hardworking women (wed to lazy husbands) in the southern, *minnanhua*-speaking part of the province, whereas in the northern provincial capital of Fuzhou, men are said to fear their wives and contribute more to domestic work than men in the south. These are, of course, only popular accounts of regional differences in gender roles; their validity has not been examined systematically to date.[97] My own survey found that participation in *hui* was more commonplace in southern Fujian, where women have traditionally played a more active role in economic production and were therefore, not necessarily subject to some of the misogynistic Confucian practices such as footbinding.[98]

95. This is especially puzzling because early ethnographic studies of China indicate that indigenously organized credit groups such as rotating credit associations in the pre-Communist era were dominated by men. Early studies include Hsiao-Tung Fei, *Peasant Life in China: A Field Study of Country Life in the Yangtze Valley* (London: Routledge and Kegan Paul, 1939); Sidney D. Gamble, "A Chinese Mutual Savings Society" *Far Eastern Quarterly* 4 (1944): 41–52; J. H. Goh, "A Note on the Chinese Lun-Hui or Rotating Credit Society," *Economics* 5, 1 (1964): 64–72; Emile W. Jacques, "A Chinese Loan Society," *Man* 31 (1931): 225–26; Daniel H. Kulp, *Country Life in South China: Phoenix Village, Kwantung, China,* vol. 1 (New York: Teachers College, Columbia University, 1925).

96. This calculation is based on the 273 valid survey responses in the south. The bivariate correlation between "GENDER" and "ANYHUI" (the variable measuring *hui* participation), yielded a coefficient of −0.1356 at the 0.5 level of significance. The negative sign of the coefficient indicates that women have higher rates of participation in *hui* than men do.

97. The 1990 province wide survey of women's social status focused on urban-rural differences rather than north-south, regional ones. See *Fujian funü shehui diwei diaocha* (Survey of women's social status in Fujian) (Fujian: Zhongguo funü chubanshe, 1995). National surveys administered in preparation for the Fourth World Conference on Women in Beijing, 1995, similarly focused on urban-rural cleavages. See, e.g., Tao Chunfang and Jiang Yongping, eds., *Zhongguo funü shehui diwei gaikuang* (Overview of the social status of Chinese women) (Beijing: Zhongguo funü chubanshe, 1993); Zhongguo shehui kexueyuan renkou yanjiusuo [Institute of Population Studies, Chinese Academy of Social Sciences], *Dangdai zhongguo funü diwei chouyang diaocha ziliao* [Sampling survey of women's status in contemporary China] (Beijing: International Academic Publishers, 1994).

An overview of the results from the Women's Federation and Institute of Population Studies surveys is Jean K. M. Hung, "The Family Status of Chinese Women in the 1990s," in Lo Chi Kin, Suzanne Pepper, and Tsui Kai Yuen, eds., *China Review 1995* (Shatin, Hong Kong: Chinese University Press, 1995), chap. 12.

98. For more detail on the influences of Hakka customs on gender norms in Huian and elsewhere, see Li Yongji, *Xingbie yu wenhua: kejia funü yanjiu de xin shiye* (Gender and culture:

Indeed, contrary to most Western notions of the passive and subjugated role of women in traditional Confucian Chinese society, Fujianese folk tales dating back to the Song dynasty (960–1279) reveal that women in Fujian were not universally portrayed in strictly submissive terms. In fact, as Karen Gernant points out, the combination of geographical distance from the imperial capitals and the poverty of the province led to substantial deviations from ideal-typical Confucian gender roles in everyday life. Ordinary women in Fujian had to contribute to economic production, and popular tales provide many accounts of women giving wise advice and helping their families to alleviate misfortune. Here are two examples of the positive portrayal of women in such tales.

Golden Cup and Hundred Leaves tells the story of a brother and sister who lived in Zhangzhou's South Village, where people depended on growing flowers, fruit trees, and high-quality rice around the Immortal Lake. One day a hurricane blew a mountain on top of Immortal Lake, and the village subsequently suffered from an extreme drought. The brother, Golden Cup, dreamed about an old man who told him how to release water from the mountain, and he decided to go and dig for water in order to save the village. When he didn't return after one year, his sister Hundred Leaves went looking for him and discovered that he had frozen to death with a hammer in his hand. Despite her sorrow for Golden Cup, she proceeded to work day and night and ultimately succeeded in chopping the mountain open and freeing the water. The village became fertile once again, and famine-stricken families returned home. Hundred Leaves died a heroine.

Widows' Pagoda is a tale about how a seven-story granite pagoda came to be built on Turtle Peak overlooking the port of Shangjing in Fuqing County. Every spring the men from eighteen families named Lin would load a boat, which they had built collectively, with silks from Hangzhou and Suzhou and cross the ocean to engage in trade in Southeast Asia. Shortly before Spring Festival the men would return with Southeast Asian products and celebrate the New Year with their families. One year the boat did not return, and the wives of the boatmen learned that it had crashed. Elder Sister Ou, whose husband had been the boat captain, decided that the tragedy should not prevent others from venturing to Southeast Asia. She therefore offered to use her savings toward building a pagoda lighthouse on Turtle Peak and convinced the other seventeen widows to donate their savings as well. With the collective savings and contributions mobilized from neighboring villages, the women employed stonecutters from Huian and supervised the construction process. After the pagoda was built, every night the eighteen widows would climb the 900-foot pagoda to light the lamp at the top so that passing boats could steer their way to safety.[99]

New perspectives in the study of Hakka women) (Guangzhou: Guangdong renmin chubanshe, 1996).

99. Drawn from Karen Gernant, *Imagining Women: Fujian Folk Tales* (New York: Interlink Books, 1995).

Table 3.5 Participation in Rotating Credit Associations

Research Site in Fujian	Local Term for Rotating-Credit Associations	Overall *hui* Participation Rate (%)	% of Women among *hui* Participants	n
Fuzhou	*biaohui*	20.7	64.4	145
Changle County/City	*biaohui*	42.2	68.4	46
Quanzhou	*biaohu*			
	huzhuhui	55.6	90.0	14
Huian County	*biaohui*			
	huzhuhui	88.0	68.1	25

Source: Tsai surveys, 1996–97.

Ultimately, however, I found that the relative popularity of *hui* tended to correspond with the structure of the local economy and demographic trends. As shown in Table 3.5, *hui* participation among micro-entrepreneurs is especially strong in Changle, Quanzhou, and Huian, while *hui* are less popular in Fuzhou.[100] The fourth column shows that the majority of *hui* participants in the four areas are women.

The table does not include Jinjiang, Anxi, and villages outside of Changle because *hui* participation is minimal in those areas: the latter two are practically devoid of informal finance in general; entrepreneurs in Jinjiang rely on high-interest interpersonal lending, loan sharks, or more formal sources of credit such as RCFs or RCCs.

Why are women more likely than men to organize rotating credit associations in South China?[101] Conventional political economy frameworks do not specifically seek to explain the dynamics of informal finance or gender differences in market behavior, but explanations derived from *structural* and *cultural* perspectives offer a more interdisciplinary explanation for the dominance of women in *hui*.

Structural Barriers to Formal Credit for Women

A basic explanation for why women are more likely to rely on rotating credit associations (RCAs) than men may be *structural*. It is clear that women and men have different resource endowments in China; that is, perhaps women turn to RCAs because official banks have more male customers, and women are less likely than men are to have acceptable forms of collateral. Relatedly, women may have no choice but to engage in mutual

100. The bivariate correlation between specific sites (PLACE) and participation in *hui* (ANYHUI) yielded a coefficient of 0.2200 at the .01 level of significance.

101. Female-dominance in rotating savings and credit associations (ROSCAs) are not unique to China; Appendix E provides a comparative summary from around the world.

assistance for capital-raising purposes because their higher rates of illiteracy preclude them from applying for loans. Or perhaps male credit officers tend to discriminate against women clients out of habit. As it turned out, virtually all the bank and credit cooperative managers whom I interviewed reported that the preponderance of their borrowers were men—though many also took care to point out the "model" exceptions of particularly successful women entrepreneurs who had good relationships with the financial institutions. The results of my survey reinforce the interview findings: 18.2 percent of the male respondents had received loans from official financial institutions as compared with 6.4 percent of the female respondents. Put differently, 70 percent of the respondents who had borrowing experience with state banks were men.[102]

The structural explanation would be plausible if it were found that women are also more active than men in the informal financial sector in general. The survey results do not fully support this, however. In fact, the data revealed that women and men had engaged in informal borrowing with nearly equal frequency. Specifically, 56.8 percent of the female and 57.5 percent of the male respondents had borrowed from informal sources ($n = 263$). In light of potential measurement error, the percentage difference of 0.7 is negligible. When it came to informal *lending*, however, more men than women had lent to friends, relatives, acquaintances, or other merchants: 70.2 percent of male respondents versus 56.3 percent of female respondents.[103] The discrepancy in lending habits may be attributed to a substitution effect such that women actually do "lend" to others as frequently as men but do so more within the institutional confines of rotating credit associations rather than on a strictly bilateral basis. Be that as it may, the point remains that women are no more likely than men to draw on informal sources of credit in general, even though women face greater structural barriers to the formal financial sector.

Gendered Economic Culture

A second possible explanation for the dominance of women in RCAs may be broadly categorized as *cultural* in the sense that women and men in China have for centuries been subject to different constructions of

102. Bivariate correlations between GENDER and "FORMALCR" (the label for experience with "formal credit") yielded a coefficient of 0.1823, which was found to be significant at the .01 level.

103. The coefficient of 0.1685 from the bivariate correlation run between GENDER and "INFLEND" (the label for having engaged in informal lending) is statistically significant at the .01 level. When the correlation between GENDER and INFLEND is run, controlling for income level (GROSSY), the relationship remains statistically significant at the .01 level; the coefficient decreases slightly to 0.1378.

gender.[104] Despite the ideological and mobilization efforts of the Maoist regime, few would dispute that on the whole, Chinese society continues to value women less than men and that this has implications for the sexual division of labor in the economy. Since the late 1970s, reform has revived the centrality of household production in rural areas, and in many regions women are directly encouraged to participate in domestic sideline production. Unlike small-scale commodity production, domestic sidelines "serve the public interest by using only spare household time and labor"— that is, the work of women.[105] In many villages, nearly 80 percent of peasant women are involved in weaving, embroidery, and other handicraft activities alongside farm work. Given that women clearly play substantial though not necessarily highly valued productive roles in China, it is not obvious how patriarchal biases against women translate into higher rates of participation in *hui*. Like the structural explanation, the cultural approach tells us why men may have an advantage over women in tapping official sources of credit, but not why women would be more likely than men to organize and participate in indigenous credit groups. If anything, a crude cultural approach might predict the opposite outcome, male dominance in *hui*, since women might not be expected to take the initiative in engaging other households in collaborative economic arrangements.

A more political economic approach that takes culture into consideration would examine how local conditions facilitate the spontaneous development of collective action solutions in the absence of third-party enforcement. Most theorists highlight norms such as trust and reciprocity as permissive cultural factors and then trace them back to personal and social networks.[106] In other words, it is possible that women in China are more likely than men to organize *hui* because they possess a greater stock

104. For an excellent collection of writings by Western and Chinese scholars on the construction of gender (from the sixteenth century to the present), see Christina K. Gilmartin, Gail Hershatter, Lisa Rofel, and Tyrene White, eds., *Engendering China: Women, Culture, and the State*, Harvard Contemporary China Series, No. 10 (Cambridge: Harvard University Press, 1994).

105. Elisabeth J. Croll, *Chinese Women since Mao* (London: Zed Books, 1983) 31–32; Barbara Entwisle, Gail E. Henderson, Susan E. Short, Jill Bouma, and Zhai Fengying, "Gender and Family Businesses in Rural China," *American Sociological Review* 60 (February 1995): 36–57; and Tamara Jacka, *Women's Work in Rural China: Change and Continuity in an Era of Reform* (New York: Cambridge University Press, 1997).

106. E.g., Mark Granovetter proposes that the degree of trust among individuals is related to the "social embeddedness" of their interaction: "Economic Action and Social Structure: The Problem of Embeddedness," *American Journal of Sociology* 91 (November 1985): 481–510. For an earlier articulation of embeddedness theory, see Karl Polanyi, *The Livelihood of Man* (New York: Academic Press, 1977), chap. 4. Different motivations underlying trust are discussed in Diego Gambetta, ed., *Trust: Making and Breaking Cooperative Relations* (Oxford: Basil Blackwell, 1988). cf. Francis Fukuyama, *Trust: The Social Virtues and the Creation of Prosperity* (New York: Free Press, 1996).

of interpersonal trust or stronger sense of community than men.[107] Ethnographic research reveals that since economic production in rural areas is now organized on a household rather than a communal basis, peasants in general are less likely to have close relations with other villagers than during the collective era.[108] The exceptions to this trend are individuals, usually men, who have political or commercial status within or beyond the village. But the sort of cooperation that occurs among them tends to be along the lines of particularlistic patron-client ties rather than horizontal arrangements. Next in line in terms of local ties are young unmarried women, who tend to have strong social networks in their natal villages. They are also more likely than married women to engage in collaborative business ventures. For example, a group of young women may travel to neighboring areas to purchase raw materials in bulk or to market their products. Older women in households with at least one daughter-in-law are also found to possess a relatively high degree of autonomy for extra-household social and economic activities. Married women of childbearing age generally have the least developed social ties, since they marry into their husbands' villages and have less time to participate in extra-household activities. Yet I found that married women with children in peri-urban areas are also the most likely to organize and participate in rotating credit associations.

Despite the fact that intra- and inter-household relations have experienced increased commercialization since reform, a sense of reciprocity still exists among villagers.[109] Neighbors are expected to make generous donations for financing weddings, funerals, and building new homes (e.g., upon a son's marriage).[110] Ellen Judd points out that "these are circumstances every household expects to face . . . so more or less balanced reciprocity" is assumed.[111] The need for working capital and related household invest-

---

107. In another context, Robert D. Putnam argues that civic associations and other community organizations (including rotating credit associations) are more popular in northern Italy because of the greater stock of social capital in the north: *Making Democracy Work: Civic Traditions in Modern Italy* (Princeton: Princeton University Press, 1994). On social capital, see James C. Coleman, "Social Capital in the Creation of Human Capital," *American Journal of Sociology* 94 (1988): S95–S120.

108. Ellen R. Judd, *Gender and Power in Rural North China* (Stanford, Calif.: Stanford University Press, 1994), 208–9.

109. Sha Jicai, *Dangdai zhongguo funü jiating diwei yanjiu* (Women's domestic status in contemporary China) (Tianjin: Tianjin renmin chubanshe, 1995). Cf. Nahid Aslanbeigui and Gale Summerfield, "Impact of the Responsibility System on Women in Rural China: An Application of Sen's Theory of Entitlements," *World Development* 17, 3 (1989): 343–50. They employ Amartya Sen's theory to illustrate that under the household responsibility system, a woman's controllable income may differ from her contribution to production inside and outside the household.

110. Yunxiang Yan, *The Flow of Gifts: Reciprocity and Social Networks in a Chinese Village* (Stanford, Calif.: Stanford University Press, 1996).

111. Judd, *Gender and Power*, p. 205.

Selling spices to send a grandson to school. Quanzhou, Fujian, November 1996.

ments would also seem to fit into the category of "circumstances every household expects to face," yet the paradox remains: women are more likely than men to engage in local credit groups that provide financing for such purposes. I would argue that trust and reciprocity are necessary but not sufficient determinants of local cooperation in the form of *hui*. Three additional variables that complement trust and reciprocity relate to the patriarchal construction of gender in China: the ability to make credible commitments for monthly payments, the expression of agency in organizing informal grassroots projects, and the social cost of accessing female-dominated networks.

Making Credible Commitments in Grassroots Credit

Studies of collective action in general and rotating credit associations in particular have noted that the ability to make credible commitments— or at least to project credibility—is essential to contractual exchanges.[112] Ironically, a strong case could be made that it is precisely because of the patriarchal reinforcement of women's domestic position since reform that

112. E.g., Michael Hechter, *Principles of Group Solidarity* (Berkeley: University of California Press, 1987), 107–11.

women are in a better position than men to make credible commitments. Since women, once married, are less likely than men to leave the village to pursue education or alternative forms of employment, in areas such as Changle and Huian (married) women account for 70 to over 80 percent of annual production.[113] The relative immobility of married women thus decreases the risk that they would default in a *hui*, which usually requires monthly meetings.[114] In addition, as other studies of rotating credit associations have found, members of society who are de facto excluded from formal financial institutions and bureaucratic channels in general are more likely to organize rotating credit associations.[115] Before their closure in 1999, the rural cooperative foundations operated by township and village governments represented the primary source of formal credit for private income-generating activities in rural China, but in the absence of inter-mediation by the local Women's Federation, women lacked regular access to the RCFs and higher-level banks.[116] For women without formal political status, participation in rotating credit associations serves (other than borrowing from relatives) as their main source of finance. Given the limited supply of credit available to women, a standard rational choice explanation would also point to the importance of maintaining a reputation for compliance in the community, since defaulting in one RCA would preclude participation in others.[117]

113. This phenomenon is also documented in Croll, *Chinese Women Since Mao*, 31–32; Margery Wolf, *Revolution Postponed: Women in Contemporary China* (Stanford, Calif.: Stanford University Press, 1985), 103–11. In the case of business owners from Wenzhou, however, the entire family tends to relocate at the same time, since the nature of their business relies on the labor of women and children. See Li Zhang, "The Interplay of Gender, Space, and Work in China's Floating Population," in Gail Henderson and Barbara Entwisle, eds., *Redrawing Boundaries: Work, Households, and Gender in China* (Berkeley: University of California Press, 2000).

114. Women account for 90 percent of the Chinese Grameen Bank replications' members, since they are deemed to be better credit risks than men. Interview Nos. 42, 158–66.

115. The primary reasons for exclusion are poverty and other indicators of social marginalization such as gender and ethnicity. E.g., see F. J. A. Bouman, "Rotating and Accumulating Savings and Credit Associations: A Development Perspective," *World Development* 23, 3 (1995): 371–84; Roger L. Janelli and Dawnhee Yim, "Interest Rates and Rationality: Rotating Credit Associations among Seoul Women," *Journal of Korean Studies* 6 (1988); Donald V. Kurtz, "The Rotating Credit Association: An Adaption to Poverty," *Human Organization* 32, 1 (1973): 49–58; Edward S. Maynard, "The Translocation of a West African Banking System: The Yoruba *Esusu* Rotating Credit Association in the Anglophone Caribbean," *Dialectical Anthropology* 21, 1 (1996): 99–107; and David Y. H. Wu, "To Kill Three Birds with One Stone: The Rotating Credit Associations of the Papua New Guinea," *American Ethnologist* 1 (1974): 565–84.

116. The RCFs were established by the Ministry of Agriculture in 1978 to provide a grass-roots source of credit to rural households; the People's Bank of China does not recognize them as legitimate financial institutions, however.

117. This point is made in Sidney Ardener, "The Comparative Study of Rotating Credit Associations," *Journal of Royal Anthropology*, no. 94 (1964): 201–29; and Hechter, *Principles of Group Solidarity*, 108–11.

Expression of Agency in Grassroots Organization

Greater permanence in the community and lack of institutional alternatives may bolster the creditworthiness of women, but their advantage in credibility does not explain why women would actually undertake collective action. A second variable often overlooked in structural approaches is the role of human agency: the self-perception of individuals as autonomous actors who do not passively accept structural constraints but, rather, devise ways to get around them. Many scholarly and journalistic accounts in the West have depicted women in China as chronically oppressed victims of state policy, thereby implying that women themselves do not (or are unable to) formulate ameliorating strategies to cope with everyday life.[118] In contrast, Judd's ethnographic research in Shandong Province (northern China) during the late 1980s provides interesting insights on women's agency as revealed by women themselves. First, women with recognized positions in the public realm of politics and business are modest about their own accomplishments and describe men as having more ability. That relative sense of inferiority, however, refers only to the two specific, highly valued spheres from which women have been excluded by male-dominated networks. Judd writes, "I was assured that while a woman might be able to manage a rural industrial enterprise, the outside arrangements crucial for supplies and marketing would have to be done by a man . . . and this would have to be a related man, given the pressures for 'respectability.'" Second, women in leadership positions perceive themselves as agents, "but only in relation to other women, and not to men." Achieving prominence in women's organizations, as opposed to local government, is not only more feasible, but more conducive to a woman's sense of agency. Third, at the household level, women's authority is recognized tacitly, as expressed by the popular saying, "men reside outside; women reside inside" (*nan zhu wai nü zhu nei*).[119] Yet women do play a salient role in the public sphere: since many villages are structured by kinship ties, the function of women as matchmakers or "introducers" (*jieshaoren*) would seem to be quite impor-

118. The fact that China has the highest female suicide rate in the world adds to this perception. Chinese women account for 56.6 percent of all female suicides, and China is the only country where women are more likely to commit suicide than men: Lijia MacLeod, "The Dying Fields," *Far Eastern Economic Review* 161 (1998): 62–63. Cf. Sing Lee and Arthur Kleinman, "Suicide as Resistance in Chinese Society," in Elizabeth J. Perry and Mark Selden, eds., *Chinese Society: Change, Conflict, and Resistance* (New York: Routledge, 2000), 221–38.

119. Judd, *Gender and Power*, 212–39; and Ellen R. Judd, "'Men Are More Able': Rural Chinese Women's Conceptions of Gender and Agency," *Pacific Affairs* 63, 1 (1990): 40–61. A revealing volume on the experiences and representation of women in urban areas is Emily Honig and Gail Hershatter, *Personal Voices: Chinese Women in the 1980's* (Stanford, Calif.: Stanford University Press, 1988); and Ford Foundation, *Reflections and Resonance: Stories of Chinese Women Involved in the International and Preparatory Activities for the 1995 NGO Forum on Women* (Beijing: Ford Foundation, 1995).

tant. This form of networking does not appear to yield much advantage in terms of women's agency or public recognition, however.[120]

On the other hand, in areas where large numbers of men reside and work outside the village, women are in fact taking on leadership roles. In some villages the Women's Federation mobilizes women for economic production on behalf of women, identifying underutilized resources and recommending means for increasing household income in a way that does not interfere with the productive activities of men. In effect, a "feminized," political economic niche is emerging in certain villages. Judd offers an important observation:

> In contrast with concerns expressed outside China about the disadvantages for women of a household-based economy following decollectivization, there are indications that rural Chinese women find the household posing fewer problems for them than larger-scale productive units. Advantages which Western feminists see for Chinese women in all-women workgroups in a collective economy do not seem valued by rural Chinese women, who did not find these workgroups necessarily supportive or enhancing.[121]

Indeed, regardless of the particular year-round ratio of women to men, there are indications that women's sense of agency derived from success in domestic sideline production may be expressed in organization "from below."[122] Beyond the Women's Federation and other elite groups, perhaps the most instrumental manifestation of women's agency—even if only with respect to other women—is their organization of rotating credit associations.[123] The *hui* organizers that I interviewed did not do it "just for fun."

120. In Korea, Laurel Kendall finds that the perception of women as matchmakers is highly polarized: the Evil versus the Good Matchmaker. Yet they perform an integral function within the constructed centrality of family involvement in social weddings. Laurel Kendall (curator, Museum of Natural History, and adjunct professor at Columbia University), "Ambiguous Heroines or What Korean Matchmakers Taught Me About the Crisis in Anthropology" (presentation at Columbia University, December 12, 1994).

121. Judd, "Men Are More Able," 55.

122. Cf. Kate Xiao Zhou, *How the Farmers Changed China* (Boulder, Colo.: Westview Press, 1996). For a case in another context of how the confinement of peasant women to small-scale agriculture may paradoxically increase their confidence and foster organization into labor gangs, see Gillian Hart, "Engendering Everyday Resistance: Gender, Patronage, and Production Politics in Rural Malaysia," *Journal of Peasant Studies* 19, 1 (1991): 93–121. Hart finds that men are more subservient to their employers than women because of their exposure to political patronage relations and inability to fulfill societal standards of male household responsibilities (114).

123. Most recent women-run NGOs involve successful women entrepreneurs or leaders who seek to help other women by sharing information and ensuring the protection of women's rights and interests. For a working list of women's NGOs in China, see Ford Foundation, *Interim Directory of Chinese Women's Organizations* (Beijing: Ford Foundation, 1995); and United Nations Development Programme, *Gender and Development in China: A Compendium of Gender and Development Projects Supported by International Donors* (Beijing: UNDP, 1998).

Needing capital to run their businesses, they strategically identified other women who faced similar working-capital constraints and persuaded them to take part in a group effort that would systematically help each member. They exercised agency.[124]

The Social Cost of Collecting Spare Change

The ability of women to make credible commitments combined with a sense of agency provides only a partial explanation for the emergence of female-dominated *hui*. Why do the men who remain in the village year round and presumably possess an equal, if not greater, sense of agency than women not organize *hui* themselves? In my interviews, a common explanation among men for the popularity of *hui* with women was that women have more time and patience to save spare change and keep track of the often complex flows of money involved in *hui*. Male respondents generally felt that it was not worth their time to deal with such "small" sums. But as shown in case studies of *hui* participants, the monthly contributions are often not as small as such responses would suggest. Financing illegal immigration is comparable to financing a luxury car in advanced industrialized countries, and small-business owners frequently participate in *hui* precisely because the collective pot may reach several "ten thousands" (*wan*) of *yuan*. In short, the smallness of *hui* is not a convincing answer for its relative lack of popularity among men.

A complicating but important factor is that according to female interviewees, men sometimes encourage their wives to participate so that they themselves will not lose face. Evidently, men may also reap the benefits of *hui* money—especially when it is reinvested into a family-run business. Regardless of whether this explanation is rational in the *homo economicus* sense, it is apparent that the social cost for men of losing face is sufficiently high to discourage them from participating in *hui*.[125] To the question whether women are also perceived to lose face through *hui* involvement, a typical dismissive or evasive male response was that "women can partake in *hui* since they control the family purse strings anyway."[126] Even if women are more likely to manage household finances (during the absence of their

124. I do not assume that agency necessarily leads to normatively positive outcomes for the actors. For example, women in Huian also exercise agency in organizing sister societies, which represent a source of comfort and camaraderie for women but have also ended in collective suicides.

125. For a discussion of how emotional deviations from calculating self-interest have been explained by Adam Smith, David Hume, and others, see Stephen Holmes, "The Secret History of Self-Interest," in Jane J. Mansbridge, ed., *Beyond Self-Interest* (Chicago: University of Chicago Press), 267–86, esp. 275–80.

126. A 1992–93 survey finds that this is more likely in urban than rural areas: Xu Yang, "Chinese Women Enjoy Equal Say," *China Daily*, January 15, 1994, 3.

husbands, for example), the gender difference in social cost remains.[127] Characterizing the exact nature of this social cost is challenging. Part of it works through external pressures: for example, men may face more social sanctions than women for joining RCAs; villagers might laugh, gossip, or treat men differently. As one male respondent put it, "When I participated in a *hui* last year, there was only one other man in the group, and people would ask us why we were spending so much time with old ladies in the neighborhood. . . . People looked down on us for doing it."[128] The perception of social cost may also be internalized, making men somehow more susceptible to the implicit shame or humiliation associated with *hui*. In a different context, Jon Elster has suggested, "Shame, or anticipation of it, is a sufficient internal sanction. . . . People have an internal gyroscope that keeps them adhering steadily to norms, independently of the current reaction of others."[129] If so, then it is relevant to inspect the social construction of "internal gyroscopes" in the first place. Perhaps women in China simply have less face to lose after centuries of social marginalization. Women may experience less risk in *hui* activities because they are not expected to try to save what limited face they possess. Yet the cost of losing face cannot be measured along the single dimension of perceived quantity. For example, chastity is very important for women before marriage. If a woman is known to have engaged in premarital sex or an extramarital affair, the whole family loses face. Even in cases of rape, women have been ostracized to the point of being driven to suicide.[130] In short, women do have face to lose, but in ways different from men, and these differences directly reflect the patriarchal construction of gender in China.[131] It is important to recognize, however, that although gender norms remain patriarchal in the sense that activities and behaviors commonly associated with men are more highly valued than those associated with women, gender norms have in fact changed over time. The gender reversal in *hui* participation is only one manifestation of how an activity once dominated by men is now perceived as women's activity.

The irony of this gender cleavage in *hui* participation during the reform era is that some women are indeed losing "face" by engaging in a form of informal finance that may jeopardize rather than enhance the household's

127. Kendall, "Ambiguous Heroines," raised the issue of social cost in the context of why women are more likely than men to perform the role of matchmaking in Korean society.

128. Survey No. 83.

129. Jon Elster, *The Cement of Society* (New York: Cambridge University Press, 1989).

130. See Christina Gilmartin, "Violence against Women in Contemporary China," in Jonathan L. Stevan Lipman and Harrel, eds., *Violence in China: Essays in Culture and Counterculture* (Albany: State University of New York Press, 1990), 203–26; and Honig and Hershatter, *Personal Voices*, 277–86.

131. See citations in Kellee S. Tsai, "Women and the State in Post-1949 Rural China," *Journal of International Affairs* 49, 2 (1996): 493–524.

financial position. Every time an organizer runs off with the collective pot, or individual members default on a payment, the practice of *hui* is delegitimized. In places such as Quanzhou (and Wenzhou in the next chapter) where *hui* collapses have reached crisis proportions, the bonds of trust and reciprocity that rotating credit associations depend on have been so weakened that the women who continue to participate in them are seen as exercising poor judgment.

Fujian's Multiple Realities

The foregoing discussion also relates to the other informal credit institutions in China. Although the particular explanatory role of credibility, agency, and social cost will clearly differ from that delineated for rotating credit associations, the underlying logic of agency within a socially constructed environment remains. Instead of gender roles in the patriarchal household, for instance, other social constructions of authority and normative sanctions may affect credit solutions where third-party enforcement is embodied in preexisting state institutions such as the unit structure (*danwei*) or rural cooperative foundations run by village committees. Ultimately, economic actors have to do more than exercise agency in devising or accessing credit. They also have to project credibility to the institutions or individuals responsible for enforcing the financial transactions. Gender is only one of multiple social categories that affect the "calculation" of creditworthiness by potential creditors.

For example, we saw that the use of *hui* in Fuzhou's urban center was limited to discrete immigrant enclaves of private entrepreneurs. Unlike small-business owners indigenous to Fuzhou, who are able to access more institutionalized sources of financing (e.g., credit cooperatives and private banks), immigrants from other parts of Fujian rely almost exclusively on less formal financing mechanisms. Political ties also define the nature of the networks involved in sustaining various financing mechanisms.

Ecological analysis of the research sites in Fujian demonstrates the wide range of intraprovincial variation in private-sector development and financial institutional diversity. Even though Fujian Province as a whole reported double-digit growth rates during the first two decades of reform, a closer look at the spatial patterns of development shows substantial divergence in output value, economic structure, and per capita income. Some of these differences were already apparent at the outset of reform. Of the county-level localities discussed here, for example, Fuzhou and Quanzhou were among the ten wealthiest counties with gross output value (GV) per capita of over 1,000 *yuan* in 1978–80. At the other end of the productive spectrum, Anxi, with a GV per capita of 165 *yuan,* was the poorest of sixty-eight counties, and Huian was fourth from the bottom.[132] By the end of the 1990s, Fuzhou and Quanzhou still ranked very high in GV per capita terms and had developed substantial private sectors, while Anxi remained relatively less developed. Yet a number of counties had climbed from the lowest quintile of county rankings to the middle or higher. In other words, economic conditions at the outset of the reform era correlate with the developmental performance of some localities but not all of them.

Examining the orientation of the local government toward the private sector is central to an understanding of developmental diversity under apparently similar macro-policy conditions. Even within a single province, different developmental paths are discernible. First, all the coastal cities and counties across from Taiwan had minimal infrastructural and industrial development at the outset of reform. With the introduction of the Open Door Policy and relaxation of military tension across the Taiwan Strait, however, governments in these localities actively encouraged foreign and Taiwanese investment in local industry, while allowing small private businesses and a variety of "popular" (*minjian*) financing mechanisms to proliferate. Not surprisingly, the scale of private-sector development in the urban centers of Fuzhou and Quanzhou and the Xiamen SEZ outstripped that of the other coastal localities. Less predictably, however, local governments in the smaller rural counties of Changle and Jinjiang leveraged their kinship ties with overseas Chinese to mobilize massive sums of capital for investment in local infrastructure and the private economy. Factories, ancestral temples, schools, clinics, and even roads in these localities proudly bear the names of charitable relatives living abroad (*qiaoxiang*). Virtually every private business in Changle and Jinjiang benefits from such capital—either directly or indirectly through curb market practices.

Second, at the same time, some localities have clearly been left behind amid this explosion of private entrepreneurship and capital flows from abroad. Geographically remote areas in southwest and northern Fujian remain impoverished.[133] Furthermore, deep pockets of poverty can be found in mountainous areas even within the eastern coastal counties. Local governments in such areas are not opposed to private-sector development, but the remaining able-bodied adults working in subsistence-level agriculture, hope to migrate elsewhere rather than invest in the barely extant local economy.

132. Thomas P. Lyons, "Regional Inequality," in Y. M. Yeung and David K. Y. Chu, eds. *Fujian: A Coastal Province in Transition and Transformation* (Shatin, N.T., Hong Kong: Chinese University Press, 2000), 330.

133. Technically, no single county in Fujian fell under the 750 *yuan* (approx. US$91) per capita per year standard for poverty in 1995, but other developmental indicators officially qualified, four counties in the southwest and four in the far north as impoverished (*pinkun xian*) (ibid, 346).

Third, Fujian had a modest share of state-directed Third Front industrialization, called the "small Third Front" (*xiao sanxian*), during the Cultural Revolution (1966 to 1976). In preparation for potential warfare, heavy industry was concentrated in the inland areas of Jianyang, Sanming, Yongan, and Longyan, which meant that in aggregate these areas accounted for 71 percent of Fujian's GDP at the end of the 1970s, while coastal areas accounted for only 29 percent.[134] Because of the dominance of the state sector, however, non-state industry and private commerce developed at a much slower pace than in the previously disadvantaged coastal areas in the east. By 1990, coastal counties accounted for 80 percent of the provincial GDP. Although I did not conduct research in Fujian's interior industrial belt, on the basis of findings from the main Third Front centers of Henan (see Chapter 5), I would expect local governments in Fujian's "small Third Front" to have permitted private business activity through creative means, while under pressure to reform large state-owned enterprises and to reemploy state workers.

Fourth and finally, some localities in Fujian have evolved along the collectivist path of development similar to the Sunan model, associated with Wuxi in the south of Jiangsu province. Mountainous Anxi, for example, went from being an officially designated impoverished county to one where collective enterprises accounted for 90 percent of local industrial and agricultural output—albeit on a less than impressive scale. With formal sources of credit devoted to township and village enterprises, Anxi's private sector remains negligible compared with its coastal neighbors, Quanzhou and Xiamen. Meanwhile, local governments in Huian have channeled official bank credit and overseas capital to collective enterprises, while women micro-entrepreneurs rely primarily on rotating credit associations.

These four developmental paths, broadly defined, demonstrate how the attitude of local governments toward the private sector influences the character of curb market finance at the grassroots level. They do not capture finer differences among localities, such as ethnic composition (e.g., Han versus Hakka versus She) or social organization (single-surname versus mixed-surname villages).[135] Be that as it may, the main point is that the orientation of the local government toward the private sector has better predictive power than do purely economic explanations. Political intricacies, however—even under conditions that would seem conducive to the emergence of informal financial intermediaries—greatly complicate the story.

134. Toyojiro Maruya, "An Economic Overview," in Yeung and Chu, eds., *Fujian*, 183.

135. Fujian is known for having particularly strong patrilineal kinship lineages, as seen in the prevalence of single-surname villages: Maurice Freedman, *Chinese Lineage and Society: Fukien and Kwangtung* (London: Athlone Press, 1966).

4

Financial Innovation and
Regulation in Wenzhou

> Our country does not permit the establishment of private banks.
> We must continue to investigate and impose discipline on
> nonbanking financial institutions and other creditors that charge
> high interest rates. This is clearly one of the most important
> measures for ensuring order in the entire financial system.
>
> —Beijing Central Office, People's Bank of China

> The credit services performed by [unsanctioned] financial
> institutions in Wenzhou are essential for the development of
> market socialism. . . . Private money houses should be considered
> within the range of "popular" credit activities that are legal. . . .
> Allow private money shops to emerge from the underground and
> operate at the ground level. Legalize them. Acknowledge their
> existence publicly.
>
> —Wenzhou City Branch, People's Bank of China

In Wenzhou, a southern coastal district in Zhejiang Province, local governments have generally supported private enterprise. Because of that support, one would expect to find a wide range of informal financial intermediaries. Sure enough, years before China's state-controlled banking system announced commercializing reforms, local officials in Wenzhou had a permissive attitude toward private-sector development, and rural entrepreneurs wielded an impressive repertoire of savings and credit mechanisms. But the very process through which these financing arrangements

An earlier version of this chapter appeared as, "Curbed Markets? Financial Innovation and Policy Involution in China's Coastal South" (Weatherhead Center for International Affairs Working Paper Series No. 98–6, Harvard University, May 1998).

120

were established, maintained, regulated, and sometimes banned has been fraught with political tension, for most of the financial innovations were not sanctioned by central banking policies at the time of their inception. Local battles over financial institutions that were initially waged between entrepreneurs and Wenzhou's bureaucrats escalated into controversial national debates about the scope and pace of economic reform in China as a whole.[1] Moreover, as implied by the juxtaposition of the epigraphs above, Wenzhou's apparent disregard for national banking regulations reinforced the central government's anxiety about its capacity to maintain financial order in a rapidly developing and decentralizing economy.[2] By the late 1980s a two-track pattern had emerged whereby financial innovations would develop, regulators from the center would notice, and then they would either attempt to ban the unusual financial practices, or sanction them as if the center had proposed such advanced reforms in the first place. In the first pattern, the case of Wenzhou suggested that the balance of central-local dynamics in China was tilting toward the localities because curb market activity would revive even after being outlawed.[3] But the second pattern revealed the experimental, incremental, and reactive nature of the economic reform process; certain economic innovations appeared at the ground level in places like Wenzhou well before they were officially acknowledged in Beijing.[4] As one local cadre put it, "If we had waited for the central government to allow certain practices, there would not be economic reform."[5]

Thus far, most scholarly analyses of Wenzhou have only highlighted the localized nature of its reform experience and emphasized the apparently

1. Articles written in 1986 by members of the Economic Research Institute of the Chinese Academy of Social Sciences are translated into English and compiled in Peter Nolan and Dong Fureng, eds., *Market Forces in China: Competition and Small Business—The Wenzhou Debate* (London: Zed Books, 1989). For early journalistic discussions, see *Jingji ribao* (Economic daily), July 1986, and 1988 newspaper articles collected in Yu Shizhang, ed., *Wenzhou gaige moshi yanxin yinxiang* (New reflections on Wenzhou's reform model) (Wenzhou: Zhonggong wenzhoushi weixuanchuangu, 1989).

2. See Huang Weiting, *Zhongguo de yinxing jingji* (China's hidden economy) (Beijing: Zhongguo shangye chubanshe, 1996), 259; and Gao Feng, Huang Chonggu, Zhang Zhenyu, Wang Feng, and Mao Chunhua, "Wenzhou minjian xinyong diaoyan" (Investigation of Wenzhou's folk credit activities), *Jinrong yanjiu* (Financial studies), no. 2 (February 1993): 71.

3. Broader debates on central-local relations include Jia Hao and Lin Zhimin, eds., *Changing Central-Local Relations* (Boulder, Colo.: Westview Press, 1994); Susan Shirk, *The Political Logic of Economic Reform in China* (Berkeley: University of California Press, 1993); Dali L. Yang, "Reform and the Restructuring of Central-Local Relations," in David S. G. Goodman and Gerald Segal, eds., *China Deconstructs: Politics, Trade, and Regionalism* (New York: Routledge, 1994).

4. This sequence is consistent with the pattern of reforms described in Barry Naugton, *Growing Out of the Plan: Chinese Economic Reform, 1978–1993* (New York: Cambridge University Press, 1996).

5. Interview No. 160.

unique cultural proclivity of its people to engage in commerce and evade central governance. These largely descriptive accounts succeed in capturing the political delicacy of Wenzhou's early start on economic reform but, because they focus on Wenzhou's renegade qualities, yield limited comparative insights. Other municipalities and southern coastal areas in China have operated under similar policy environments and sparked their share of political economic intrigue.[6] In fact, most transitional economies probably possess pockets of local initiative that flirt with regulatory intervention. As such, this chapter focuses not on why Wenzhou is so special, but rather, the logic that underlies the emergence of community-based financing institutions, and the basic political economic conditions under which these institutions are either permitted to flourish or subjected to regulatory intervention. More simply, what are the origins of local financial institutions and, once they are established, why do some last longer than others? Further, what is the role of entrepreneurs' political ties in shaping their choice of financing arrangements?

Wenzhou and Its Puzzles

Wenzhou had been a vibrant trading port up through the Republican era.[7] For the first thirty years of PRC governance, however, its economy was stagnant and the standard of living poor in both relative and absolute terms. Its underdevelopment was not accidental. As with other southern coastal cities, Wenzhou's proximity to Taiwan made it a high-risk district geostrategically speaking. Hence, neither the central nor the provincial (Zhejiang) government was inclined to devote its limited resources to Wenzhou's infrastructural and industrial development.[8] Although Wenzhou accounts for 11 percent of the province's land mass and 15 percent of its population, it received only 1 percent of Zhejiang's fixed capital investment throughout

6. See, e.g., Ezra F. Vogel, *One Step Ahead in China: Guangdong under Reform* (Cambridge: Harvard University Press, 1989).

7. During the Sino-Japanese War, China's coastal ports were blockaded with the exception of Ningbo, Wenzhou, and a few others; as a result, Wenzhou rapidly developed into a key port for the province. After the Pacific war started in 1941, the KMT attempted to impose an economic blockade on Shanghai, but trade continued between Shanghai and Wenzhou: Zhang Zhenning and Mao Chunhua, *Wenzhou jinrong xianxiang toushi* (Perspectives on the phenomenon of finance in Wenzhou) (Hangzhou: Zhejiang daxue chubanshe, 1993), 61–62.

8. Despite Wenzhou's spectacular economic performance since reform, local officials and business people still express bitterness mixed with pride about its developmental history. Since it is flanked by mountains and the East China Sea, a 500-kilometere ferry ride from Shanghai was the primary way to reach Wenzhou until a small airport was built (with private capital) in 1990. A railway from Wenzhou to Jinhua City in Zhejiang, opened in 1998, linked Wenzhou with central and western Zhejiang and portions of Jiangxi, Hunan, and Fujian.

the Mao era.[9] Adding to the disadvantage of official neglect was its scarcity of arable land: only 0.42 *mu* per capita, as compared with 0.65 *mu* for the province and 1.4 *mu* countrywide.[10] The ecological limitation on Wenzhou's labor-land ratio meant that 44 to 49 percent of the rural labor force (790,000 to 880,000 of 1.8 million working-age people) was unemployed or underemployed at the beginning of reform.[11]

Given this developmental legacy, local officials express pride that the emergence of a de facto private economy of petty commodity producers, retail vendors, and wholesale traders in Wenzhou was early and vigorous, relative to the rest of China. At the formal commencement of rural reform in 1979 there were already an estimated 1,844 micro-entrepreneurs in the area; three years later the number had multiplied eleven times, to 20,363 entrepreneurs.[12] Despite the dynamism of its private economy, the state banking system was neither willing nor juridically able to meet the credit needs of the new generation of individual entrepreneurs.

Ultimately, Wenzhou's private economy flourished to publicity proportions in tandem with the its informal financial sector, which both defied and competed with formal financial institutions. When private finance in Wenzhou attracted the most domestic attention in the mid-1980s, the capital-raising strategies employed by entrepreneurs ranged from ad hoc, interest-free lending among relatives, neighbors, and local merchants to more institutionalized and controversial arrangements such as private money houses that operated around the clock, seven days a week. If the early 1980s were about nongovernmental financial *innovation* in Wenzhou, a decade later the original innovations were being curbed, incorporated, or redirected by financial system *reform*, promulgated by administrative levels above Wenzhou. This is not to say that official reform policies thwarted the development of additional innovations during the 1990s. Rather, both the market and the financial institutional environment in which economic actors were operating had changed, and the net effect of that change was to redefine the terms of the economic playing field.

9. Wang Yongfen and Li Ning, "Buttons Work Miracle in Wenzhou," *Beijing Review*, no. 42 (October 20, 1986): 14, cited in Keith Forster, "The Wenzhou Model for Economic Development: Impressions," *China Information* 5, 3 (1990–91), 56 n. 14.

10. Only 2 percent of Wenzhou's total surface area is used for farming because of its mountainous terrain. See Forster, "The Wenzhou Model," 56; and Chris Bramall, "The Wenzhou 'Miracle': An Assessment," in Nolan and Dong, *Market Forces in China*, 49.

11. Bramall, "Wenzhou 'Miracle'"; 81; Zhang Lin, "Developing the Commodity Economy in the Rural Areas," in Nolan and Dong, *Market Forces in China*, 97.

12. In comparison, Beijing did not even start keeping track of private businesses until 1980: *Beijingshi gaige shinian* (Ten years of reform in Beijing) (Beijing: Beijing chubanshe, 1989), 936. By 1982, Beijing had 13,210 registered private businesses: *Guoming jingji he shehui fazhan gaikuang, 1981–1985* (Developmental conditions of the Republic's economy and society) (Beijing: Zhongguo tongji chubanshe, 1987), 228.

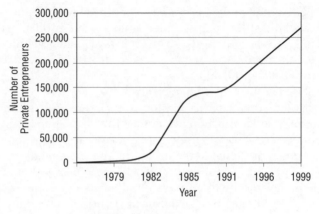

Source: WZNJ, various years.

Figure 4.1 Growth of Private Entrepreneurs in Wenzhou, 1979–1999

To illustrate more concretely, using the periodization of official statistics, Figure 4.1 shows that the ranks of private entrepreneurs increased substantially within the first six years of reform (1979–85), expanded at a lower rate during 1986–91, and picked up slightly in the 1990s.[13] Figure 4.2 reveals that the capital intensity of private operations grew through the mid-1980s and slowed down during the latter part of the decade. Unlike the more modest growth in the nominal volume of private entrepreneurs during the 1990s, however, the per capita capitalization increased by a large factor, and by 1999 the private sector accounted for over 96 percent of the city's total industrial production.[14] A visual comparison of the two graphs shows more vividly the divergence in the growth rates of entrepreneurs versus their average level of capitalization.

Although it is difficult to verify the volume of credit supplied by nongovernmental sources, Chinese economists estimate that on the high end, as much as 95 percent of the capital flows in Wenzhou during 1983–85

13. The following periodization is adopted from the sources cited in note 1 of this chapter, as well as the author's personal interviews with cadres in the Wenzhou City ICMB in March 1997. Although the numbers of private entrepreneurs and their capitalization have undoubtedly increased rapidly since reform, these numbers may overestimate their growth rate (and perhaps underestimate their nominal volume) because of underregistration of private businesses in the early years. In other words, part of the growth in numbers may derive from late registration of preexisting businesses rather than reflect the sudden appearance of new businesses.

14. According to the *WZNJ 2000* (Wenzhou yearbook 2000), SOEs contributed only 3.4 percent to Wenzhou's industrial output in 1999. By 1997, Wenzhou's private sector accounted for over 90 percent of GVIO, compared with 38.8 percent in Zhejiang: "Zhejiang Meeting on the Individual Economy," *Zhejiang ribao* (Zhejiang daily), October 24, 1998, reported in FBIS-CHI-98-320.

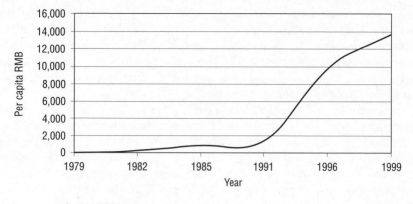

Source: WZNJ, various years.

Figure 4.2 Average Capitalization of Private Businesses in Wenzhou, 1979–1999

occurred among nongovernmental financial actors and institutions.[15] Even on the lower end, the estimated share of the informal financial sector as a function of total capital volume in Wenzhou during the same period was 80 percent.[16] The nongovernmental financing practices and mechanisms in Wenzhou include trade credit (*hangye xinyong*); professional money lenders, middlemen (*yinbei*); raising capital from banks and state-owned enterprises by posing as a collective enterprise (*dai hongmaozi, guahu qiye*); pooling capital and issuing shares in the form of shareholding cooperative enterprises (*gufen hezuo qiye*); credit associations (rotating—*lunhui*, bidding—*biaohui*, escalating—*taihui*); private money houses (*qianzhuang*); rural cooperative foundations (*nongcun hezuo jijinhui*); and pawnshops (*dangpu*).

That such a diversity of nongovernmental financing mechanisms could develop is consistent with the broader argument that localities where the government has been supportive of the private sector will also have a wider range of financial institutions. But the case of Wenzhou presents an opportunity to delve deeper into the local political economic dynamics that lead to such an outcome. In reality, "local government" in China is neither a unitary actor nor an independent administrative entity that can always

15. Ya-Ling Liu, "Reform from Below: The Private Economy and Local Politics in the Rural Industrialization of Wenzhou," *China Quarterly* 130 (June 1992): 298.

16. Some Chinese economists distinguish between "funds privately raised by managers" and "popular credit." E.g., as of 1992, economists in the Wenzhou PBOC estimated that banks and UCCs accounted for 20 percent of the total capital in Wenzhou; "funds privately raised by managers" for 40 percent; and popular credit for the other 40 percent. Gao et al., "Wenzhou," 66; and Zhang and Mao, *Wenzhou,* 9.

resist policy mandates from higher governmental levels. Given that the state banking system attempts to monopolize the supply of credit in the economy, informal financial institutions by definition almost always run the risk of official interference. Official intervention in private financial activities has in fact occurred in Wenzhou but only in a selective manner and by selected governmental entities.

Furthermore, to the extent that certain institutional innovations have been subject to regulation, financial entrepreneurs have devised creative ways to evade or adapt to regulatory constraints, which in turn have triggered additional attempts at regulation.[17] At the broadest level, therefore, a cyclical dynamic of innovation (I) and regulation (R) may be discerned in certain cases where $I \to R \to I' \to R'$ and so forth. But not all innovations have attracted regulatory intervention, and not all regulatory measures have failed. In order to explain the finer variation in both financial innovations and official intervention, one can expect that, other things being equal, government cadres are most likely to exercise their regulatory authority and interfere with private financial activities when (a) they are not able to extract rents from the financial entrepreneurs; (b) the financial activities are highly visible; and (c) they possess clear indicators that exercising their regulatory powers would be politically advantageous. These sub-hypotheses are meant to anchor the broader argument about institutional emergence to specific financing practices and add a temporal element to the analysis. Specifically, the durability of private financial institutions over time may be seen as a function of official interference. The alternative economic argument would be that the durability of financial institutions hinges upon their profitability, which is certainly relevant for the day-to-day viability of a financial business, but political tolerance for a financial institution is an even stronger influence on its chances for survival. On the demand side, the case of Wenzhou illustrates the role of local political relationships in shaping the financing choices of private entrepreneurs. Again, ceteris paribus, private entrepreneurs who have close ties to political cadres or are cadres themselves are more likely to employ highly institutionalized financing practices, whereas those with few political connections are more likely to use financing practices with low and medium degrees of institutionalization.

Illustrating these contentions requires examining the political and economic context in which various private financing strategies developed and the consequent governmental reaction to each of them. In many cases, the

---

17. In his discussion of regulatory efforts in U.S. banking, Edward J. Kane refers to this phenomenon as the "regulatory dialectic": "Impact of Regulation on Economic Behavior: Accelerating Inflation, Technological Innovation, and the Decreasing Effectiveness of Banking Regulation," *Journal of Finance* 36, 2 (1981): 355–93.

supply and demand for particular forms of private finance are closely linked. Private entrepreneurs have to work around political and regulatory constraints in devising financing mechanisms. At the same time, state bureaucrats have political incentives for carrying out their regulatory mandates, as well as economic incentives for collaborating with private entrepreneurs who may attempt to evade regulations. In other words, certain informal financial institutions may be seen as deriving from an iterative process of mutual monitoring between profit-seeking economic actors and rent-seeking regulators. Taking into account this interaction between entrepreneurs and cadres complicates the story, but it is key for understanding the prevalence of some financing practices over others.

From Extorted Harmony to Cadre Careerism

What is now known as the "Wenzhou model of development" may be classified broadly into three phases since reform (1979–85, 1986–91, 1992–). During the first phase the private economy was centered on household production in the handicraft industry. Such production required minimal capital, since it used simple production machinery and few fixed assets. To the extent that rural households were prepared to increase their scale of production, they relied on private borrowing, sometimes facilitated by financial middlemen or brokers (*yinbei*).

The experience of Mr. Li is typical in this regard.[18] Like most middle-aged people in Ouhai County, he grew up impoverished. He and his five brothers shared half of a room, and he did not have the chance to attend elementary school until the age of eleven. After graduating from primary school at the age of seventeen, he served as a soldier for three years during the Cultural Revolution, from 1967 to 1970, and then worked on a commune until 1982, when he decided to undertake nonagricultural activities. Since his salary on the commune was only 42 *yuan* per month, Mr. Li borrowed 4,000 *yuan* for one year at 4 percent interest to start up his first business, a small electrical components factory. His grandmother brokered the loans from various people for him; apparently she had been an informal money lender since 1949 and had a good reputation in the community. He did not register the business until 1984, though its output value reached 100,000 *yuan* the first year.

In addition to borrowing from moneylenders, the earliest group of entrepreneurs in Wenzhou also participated in rotating credit associations. Depending on the particular locality, the most basic types of *hui* were called *chenghui, hehui,* or *juhui,* which can be translated as a "favor-providing asso-

18. Interview No. 185.

ciation," "contractual association," and "cooperative association." Notwithstanding nuances in local dialects, the mechanics of all three were quite similar: ten to fifteen people would agree to contribute a fixed amount of money to the collective pot every month; the *hui* organizer (*huitou*) would collect all the money during the first meeting; and in subsequent months the collective pot would either be rotated to the remaining members in turn according to a predetermined schedule, as in a "rotating association" (*lunhui*), or given to the member offering the highest bid in interest payments to the other members, as in the "bidding association" (*biaohui*).[19] Small-scale retail vendors were most likely to participate in *hui* during either the start-up or major expansionary phases of their operations in order to finance licensing fees (and associated expenses) and fixed assets. In the course of ordinary business periods, however, their short-term capital requirements were better served by trade credit (*hangye xinyong*); that is, developing ongoing relationships with wholesale suppliers who would deliver the merchandise first and then collect their payments a few hours, days, or sometimes weeks later.

During the early 1980s, private credit activities such as *hui* and financial brokering remained dispersed and confined to discrete social networks of rural entrepreneurs. Officials in Wenzhou and Hangzhou (the capital of Zhejiang Province) generally maintained a hands-off attitude, even though rumors circulated that petty capitalists in Wenzhou's countryside were engaging in illegal loan-sharking activities. Upper-level officials viewed Wenzhou with curiosity as an apparently self-propelling capitalist experiment in a remote, coastal region. Local cadres, who saw a remarkable transformation in the lives of the early entrepreneurs, seemed to be more interested in identifying potential rents for themselves than interfering with informal financing practices.[20] In other words, the price that private entrepreneurs had to pay to ensure political protection was in the form of de facto extortion on the part of cadres, which arguably represented a grosser violation of the broader legal framework than the entrepreneurs' localized forms of financial mutual assistance. By paying and receiving rents, respectively, both cadres and entrepreneurs were implicated in corruption which, if revealed, might have had disastrous consequences for

19. This is the form discussed in Chapter 3.
20. In addition to the arbitrary collection of taxes and fees, the rents also took the form of goods and services. In China the line between corrupt rent-seeking behavior and the instrumental cultivation of strong social relationships (*guanxi*) is at times thin, but important distinctions are made in practice between instrumentally motivated gifts and those based on "human feeling" (*renqing*). See Mayfair Yang, *Gifts, Favors, and Banquets: The Art of Social Relations in China* (Ithaca: Cornell University Press, 1994). Cf. Yunxiang Yan, *The Flow of Gifts: Reciprocity and Social Networks in a Chinese Village* (Stanford, Calif.: Stanford University Press, 1996).

both.[21] As a result, entrepreneurs preferred to pay the bribes and not report cadre corruption rather than report them and call attention to their own income-generating activities, and cadres preferred to profit from the entrepreneurs rather than interfere with a lucrative source of rents.[22]

This situation was not unique to Wenzhou during the early years of reform. As Dorothy Solinger observes, "Seeing an opportunity to collect extra income, various city government departments, including those for sanitation, urban construction, transport, and weights and measures, charged the firms different sorts of fees, which sometimes amounted to nearly the total of the net profits the firms had taken in."[23] Nonetheless, to a formerly underemployed peasant, continuing to eke out a modest profit from private peddling seemed preferable to tilling land. And in many cases the self-reported profit was more than "modest" in relative terms.[24]

During the second phase (1986–91), private-sector growth stabilized as the rest of the country grappled with episodes of high inflation, especially in 1988. The political crisis of 1989 had an immediate short-term effect on Wenzhou's private sector, as both economic and political actors faced renewed uncertainty about the central government's commitment to continued reform. After June 4, many entrepreneurs decreased their scale of production and transferred their productive capital into bank savings

21. In recent years, ongoing anticorruption campaigns have targeted local officials and cadres. In 1997, e.g., the anticorruption drive "was aimed at crimes like accepting bribes, embezzling public funds and leading a rotten life-style committed by officials and cadres in the administrative, law enforcement, judiciary, and economic departments while dealing with financial affairs": "Results of Wenzhou Anti-Corruption Drive Outlined," *Zhongguo xinwenshe*, October 24, 1997, reported in FBIS-CHI-97-297.

22. This game resonates with Lisa L. Martin's conceptualization of the "coercion problem," where the equilibrium outcome is mutual cooperation but only because the more powerful player (the cadre) employs coercive tactics (extortion) to ensure an optimal outcome: *Coercive Cooperation: Explaining Multilateral Economic Sanctions* (Princeton: Princeton University Press, 1992), 20.

23. Dorothy J. Solinger, "The Private Sector: The Regulation of Small Rural Traders," in *Chinese Business under Socialism: The Politics of Domestic Commerce, 1949–1980* (Berkeley: University of California Press, 1984), 196 n. 147, citing Xiao Xiangzi, "Obstacles to the Development of the Chinese Individual Economy," *Zheng Ming* (Contend), no. 48 (October 1981); and *Shichang* (Market), no. 20 (July 25, 1980), 1. Cf. Ole Odgaard, "Collective Control of Income Distribution: A Case Study of Private Enterprises in Sichuan Province," in J. Delman, C. S. Østergaard, and F. Christiansen, eds., *Remaking Peasant China: Problems of Rural Development and Institutions at the Start of the 1990s* (Aarhus, Denmark: Aarhus University Press, 1990), 106–24; and Jean C. Oi, "Market Reforms and Corruption in Rural China," *Studies in Comparative Communism* 22, 2–3 (1989): 221–34. I found that similar practices continue in the Fujian and Henan Provinces (Chapters 3 and 5). Even former SOEs that are now publicly traded on the Hong Kong Stock Exchange are subject to such apparently indiscriminant taxation. See Edward S. Steinfeld, *Forging Reform in China: The Fate of State-Owned Enterprises* (New York: Cambridge University Press, 1998), 124–64.

24. As of 1998, the per capita GNP in Wenzhou was 75 percent higher than that of the average urbanite in China. "Boom Time in Capitalist Wenzhou," *Economist*, May 30, 1998, 43.

deposits to earn interest. Correspondingly, the scale of popular credit also decreased. Those who had made a business out of loan-sharking activities, seeing that the market was sluggish, poured their money into banks and, especially, urban credit cooperatives (UCCs). From 1989 to the end of 1991 the city's savings deposits increased by 3.2 billion *yuan*, the most dramatic increase in PRC history. The Wenzhou PBOC attributes at least 50 percent of that increase to cash formerly invested in private enterprises and funds from the business of private finance.[25]

Nonetheless, during the third phase, beginning in 1992, production became more capital-intensive as the quality of the products improved, household industry expanded in scale, specialized markets flourished, and Wenzhou began attracting cheap labor from less developed parts of China.[26] The developmental dynamics underlying the following financing mechanisms from these periods are analyzed below: public or collective registration of private and shareholding firms; the rise and fall of pawn-shops; the mutation of rotating credit associations into pyramidal invest-ment schemes (*taihui/paihui*) and their subsequent domino-style collapse; the emergence of privately owned banks (*qianzhuang*); and the semilegal-ity of rural cooperative foundations (*nongcun hezuo jijinhui*).

Red Hat Disguises, Hang-on Households, and Shareholding Cooperatives

Local entrepreneurs devised an elusive way to raise capital from the offi-cial banking system by becoming affiliated with public enterprises or reg-istering as collective enterprises, even though they were really privately owned. Those that pursued the former strategy were called "hang-on household enterprises" (*guahu qiye*), since they attached themselves to state-owned enterprises by paying to use their name, stationery, receipts, and account numbers to evade taxes and other requirements that regu-lated private businesses more stringently than SOEs. Those that chose to register as collectives with neighborhood or village committees were said to "wear a red hat," since the businesses wore a collective label only for access to bank credit, preferential tax treatment, and other advantages denied openly private enterprises.[27] By the mid-1980s approximately 62

---

25. Gao, et al., "Wenzhou," 70.

26. As of 1997 there were over 800,000 rural migrants in Wenzhou: "Wenzhou City Not Afraid of Unemployment," *Xinhua News Agency*, October 30, 1997, reported in FBIS-CHI-97-302.

27. Registering as a collective enterprise was especially advantageous for private businesses with eight or more employees, since "private enterprises" (*siying qiye*) were not legally sanc-tioned by the State Council until 1988—and even then, they were subject to 35 percent tax-

percent of household enterprises were hang-on households, and 80 percent of the neighborhood and district enterprises in Wenzhou City wore red hats.[28]

The red hat enterprises and hang-on households represent the least conspicuous capital-raising strategy since it basically entails securing the necessary registration status for accessing bank credit. Owners of "fake collectives" are typically either political cadres themselves—which makes the red hat even redder—or well connected to local cadres, socially or through family.[29] The difference between the private entrepreneurs in the first situation and those with a politically and economically convenient registration status is that the latter may bypass the private entrepreneur–political cadre interaction by subscribing to the old rules of the game (collective/cooperative/public ownership) and reducing the incentives of cooperating cadres to jeopardize their share of the rents by confessing their complicity in the arrangement. Unlike the first situation, where both the private entrepreneur and cadre (or SOE manager) are uncertain about the net cost or benefit of reporting the other, here the mutual dependence may be deeper and have larger stakes. Two types of interactive patterns— or, in rational choice vernacular, games—may be discerned. The first is essentially a game of Red Hat Harmony, in which mutual cooperation is the dominant strategy for both actors and, unlike Extorted Harmony, the price that entrepreneurs pay for cooperation is negotiated rather than

---

ation and required to reinvest half of their after-tax income in production. In practice, the color of the cat (or hat) continued to matter, despite Deng's oft-quoted black cat/white cat saying that encouraged economic pragmatism over ideological battles.

28. In some areas, it is estimated that as many as 90 percent of household enterprises were *guahu* firms: Huang Jiajin, "The Problem of Wenzhou's Hang-on Household Management," *Zhejiang xuekan* (Zhejiang studies), no. 2 (1986): 16, cited in Kristen Parris, "Local Initiative and National Reform: The Wenzhou Model of Development," *China Quarterly* 134 (June 1993): 245–46 n. 15. Also see *Jingji ribao* (Economic daily), November 26, 1987, 2.

29. See Victor Nee, "Social Inequalities in Reforming State Socialism: Between Redistribution and Markets in China," *American Sociological Review* 56 (1991): 267–82; David L. Wank, "Bureaucratic Patronage and Private Business: Changing Networks of Power in Urban China," in Andrew G. Walder, ed., *The Waning of the Communist State: Economic Origins of Political Decline in China and Hungary* (Berkeley: University of California Press, 1995), 153–83; and Victor Nee, "Peasant Entrepreneurship and the Politics of Regulation in China," in Victor Nee and David Stark, eds. *Remaking the Economic Institutions of Socialism: China and Eastern Europe* (Stanford, Calif.: Stanford University Press, 1989), 167–207.

The proportion of cadres and former cadres among entrepreneurs, however may not be as high as typically assumed, since "cadres" includes people in professions with no particular advantage in political status. See Ole Odgaard, "Entrepreneurs and Elite Formation in Rural China," *Australian Journal of Chinese Affairs*, no. 28 (July 1992): 89–108. His survey of cadre attitudes toward different categories of rural private enterprises found that joint household enterprises (*lianhu qiye*) received the most support from cadres, and individual enterprises (*geti qiye*) had broad cadre support; large private enterprises (*siying qiye*) received the most criticism by cadres who lacked special connections to them.

extracted coercively.[30] Red Hat Harmony does not necessarily imply a static operational situation. For example, a cooperative relationship between cadres and entrepreneurs in a hang-on enterprise could evolve into one where the SOE would enter into a contracting arrangement with private operators (*siren chengbao*) such that even the public portion of the *guahu* agreement would become increasingly privatized by mutual consent.[31] In such arrangements, SOEs would agree to hand over managerial responsibility of their production to individual entrepreneurs in exchange for a flat monthly fee, and the latter would pocket the remaining profits.[32]

In the second game, SOE managers or local cadres permitting the sale of red hats may attempt to increase the cost of the red hat (i.e., the price of protection) or insist that private businesses wear a red hat.[33] By the same token, entrepreneurs may threaten to terminate their association with the public enterprise and switch to a different red protector. This situation would not be relevant in situations where the cadre and the entrepreneur are essentially one and the same. Therefore, assuming that the cadre and the entrepreneur do not have interdependent utility functions, whether or not the red hat relationship escalates in cost and tactical asymmetry depends on the mobility of the red hat enterprise and the relative dependence of the grassroots government or public enterprise (red hat protector) on the particular private firm, as measured by the market availability of private firms.[34]

Ceteris paribus, two expectations follow. First, the more mobile the red hat enterprise, the more leverage it will possess in negotiations with red hat suppliers and vice versa; second, the more dependent the red hat supplier on the red hat enterprise, the less leverage it will have in relation to the red hat enterprise and vice versa. The matrix in Figure 4.3 illustrates the range of resulting possibilities.

The two dimensions of mobility and dependence provide a basic means of predicting the relative bargaining strength and potential outcomes of red hat arrangements at the most cursory level: that is, the terms under which cooperation may ensue and the degree of asymmetry in payoffs in

30. Cf. David L. Wank's concept of "symbiotic clientelism" in *Commodifying Communism: Business, Trust, and Politics in a Chinese City* (New York: Cambridge University Press, 1999).

31. Parris, "Local Initiative," 247. The ultimate issue of ownership, however, would remain murky.

32. This mirrors the household responsibility system of rural reform, whereby plots of collectivized land were divided up and contracted to individual households in exchange for a fixed quota of grain; peasants were permitted to sell above-quota grain on the market.

33. Cases of local governments penalizing attempts by managers and workers in the collective sector to join the private sector are discussed in David Zweig, "Rural People, the Politicians, and Power," *China Journal* 38 (July 1997): 153–68.

34. Cf. Jeffry A. Frieden's analytic use of asset specificity in *Debt, Development, and Democracy* (Princeton: Princeton University Press, 1991).

		Red Hat	Mobility
		Low	High
Dependence of Red Hat Protector	Low	Extorted Harmony[a]	Red Hat Harmony
	High	Red Hat Harmony	Entrepreneur has leverage

[a] Since the red hat protector would have leverage over the entrepreneur in this situation, the resulting situation would be Extorted Harmony.

Figure 4.3 Summary of Red Hat Situations

the equilibrium situation. They do not, however, specify the institutional form that a private entrepreneur will choose if he or she has leverage (the situation in the lower right-hand quadrant). In addition to the hang-on and contracting arrangements, other quasi-legal corporate forms that wore the collective label in Wenzhou included partnership households (*hehuo hu*), shareholding cooperatives (*gufen hezuo qiye*), and shareholding companies (*gufen hezuo gongsi*). Partnership households were privately owned by two or more people with preexisting social or familial ties. Shareholding enterprises sometimes involved the actual distribution of shares among several proprietors of the corporation, who did not necessarily participate in its management; as in the modern corporation, a board of directors would elect a manager, who was held accountable for business performance and, ultimately, the market value of the shares.[35] Other shareholding cooperatives were essentially the same as partnerships; that is, they were owned and managed by one or two principals.[36] In short, the "collective" sector in Wenzhou and other parts of China encompassed, and continues to encompass, a wide range of institutional expressions with different implications for its capitalization.[37] Examining a business's particular appellation is not a reliable way to assess its actual ownership structure.

35. Of course, the earliest shareholding enterprises did not issue publicly traded shares, but their ownership structure was quite controversial. Not until the Fifteenth Party Congress in September 1997 were stock-issuing public corporations encouraged as a means to reform SOEs.

36. For more on how shareholding cooperatives became a more secure registration status for property rights than "fake collectives," see Susan H. Whiting, "The Regional Evolution of Ownership Forms: Shareholding Cooperatives and Rural Industry in Shanghai and Wenzhou," in Jean C. Oi and Andrew G. Walder, eds., *Property Rights and Economic Reform in China* (Stanford, Calif.: Stanford University Press, 1999), 171–200.

37. See, e.g., Victor Nee, "Organizational Dynamics of Market Transition: Hybrid Forms,

Since red hat strategies are among the least "visible" financing strategies, one would expect minimal official interference in red hat businesses. Yet this prediction is complicated by the notion that official interference is also a function of rent-seeking opportunities. The dimensions of dependence and mobility show that the benefits accruing to cadres and entrepreneurs in red hat arrangements may vary. In other words, the price of keeping a low profile is not a constant. If an entrepreneur does not already have a strong political tie to a cadre, then it is relevant to look at the structure of opportunity facing both cadres and entrepreneurs in order to understand the nature of the resulting red hat disguise. In situations where the interaction between entrepreneurs and cadres extends beyond the scenarios of Extorted Harmony, Cadre Careerism, and Red Hat Harmony, it is necessary to examine the broader set of relationships among cadres from different bureaucratic hierarchies. In addition, official interference in curb market activities is also a function of their visibility. Even in the absence of direct rents, officials may exercise their regulatory authority if certain financing mechanisms threaten local economic stability (the case of rotating credit associations, below), flagrantly violate state banking laws (money houses), or simply call for prudential supervision (pawnshops, rural cooperative foundations). Just as political actors may mediate—or cash in on—the development of economic institutions, the economic performance of financial institutions may inspire political intervention.

From Rotating Credit Associations to Pyramidal Investment Schemes

As previously noted, rotating credit associations reemerged during the early years of reform as a grassroots strategy to provide rural households with a community-based source of savings and credit. As more and more households turned to petty commodity production in Wenzhou, *hui* became an important source of capital for investing in fixed assets, mass purchase of raw materials, and other production-related costs. The monetary scale of *hui* also increased dramatically. Initially, the monthly contribution of each member typically ranged between 100 and 500 *yuan* a month; by the mid-1980s the monthly payments had crept up to 1,000,

Property Rights, and Mixed Economy in China," *Administrative Science Quarterly* 37 (1992): 1–27; Su Si-jin, "Hybrid Organizational Forms in South China: "One Firm, Two Systems," in Thomas P. Lyons and Victor Nee, eds., *The Economic Transformation of South China: Reform and Development in the Post-Mao Era* (Ithaca: Cornell East Asia Program Series, 1994), 199–213; and Hu Xiongfei, *Qiye zuzhi jiegou yanjiu* (Research on the organizational structure of enterprises) (Shanghai: Lixin kuaiji chubanshe, 1996).

5,000, 10,000, and even 100,000 *yuan*.[38] Meanwhile, the uses of *hui* funds evolved from financing consumption requirements and investment in productive assets to serving as a profitmaking end in itself.

Hui organizers quickly realized that they could earn interest by on-lending the pot that they collected in the first month. Consider, for example, the case of a 10,000 *yuan chenghui* with eleven participants where the organizer collects the pot in the first month and the order of the rotation for the remaining ten months is established at the outset. At the first meeting, ten participants would each contribute between 600 and 1,500 *yuan* depending on their position in the *hui*; i.e., the member slotted to receive the pot in the second month would contribute 1,500 *yuan*, the third member would contribute 1,400 *yuan*, the fourth would contribute 1,300 *yuan*, and the last member would contribute 600 *yuan*. This means that the organizer would receive a total of 10,500 *yuan* in the first month. If she onlent the money at 3 percent interest per month for six months, she would receive 1,890 *yuan* in interest and have a net profit of 390 *yuan* after subtracting her 1,500 *yuan* contribution in the second month.[39] If the organizer continued to on-lend the 10,500 principal plus accrued interest every six months, in five and a half years, she could earn 27,185 *yuan* (23,547 + 3,638; see Table 4.1).[40]

If the second recipient of the collective pot similarly used the money for on-lending, in this example, she would receive 17,936 *yuan* (16,472 + 1,464), and net 16,436 *yuan* after subtracting the initial 1,500 *yuan* contribution. This would work out to a de facto interest rate of 1.8 percent per month (or 21.6 percent annually), which was lower than the market rate but higher than the interest paid by a state-owned bank (about 0.5–1 percent per month). In theory, all members of a standard *chenghui* or *juhui* could profit from the credit association, provided that none of them defaulted.

Problems emerged when certain organizers started managing several *hui* simultaneously and ran into short-term liquidity constraints. An organizer who defaulted, affected hundreds of households. According to transcripts from the 1984 "Huanghua" court case, for example, a person named Nan started organizing *juhui* in 1977 to alleviate poverty in Huanghua Township, Yueqing County. By 1982, Nan was involved in several *hui*, lost the ability to keep track of them, and at year's end became completely

38. Even monthly payments of only 1,000 *yuan* were considered extremely high in 1985, given that the average rural salary in Zhejiang Province at the time was 547 *yuan* and the average Wenzhou salary was 527 *yuan*: *Zhejiang jingji nianjian 1986* (Zhejiang economic yearbook) (Hangzhou: Zhejiang renmin chubanshe, 1986), 346.

39. Example given in Zhang and Mao, *Wenzhou*, 16–18.

40. A popular saying was coined to describe such profit by *hui* organizers: *wuben wanli*, or more awkwardly in English, "earning 10,000 in interest without a principal investment."

Table 4.1 Summary of Cash Flow for Organizer of a 10,000-*yuan chenghui*

	Month									
	1	2	3	4	5	6	7	8	9	10
Cash received (cum.)	10,500	10,890	11,450	12,211	13,209	14,487	16,095	18,092	20,548	23,547
Interest received[a]	1,890	1,960	2,061	2,198	2,378	2,608	2,897	3,256	3,699	4,238
Contribution to *hui*	1,500	1,400	1,300	1,200	1,100	1,000	900	800	700	600
Net income every 6 months	390	560	761	998	1,278	1,608	1,997	2,456	2,999	3,638

[a] Assuming 3% interest/month on a 6-month loan. Source: Zhang and Mao, *Wenzhou*, 16–18.

illiquid. Nonetheless, Nan continued to participate in *hui* in order to finance the other *hui*. During the spring of 1984, they completely collapsed, bringing 367 households into 1.1 million *yuan* of collective debt. As of 1991, 60 percent of Nan's debt remained outstanding.[41]

The most serious cases of domino-style financial collapse involved *taihui* and *paihui*, hybrid types that mutated from the relatively innocuous community-centered, institutional expression of mutual assistance to a more insidious, destabilizing form: the pyramidal investment scam. Unlike *chenghui* and *juhui*, which depended on reciprocity among *hui* members to provide a bureaucracy-free means of savings mobilization and credit delivery, *taihui* and *paihu*: literally, "escalating association" and "lining-up association"—were based on bilateral relationships between the organizer and the investor, with the organizer promising an impressively high rate of return on the initial investment. The problem with these variants was that the capital was not truly being invested in productive business ventures; prospective "investors" were basically speculators who were lured by the appeal of quick money. Table 4.2 provides a sampling of different versions of *taihui* that were identified in Wenzhou in 1985.

A quick glance down the far right column shows that either the returns were either extremely inflated or else the investors were set up for losses in the medium term.

The typical *taihui* organizer was not a commercial entrepreneur per se but rather what became known as a "briefcase merchant" (*pibao shang*). Briefcase merchants were generally poorly educated women from rural areas who did not have any capital of their own and relied on social networks to enlist investors.[42] Given that the "investment" base was not

41. Zhang and Mao, *Wenzhou*, 21.
42. A local writer who studied the development and collapse of *taihui* in Yueqing County found that 80 percent of the *taihui* participants were women. Interview with Mr. Li Tao, Wenzhou (March 18, 1997), who coauthored a fictional account of the *taihui* crisis in Yueqing: Xu Guangyue and Li Tao, *Guai Tai* (Strange fetus) (Zhejiang: Zhongguo qingnian chuban-she, 1988).

Table 4.2 Main Variants of *taihui* in Wenzhou, 1985

Type	Initial investment	Interest Payment to Investor Starting 2nd Month	Interim Return on Investment	Additional Investment	Final Return on Investment[a]
I	30,800	9,000	By 10th month, investor has received net total of 90,000 = 163% or 16.3%/month	1,500/ month starting 11th month	90th month: total investment 135,000; total return negative
II	50,000	9,000	NA	NA	8th month: investor has received total of 72,000 = 44% or 5.5%/month
III	11,600	9,000	By the 12th month, investor has received net total of 108,000 = 831% or 69.3%/mo.	3,000 starting 13th month	88th month: total investment 260,000; total return negative
IV	12,000	9,000	NA	NA	3d month: investor has received total of 18,000 = 50% or 16.7%/month

Source: Zhang and Mao, *Wenzhou*, 21–22.
[a] Calculated by author.

premised on tangible production, several layers of organizers emerged to sustain the mammoth payment streams. For example, in a Type III *taihui*, where the organizer raises 11,600 each from its members, by the sixth month there would be 22 organizers, 691 organizers by the twelfth month, and 20,883 organizers by the eighteenth month.

With the exponential growth of *taihui* from 1985 to the spring of 1986, chaos swept the informal financial markets in Wenzhou, with particular intensity in Yueqing, Pingyang, Cangnan, Yongjia, Dongtou, Taizhou, and Lishui. The aggregate capital involved exceeded 100 million *yuan* (approximately US$33 million at the time), and ultimately, people from every sector of the population were affected, including workers, peasants, doctors, teachers, and even policemen and cadres. Once investors started

---

A broader study found that of the organizers of the largest *hui* (more than 10 million *yuan*), "well over half" were women, and eleven of the twelve largest were illiterate or semiliterate. Zhang and Mao, *Whenzhou*, 23.

Table 4.3 Main Variants of *paihui* in Wenzhou, 1986

Number of Shares	Length	Cost per Share	*hui* Total	Other Names
18	4 years, 3 months	600 or 1,200	10,200 or 20,400	NA
21	3 years, 4 months	500	10,500	*wanyuan hui* (10,000-*yuan* assoc.)
21	3 years, 4 months	1,000	21,000	*shuangwan hui* (double 10,000 *hui*)

running their own *taihui* in order to participate in those yielding higher interest, most participants were in the end both investors and organizers who were also indebted to others.

Just as the *taihui* were collapsing en masse in early 1986, participation in *paihui,* a close cousin of *taihui,* reached its peak.[43] Like *taihui, paihui* began as a bilateral relationship between a head organizer and a participating investor. But then it grew increasingly complicated in anatomy such that the most complex *paihui* consisted of a head (*tou*), belly (*du*), and tail (*wei*). Members in each of the parts would end up with very different financial outcomes; the head would be the first to receive the collective pot of money. *Paihui* came in varying lengths and amounts, as shown in Table 4.3. Moreover, unlike the other *hui, paihui* accounts were not always settled in cash, and sometimes interest rates were compounded on debts.[44] For example, in a *taihui* with twenty-one shares called *shuangwan hui* (double 10,000 *hui*), involving 15,297 *yuan*, the head would earn a total of 20,283 *yuan*, the second and third members would earn a total of 32,555 *yuan*, the belly (holders of the fourth through thirteenth shares) would earn 25,904; and the tail (holders of the fourteenth through eighteenth shares) would *lose* 63,445 *yuan*. The tails, of course, did not realize that they were getting the raw end of the deal; to sustain their earlier payments, the tails would

43. *Paihui* derived from popular local forms of credit associations called *sannian sihui* (three years, four associations) and *qianyuan, shuangyue, shuangwan hui* (1,000 *yuan,* double months, double ten 10,000 association).

44. In the example of a *taihui* with "18 shares plus 7 shares," the total amount distributed in each period would be 20,400 (at 1,200 per share). When the head collects the pot in the first month, the members who "eat second and third" (*chi er, san,* a.k.a. the belly), give the head 8,400 in credit (in writing) at a rate of 4.5 percent interest per month (378 *yuan*). In the second meeting, on paper, the second and third members receive the pot, and the head repays the 8,400 loan plus 378 *yuan* in interest, which reduces the contribution of each member to 6,600 *yuan*. In the end, the second and third members receive only a net of 5,022, since they still have to contribute 6,600 yuan. Calculation of the second and third members' net receipt in the second month is as follows: (size of the pot [20,400]) − (contribution to the pot [6,600]) − (repayment of loan to the head + interest [8,400 + 378]) = 5,022.

end up organizing additional *hui*, which put them in a favorable cash situation. As a result, the networks of debtors and creditors became more and more intricate.

In May and June 1986 the *paihui* in Pingyang and Cangnan counties started to collapse. There were 170,000 *paihui* participants in Pingyang with 104 million *yuan* (US$30.1 million) wrapped up in *hui*; in Cangnan, 35,000 *paihui* participants had 91 million *yuan* (US$26.4 million) at stake. Various county governments attempted to deal with individual *hui* organizers in a confidential manner (*neibuchuli*), but *hui* continued to proliferate, rendering damage control difficult. In some cases, government intervention had the perverse effect of fomenting participation in *hui*. At one point a printed public announcement forbidding participation in *hui* appeared in Yueqing County, but it was missing the stamped red seal that appears on all official government and party documents; in other words, the warning was only semiofficial. Nonetheless, local citizens apparently viewed the notice as reflecting the party line and acted contrary to its admonitions, reasoning that anything the Chinese Communist Party opposed must be profitable.[45] People literally rolled carts of 10-*yuan* bills to *hui* organizers, while others delivered money by boat via the canals that criss-cross Wenzhou. The organizers no longer had to leave their homes to mobilize participation in their *hui*. Strangers approached well-known organizers with cash in hand, eager to partake of this apparent financial miracle. As recordkeeping grew sloppy, with large transactions noted on random scraps of paper, accounting grew extremely complex, and by this time *none* of the money was being invested for productive purposes. The supposed investment returns were being sustained only by leveraging off of other *hui*.

It is estimated that by 1986, over 95 percent of households in Wenzhou were participating in *hui* (with the exception of those in two small northern counties).[46] Given this enormous scale, when individual people started to default on payments, entire networks of participants were driven to bankruptcy.[47] The organizers and their families became targets of vandalism, kidnapping, and physical and sexual violence, though no one actually attempted to murder the organizers themselves since they were indebted to so many people. When court trials of the organizers were being held in 1986, about twenty-five people committed suicide, and several relatives of

45. In Chinese, *dang fandui douneng zhuanqian*. Interview No. 164.

46. Li Yu, "Jinrong wanhuatong" (Financial kaleidoscope), in Yu Shizhang, *Wenzhou*, 49–62.

47. For example, if the organizer of a 10,000-*yuan hui* defaulted, at least eleven households would be affected. If the organizer of a million-*yuan hui* defaulted, then at least fifty 10,000-*yuan hui* (at least 550 households) would be dragged down. The largest reported *hui* involved 100,000 participants and 100 million *yuan* (nearly US$30 million): Ma Jinlong, "Wenzhou jinrong shichang" (Wenzhou's financial market), in Zhang Xu and Zheng Dajiong, eds, *Wenzhou shichang* (Wenzhou's market) (Beijing: Zhonggong dangshi chubanshe, 1995), 414.

organizers were murdered.[48] In an ad hoc attempt at crisis management, Wenzhou established an "eradicate *hui*" office (*qinghui bangongshi*) to implement a class action settlement; the office collected as much money as possible from *hui* organizers and participants and then distributed an equal sum to all *hui* victims. Ironically, in cases where victims continued to hold organizers responsible for repayments, one-shot *hui* called "life saving associations" (*jiuming hui*) and "single 10,000 associations" (*danwan hui*) were established.[49]

Despite the obvious scale of distress in Wenzhou's informal financial market, the *hui* collapses were never reported in official newspapers.[50] It was an embarrassment to local cadres. Upper-level officials in the banking administration (*xitong*) nonetheless found out about it, and Wenzhou received a steady stream of upper-level cadres and economists from Beijing, Hangzhou, and Shanghai who sought to eradicate the practice of *hui* as well as to understand how an informal financing mechanism could snowball into such chaotic proportions. According to some local intellectuals and cadres, in the early 1980s many people in Wenzhou had said that financial reform had to accompany economic reform, but no one would listen.[51] In retrospect, local observers believe that it took something as extreme as the *hui* collapses to stimulate official reconsideration of reform policy and its sequencing.

Analytically speaking, the nature of government intervention in *hui* is consistent with the sub-hypotheses delineated earlier. When participation in *hui* was limited to small networks of women entrepreneurs and the money employed for productive purposes, the visibility of *hui* was low, and local cadres lacked both economic and political incentives for interfering with their operations. When Wenzhou's broader population became swept up in the speculative fervor of *taihui* and *paihui*, however, they became highly visible and destabilizing. Even though it was mainly the *taihui* and *paihui* that caused serious trouble, the local government banned all forms of *hui* as a precaution against future outbreaks of chaos in the informal financial markets.

No Hat, Red Hat, Hard Hat

The story of how thirty-year-old Fang Peilin left his administrative job in a hospital and opened the PRC's first private money house in a small rural

48. Interview Nos. 160, 164.
49. Zhang and Mao, *Wenzhou*, 31.
50. The aggregate scale of *hui* reached 1 billion *yuan* (over US$330 million). But the *hui* collapses were not mentioned in the local press because the matter was "dealt with internally" (*neibu chuli*). According to Li Tao, the coauthor of *Guai Tai*, a Shanghai TV station wanted to turn his book into a movie, but the Wenzhou City government would not allow it.
51. Interview Nos. 160, 161, 162, 163, 164.

county of Wenzhou on September 29, 1984, has become a central part of the local lore about Wenzhou's economic ingenuity.[52] It may also be seen as a case study in bureaucratic and central-local politics. The Ascendent Money House of Cangnan County, Qianku Township, had operated for only five years when upper-level banking officials forced it to close down. Nonetheless, Fang's money house had a lasting impact on the commercial practices of official financial institutions in and, arguably, beyond Wenzhou.

Given that private ownership of enterprises employing more than eight employees had appeared radical—in the sense of being officially defined as capitalistic and exploitive[53]—during the early years of reform, overtly institutionalized, private profit making from financial services seemed even more aggressive and extreme. Moreover, the Communist judgment of the private money houses in imperial China was that they represented tools of bourgeois greed and manipulation. As the founder of the first registered private money house under Communist rule, Fang attempted to justify his operations by appealing to a 1984 central policy document that expanded the scope of reform. He found one sentence particularly malleable in interpretation: "Encourage peasants to raise capital collectively in running various types of businesses, and especially in open-minded professions."[54] Fang reasoned that "raising capital collectively" (*jizi*) entailed issuing shares (*rugu*), and, by definition, shares may distribute dividends (*guxi*); therefore, earning dividends was a legal activity. Following his logic, if dividends were legal and were essentially the same as interest payments (*lixi*), then earning interest should be legal as well.[55]

52. The history of money houses or native banks in Wenzhou dates back to the mid-nineteenth century, when they were essentially "governmental silver houses" (*guan yinhao*), responsible for collecting local tax payments, accepting savings deposits, and serving as the local silver house (*yinkui*). By the turn of the century many had evolved into genuinely privately owned money houses (*qianzhuang*) that provided commercial financial services to merchants, official gentry, and landlords: Zhang and Mao, *Wenzhou*, 56–66. Cf. Susan Mann Jones, "Finance in Ningpo: The *ch'ien chuang*, 1750–1880," in W. E. Willmott, ed., *Economic Organization in Chinese Society* (Palo Alto, CA: Stanford University Press, 1972), 44–77; Lien-Sheng Yang, *Money and Credit in China: A Short History* (Cambridge: Harvard University Press, 1952) chap. 8.

Jones cites Frank Tamagna's definition of *qianzhuang* as "a financial firm extablished in the form of a single proprietorship or partnership by members of a family, a clan, or a closed circle of friends, for the purpose of handling deposits, lending, remittances, and exchange of money, with unlimited responsibility guaranteed by all resources of the proprietor or of the partners": *Banking and Finance in China* (New York: International Secretariat, Institute of Pacific Relations, 1942), 57.

53. The ideological rationale was that Marx's *Das Kapital* specified any enterprise with over eight employees as exploitive.

54. Zhang Heping, "Qianzhuang 'laoban' Fang Peilin" (The money house "boss," Fang Peilin), in Zhang Zhiren, ed., *Wenzhouchao* (Wenzhou tide) (Beijing: Wenhua yishu chubanshe, 1989), 90–110.

55. Of course, in tax treatment, corporate valuation, and capital structure, interest payments and the distribution of dividends are quite distinct in advanced industrialized

When local officials first heard about Fang's plan, they said that the government was unlikely to permit the establishment of money houses, which had been denigrated by the CCP as a "feudal vestige of old China." At first, though, Fang seemed to succeed in securing approval from his well-placed friends, the party secretary of Qianku Township and the mayor of Cangnan County. But then the former got cold feet and recommended that he solicit permission from higher administrative levels or at least produce an official red-sealed policy document (*hongtou wenjian*). Since the county government refused to issue the document, Fang applied to the Industrial and Commercial Management Bureau (ICMB) for a regular business license and received it. This full-fledged, for-profit seal of approval meant that the Ascendant Money House was registered as a private enterprise, not as a financial institution—an administrative bureaucracy in charge of commerce had approved the operations of an institution whose activities technically fell under the jurisdiction of the financial administrative hierarchy. In other words, the ICMB had ignored policies and procedures governing financial practices. In retrospect, people have speculated that Fang Peilin either had good relationships or *guanxi* with ICMB officials or paid them more than necessary for a basic business license.[56] Not surprisingly, as soon as the money house opened its doors for business, the four highest leaders of the Wenzhou Agricultural Bank immediately warned Fang that the central government had yet to issue an official policy sanctioning the establishment of private banks. Fang boldly retorted that the bankers knew very well the scale of underground credit activity going on in Wenzhou; all he intended to do was to bring underground activities to the surface. He accused the officials of "ignoring the ox that walks by, but shaking a climbing louse really hard," meaning that the scale of Fang's money house would be minuscule compared to all the other nongovernmental financing activities that were flourishing in Wenzhou. In any case, the money house operated in a rather gray zone of legality—approved by the ICMB but not by the banking bureaucracy.[57]

Fang's money house opened with only 5,000 *yuan* (US$2,155) of working capital and a 100,000-*yuan* (US$43,103) capital base. The scale of his operations increased rapidly, however. The money house appealed to a client base whose financing needs were not being met by the state banks. Working from the (capitalistic) notion that "time is money," Fang calculated interest rates on an hourly basis and coined the motto "time is interest."

---

countries. Given the virtual absence of either in China in 1984, however, it is plausible that the two types of financial flows seemed to share a similar logic.

56. Interview Nos. 160, 164.

57. On top of the local controversy, it is worth noting that the establishment of Fang's money house predated the Third Plenum of the Twelfth Central Committee meetings in October 1984, which extended economic reform to urban areas.

Table 4.4 Comparison of Monthly Interest Rates

Financial Service	Fang's Money House	State Banks/ Credit Cooperatives	Spread (basis points)[a]
Savings—call deposit	1%	0.24%	83
Savings—fixed term, 3 months	1.2%	1%	20
Borrowing	3–5%	1.5%	15–35

[a] Basis points are standard units of measuring interest rate spreads and bond yield differentials in finance. One basis point is equivalent to one hundredth of a percentage point (0.01 percent).

Whereas banks and credit cooperatives were open for only eight hours a day,[58] the money house operated twenty-four hours a day, seven days a week. Fang had noticed that the prime time for borrowing was early in the morning, and the most popular time for people to deposit their savings was late in the evening, so he operated in a manner that suited the daily borrowing and savings cycles of local merchants. He brokered money between those with extra cash on hand and those who needed it, thereby turning "dead money" into "live [interest-earning] money."[59] Moreover, the money house's interest rates took advantage of the market gap in the local supply and demand of capital by offering savings rates slightly higher than that of the banks and lending rates lower than those of other nongovernmental forms of finance (see Table 4.4). Given the rapid turnover of capital at lucrative spreads, at its peak the volume of the money house's transactions in one day reached 700,000 *yuan*, with monthly deposits of over one million *yuan* and monthly earnings exceeding 60 million *yuan*.[60]

In May 1986, two years after Fang's money house opened its doors, the director of the central PBOC at the time, Chen Muhua, visited Wenzhou and admonished the Wenzhou PBOC for not keeping a tighter rein on illegal financing activities such as *taihui*, which were collapsing at the time.[61] He also publicly announced that national banking laws did not allow governments, enterprises, and private individuals to run financial institutions.[62] Despite this warning, private money houses continued to conduct

58. Actually, they were probably open for only six hours a day, since government offices take two hours off for midday lunch and a nap.

59. For example, a client might call at 10:00 A.M. and ask to borrow 10,000; if Fang did not have enough cash on hand, he would go and borrow it from someone who did have it because he was waiting to pay someone else 10,000 at 2:00 P.M. that day. Fang would take the money, lend it out, and by 2:00 P.M., he would not only return the 10,000 as promised but would have turned it over three times already: "Exploiting Loopholes in a Positive Manner," in Ou Ren, et al., *Nanshang yu beishang* (Southern merchants and northern merchants) (Zhengzhou: Hainan guoji xinxi chubanshe, 1996), 70–77.

60. Li Yu, "Jinrong wanhuatongs" 51.

61. Zhang and Mao, *Wenzhou*, 8.

62. Zhang Heping, "Qianzhuang 'laoban' Fang Peilin," 110.

their businesses openly for another three years. Their elimination was not implemented locally until 1989, when the national political crisis triggered a period of economic retrenchment and uncertainty about the future of reform. By the time money houses were effectively banned in Wenzhou, there were 27 of them, which people openly referred to as "private banks."[63]

The delay in closing down money houses did not prevent bankers from attempting to sabotage their business in the interim. Shortly after Fang started operating, for instance, managers from the Agricultural Bank of China and rural credit cooperatives (RCC) in Qianku Township held secret deliberations on how to "extinguish" the money house. They decided to recall all outstanding loans from state units within three days, thereby flooding the money house with requests for loans. Fang's clients and friends helped him to raise 100,000 *yuan* for on-lending purposes; but then the RCC returned Fang's 50,000-*yuan* savings deposit and suspended his borrowing privileges, claiming that they had a business "conflict." The RCC manager explained that "a car," meaning the financial system, "cannot have two steering wheels."[64] When Fang pointed out that RCCs have a written policy indicating that savers are entitled to leveraged lines of credit, the manager responded that Fang's lending habits were too troublesome: he would borrow for only two or three days at a time and require up to ten borrowing transactions in any given month. In effect, they were saying that the transaction costs of serving Fang were prohibitively high because of the frequency and volume of his business. Retorting that his type of business required rapid and frequent turnover in capital, Fang accused them of being jealous, since he was willing to provide services that official banks deemed to be too troublesome and was able to do so in a highly profitable manner. Throughout the five years of the money house's operation, many more attempts were made by bankers at different administrative levels to restrict its activities. The ICMB stubbornly protected them, however.

In light of the official banks' opposition to money houses, financial entrepreneurs turned to a less controversial option for engaging in financial brokering. Rather than directly confronting officials in the financial hierarchy with a corporate institution of questionable legality, they chose an organizational form that was more palatable to the formal financial sector: the credit cooperative. Just as privately owned businesses found it more convenient politically to register as collectives, would-be managers of money houses organized their operations as credit cooperatives. Because they were structured as stock-issuing financial institutions, credit cooperatives provided the institutional appearance of being collectively held even

---

63. "Wenzhouren banqi zhongguo shoujia siying yinhang" (Wenzhou people run the first private banks in China) in Yu Shizhang, *Wenzhou gaige moshi yanxin yinxiang*, 63–64.
64. Ibid., 113.

if the actual distribution of shares was dominated by only two or three people (who might also happen to be related). In theory, their performance would directly affect the UCC shareholders and staff wages.

Urban credit cooperatives were first established in Wenzhou in 1984. By 1989 there were twenty-six, sixteen of which were in the city center; by 1992 there were forty-three UCCs, including fourteen "rural financial service societies" (*nongcun jinrong fuwushe*) that accounted for one-third of the total in Zhejiang province.[65] Like the money houses, they worked extended hours to serve the financing needs of private businesses. Moreover, they offered rates as competitive as those of the money houses, even though they should have been subject to the interest rate limits defined by the state banking system. Bankers, officials, and merchants all understood that while the UCCs were registered as collective financial organizations, they were in fact privately owned. They did not report to other state units, raised their own capital, operated as independent accounting entities, and shouldered complete responsibility for their own profits and losses. UCCs enjoyed a period of relative autonomy and flexibility in their operations throughout the 1980s.

In 1990, however, the Wenzhou branch of the People's Bank of China investigated the UCCs and discovered a number of cases where managers were being overcompensated or dividends were not being properly distributed to shareholders. One year later the Wenzhou PBOC issued a policy ruling that placed UCCs and rural financial service societies under the management of the PBOC. But local officials openly admit that UCCs continued to act independently: their interest rates remained higher than those of the state banks; they retained autonomy in personnel appointments and lending decisions, and essentially continued to operate business-as-usual.[66]

In March 1997 the financial hierarchy attempted once again to govern UCCs more stringently by forcing them to convert into Urban Cooperative Banks (UCBs, *chengshi hezuo yinhang*), which are considered stock-issuing commercial banks.[67] The stated rationale for their creation was to increase

---

65. Unnamed Hong Kong newspaper, "Xinyong hezuoshe yinyunsheng," November 28, 1988, reprinted in Yu Shizhang, *Wenzhou gaige moshi yanxin yinxiang*, 65–66; Zhang and Mao, *Wenzhou*, 124.

66. In an interview with the *Far Eastern Economic Review*, however, a prominent UCC director described Wenzhou's UCCs as the "Eighth Route Irregulars of Banking" and then claimed that UCCs no longer competed for deposits and had limited their lending activity to four-month working-capital loans that are collateralized by real estate at 50 percent of the purchase price: "Policies: Too Hot to Handle," *Far Eastern Economic Review*, January 28, 1993, 39.

67. The first Urban Cooperative (Commercial) Bank was established in Shenzhen in June 1995 by consolidating the capital of sixteen preexisting UCCs: "First Urban Cooperative Bank Opens in Shenzhen," *Xinhuashe* (New China news agency), June 28, 1995, 54. The four other pilot cities chosen for the establishment of UCBs were Beijing, Tianjin, Shanghai, and

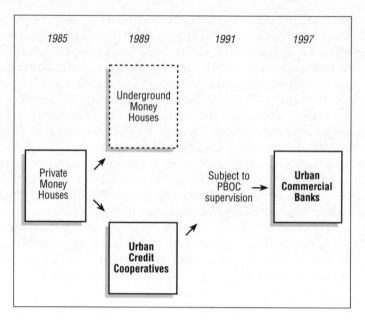

Figure 4.4 No Hat → Red Hat → Hard Hat: The Fate of Private Money Houses in Wenzhou

the efficiency of UCCs by consolidating them into standardized commercial banks. As the UCBs were being established, both bankers and local officials believed that the de facto privately run UCCs, as outgrowths of the private money houses, would finally have to relinquish their majority stakes and operational autonomy.[68] Former owners of UCCs were informed that they could retain a 50 to 60 percent share of the new entities; the local government would hold 30 percent of the stock, and the remaining 10 to 20 percent would go to other individuals and units.[69] Furthermore, since UCBs were formed by merging all the UCCs in Wenzhou, the UCB branches now report to a central office that monitors their management and business practices. In effect, the red hat that would-be managers of money houses wore to evade official interference turned into a hard hat.

Figure 4.4 summarizes the organizational progression of money houses over time. Their highly controversial history in Wenzhou has two main implications. First, financial entrepreneurs who are resourceful in cultivat-

---

Shijiazhuang: "Urban Cooperative Banks Set Up Instead of Private," reported in July 6, 1995, FBIS-CHI-129.

68. Interview Nos. 160, 161, 162, 163, 164.

69. "Wenzhou to Accept Urban Cooperative Bank," *Xinhua News Agency*, March 15, 1997, reported in FBIS-CHI-97-073.

ing political ties beyond the banking bureaucracy may succeed in establishing private financial institutions by registering them through other agencies (the next chapter provides additional examples). Second, political ties may help in getting past initial bureaucratic obstacles to the *establishment* of a novel financial institution but are likely to be insufficient in guaranteeing the *survival* of the business. To the extent that private financial institutions are highly visible—as the private money houses were in Wenzhou—their unconventional financial practices are bound to prompt interference from banking authorities. This does not mean that financial entrepreneurs will cease to engage in private finance—many private money houses continue to operate underground—but it is becoming increasingly difficult to run a nongovernmental financial business in a public manner without wearing one of the state-sanctioned disguises. Virtually all the financial institutions operating aboveground in Henan (see Chapter Five) wear legal hats of some sort.

Pawnbrokering Cycles

Establishing pawnshops represented another attempt by Wenzhou's financial entrepreneurs to choose a less contentious organizational form than money houses for providing nongovernmental financial services to local merchants. Because private individuals are not allowed to own pawnshops, they had to register as collective enterprises. Organizationally, the pawnshops seemed no different from other red hat businesses: they had a board of directors, a manager, an appraisal office, and other technical offices with a staff of about ten to twelve. The founders of the shops generally came from high positions in other commercial enterprises and possessed an extensive network of friends engaged in business. These connections also put pawnshop owners in a position to violate certain laws quite flagrantly, including, for example, accepting real estate titles from customers, borrowing from credit cooperatives, and acting as depository institutions for everyday savers.

Since pawnshops by definition provide collateralized credit, their operations would appear to entail less risk than those of the financial brokers and money house bosses. Furthermore, unlike the pawnshops in pre-Communist China, their main client base consisted of relatively well-off businesspeople rather than impoverished peasants.[70] According to a survey

---

70. Contemporary writings about pawnshops are careful to distinguish the "usurious practices" of the old pawnshops from the methods of those that serve small businesses today. See, e.g., Sun Xiaocun, *Jindai zhongguo diandangye* (Pawnbrokering in contemporary China) (Beijing: Zhongguo wenshi chubanshe, 1996); and Xin Jing, *Diandangshi* (History of pawnbrokering) (Shanghai: Shanghai wenyi chubanshe, 1993).

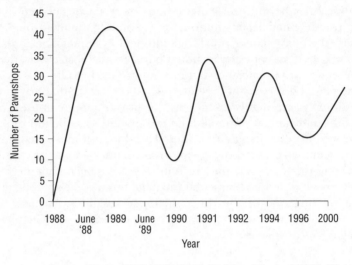

Sources: Wenzhou PBOC (1993), 67–73; Ma Jinlong "Wenzhou" (1995), 415; Interview Nos. 160, 186.

Figure 4.5 Pawnshops in Wenzhou, 1988–2000

of pawnshops in the early 1990s, about 97.9 percent of the clients used the cash for productive or business purposes; only 2.1 percent pawned items to alleviate cash constraints in everyday life.[71] Yet their performance as businesses in Wenzhou has been cyclical since the first pawnshop opened in early 1988.[72] By the end of the year, forty-two shops had registered with the Wenzhou ICMB, accounting for 20 percent of all pawnshops in China at the time—but fifteen of them closed down within a year. By the beginning of 1991 the number of pawnshops had risen to thirty-four, then fell to nineteen by 1992, only to increase again to thirty in 1994 (see Figure 4.5).

71. Gao, et al. "Wenzhou," 70. During my follow-up visit of pawnshops in early 2001, however, it was apparent that migrant workers from other provinces were also using them to get enough cash to go home for Spring Festival.

72. Wenzhou's first pawnshop opened on February 9, 1988, which locals claim was only one month after the first pawnshop in PRC history was opened in Sichuan Province: Zhang and Mao, *Wenzhou*, 66. In actuality, the first one was established in November 1987 in Shaoyang, Hunan Province, according to Beijing Institute of International Finance, *The Banking System of China* (Beijing: China Planning Press, 1993), 240. Like the other nongovernmental financial institutions discussed, however, pawnshops were by no means "new" in Chinese history. The earliest pawnshops in China, called *zhiku*, operated out of Buddhist monasteries during the Northern Dynasty. Partial statistics in 1935 estimate that there were approximately 1,100 pawn shops in Shanghai, Beijing, Tianjin, and eight other major cities, as well as 3,500 shops in rural areas. They were forced to shut down after 1949. Despite this history, the founder of Wenzhou's first pawnshop in 1988 decided to experiment with pawnbrokering because he had first read about the popularity of pawn shops in Italy in the magazine *Shijie zhihu* (Windows of the world), and later heard more about pawnshops in Mexico. Li Yu, "Jinrong wanhuatongs" 62.

The proximate cause of the pawnshops' uneven business performance may be traced to their inability to fulfill debt obligations. Local economists who have studied Wenzhou's pawnshops suggest that their instability was rooted in fundamental operating deficiencies. First, there was poor appraisal of fixed assets. The real estate that (illegally) represented most of the shops' portfolios put them at greater risk. Shops tended to focus on the pawned item itself rather than the person pawning it, and in the case of real property the customer often did not even possess property rights (i.e., usufruct rights in China), or might submit false identification, or pawn a building whose legal status was in dispute.

Second, a one-dimensional pursuit of business volume often tended to blind owners to a customer's reasons for pawning the object and led them to overlook the security of the loan. Especially during the initial period of operation, owners were concerned to increase their scale in order to grow profitable. In some cases, pawnshops would thus extend millions of *yuan* in loans within days of opening shop.

Third, internal operating procedures were frequently shoddy, since the paid staff were often friends and relatives of the owner who were not qualified for the work. Examples abound of staff mistaking gold-plated objects for real gold and in-house accountants who could not distinguish between debits and credits on pawned objects.

To capitalize their businesses, pawnshops generally relied on loans from nonbanking financial institutions such as UCCs and rural financial societies, unofficial borrowing from enterprises and state units (*neibujin*), and wealthy merchants with cash on hand. The share of each of these sources is illustrated in Figure 4.6.[73]

In order to maintain their liquidity, many pawnshops used their capital base to repay debts and, of greater concern to the formal banking system, accepted savings deposits from private entrepreneurs in order to stay afloat. One shop in Cangnan County, for example, relied solely on savings deposits for its capitalization of 800,000 *yuan*. In another shop, over 82 percent of its capitalization came from savings (some 7 million *yuan*), which exceeded the deposit level of the local rural financial society by 75 percent.[74] Pawnshops offered interest rates on savings that were 20 to 66 basis points higher than those of UCCs and rural financial societies (0.9–1.2 percent verse 0.24–1.0 percent per month), which made them as competitive as the private money houses relative to official financial institutions.

Shortly after the initial surge in the growth of pawnshops, the Wenzhou city government, the Zhejiang provincial PBOC, and the Wenzhou PBOC

73. Zhang and Mao, *Wenzhou*, 74.
74. Ibid.

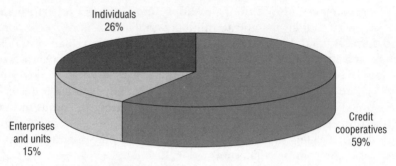

Source: Wenzhou PBOC (1993), 74.

Figure 4.6 Sources of Loans for Pawnshops in Wenzhou

agreed to issue new regulations to govern their operations.[75] In September 1988 the Wenzhou city government issued policy statement 209, which formally assigned responsibility for overseeing pawnshops to the Wenzhou PBOC, forbade all banking and nonbanking financial institutions from extending additional credit to pawnshops, and stipulated that the pawnshops could not raise capital from the public (*xiang shehui chouzi*). Two months later the Wenzhou PBOC issued statement 427, reiterating the spirit of 209, which authorized a thorough investigation of all existing pawnshops to ensure their compliance with financial and operational regulations. It was not until July 1989, however, that the Zhejiang PBOC actually issued its own statement 12, regulating all pawnshops in the province—at a time when most of the pawnshops in Wenzhou and elsewhere were not even operating because of the political and economic repression of 1989. The local PBOC had been slow in banning the private money houses as directed by the central PBOC, but here the city government was more proactive in establishing an official policy on a "new" financing practice; it was the provincial government that lagged behind. Although the provincial PBOC's delay may not seem significant in retrospect, the fact that it ultimately issued regulations at all is telling of the broader political environment during that period. Initially, the PBOC was content to devolve the responsibility for regulating pawnshops to Wenzhou's financial bureaucracy. With the double-digit inflation of 1988 and political instability of 1989, however, provinces were pressured to recentralize their regulation of local economic activities or at least demonstrate their attempts to do so by issuing policy documents.

In sum, the experience of pawnshops in Wenzhou shows that the

---

75. This paragraph draws from Gao, et al., "Wenzhou," 80–85.

Quick cash from Wenzhou's oldest pawnshop. Wenzhou, Zhejiang, January 2001.

durability of nonbanking financial institutions also depends upon their profitability, as a market-based explanation would expect. Fluctuations in the scope and scale of financial businesses are not always rooted in politics. At the same time, however, the fact that the performance of Wenzhou's pawnshops proved to be so aberrant led the local PBOC to be more proactive in devising standards for regulating them. The regulatory efforts occurred after the *hui* disasters and as part of the broader crackdown on private finance (especially the money houses).[76]

76. Note that in August 2000 the PBOC and State Economic and Trade Commission jointly issued "Notice on the Transfer of Management Responsibility for Pawnbroking," which declared that pawnshops would no longer be considered "financial institutions" but rather a "special kind of industrial and commercial enterprise": "China Reclassifies Pawnshops," *Jingji ribao* (Economic daily), August 7, 2000.

Rural Credit Cooperatives and Rural Cooperative Foundations

As holdover institutions from the cooperative movement of the Mao era, RCCs experienced more competition from the full range of nongovernmental financing mechanisms than did UCCs, largely because Wenzhou was predominantly rural at the beginning of reform. In 1980, when the ranks of private entrepreneurs were growing exponentially in rural Wenzhou, 83 percent of the RCCs were operating at a loss. Meanwhile, financial brokers and *hui* organizers were busy juggling vast networks of savers and borrowers. The RCCs knew that their interest rates were vastly depressed relative to the rates offered in the informal financial markets operating right outside their offices. Without consulting upper-level banks, in October the Jinxiang Township RCC in Cangnan County became the first formal financial institution to float its interest rates. The rates on one-year fixed deposits for individual accounts increased from 4.5 percent to 10 percent; and the annual lending rate to private businesses and TVEs went from 6 to 15 percent.[77] The Jinxiang Township RCC was able to break even again by the end of the year, and seeing its sudden success, RCCs in other areas followed its example. By 1986, 88 percent of the RCCs in Wenzhou had floating interest rates. Yet the central-level PBOC did not endorse Wenzhou as an experimental district (*shidian diqu*) for interest rate reform until September 1989.[78] Again, official policy followed, rather than led, the direction in liberalizing reforms.

Even though RCCs were intended to serve as a localized means for the ABOC to provide credit, they were not able to meet the demand for rural credit. After the Cangnan County economic reform committee issued a public announcement titled "Views on the Experiment of Rural Cooperative Stock Foundations" in August 1992, rural cooperative foundations (RCFs) developed as an additional player in commercial finance in Wenzhou's countryside.[79] Unlike RCCs, which were technically regulated by the ABOC until their transfer to the PBOC in 1996, RCFs were not even considered "financial institutions" because they were originally sanctioned by the Ministry of Agriculture. RCFs fell under the administrative jurisdiction of village and township governments; depending on the area, they were approved by such various administrative bodies as the county-level

77. Ma Jinlong, "Wenzhou jinrong shichang," 416.

78. By the summer of 1985 the ABOCs had started floating their interest rates for savings, and after 1987 the specialized banks increased their one-year and fixed-term savings rates to a level twice as high as the upper end of the state regulations: Gao et al., "Wenzhou," 70.

79. Chen Guoxing, "Wenzhou nongcun hezuo jijinhui diaocha baogao" (Report on the investigation of rural cooperative foundations in Wenzhou), *Nongcun jinrong yanjiu* (Research on Rural Finance), No. 11 (1993), 25.

Economic System Reform Bureau, township-level Agricultural Bureau, village-level rural committees, and even labor unions. They also had a wide range of names, but structurally they were all established as shareholding (*gufenzhi*) or shareholding cooperative (*gufen hezuozhi*) organizations. As in the UCCs and RCCs, the shares were concentrated in the hands of a few individuals. The RCFs grew even faster in number and scale than the money houses or pawnshops—and this surge in growth actually occurred *after* the central government had issued restrictive macrofinancial regulations in 1993. By the end of that year, 89 RCFs had been established, holding aggregate savings deposits of more than 600 million *yuan* (US$103 million at the time).[80] When restrictive monetary policies were imposed on banks from above, Wenzhou's official banks were able to attract savings deposits but remained limited in their scale of lending. By 1993 their savings-lending gap had reached 5.6 billion *yuan* (over US$965 million).[81] Fearing another explosion in *hui*, local governments gave RCFs the green light to relieve the capital shortage.[82] Even though the RCFs offered the same services as banking institutions, they evaded official PBOC regulations and avoided the use of financial jargon. For example, loans were called "capital managed by another person" (*daiguanjin*), savings deposits became "invested money" (*toufangjin*), and interest was called "adjusted capital fee" (*zijin tiaoji feilü*) or "capital use fee" (*zijin zhanyong feilü*).[83] These euphemistic terms did not alter the economic attractiveness of RCFs to local entrepreneurs, however.

In other provinces there were repeated attempts either to standardize or to eliminate RCFs because they have always been illegal in the eyes of China's central bank.[84] In Wenzhou, bankers and economists had their share of controversy over how to reform the RCFs. On the one hand, they provided a much-needed source of grassroots credit; on the other hand, if left unregulated, they would continue to offer higher interest rates and

80. Ma Jinlong, "Wenzhou jinrong shichang," 415. In the last quarter of 1993 the exchange rate was US$1 = 5.8 RMB.

81. Chen Guoxing, "Wenzhou nongcun hezuo jijinhui," 25.

82. The lending volume of RCFs increased dramatically. In 1993 alone, the eighteen in Cangnan County were lending three times more than the county-level People's Construction Bank of China (now called China Construction Bank), at about half of the ABOC's volume, and about the same level as the ICB. Before it was shut down in 1999, the capitalization of the first RCF in Cangnan exceeded that of the local RCCs and UCCs.

83. RCFs first emerged in 1985: Kuang Xuzhong and Xia Zongyu, "Jiaqiang nongcun hezuo jijinhui de guanli shizai bixing" (strengthening the management of RCFs is imperative), *Nongcun jinrong yanjiu* (Research on rural finance), no. 9 (1993): 33–38. Starting in 1988 they grew particularly rapidly in Sichuan, where they also employed such euphemistic terminology to disguise their financial transactions. See Guo Xiaoming, "Emergence and Development of Rural Cooperative Fund in Sichuan," Rural Economy Institute, Sichuan Academy of Social Sciences, October 1996.

84. Most of the debate has focused on Sichuan.

accept savings deposits not protected by the official banking sector.[85] As part of the central government's attempts to rationalize the financial system, in March 1999 the State Council announced that RCFs would be shut down or taken over by RCCs. This announcement triggered protests in at least four provinces and one municipality (Sichuan, Hunan, Henan, Guangxi, and Chongqing).[86] In contrast, the "rectification" of 225 RCFs in Wenzhou was carried out by the end of 1999 without inspiring social unrest because most of Wenzhou's RCFs were able to compensate their depositors.[87]

RCCs are next in line for rationalizing reforms. Some ABOC officials have proposed establishing a "one bank, two systems" (*yihang liangzhi*) solution by turning the RCCs into a rural cooperative bank which, above the county level, would be treated as a state-owned commercial bank; at the county level it would be a "united bureau" (*jiehebu*) jointly financed by the ABOC and grassroots cooperative financial organizations; and below the county level it would be a cooperative financial organization. At the same time, some local governments would prefer to turn RCCs into local commercial banks to promote local economic profit. As one Chinese economist has observed, "Everyone is discussing [the reform of RCCs] from the perspective of how they would benefit from it, rather than how to reform RCCs into a truly cooperative financial organization that best serves the development of the rural commercial economy."[88]

Official Intervention and Regulation of Nonbanking Financial Institutions

After the initial cycle of cadre collaboration and defection in the early 1980s, the terms of cadre-entrepreneur interaction became more nuanced and issue-specific. As a richer range of private financing strategies emerged, local cadre interference or noninterference retained the same interest-driven logic, but as I have attempted to illustrate with regard to different financing mechanisms, these interests were specified more finely by the nested identities of actors in their layered institutional environments. More concretely, the sub-hypotheses set forth at the beginning of the chapter

85. Zhang Huiru, "Nongcun hezuo jinrong de fazhan zhangai ji duice" (Obstacles and countermeasures in the development of rural cooperative finance) *Dangdai jingji kexue* (Modern Economic Science), no. 1 (1996): 92–95.

86. "China Closes Credit Coops," *Associated Press Wire*, March 22, 1999.

87. *WZNJ 2000* (Wenzhou yearbook 2000), 254.

88. Han Lei, "Guanyu nongcun xinyongshe gaige yu jianli nongcun hezuo yinhang wenti" (On the reform of RCCs and the issue of establishing a rural cooperative bank), *Nongcun jingji yu jinrong* (Rural economy and finance), no. 6 (1996): 5.

Table 4.5 Summary of Official Regulation of Private Financing Arrangements

Financing Mechanism	Availability of Rents	Visibility of Financing Practice	Political Pressure to Intervene	Responsible Bureaucracy	Nature of Intervention
Trade credit	no	low	no	none	none
Brokers; middlemen	no	low	no	none	none
Red hat/hang-on enterprises	yes	low	no	county and township governments	none
Shareholding cooperatives	yes	low	no	county and township governments	none
Rotating credit associations	no	low/medium	no	none	banning
Pyramidal investment scams	no	high	yes	none; then county gov't	banning
Money houses	yes	high	yes	ICMB; then PBOC	conversion into UCCs; merger with UCBs
Pawnshops	yes	high	yes	ICMB; county gov't; then PBOC	formal regulation
Rural cooperative foundations (RCFs)	yes	high	yes	MOA; township and village gov'ts	disbanding or merger with RCCs

posited that official intervention in private financing practices would depend on: (a) the availability of rent-seeking opportunities, (b) the visibility of the financing activities, and (c) the political benefits of intervention.

Empirically, the situation for each of the financing mechanisms is summarized in Table 4.5 with regard to official intervention. A quick comparison between the Availability of Rents and the Nature of Intervention columns shows that the former is not a particularly robust indicator for lack of governmental intervention. In other words, financial entrepreneurs may pay rents to various bureaucracies for protection purposes, but if their operations become highly visible or controversial, responsible bureaucracies that experience political pressure to intervene find it difficult to continue looking the other way. It is also important to reiterate that the wave of regulatory intervention in Wenzhou's curb market occurred in an environment marked by intense competition both within the curb market and

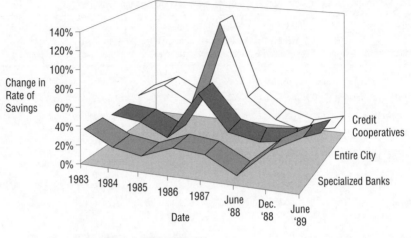

Source: Wenzhou PBOC (1993), 111.

Figure 4.7 Savings Deposit Fluctuations in Wenzhou's Banks and Credit Cooperatives

between the formal and informal financial sectors. In other words, the nature of intervention in each of the particular financing mechanisms should be viewed as part of a broader effort by local governmental and banking authorities to minimize financial speculation and promote local economic stability. The ban on *all* types of *hui* is one example of how the chaos in *taihui* and *paihui* had spillover effects on the perception and regulation of the more "normal" types of *hui*. Before disaggregating the bureaucratic actors (government, banking, industry and commerce) that stepped in to regulate the financing arrangements—and their rationale for doing so—it is worth reiterating that each of the private financing practices discussed above preceded any debate among official authorities about their particular utility or infringement on existing policy. The logic of intervention by governmental organs was therefore based on the perceived impact of each practice on the political and economic interests of each official actor.

Since banks were not in a position to provide credit to private businesses, the level of savings deposits represents the central indicator of the sheer economic impact of nongovernmental forms of finance on local state banks. Based on data compiled from the Wenzhou PBOC, Figure 4.7 shows that savings deposit rates in the official banks indeed fluctuated quite frequently during the 1980s.[89] Savings deposits in official banks declined when savings and investment opportunities in the nongovernmental financial

89. Zhang and Mao, *Wenzhou*, 111. Data were available only for *change* in the rate of savings deposits.

sector were most accessible; as a result, state banks switched to floating interest rates in order to compete with private financiers.[90]

In addition to illustrating the cyclical pattern of aggregate savings levels, Figure 4.7 shows the divergent impact of fluctuations in savings on the specialized banks as compared with credit cooperatives. Ultimately, credit cooperatives experienced the most extreme waves of capital in- and outflow, yet it was the state banks that objected most vocally to the underground or disguised financing practices of nongovernmental financial actors. Since the de facto ownership of credit cooperatives themselves was either nearly or completely private, it is not surprising that their directors remained silent amid tumultuous financial shifts. They could not legitimately complain about private moneylenders and loan sharks when they too were offering inflated interest rates by official standards. It is not so obvious, however, why state banks would express concern about the impact of private finance on their own operations, given their soft budget constraints. In other words, with virtually guaranteed lifetime employment in their respective banks, why would they care about their banks' profitability?

First of all, the extent to which local state banks exercised the "voice" option varied.[91] It depend on the degree of institutional formalization that the nongovernmental financing practices possessed and the administrative level at which banks could be held responsible for permitting unusual financing practices. They did not, for example, complain about the *taihui* or *paihui* that clearly wrecked havoc with the local financial markets. But when the first money house was only in the preparatory stages, the ABOC withdrew its support, and the PBOC would not recognize it as a valid financial institution. As players in the official banking system they could not directly authorize the establishment of a de facto private bank, even if they wanted to, without the risk of eliciting upper-level censure. The highest-ranking PBOC director himself came down from Beijing to admonish Wenzhou's state bankers.

What local banks could and did do, however, was to engage in an intellectual lobbying effort to persuade upper-level banks that nongovernmental, "popular" (*minjian*) finance played a central role in local economic development.[92] By "intellectual lobbying effort" I mean that local banking officials and managers wrote academic articles in journals—*Nongcun jinrong*

90. This could be termed the "if you can't beat them, join them" strategy.

91. Albert O. Hirschman, *Exit, Voice, and Loyalty* (Cambridge: Harvard University Press, 1970).

92. An in-depth analysis of one of the key think tanks involved in such research and policy advocacy, the Economic System Reform Institute, is Catherine H. Keyser, *Professionalizing Research: The System Reform Institute and Policymaking in Post-Mao China* (Armonk, N.Y.: M. E. Sharpe, 2002).

yanjiu (Research on Rural Finance), *Zhejiang xuekan* (Zhejiang Academic Journal), and *Jinrong yanjiu* (Financial Studies)—which "objectively" analyzed Wenzhou's financial environment and made policy recommendations regarding the course of financial system reform. If money houses could operate openly, they reasoned, then formal financial institutions could attempt to regulate them by requiring, for example, that a certain level of loan loss reserves be deposited in a state bank, or that money houses share their client base with banks in a more transparent manner. As it was, red hat enterprises were more likely to employ the financial services of state banks, while hatless ones depended on (illegal) private banks. The intellectual lobbying was also an indirect way of calling attention to the perceived deficiencies of the existing banking system. More prosaically, they were basically saying, if you will not permit us to meet the credit needs of private entrepreneurs directly, then let other institutions do so with our oversight, we want to, but lack the mandate and infrastructural capacity; yet the demand for financial services by a burgeoning market of private entrepreneurs clearly exists. By lobbying for the legal recognition of money houses, the banks hoped to be assigned official authority over their management, with ensuing institutional (albeit illegal) access to rents.

The Industrial and Commercial Management Bureau was the main rentier beneficiary of highly institutionalized financial entities: namely, registered private businesses, including the money houses and pawnshops. The ICMB certainly did not complain about the financing practices of *its* registered enterprises, for that bureaucracy could depend on a steady stream of payoffs from Extorted Harmony.[93] Similarly, Wenzhou's banks dragged their feet on eliminating the money houses because they perceived the economic advantages of incorporating them into their administrative jurisdiction instead. They tried to encroach on the money houses' market share via sabotaging tactics, and when that had limited impact, they lobbied for official authority over their business.[94] Ultimately, the Wenzhou banking bureaucracy succeeded in eliminating *registered* private money houses. The nationwide political economic retrenchment in 1989 elicited their compliance, as private entrepreneurs redirected their capital from their businesses to state banking institutions.

When former owners of money houses established themselves as UCCs, Wenzhou's banks were content to raise their own interest rates and compete with them as near-equals in the local financial market. As long as they could extract rents from their administrative underlings—the UCCs, now UCBs—they were content. Upper-level banks, on the other hand, saw

93. Cf. Melanie Manion, "Corruption by Design: Bribery in Chinese Enterprise Licensing," *Journal of Law, Economics, and Organization* 12 (April 1996): 167–95.
94. Interview No. 160.

the growth in nonbanking financial institutions as an encroachment on the degree of control they had over the volume and cost of capital in the economy. Central-level banks have attempted repeatedly to enforce the State Council's mandates on restricting credit during inflationary periods. But compliance from progressively marketized districts like Wenzhou has proved to be challenging since lower administrative banking levels realize the local impetus for continued economic expansion, and the consequences of restricting official sources of credit.[95]

In the case of local governmental (city, county, township, village) interference, each level's strategies for dealing with different financing mechanisms depended on its institutional and economic interests. Township and village governments, for example, had direct stakes in RCFs and thus supported their operations. City and county governments knew that they were problematic from the perspective of higher banking levels; but at the same time they understood why RCFs existed (i.e., market demand) and thus silently left the financial hierarchy with the burden of reforming them. Unless they could bring the RCFs under their immediate jurisdiction, they lacked the incentive for regulating them. By the same token, township and village cadres would not be expected to expose the red hats, given that they played a direct role in registering private enterprises as collective ones. In Red Hat Harmony they literally sold the collective label for a monetary sum, conveniently called the collective enterprise management fee. In the case of private money houses, most township and county governments were reluctant to register such overtly controversial businesses but did not publicly oppose them either, for the cadre-entrepreneur networks were sufficiently interdependent to ensure a cooperative equilibrium. For example, just as private money houses bypassed the banking hierarchy for a time by registering through the ICMB, red hat enterprises could evade the ICMB by claiming a collective ownership status.

Ultimately, local governments never objected to financing mechanisms that facilitated the continued growth of private businesses and their tax revenues, for local growth served their economic interests.[96] When financing practices threatened social order at the grassroots level, however, as in *taihui* and *paihui*, township and county governments attempted to limit their damage and thus restore social order and prevent higher-level gov-

95. A former banker revealed that the banks are well aware of the comparative advantage of UCCs over the state's specialized banks; in 1994 figures, e.g., UCCs had a late repayment rate of only 2.6 percent, while the rate of overdue loans for specialized banks in Wenzhou exceeded 10 percent. Interview No. 160.

96. Politically, Wenzhou's capitalist infamy was not always advantageous. But all that the city government could do during restrictive times was to parrot the ideological line against usurious practices by local capitalists until the national priority shifted back to economic growth.

ernments from getting involved. Wenzhou City did of course step in to prosecute the largest *hui* organizers and launch a campaign to eliminate *hui*.
But the visits by higher-level officials and academics only impressed upon
city officials the importance of allowing private financing mechanisms to
operate in a more institutionalized and transparent manner.

In recent years the city government has actually encouraged creative
means of capital formation among private enterprises to the extent that
they are not overtly illegal. When the Wenzhou City Party Central
Committee and People's Government launched the "second pioneering"
growth campaign at the beginning of 1994, the policy document announc-
ing its objectives clearly advocated the continued development of different
financing mechanisms.[97] In addition to recommending the conversion of
UCCs and RCCs into commercial banks before the pilot UCBs were
launched in Beijing, Shanghai, Tianjin, and Shijiazhuang, the second
pioneering strategy encouraged local enterprises to issue negotiable
stocks and securities in a public, as opposed to underground, manner. That
announcement, however, came two years after the Wenzhou International
Trust Company first issued shares on the Shanghai Stock Exchange in
November 1992: that is, at a time when 33,000 other Wenzhou companies
had already issued shares. By 1994, Wenzhou's companies had already
issued an aggregate of 180 million *yuan* in negotiable securities, which were
being traded in twenty-seven local markets.[98]

Despite a reputation for financial daring and innovation, Wenzhou's
entrepreneurs have not jumped into the stock market with the fervor that
has swept such other cities in the region as Hangzhou and Shanghai.
Instead, closely held shareholding cooperatives and enterprises (*gufenzhi
hezuo qiye* and *gufenzhi qiye*) have emerged as the corporate form of choice.
Since the late 1990s the debate among provincial policymakers and academics has centered more on the managerial problems encountered in the
intermediate years of operation than on their relative legality and administrative allegiance.[99] Meanwhile, local branches of state banks have

---

97. The "second pioneering" (*dier chuangye*) stage of Wenzhou's growth was initiated as a
development strategy that emphasized increasing the city's technology base, upgrading transportation and infrastructure, and improving the quality of its products. The decision was formally passed by the Wenzhou City Central Committee and People's Government in the No.
1 policy document issued January 5, 1994, reprinted in Zhang and Zheng, eds., *Wenzhou
shichang*, 180–85: Zhang Minjie, "Wenzhou 'dierci chuangye' kaocha" (An investigation of the
second pioneering in Wenzhou), *Shehuixue yanjiu* (Sociological research), no. 4 (May 20,
1996): 64–74.

98. Ma Jinlong, "Wenzhou jinrong shichang," 417.

99. Research Group on Rural Stock Cooperative Ownership, Zhejiang Academy of Social
Sciences, "Zhejiang nongcun gufen hezuozhi de jueqi beijing yu yunzuo fangshi" (Crisis environment and operation of Zhejiang's rural cooperative stock ownership system), *Zhejiang
xuekan* (Zhejiang academic journal), no. 1 (1996): 48–57.

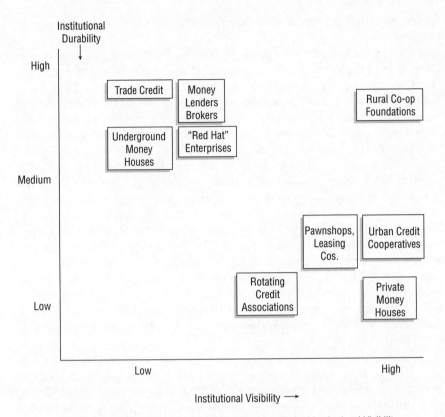

Figure 4.8 Relationship between Institutional Durability and Institutional Visibility

proliferated, and competition for savings deposits has intensified, leading one official to exclaim, "There are more banks than toilets in this city."[100]

Private Entrepreneurs' Choice of Financing Mechanisms

The expectation that entrepreneurs with stronger political ties will choose financing mechanisms with higher degrees of institutionalization is borne out in the Wenzhou context at the most basic level. The logic of this argument is that entrepreneurs with better political ties (*guanxi*) will incur lower transaction costs and experience less uncertainty in institutionalizing their financing arrangements in the form of registered businesses. Therefore, it is worth highlighting in brief the primary variables that

100. Interview No. 157.

determine the degree of uncertainty and transaction costs for private entrepreneurs.

First, the most basic distinguishing characteristic among entrepreneurs is their registration status. Enterprises that are privately owned but registered as collectives possess greater access to state banks and other resources available to SOEs than those without the collective label. The foregoing discussion of red hat enterprises suggests that the stability of the red hat relationship depends on the two dimensions of *mobility* and *relative dependency* on the red hat supplier. If the red hat supplier attempts to increase the cost of protection and the enterprise is relatively mobile, then the preferred alternative is not necessarily switching to a different red hat protector but pooling resources with other private enterprises to form shareholding and limited liability corporations. That strategy has become increasingly popular as the stigma against private enterprise has tempered over time and the preponderance of Wenzhou's population has become involved in private economic activities in one form or another. In the 1980s, wearing a red hat carried many advantages that came with having a public patron. By the mid-1990s, however, many larger-scale enterprises had in effect grown out of red hat relationships and found it more efficient to cooperate with other like-minded entrepreneurs in approaching specialized banks for loans.[101]

The case of Mr. Pi, a thirty-five-year-old owner of a leather factory in Yongzhong Township shows how the combination of extensive business experience and good political ties has enabled private entrepreneurs to tap even official sources of credit.[102] Before establishing his current leather factory, Mr. Pi was involved in a variety of nonagricultural activities. In 1983 he and his three brothers pooled 6,000 *yuan* to start engaging in petty trade. Over the years they sold, among other things, lumber, steel components, and bicycles. In 1998, Mr. Pi and six partners established a leather factory registered as a shareholding enterprise with a capitalization of 3.58 million *yuan*. Initially, he contributed 4 million *yuan* and his friends and relatives an additional 2.5 million. Later on, the factory was able to get a loan from the ABOC for 5 million (at 5.5 percent per year for six months) and 1 million from an RCC (at 5.8 percent per year for four months). As of 2001 the factory had 136 employees, including Mr. Pi's spouse and five relatives, and the total output value in 2000 exceeded 60 million *yuan*. Each of the seven partners takes 1,500 *yuan* a month from the factory in the form of salary, and additional profit is automatically reinvested.

Mr. Pi is clearly well connected and respected locally. He is the head of

101. For a more extensive discussion on privatization in the 1990s, see Susan H. Whiting, *Power and Wealth in Rural China: The Political Economy of Institutional Change* (New York: Cambridge University Press, 2001).

102. Interview No. 184.

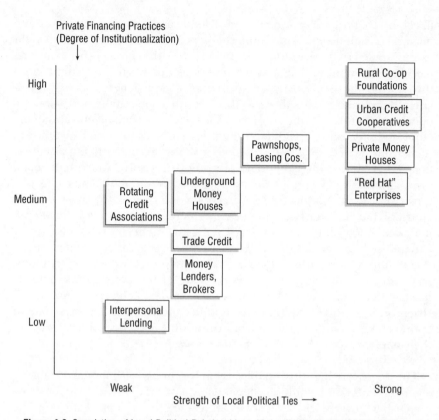

Private Financing Practices
(Degree of Institutionalization)

Figure 4.9 Correlation of Local Political Relationships with Institutionalization of Private Finance

the local leather trade association (*shanghui*), which deals with shared industry concerns such as marketing and price-setting. Meanwhile, his father is the head of the local Individual Laborers Association, and many of his relatives work in the government and are CCP members. (Mr. Pi is not a Party member himself, but his three brothers are busy applying for admission.) The government offices that help the factory most are the banks, the village committee, and the township government. Township officials, for example, visit their factory twice a year.

Although the leather factory has no difficulty in getting loans from the ABOC, Mr. Pi and his partners continue to use informal sources of finance, including private money houses, for short-term working-capital needs. "It is still faster and more convenient than applying for a formal bank loan," he explained.

Smaller businesses registered as "individual households" (*getihu*) generally had fewer institutionalized options in the early 1980s. They were more likely to rely on informal loans from friends and relatives, or to cultivate bilateral relationships with moneylenders and wholesalers who would extend trade credit, than to try to curry favor with lending officers in state banks. Many vendors felt that it simply was not worth their time to go through all the paperwork, gift-giving, and waiting necessary for a collateralized loan.[103] With the growth of credit cooperatives and rural cooperative foundations at the grassroots level, individual entrepreneurs employed their services with less hesitation. Not only were such institutions specifically geared toward serving the local private economy, but also business owners were more likely to possess preexisting social ties with the managers and staff of local nonbanking financial institutions. Hence, gifts to a credit officer at the local RCF were not necessarily given prior to loan approval, but afterward, and were thus perceived more as a gesture of gratitude and goodwill than as a bribe. Even if the monetary value of a gift or banquet held on behalf of an RCF loan officer was roughly equivalent to that required for securing a loan from, for instance, the county-level Industrial and Commercial Bank, the perception of the transaction would be fundamentally different. This is not to say that rural entrepreneurs valued "friendship" to the exclusion of economic concerns, but the social ease of approaching a particular financial institution for services did factor into their implicit calculation of transaction costs.

The logic driving the establishment of nongovernmental financing arrangements and institutions depends in part on the regulatory environment that governs the availability of capital in various sectors of the economy. Capital scarcity in rapidly developing areas such as Wenzhou may be the initial economic impetus for turning to unofficial sources of credit, but the various branches of the local government also play key roles in facilitating or obstructing the emergence of informal financial institutions. The process of institutional supply and maintenance is fundamentally political, though the economic performance of the actual institutions also influences their capacity to survive over time. On the demand side the particular financing practices and institutions that economic actors choose hinges on their perceived alternatives. The array of financing mechanisms that have emerged in Wenzhou demonstrates that private entrepreneurs' choices of financing arrangements depend on their scale and relative access to local political and social resources. Market women, for example, finance their businesses quite differently from well-placed cadres or the moonlighting SOE manager.

---

103. The gifts of potential borrowers to credit officers can often exceed the value of the loan itself. In such cases, the implicit understanding is that the loan may not be repaid on time, if ever: Interview No. 101.

Further, in the course of pursuing various financing options, these entrepreneurs' aggregated acts of agency transformed the local financial institutional environment and influenced the enactment of broader-level financial reform measures. A popular Chinese saying about the reform process captures the essence of this dynamic: "Whenever there are policies from the top, the bottom produces counterstrategies" (*shangyou zhengce xiayou duice*). In Wenzhou, local economic practices also elicit counterstrategies from higher administrative levels.[104] Since socialist development was subject to centralized planning, institutional tendencies to mandate reform from above continue. Yet the empirical experience of China and other transitional economies demonstrates that the reform process is fraught with unanticipated consequences. For one thing, divergent interpretations and implementation of policies by competing bureaucratic actors may have varying implications for preexisting and new forms of entrepreneurship at the local level; they may preempt, anticipate, or even inspire additional reform measures. The ability of particular financial institutions to survive in this context depends on what each actor has at stake and what resources are available for adapting old exchange relationships to changed rules of the game.

The next chapter turns to a province where, although local governments have been more ambivalent toward private-sector development than in Wenzhou, informal financial institutions have nonetheless emerged in the form of clever disguises that are sanctioned by bureaucratic agencies outside of the financial hierarchy.

104. Cf. Kane, "Impact of Regulation"; and Parris, "Local Initiative."

5

Creative Capitalists in Henan

> It's the cradle of Chinese civilization. The Silk Road started from here. The Four Great Inventions spread from here. You are welcome to invest here and go sightseeing.
>
> —*Henan Province Homepage, 1998*

> "Northerners are more conservative than people in the coastal south. We aren't as adventurous or entrepreneurial as southern merchants."
>
> *Why is that?*
>
> The bicycle vendor smiled and patiently explained, "Northerners value their families and land more highly, so they are not willing to leave home for long—even if it means making a profit. People in the south think that we are quite friendly, but we are still basically country bumpkins. Southerners are shrewd in business."
>
> *Do you consider yourself a "country bumpkin"?*
>
> "I've done all right for myself in this small operation. Here I have a stable group of customers who only have their bikes fixed at my street corner. There's no reason for me to go down to a fancy place like Shanghai. I heard that they don't even ride bikes down there anymore. So I guess you could say that I play it safe."
>
> *But you said that you invest in futures through a local credit cooperative. Isn't that a bit risky?*
>
> "Not really. Everyone is doing it, so it would be riskier *not* to play the stock market."
>
> —Fieldnotes from Zhengzhou, Henan, 1996

In southern coastal areas local governments and cadres saw more to gain than lose from initiating and implementing economic reform.

Since the northern interior of China experienced the preponderance of "socialist construction" during the Mao era, standard political economic analyses would expect cadres in those areas to exhibit more resistance to marketizing reforms. Even in places like Henan, where cadres would appear to have a greater stake in preserving their state-subsidized positions, in many cases local cadres and entrepreneurs have succeeded in striking mutually profitable bargains. To be sure, substantial structural differences exist between the southern coastal and northern inland provinces, but such regional variation does not detract from the broader logic of financial institutional development. If anything, the spectrum of financial institutions run by private entrepreneurs in Henan lends even stronger support to the argument than to notoriously exceptional places like Wenzhou, which are known for their experimental tendencies. Given their proximity to Taiwan and Hong Kong, it is not surprising that provinces in the coastal south are more advanced commercially than the rest of the country. Likewise, the existence of creative financing mechanisms in the coastal south is consistent with the economic logic that areas with vibrant commercial sectors are more likely to require and spawn private financing arrangements. In contrast, entrepreneurs in a northern central province like Henan would not be expected to devise such creative forms of financing, and local governments might not be expected to be as tolerant toward private finance. After all, Henan represented a core province during the years of Mao's Stalinist-style industrial development strategy and was held up as a model during the Great Leap period (1958–61). This is not to say that Henan did not also suffer immensely from Maoist policies. It did.[1] But under Communist rule Henan had a more conservative (or "leftist") reputation than the southern coastal provinces.[2] As one historian put it, during the first decades of PRC rule, "politically, Zhengzhou (the capital of Henan) was simply a suburb of Beijing."[3] In other words, provincial leaders were especially sensitive to politics and demands emanating from the center.[4] Henan

1. For an account of Henan's tragic experience of 1958–61, see Jasper Becker, *China's Hungry Ghosts: Mao's Secret Famine* (New York: Free Press, 1996), 112–29. Estimates of the provincial death toll range from 2 to 8 million people. Ironically, the famine was most extreme in Xinyang, the model, first people's commune in China, where the most conservative estimate of a million deaths is equivalent to one-eighth of the population at the time.

2. The CCP also faced less difficulty in consolidating power in the northern central provinces. For Henan, see Odoric Y. K. Wou, *Mobilizing the Masses: Building Revolution in Henan* (Stanford, Calif.: Stanford University Press, 1994).

3. Jean-Luc Domenach, *The Origins of the Great Leap Forward: The Case of One Chinese Province*, trans. A. M. Berrett, (Boulder, Colo.: Westview Press, 1995), 158.

4. Dali Yang points out one reason that the Great Leap Forward was so devastating in Henan: the CCP had weak roots there, so provincial leaders were especially attuned to Beijing: *Calamity and Reform in China: State, Rural Society, and Institutional Change since the Great Leap Famine* (Stanford, Calif.: Stanford University Press, 1996).

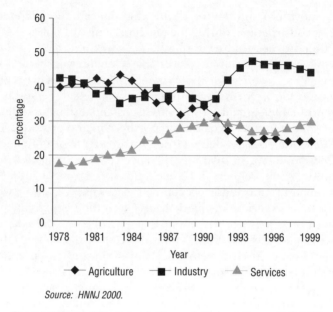

Source: HNNJ 2000.

Figure 5.1 Share of Production by Economic Sector in Henan, 1978–1999

may thus be viewed as a "least-likely case" comparison in my research design.[5]

Henan's Economic Structure and Developmental Challenges

On the eve of reform, as illustrated in Figure 5.1, economic production in Henan was dominated by industry and agriculture, as was the case in the rest of China. By 1992, however, services surpassed agriculture's contribution to Henan's economic output. Note that the share of industrial output actually increased slightly in the post-Mao years. But the increase in industrial production did not derive from the state-owned sector. Instead, as seen in Figure 5.2, collective and private enterprises played increasingly dominant roles in industrial production after the commencement of reform. The state sector declined from 74 percent of industrial output in 1978 to 28.8 percent in 1998. In other words, within the first two decades of reform, Henan's non-state sector increased to over 70 percent of industrial production.

The rise of the private sector in Henan has been most apparent in

5. Harry Eckstein, "Case Study and Theory in Political Science," in Fred I. Greenstein and Nelson W. Polsby, eds., *Handbook of Political Science*, vol. 1, *Political Science: Scope and Theory* (Reading, Mass.: Addison-Wesley, 1975).

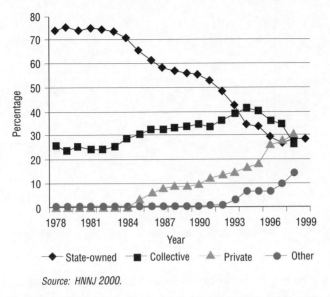

Source: HNNJ 2000.

Figure 5.2 Industrial Production by Ownership Type in Henan, 1978–1999

the production of retail consumer goods. In 1978 private enterprises accounted for only 0.2 percent of retail goods, while state enterprises accounted for 69.7 percent. By 1998 the share of the private sector had increased to 48.1 percent—larger than the state (18.8 percent), collective (16.1 percent), or other (16.9) sectors. Although the collective sector has taken on a greater share of industrial production in Henan since the beginning of reform, in the consumer retail sector it actually declined by over 12 percent, from 28.3 percent in 1978 to 16.1 percent in 1998 (see Figure 5.3). The "other" category, which emerged in Henan's official statistics after reform, includes joint ventures, which are technically classified as "foreign-invested enterprises." It was not until 1994 that provincial regulations were passed regarding the treatment of foreign investment.[6]

According to provincial statistics, by the beginning of 2000 the number of "individual commercial households" (*geti gongshang hu*)—small businesses with fewer than eight employees—reached 2.04 million, representing an increase of 62.5 percent since 1995 and an average annual growth rate of 12.5 percent in that five-year period.[7] Small businesses also reported

6. The "Regulations of Henan Province to Encourage Foreign Investment" were passed at the Eighth Session of the Standing Committee of the Eighth NPC of Henan Province on June 23, 1994. They were available on-line at <http://china-window.com/Henan_w/finance/frame1e.htm>, December 17, 1998.

7. Guo Lingling with Hu Guolei, "Wosheng fei gongyouzhi jingji fazhan taishi lianghao," (Our province's non-public economy is developing well), *Henan ribao* (HNRB–Henan daily), March 18, 1998; and *HNNJ 1999, 2000.*

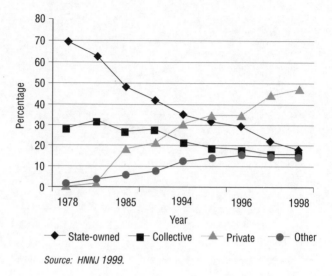

Source: HNNJ 1999.

Figure 5.3 Production of Retail Consumer Goods by Ownership Status in Henan, 1978–1998

significantly higher levels of registered capitalization in the second half of the 1990s: the total registered capitalization of *getihu* went from 6.2 billion to 13.4 billion *yuan*, which translates into a 25 percent annual growth rate over the five years.

Meanwhile, the number of "private enterprises" (*siying qiye*)—businesses employing more than eight persons—grew even more rapidly. By 2000 there were 45,172 registered *siying qiye*, representing an increase of 73.3 percent since 1995 and an annual average growth rate of 14.7 percent. Larger businesses also grew substantially in capital intensity: the total registered capitalization of *siying qiye* increased from 11.6 billion *yuan* at the end of 1995 to 28.7 billion *yuan* by the beginning of 2000, an average annual increase of 36.9 percent over that four-year period.[8] In 1998 the *Henan Ribao* (Henan Daily) reported that the pace of growth in the province's private sector ranked it among the top ten fastest-growing provinces in the country. As of year-end 1997, Henan ranked fifth of the country's thirty provincial units (i.e., twenty-two provinces, three municipalities, and five autonomous regions) in terms of *getihu* growth, and ninth in terms of *siying qiye* growth.[9]

Although the non-state sector already accounted for over 70 percent of

8. It is worth pointing out, however, that larger private enterprises have not become more labor-intensive. The number of people employed in *siying qiye* increased at a more modest annual rate of 3.8 percent over the same period. In contrast, the number of people employed in the *geti* sector grew at an annual rate of 14.9 percent. *HNNJ*, various years.

9. *HNRB*, March 18, 1998.

the industrial workforce as of 1998, the provincial government remains keenly aware of the fact that Henan has been more of national laggard in implementing state sector reform and attracting foreign investment.[10] The former problem is evidenced most vividly by the increasing incidence of strikes and protests by state workers in recent years—and foreign investment is viewed as a potential panacea to mass unemployment.[11] In the 1998 conference "Opening Up to the Outside World," Ma Zhongchen then secretary of the Provincial Party Committee and governor, observed,

> The problems that [have] emerged in our current economic life are contradictions that have accumulated over a long period, and they are problems exposed in a concentrated manner, indicating that the province's economy is in a fairly difficult period in which systems and structures are being changed. . . . [Therefore,] we should attach importance to introducing foreign capital and strategically reorganizing the state-owned economy.[12]

Governor Ma added that Henan faces challenges in attracting foreign investors, however, because "the province lacks new hot spots for investment, essential demand is inadequate, and the employment contradiction is prominent." His proposed solution was to play up Henan's attractiveness as an international tourist destination, while continuing to hold international and investment fairs.[13]

Apart from relatively recent efforts at attracting foreign capital, during the reform era the province has focused more on creating internal solutions for internal developmental dilemmas. With a population of over 92 million people, Henan became the most populous province in China after Chongqing was administratively separated from Sichuan in 1997. Yet Henan's total economic output in the same year ranked seventh in the country, and its per capita GDP ranked even lower at the twentieth position.[14] As *Henan Ribao* reporters put it, "The large population is like a large and cruel 'denominator.' "[15] Since the gap between its large population and

10. "Henan Non-State Industries Enjoy Boom Cycle," *Xinhua News Agency*, September 17, 1998, reported in FBIS-CHI-98-260.

11. According to the General Office of the Henan Federation of Trade Unions, in 1998 there were 247 street protests and demonstrations in Henan, involving 33,318 people—an increase from the previous year of 100.8 percent in the number of protests and 79.4 percent in the number of people involved from the previous year: *Gonghuixinwen* (Trade union news), no. 4 (1999).

12. "Henan Holds Meeting on Opening Up," *HNRB*, May 28, 1998, 1–2, reported in FBIS-CHI-98-161.

13. E.g., Henan started holding Commodities Fairs in 1996 and has hosted many other specialized trade shows since then: "Zhengzhou Commodities Fair Attracts Foreign Investment," *Xinhua News Agency*, September 3, 1996, reported in FBIS-CHI-96-171.

14. Henan Window, ⟨http://china-window.com/Henan_w/finance/zhsle.htm⟩, December 17, 1998.

15. Li Peng, Wang Xuefei, and Wang Binglong, "Display New Achievements in the 15th

modest economic performance was flagged at the Fourteenth National Party Congress in October 1992, the provincial government initiated a development strategy dubbed "one high and one low" to increase the rate of economic growth and decrease the rate of population growth. The economic component of the strategy included promoting key projects in energy, communications, and infrastructure development, as well as encouraging TVEs, the upgrading of agricultural technology, and heightened efforts to alleviate poverty in Henan's thirty-four officially impoverished counties. At the Fifteenth National Party Congress in 1997, Henan was able to report success in keeping its population growth below the national average and maintaining above-average growth rates; and by the end of 1998 it could report that the impoverished population had been reduced to 3.16 million people from 25 million in the late 1980s.[16] Nonetheless, the disparity between its population and productive output remains.

Zhengzhou City

Once an imperial seat of the Shang Dynasty (1766–1122 B.C.), Zhengzhou has been continuously populated for over 4,000 years; its earliest settlement dates back to 2100 B.C. After the Shang period, neighboring Anyang emerged as a dynastic capital, but after the PRC was established, Zhengzhou regained its stature as the provincial capital of Henan.[17] The city started to develop as an industrial center in 1898 when foreign contracts were granted for the building of two strategic railway lines: the north-south Beijing-Guangzhou express route and the east-west Shanghai-Xi'an route. Because of its importance as a railway center, Japanese forces targeted Zhengzhou during the 1937 offensive. Since 1949 it has developed into an industrial center, as evidenced by the mammoth Soviet-style facto-

National Party Congress: Brilliant Achievements in 'One High and One Low,'" *HNRB*, August 23, 1997, 1–2, reported in FBIS-CHI-97-266. Cf. Sun Jie and Wang Amin, "Henan Party Secretary on Being Most Populous Province," *Xinhua News Agency*, March 14, 1997, reported in FBIS-CHI-97-081.

16. Since 1996, Henan has spent over 1.7 billion *yuan* (US$200 million) on poverty alleviation: "Henan Province to Implement Poverty Reduction Program," *Xinhua News Agency*, February 26, 2001, reported in FBIS-CHI-2001-0226. Note that the central government's poverty line is set at a per capita income of 550 *yuan* per year: "Henan Cites Success in Poverty Elimination Efforts," *Xinhua News Agency*, August 2, 1999, reported in FBIS-CHI-1999-0801; and "Henan Reports Success in Drive against Poverty," *Xinhua News Agency*, January 26, 1998, reported in FBIS-CHI-98-025. The province, however, set the standard somewhat lower, at 450–500 *yuan* per year, to reflect local prices and consumption: "Henan Sets Minimum Living Standard for Farmers," *Xinhua News Agency*, July 6, 1997, reported in FBIS-CHI-97-187.

17. Zhengzhou was officially liberated by the CCP on October 22, 1948. The Henan Provincial People's Government moved from Kaifeng to Zhengzhou in 1954.

ries lining block after block in the western part of the city. The factories produce electrical equipment, textile machinery, agricultural tools and machinery, and aluminum products. As in other provincial capitals, citizens of Zhengzhou did not suffer as extensively from the Great Leap famine as their counterparts in rural Henan. In the reform era, however, the apparent benefits of heavy industrialization have brought their share of developmental dilemmas. The first phase of reform—agricultural decollectivization—had the effect of flooding the streets of Zhengzhou with surplus labor from the countryside.[18] These earliest migrants became vegetable vendors, peddlers, and, many locals claimed, "criminals."

Although official recognition of private enterprise in Henan lagged behind the southern coastal provinces, Zhengzhou's government was still a few steps ahead of the central government in issuing rules to regulate the reemergence of private entrepreneurs. The provincial Industrial and Commercial Bureau (ICMB) was reestablished in 1979, and the Individual Laborers' Association (ILA)—the mass organization meant to represent the interests of *getihu*—was established in 1984. By the beginning of 2000 the Zhengzhou City ICMB reported that there were 158,378 individual businesses (*getihu*) and 6,631 private enterprises (*siying qiye*), more than double the number in 1995.[19] The total reported capitalization of *getihu* and *siying* businesses at the outset of 2000 was 2 billion and 3.27 billion *yuan*, respectively, for an average annual increase of approximately 20 percent since 1995.

Despite Zhengzhou's reputation as the bastion of Maoist heavy industrial complexes, the liberalizing effects of reform are evident in the proliferation of specialized wholesale and commercial retail markets all over the city. Dilapidated factory buildings that once housed Soviet-influenced machinery have been partitioned into individual stalls and leased out to private vendors (*getihu*). Wholesale markets serving the greater city district have been established all over town, specializing in fruits and vegetables, meat, dried edibles, bottled beverages, packaged snacks, books, clothing, shoes, motorcycles, coal, agricultural implements, construction materials, electrical equipment, and assorted household products.[20] Some commer-

18. Note that Zhengzhou Municipality comprises six urban "districts" (*qu*) and six rural "counties" (*xian*). Nearly 70 percent of Zhengzhou's population of 6 million people (not including an estimated 600,000 migrant workers on any given day) are registered as residing in rural areas. "Zhengzhou Becomes Regional Commercial Center," *Xinhua News Agency*, June 20, 1998, reported in FBIS-CHI-98-171.

19. *Zhengzhou tongji nianjian 2000* (Zhengzhou statistical yearbook 2000).

20. As of 1996 there were 102 wholesale markets in Zhengzhou; before 1990 there were only nine. In 1996 about a third of them were classified as production materials markets, over half were industrial consumer products markets, and 20 percent were agricultural and related products markets. They are generally established by one of the following entities: the ICMB; industrial enterprises that have unused space on their premises; state-owned enterprises;

cial retail sections of town are also specialized—one street may have only outdoor clothing and shoe stands; the next block over, only fruit and vegetable vendors—whereas others possess a relatively balanced mix of consumer goods but may be dominated by private entrepreneurs with similar geographical backgrounds.

Although Zhengzhou's ICMB is trying to establish dedicated market areas for private entrepreneurs, seasonal *getihu* from rural areas often prefer to bypass the bureaucratic procedures required for registering with the ICMB and renting an officially designated stall. Itinerant vendors sometimes set up right at the gates of a market complex and sell the same products as the neighboring specialized market. In mid-1996, for example, outside one wholesale fruit market, my research assistant and I saw half a dozen vendors selling peaches and apples from the backs of their bicycle carts. As it turned out, they were all from the same village in Zhangmo County, outside of Zhengzhou City proper.[21] The farmers explained that it did not make sense for them to rent a permanent space inside the wholesaling market because that would cost them 500 *yuan* a month, and they typically earned only 300 *yuan* a month, since they could not sell fruit on the same scale as professional wholesalers. When asked if they had considered pooling their homegrown fruit and renting a stall together, the vendors responded that it would be difficult to rent a place in the market because none of them had urban household registrations, nor were they sufficiently literate to fill out the requisite forms. The best-educated of the group was a fifty-year-old woman who had finished elementary school; the others had completed only a few years of primary education. They had never really thought about registering with the ICMB as a realistic possibility. Instead, the farmers figured that they could simply ride their bikes into town, sell fruit casually for a few hours, and ride back home.

They quickly discovered that the life of an itinerant vendor is challenging and sometimes dangerous. The ICMB's policy on regulating "floating street peddlers" (*liudong tanr*) is that they should pay a three-*yuan* fee for

---

city/township/village governments and neighborhood street committees in collaboration with one another; national, provincial, and city-level collaboration: He Yongxin, "Zhengzhoushi pifa shichang fazhan qingkuang" (The developing conditions of Zhengzhou City's wholesaling markets), *Jingji yanjiu cankao* (Reference for economic research) 15 (January 26, 1996): 34–37. Cf. Zhengzhoushi benketizu (Study group of Zhengzhou as a trade city), "Guanyu Zhengzhoushi pifa shichang fazhan duice yanjiu" (Policy implications and research on the development of Zhengzhou's wholesaling market), *Jingji yanjiu cankao* (Reference for economic research) 1 (January 1, 1996): 2–5; and Zhengzhou maoyi cheng jianshe ketizhu (Study group on building trade in Zhengzhou City), "Guanyu jiakuai Zhengzhou maoyi cheng jianshe de sikao" (Reflections on speeding up the construction of trade in Zhengzhou), *Shangye jingji, shangye qiye guanli* (Commercial economy and the management of commercial enterprises) 4 (1993): 117–20.

21. Their hometown, Zhang Village, has a population of only 6,000 people. Survey Nos. 279, 280.

each day of operation. Similarly, the Sanitation Bureau charges floating *getihu* two *yuan* a day for cluttering up the street. In practice, this means that when ICMB and Sanitation Bureau cadres spot mobile vendors on their daily rounds, they automatically collect the daily fee. If, however, the fee collectors are "unhappy" or do not like the attitude of the *getihu*, then they may fine a vendor anywhere from 20 to 200 *yuan* and still collect the more nominal two to three *yuan* fee. When a vendor is either unwilling or unable to pay on the spot, the collectors may resort to physical coercion and confiscate the bike. In such cases, the bike-less vendor then has to go all the way home to get the money. By the time the fine is paid and the bike retrieved, all the fruit in the back of the bicycle cart will have rotted, and three days of business have been lost.

Other "*getihu* ghettos" within Zhengzhou City have concentrations of vendors from farther away. A market complex on Agricultural Road West, for example, originally consisted of migrants from Yiwu County in Zhejiang Province.[22] In mid-1995 an entrepreneur from Yiwu County traveled to Zhengzhou to see if he could start up a market that would introduce products from the coastal south to the northern interior. With the help of a friend in the Zhengzhou traffic police he tracked down an abandoned lot next to some chemical factories in the northern district of Wangshan and leased the entire property.[23] Then he went back to Yiwu and recruited local entrepreneurs with the promise of tapping a new market at low rents.[24] The Yiwu Small Commercial Products Market opened on November 8, 1995. Some three hundred vendors paid 10,000 *yuan* up front in cash to lease their twelve-by-fifteen retail lots for five years (with a tax-free grace period in the first year) and arrived with assorted low-end merchandise from Zhejiang, Fujian, and Guangdong.

When I first visited the Yiwu market during the summer of 1996, business was sluggish, and it still looked stagnant during follow-up visits in October 1996 and May 1997. Unlike the heavily trafficked market districts in more central parts of Zhengzhou, the Yiwu market clearly had more

---

22. Survey Nos. 195, 196, 197, 198, 199, 200, 201, 202.

23. The local newspaper reported the market's establishment somewhat differently. Credit was given to the highest leaders of the ICMB in Yiwu and Zhengzhou, respectively. See Wen Yong, Xiao Xu, and Jian Ling, "Jiangnan mingzhu yao zhongyuan—Yiwu xiao shangpin shichang Zhengzhou fen shichang fazhan jishi" (A bright pearl in the center of the Jiangnan region—An account of the Zhengzhou branch of the Yiwu small commercial products market), *HNRB*, July 17, 1996, 6.

24. He compared his vision with that of Zhejiang Village in Beijing; see Xiang Biao, "Beijing youge 'Zhejiangcun'" (Beijing has a 'Zhejiang Village'), *Shehuixue yu shehui diaocha* (Sociology and social investigation) 3 (1993): 36–39; Xiang Biao, "Chuantong yu xin shehui kongjian de shengcheng" (Tradition and the formation of a new social space), *Zhanlue yu guanli* (Strategy and Management) 6 (1996): 99–111; and Li Zhang, *Strangers in the City: Reconfigurations of Space, Power, and Social Networks within China's Floating Population* (Stanford, Calif.: Stanford University Press, 2001).

vendors than customers. The vendors I surveyed confirmed that business had been much better for them in Zhejiang than in Henan; many said that they were planning to return home in a few months if things did not pick up, even if it meant taking a loss on their initial 10,000 *yuan* investment. In addition to the costs of purchasing their retail space and of leaving business behind in their hometowns, the vendors continued to incur various monthly operating charges in Zhengzhou, including an average of 25 *yuan* in water and electric fees, 20 for the ICMB fee, and 100 in sales tax. Because business was so poor, when any member of the migrant market community wanted to travel back to Yiwu to visit relatives, other vendors would pool their cash and lend it to the traveler so that he or she would not have to go home empty-handed.

By June 2001 there had been substantial turnover in vendors, and the five-year rent had increased to 15,000 *yuan*.[25] Most of the Yiwu vendors had left, and the market was full of migrant entrepreneurs from Jiangsu, Shandong, and other provinces. Despite the less than ideal conditions, during my first visit in 1996 it was apparent that the non-Yiwu business owners tended to be less dissatisfied than their Yiwu counterparts. The Yiwu merchants seemed to have higher expectations than those from areas where commerce is less developed than Zhejiang. For example, I surveyed a mobile fast food vendor from a rural mountainous part of Xi'an who raved about the increase in her family's standard of living after moving to Zhengzhou.[26] As of mid-1996 the thirty-five-year-old illiterate woman had been selling soy noodles for 1.8 *yuan* a bowl for about five months. Her husband stayed at home to make the soy meal for the noodles, while she spent an average of eleven hours a day selling the bowls of noodles retail. It had cost them 500 *yuan* to purchase the mobile noodle stand, but since the business was netting about 500 *yuan* a month, it was worth the investment. Back home in Xi'an they had had only enough land to harvest food for subsistence purposes. Her younger brother had lent her 1,000 *yuan* at 30 percent interest for the couple to make the trip to Zhengzhou and start the business.

In addition to market clusters of migrant entrepreneurs, a number of specialized markets are based upon the networks connecting former workers of a particular factory. It is not uncommon to find a market filling an entire block where private entrepreneurs who were all laid off from the same factory are selling products that reflect the focus of their former employer. In such cases, the shared *danwei* experience may enhance the ability of market vendors to overcome collective action problems that store

25. By June 2001, when one of my research assistants paid a follow-up visit and interviewed several vendors, a rumor was circulating that the market had originally been established by entrepreneurs from Urumqi, Xinjiang, rather than Yiwu, Zhejiang.

26. Survey No. 198.

owners in other markets may face in case of a common grievance. My interviews in a traditional Chinese arts and crafts market illustrate this dynamic.

In mid-1996, Mrs. Hua was a fifty-year-old, high-school-educated owner of a traditional Chinese arts and crafts store.[27] She had worked as a jade sculptor for a state-owned enterprise for thirty years but retired two years before the official retirement age for women because the factory apparently went bankrupt—though it somehow manages to provide 400 *yuan* a month to the early retirees. Many retired workers from this *danwei* set up shop on the block and sold similar products.

In early 1996 the arts and crafts vendors experienced repeated harassment from various uniformed officials claiming to be tax collectors.[28] The collections seemed utterly arbitrary, and it was not clear to the owners which fees were legitimately owed. Mrs. Hua cited a litany of monthly changes: "20 *yuan* for sanitation, an environmental fee of 10 *yuan*, 30 *yuan* for a license to sell art, a 'city face lift' fee of 15 *yuan,* and 50 *yuan* for the cadres' nicotine habit, etc." Fed up with the constant demand for random fees, the arts and crafts vendors approached the Industrial and Commercial Management Bureau together and demanded that only one official be sent to their market each month to collect whatever fees were legally owed to the city government. The office agreed to their demands, and at the time of my visit six months later, the vendors said they had since succeeded in turning away opportunistic or corrupt cadres.

Kaifeng City

Kaifeng served as the capital of seven imperial dynasties and reached the peak of its imperial grandeur during the Northern Song (960–1127). Several thousand Muslims migrated from Bukhara, Uzbekistan, and settled in Kaifeng in 1070. After the Ruzhen (or Jurchen) of Manchuria invaded Kaifeng in 1126 and set up their Jin dynasty in northern China, Hangzhou became the capital of the Southern Song (1127–79). Meanwhile, Jewish migrants of Mediterranean origin migrated to Kaifeng from Hangzhou and played significant roles in banking and commerce during the fourteenth and fifteenth centuries.[29] Kaifeng became the provincial capital during the

27. Survey No. 251.

28. This was corroborated by other vendors in the market: Survey Nos. 252, 253, 254, 255.

29. Chinese historian Wang Yisha admits the possibility that Jews first arrived China in the first or second century via the Silk Road, but there is stronger evidence (based on stone inscriptions in synagogues) that Jewish cotton merchants first settled in Kaifeng during the Northern Song: Wang Yisha, "The Descendants of the Kaifeng Jews," in Sidney Shapiro, ed., *Jews in Old China: Studies by Chinese Scholars* (New York: Hippocrene Books, 1984), 167–88. Cf.

Ming (1368–1644) and Qing (1644–1911) dynasties. During the dynastic transition in 1644, local officials released the Yellow River's dikes to forestall the Manchu invasion, which resulted in a catastrophic flood that killed over 300,000 people. Since 1949, Kaifeng has developed a modest industrial base consisting of electrical, chemical, and agricultural machinery plants, as well as flour and edible oil processing mills. Locals openly admit, however, that Kaifeng's commercial impulses were never fully suppressed during the Mao era, when merchants were gradually relegated to one of the lowest tiers of Communist society and therefore disadvantaged when it came to receiving assignments in the *danwei* system. In Kaifeng, however, enterprising Muslims bore the brunt of such discriminatory employment by the state. As a result many of the *getihu* on the streets of Kaifeng in the late 1990s came from families with many generations of experience as self-employed workers.

The case of Mrs. Li, an elderly Muslim who sells Middle Eastern pastries out of the back of a bicycle cart, is not untypical.[30] When she was eighteen (in 1940, during the Anti-Japanese War), she was married off by her parents to a man twenty-one years her senior, who already had one wife. In traditional Chinese style, she did not know what her husband looked like until the wedding day. In traditional Islamic style, as the second wife she was not permitted to speak in the household and spent her days looking after the nine children (three daughters from the first wife, five daughters of her own, and an adopted son). Her husband ran a tea shop, but the People's Liberation Army destroyed it during the revolution. After liberation she and her husband pulled garbage-transporting carts for a living, and each earned one *yuan* per day. After the famine she started selling sheep brain soup on the street to support the family. Now she lives with one daughter and one son but continues to work because their collective earnings are insufficient for the whole family.

Notwithstanding the economic difficulties of vendors like Mrs. Li, locals on the whole view the Muslim population as being relatively well off. Since the beginning of reform, Muslim restaurants and stores have proliferated in the form of established storefronts and night markets, and mosques have been renovated with expensive building materials.

Jiang Qingxiang and Xiao Guoliang, "Glimpses of the Urban Economy of Bianjing, Capital of the Northern Song Dynasty," in Shapiro, *Jews in Old China*, 103–17. Jesuit accounts summarized by Marcus N. Alder conclude that Jews settled in China even earlier, during the Han Dynasty (220 B.C.–220 A.D.), probably after 34 A.D. when Jews were executed en masse in Babylon: "Chinese Jews" (lecture delivered at the Jews' College Literary Society, Queen Square House, London, June 17, 1900), in Hyman Kublin, ed., *Jews in Old China: Some Western Views* (New York: Paragon, 1971), 94–117. In the last few years Kaifeng's leaders have apparently been attempting to use the city's distant connection to Judaism as a means to attract foreign investment: "China: A Jewish Question," *Economist*, December 3, 1994, 46.

30. Survey No. 216.

The private sector in Kaifeng has grown steadily. During the early to middle 1990s the annual growth rate in small and larger businesses averaged 20 and 33 percent, respectively.[31] By 2000 there were 114,800 registered small businesses (*getihu*) and 1,955 private enterprises (*siying qiye*), representing an absolute increase of 75.1 and 244.6 percent, respectively, since 1995.[32] Although such increases sound substantial, the Kaifeng ICMB reports that private-sector growth is slower than projected and is unevenly distributed among different areas. During my first visit in mid-1996, for example, the bulk of private-sector growth was concentrated in urban and peri-urban districts of Kaifeng, while participation in the private sector actually appeared to be declining in rural areas. Official statistics are not available to track the migration of Kaifeng's entrepreneurs, but it is evident that people in the neighboring rural areas have been moving to Kaifeng, and Kaifeng's enterprising urbanites have been moving to larger cities such as Zhengzhou.

One such example is Mr. Wang, who in 1996 was a thirty-four-year-old, high-school-educated owner of a six-month-old store in Zhengzhou, where he sold rare and exotic fish for decorative or recreational (not consumption) purposes.[33] Although he and his family maintain a rural household registration status in Kaifeng, he is a seasoned *getihu*. He ran a large restaurant from 1984 to 1986, took out a 3,000-*yuan* loan from an RCC in 1986 at 9 percent interest in order to sell cloth for another six years, and went into the jewelry business for a few years before opening this fish shop with 10,000 *yuan* of his savings. Mr. Wang imports the fish from Tianjin, Guangzhou, Beijing, Suzhou, and even Brazil. The store generally earns a minimum of 1,000 *yuan* a month and sometimes as much as 5,000. Mr. Wang's parents remain in Kaifeng, and his younger brother works on the family's shared eight *mu* of land, which is scattered all over the place. They plant only enough for the family's consumption, though his eleven-year-old daughter and eight-year-old son added that they also raise pigs and cows and own one horse and one donkey.[34]

There is no dearth of ambitious entrepreneurs among the generation that was born after the Cultural Revolution and during the early years of reform. Having come of age during the first two decades of reform and experienced ongoing increases in the standard of living, this generation is

31. Kaifengshi gongshanghang zheng guanliju wenjian (Kaifeng City ICMB document [no. 201]), "Guanyu quanshi shang bannian geti jingying fazhan qingkuang de tongbao" (Circular on the situation of the developmental conditions of the private economy in the entire city during the first half of the year), July 10, 1996.

32. *HNNJ 2000.*

33. Survey No. 253.

34. The Wangs had to pay a fine of 500 *yuan* in 1988 for having an "above-quota" second child. He indicated that these days families would have to pay 10,000 *yuan*.

surrounded by evidence that self-employment may be quite rewarding, both personally and financially. Rural residents may see their relatives who have ventured to urban areas return with considerable sums of cash during the holidays, and urbanites see a wide range of private income-generating opportunities on a daily basis. A number of young business owners I surveyed in urban areas had gone through the traditional PRC channels of being assigned to a state unit upon graduation from school but then started private businesses on the side.

A particularly active entrepreneur whom we met in 1996 was Mr. Chang, a twenty-two-year-old owner of a KTV (Karaoke) club in downtown Kaifeng.[35] He greeted my assistant and me warmly at the door even though 6:00 P.M. was a bit early for such an establishment to be open for business on a Friday. Inside, it was obvious that this was not simply a bar with karaoke entertainment. The dark, foul-smelling hall was lined with spacious semi-private booths, which could be made more private by drawing close the stained orange velveteen curtains that framed them. Before we could either leave or introduce ourselves, Mr. Chang motioned to a young woman to serve us tea and lychee nuts. Our host was surprised to hear that we were academics rather than the plainclothes officials that he was expecting; apparently, a friend had tipped him off that cadres were making inspection rounds of KTV clubs that evening to search out the use of "illegal female companions." He explained that the inspectors "aren't supposed to arrive my place until 10:20 P.M., but I thought that maybe someone was doing me a favor by sending them over before my usual customers arrive." We were surprised by his candor and even more surprised by his business card, which listed him as a manager in the Kaifeng Cigarette Factory, a partner in a private futures trading company, and the owner of the KTV club. The use of a single business card to denote such varied occupations seemed odd. As it turned out, this curriculum vitae reflected Mr. Chang's confidence that people would respect his ability to wear so many prestigious hats at a young age (apparently, he had been working since the age of seventeen). Several hours into the interview he also claimed to wear a hat that was not listed on the packed business card—a plainclothes security officer.[36]

Regardless of whether that was true at the time, the information that he shared with us about the operation of the KTV den was revealing (and consistent with other accounts of running such a business). At the time of the interview, his club had been in business for only ten months. Mr. Chang explained that the actual space was state-owned, but he was able to rent it

---

35. Survey No. 232.

36. About nine months after the initial interview we discovered that he was a different type of cadre. I have changed biographical details to preserve his anonymity.

for 2,200 *yuan* per month from the Transportation Management Office because he had worked there. And because he had saved several thousand *yuan* from trading futures, he did not have to borrow money from banks or friends to start up the club. He simply took 3,000 *yuan* out of his savings account to lease the retail space and then recruited low-wage employees from the local labor market (*laowu shichang*). The club employed three permanent female hostesses and sixteenth part-timers. The full-time workers received a base salary of 300 *yuan* a month plus 20 *yuan* for "each customer she succeeds in accompanying." The part-time hostesses, some of whom were Henan University college students with extra time during their summer vacations, earned an average of 30 *yuan* per hour. On a busy night the hostesses could make 200 *yuan* plus gratuities. During peak business periods, the KTV club could net over 10,000 *yuan*, but Mr. Chang spoke like any other entrepreneur: "You have to understand that this is a seasonal business—it's best in the fall and spring, right around Spring Festival." Just as he was beginning to explain the seasonal intricacies of the demand for female escorts, a uniformed public security cadre entered the club and joined us on the rounded leatherette couch. Mr. Chang introduced his friend briefly and continued to discuss the challenges of running such a business. He explained that he would like to run a larger and fancier operation, but felt that he needed more experience before doing so. I asked him if by "experience" he meant "*guanxi*," and he nodded with a smile.

Luoyang City

Although little evidence of its rich history can be seen today, Luoyang has a past equally if not more impressive than that of Kaifeng. Luoyang dates back to 1200 B.C. and served as the capital of ten imperial dynasties. It was also the site of Buddhism's introduction from India and the birthplace of prominent scientists, astronomers, and writers. But it fell into relative obscurity after the northern Jin relocated their capital to Bian Jing (present-day Kaifeng) in 937 A.D. The CCP revitalized Luoyang by building it into a Stalinist-style industrial center. Because it lies in a river basin flanked by mountains, the city was an industrial base for the First Five-Year-Plan and the Third Front industrial development strategy as well. As one interviewee put it, "Luoyang was about as safe you could get from the American imperialists."[37] The PLA has maintained a solid presence in Luoyang as evidenced by the rows of mammoth heavy-industrial factories—chemi-

37. Interview No. 87. Note that Luoyang is on the railway line between Xi'an and Zhengzhou, so it is more accessible than many other parts of Henan.

cals, glass works, textiles, machine-building—identified only by numbers rather than proper names. The factories in Luoyang dwarf even those in Zhengzhou; some employ up to 50,000 workers.

In many ways, as of the mid-1990s Luoyang looked as if economic reform had not reached so far inland. During my visit in August 1996, bikes remained the primary means of transportation, and the only motorized vehicles on the muddy (yet dusty) roads were old buses, blue cargo trucks, and yellow van taxis (*mianbao che*).[38] An eighteenth-foot statue of Chairman Mao remained erect in front of the ten-block-long No. 1 Tractor Factory (also known as the model "East Is Red Tractor Factory"), which produced tanks for the army not too long ago. In public, people still called one another "comrade," and billboards displaying revolutionary-inspirational slogans could be seen on every other street corner. Yet despite this initial pre-reform appearance, closer inspection showed *getihu* lined up against the edges of the drab gray factory buildings and down the long alleys between them. And according to Luoyang's ICMB, the number of registered private entrepreneurs is growing, though not as fast as the city would like. Between 1995 and 1996, the number of registered *getihu* increased by 26.8 percent and the number of *siying qiye* by 62.2 percent.

The ICMB also highlighted a number of trends in the midyear progress report of 1996.[39] First, it noted that private-sector growth was concentrated in the service sector: the number of private entrepreneurs (both *geti* and *siying*) engaged in agricultural activities accounted for only 0.05 percent of the total registered entrepreneurs (94,774), and those engaged in manufacturing made up 12.1 percent, but private businesses in the service industry constituted 87.9 percent of the total. Second, the apparent growth in the absolute numbers of registered entrepreneurs should be interpreted in light of the level of business failures versus the establishment of new businesses. In other words, the nominal increase in registered entrepreneurs may have stemmed from the fact that fewer were going out of business (only 4,527 private businesses had shut down during the first half of 1996, compared with 9,199 closures during the same period in 1995). The number of newly registered businesses in 1996 had actually declined relative to the previous year (7,473 during the first half of 1996 versus 7,787 during the first half of 1995). Put another way, in 1995, 1.2 times more businesses had shut down than were newly registered, whereas in 1996 the

38. Because of their poor safety standards, *mianbao che* had already been banned from Beijing by that time.

39. Luoyangshi gongshang xingzheng guanliju (Luoyang City Industrial and Commercial Administrative Management Office), "1996 nian geti siying jingji fazhan bannian qingkuang tongbao" (The individual and private economy in 1996; circular on developments in the first half year), July 3, 1996.

number of businesses that declared bankruptcy represented only 60.6 percent of the newly established ones. Despite this apparent progress, the mid year report admitted that when the numbers of bankruptcies were taken into account, the actual growth in private enterprise was up only 2.8 percent from the previous year—far short of the ICMB's targeted growth rate of 22 percent.

By the beginning of 2000, however, Luoyang had 179,746 registered *getihu* and 7,499 *siying qiye*, which meant that its private-sector development had caught up with that of Zhengzhou or Kaifeng by the end of the 1990s. Indeed, between 1995 and early 2000, registered *geti* and *siying* businesses increased annually by an average of 29.7 and 60.6 percent, respectively. This apparent growth may be attributed to the increased efforts of the ICMB to locate and register larger private enterprises once the state-sector reforms announced at the Fifteenth Party Congress in late 1997 had acknowledged the increasing importance of the private sector to China's economy.

Given the preponderance of Mao-era heavy industry in Luoyang, it is not surprising that most of the vendors I surveyed were former employees of SOEs or administrative *danweis*. Some of the entrepreneurs went into business because they were essentially laid off from their factories (i.e., wages were not being paid). Others, were bored with their positions, decided to "jump into the sea of business" (*xiahai*) and earn more money. Mr. Shu's experience is characteristic of the latter scenario.

After working for eleven years as a midlevel accountant in a government agency, then thirty-one-year-old Mr. Shu decided to take a leave of absence (*tingxin liuzhi*) and go into private business.[40] In reality, he never had any intention of returning to work, but he gave his superiors face by not quitting outright and as of 1996 he did not think that they had missed him in his two-year absence.) His desk job was busy but boring. Since he would much prefer to spend all day reading rather than stooped over sixteen-column ledgers, he decided to open a bookstore. He had heard through a high school classmate that the old movie theater in which they used to watch revolutionary war films had been converted into a series of open-faced private market stalls—all of which sold books. During my visit, the former theater was indeed packed with vendors selling a wide range of publications, from children's books and sports magazines to hard-cover collections of classical poetry, Mao Zedong thought, and PRC tax laws.[41] Mr. Shu rents his stall for 500 *yuan* a month and pays a host of additional

40. Survey No. 265.
41. By U.S. standards, the theater would be considered a fire hazard, as one of the two exits was obstructed by high stacks of newspapers. Moreover, because the overhead light had long ceased to work, each stall used a raw wire extension that wove through makeshift bookshelves to hang a single light bulb.

monthly fees: 40 *yuan* for electricity, 10 for sanitation, 150 for the ICMB fee, 15 for security, 50 in taxes. Although he feels that there are too many fees and taxes, Mr. Shu admits that he probably pays less than some of the neighboring vendors do, for thanks to his previous employment, he is well-connected. Governmental affiliation has not only provided tax breaks but enabled him to borrow working capital from the Industrial and Commercial Bank, the Agricultural Bank, and a UCC. Initially, when Mr. Shu applied for loans as an individual entrepreneur, various banks all refused him. It was only when he convinced his *danwei* to serve as a guarantor that the ICB and ABOC approved his loan application. Running a business is definitely more challenging than his old job, but Mr. Shu feels that it is worth the hassle, financially speaking. His wife earns only 500 *yuan* a month as a manual worker in a freezer factory. He now earns three times as much as she does, thanks to the book business, and he hopes to send his seven-year-old son to college.

In cases where state workers have been laid off, the attitude toward self-employment is somewhat less positive. Ms. Yin, for example, a junior high school graduate, in 1996 was a thirty-year-old woman selling soft drinks at an outdoor stand in the commercial section of Luoyang's Old Town.[42] In 1994 the state-owned department store where she had worked for ten years simply closed down. The laid-off workers were not offered any form of unemployment compensation, and even the retirement age employees lost their pensions. Since her husband earned only 350 *yuan* a month as a railway worker and they had a five-year old son, Ms. Yin knew that she had to find another source of income immediately, so she spent the entire 6,000 *yuan* of her household's savings to purchase a mobile refrigerator and a variety of soft drinks. The initial investment quickly paid off. During summer months her net income averages 1,500 *yuan*, and even during cooler seasons she earns more than her previous income of 300 *yuan*. Nonetheless, Ms. Yin is unhappy with her life. She now works twice as long as she used to (twelve-hour days versus the leisurely pace of state employment) and worries constantly about the viability of her soft drink business. "I did not choose to become self-employed," she explained. "I was forced to jump into the sea of private business."

As in the other research sites, it was apparent that the *getihu* in Luoyang are subject to arbitrary demands for assorted fees and taxes by different bureaucratic agencies. The Industrial and Commercial Management Bureau has the authority to regulate private businesses, so its blue-uniformed staff are essentially given the freedom to extract fees by whatever means possible. Since vendors cannot always predict when the ICMB will show up, they are often caught unprepared and either do not have the cash

42. Survey No. 268.

available to make the payments or simply refuse to do so. When vendors refuse the ICMB's demands, the collecters may confiscate the store's merchandise until the fee is paid or ransack the displays to show other vendors the consequences of noncompliance. In Luoyang, ICMB personnel actually drove around the city in packs, with some riding in large blue pickup trucks and others on motorcycles. The rationale for traveling in numbers became apparent when we watched an ICMB group work through a street corner lined with sidewalk vendors selling vegetables and low-end consumer products. About six of the twelve ICMB cadres approached the *getihu* and demanded that they each pay a 10-*yuan* fine for selling merchandise without displaying the appropriate ICMB registration licenses. One vendor refused and said that the local neighborhood committee had given them permission to use that particular corner for retail space. The explanation did not suffice. The ICMB cadres motioned to the others waiting in the pickup truck, and they proceeded to confiscate the vendors' products and load them into the back of the truck. Many of the *getihu* resisted their confiscatory efforts physically but were overpowered by sheer numbers. Even the most frail-looking elderly vendors were not spared.[43]

Impoverished Counties

In 1996 Luoyang may have appeared "un-reformed" relative to urban centers such as Beijing and Zhengzhou, but at least it exhibited evidence of capital investment from the Mao era. In contrast, many isolated rural areas in Henan remain truly underdeveloped, or "backward" (*luohou*), as Chinese people would describe such places. The provincial government has designated thirty-four counties in Henan as officially impoverished (*pinkun xian*) according to the provincial criterion: an average annual per capita income below 500 *yuan* and total household assets valued at less than 8,000 *yuan*, based on 1990 prices. Since foreigners are still prohibited from entering most such areas, I was able to visit only those that had already benefited from international and government-supported microfinance programs (discussed below), specifically Yucheng County in the east and Nanzhao County in the southwest of the province. As expected, prior to

---

43. In five of my research sites, various respondents made comments such as, "Even the KMT wasn't as corrupt as cadres are these days." Some even compared the ICMB cadres to "Japanese imperialist invaders." To a certain extent, the exaction of local fees is due to the need of local governments to finance local public goods, but there are also clear cases of corruption. Local finance in the Qing Dynasty and Nanjing eras versus the reform era are discussed, respectively, in Madeleine Zelin, *The Magistrate's Tael: Rationalizing Fiscal Reform in Eighteenth Century Chi'ing China* (Berkeley: University of California Press, 1984); and Elizabeth Justine Remick, "Cadres, Clerks, and Tax Farmers: State Building in Rural China, 1927–1937 and 1982–1992" (Ph.D. diss., Cornell University, 1996).

the inauguration of these programs, private business was limited. Although I did not administer market surveys in Yucheng and Nanzhao, it was readily apparent that the vast majority of villagers in such areas had not seen the economic advantages of reform to the extent that people living closer to urban centers had. Decollectivization of agriculture had enabled some younger, able-bodied villagers to migrate and seek employment in more prosperous parts of the province, but those who remained behind had few income-generating activities in the absence of access to credit.

With the microfinance program, however, some recipients of 1,000-*yuan* loans in Dingzhuang Village, Yucheng County, for example, use them to raise pigs, which can be sold in the township center for 700 to 800 *yuan* apiece. Others buy raw materials for basket weaving and other handicrafts. An increasingly popular activity in mountainous Yang Shigou Village, Nanzhou County, is making decorative silk rugs. The process is extremely time-intensive, since the rugs have finely detailed patterns involving intricate color schemes. One loan recipient who had been working on a rug for four months reported that the materials are also quite expensive. The dyed silk and pattern for a single rug cost her over 300 *yuan*, but she was confident that the rug would sell for 800 to 900 *yuan* in the town at the bottom of the mountain. Because she had to care for her five-year-old son and her chronically ill husband, till the household's 1.5 *mu* of land, and feed the three chickens and two pigs, like most other rug-weaving women in the village, she was unable to work on the rug full time. She estimated that it would ultimately take her a full year to complete one rug. In the interim, she was making her loan repayments by selling vegetables.[44] Other participants in the microcredit schemes in Yang Shigou Village were involved "upstream" in the production of silk rugs by engaging in sericulture—raising silkworms in mulberry trees and selling the raw silk.

Financing the Non-State Sector in Henan

As in most other parts of the country, the formal financial sector in Henan provides credit primarily to state and collective enterprises rather than to private enterprises.[45] Of all the officially sanctioned banks and non-banking financial institutions, state banks allocate the lowest percentage of their short-term lending portfolios to private commercial loans. In Henan,

---

44. Interview No. 180.

45. Even so, the SOEs remain strapped for additional credit: Wang Tong and Zhu Seli, "Wo sheng jinrong bumen chutai zhichi difang jingji fazhan xin jucuo: qiye zijin jinque zhuangkuang jinqi kewang gaiguan" (Our province's financial authorities have introduced new measures to support the development of local economies: The shortage of credit to enterprises should be alleviated soon), *HNRB*, July 14, 1996, 1.

Poverty alleviation loans financed these hand-woven silk rugs. Nanzhao, Henan, May 1997.

private commercial loans accounted for only 0.1 percent of total state bank lending throughout most of the 1990s and increased to only 0.2 percent in 1998 and 1999.[46] Urban credit cooperatives on-lend more of their funds to private enterprises, but the percentage is still relatively low and has actually declined over time in the reform era—from a high of 10.4 percent of their lending portfolio in 1989 to a low of 2.8 percent in 1996 and then 3.6 percent in 1999.[47]

Indeed, 93 percent of the private entrepreneurs surveyed in Henan reported that they had never received loans from official financial institutions (i.e., state banks and urban or rural credit cooperatives), and nearly 60 percent of the business owners have borrowed money from non-state sources. In other words, the informal rather than the formal financial sector serves as the primary source of capital for private entrepreneurs. Even governmental publications recognize the shortage of official sources of credit for the private sector, and the ensuing existence of underground financial practices.[48] Be that as it may, it is worth noting that state banks

46. *HNNJ 2000.*
47. *HNNJ*, various years.
48. E.g., an article extolling the rapid growth of private enterprises in Henan also mentions that the growth is largely financed by "popular capital" or informal finance (*minjian zijin*) because governmental funds are not available to the private sector: Guo Lingling with Hu Guolei, "Wosheng fei gongyouzhi jingji."

and credit cooperatives are more likely to lend to enterprises registered as "collectives," even if they are actually privately held operations.[49] TVE loans make up more of the lending portfolio of state banks and credit cooperatives than private commercial loans do. In 1999, 4.6 percent of state bank loans and 21.3 percent of RCC loans were extended to TVEs. Consequently, to the extent that privately run businesses can access the formal financial sector, the best strategy is to falsify the enterprise's ownership structure as a collective. Even so, the share of SOEs in the loan portfolios of official banks continues to dwarf that of the non-state sector (private and collective businesses); as of 1999, SOEs accounted for 63.6 percent of state bank loans.

Most private business owners thus rely on informal sources of credit. In addition to interpersonal lending and borrowing, entrepreneurs in Henan use a variety of what I call "red" or "grey hat" financial institutions, meaning any registered corporate entities that mobilize savings and extend loans without the explicit approval of the PBOC. *Red hat institutions* register as operations that are technically legal according to the PBOC, such as the urban credit cooperatives in Wenzhou that were really run by private individuals. *Gray hat institutions*, on the other hand, are registered as private businesses or other types of social organizations but perform financial intermediation. Institutions that fall into the gray hat category include pawnshops, rural cooperative foundations (RCFs), private societies and capital mutual assistance associations (CMAs), and government-sponsored microfinance programs.

Pawnshops

Pawnshops fall under the jurisdiction of the ICMB rather than the PBOC. Although they have flourished less in Henan than in more commercialized parts of the country (e.g., Shanghai, Beijing, and Wenzhou), pawnshops did reappear in Henan in 1992 after an absence of some forty years. The first one opened in Zhengzhou, followed by others in Xinxiang, Anyang, and especially Kaifeng. The provincial ICMB readily admits that they should really be classified as "financial institutions" because they essentially offer collateralized loans at high interest rates.[50] Furthermore, they primarily serve private entrepreneurs in need of start-up or working capital and charge the necessary processing fees to make a healthy profit; aside from at-market interest rates, there are management and security fees,

49. In Henan both private entrepreneurs and bankers readily admit that wearing the red hat is a common strategy.

50. Liu Guiying and Zhao Yashan, "Tuikai dangpu shenmi de damen" (Opening the big doors of mysterious pawnshops), *Henan gongshang jie* (World of industry and commerce in Henan) 7 (1995): 17–19.

insurance charges, and storage fees. None of the vendors I surveyed had employed the services of a pawnshop, but apparently they are making a comeback in Henan.

Rural Cooperative Foundations

Rural cooperative foundations (*nongcun hezuo jijinhui*) also fall into the gray area of quasi legality. They were originally established by the Ministry of Agriculture but deemed illegal by the People's Bank of China (PBOC). My attempt to figure out which government branch is ultimately responsible for RCFs in Henan Province revealed the elusiveness of their legal existence. First, my assistant and I went to the Civil Affairs Bureau in Zhengzhou, since the RCFs we had seen all over the province displayed registration licenses indicating that they were technically "societal organizations" (*shehui tuanti*).[51] The Civil Affairs Bureau said that RCFs were supposed to register with them but never did. Next, we headed across town to the provincial branch of the Ministry of Agriculture (*sheng nongye ting;* hereafter, "Agricultural Office"), which created RCFs in the early years of reform. The director of RCFs was hesitant to speak with us initially, but her attitude changed upon hearing that we were academics rather than government cadres.[52] She explained that the Agricultural Office is protective of the RCFs because they clearly play an important role in financial intermediation in rural areas—and she thought it important for apolitical academics like ourselves to understand that. Apparently, officials from the PBOC and Zhengzhou city government had been bothering her office about the illegality and increasing popularity of RCFs. "If you were from the People's Bank, then I would give you a different set of numbers; and the city government gets yet another set of numbers," she said as she pulled out a notebook with "more accurate statistics."[53] According to the Agricultural Office's private statistics, as of mid-1996 there were sixty-five RCFs in Henan, and loans to households accounted for 70.7 percent of their total lending, while loans to TVEs and loans to rural service offices accounted for 25.4 and 3.9 percent, respectively.[54]

The director distinguished three situations under which RCFs arise. First, nearly one-third of those in Henan operate according to regulations as truly "cooperative" organizations. In other words, they are managed by cities or townships (not villages) and extend loans only to members who have savings deposits with the RCFs. Their loans range from a few hundred

51. In other words, RCFs clearly were not part of the PBOC hierarchy of legally established banks.
52. Interview No. 185.
53. In reporting to the PBOC, the director omits the RFCs that are not officially registered.
54. Interview No. 185.

yuan to over 100,000 but for the most part average around 10,000 *yuan*. Second, regions in Henan that have experienced rapid commercialization (*shangyehua*) have established RCFs more consistently than poorer areas. The director specified the rural districts of Gongyi and Xinmi as having notably growing economies, such that shareholding companies outnumber cooperatives and the market demand for capital is high. During the first half of 1996, Gongyi alone accounted for all fifteen of the new RCFs in Henan. Moreover, the scale of RCFs managed by the villages and townships in Gongyi far exceeds the minimum scale required by the Zhengzhou City government. According to the latter, RCFs run by village committees must have a minimum capitalization of 50,000 *yuan*; those managed by township and city governments, at least 100,000 *yuan*. In Gongyi, however, the scale of RCFs is over 40 million *yuan*, and most of them are run by village committees.[55] The third type of RCF in Henan comprises those in the suburbs of Zhengzhou. "Originally," the director explained, "there weren't any banks outside the city center, so RCFs basically functioned like the RCCs." The RCFs first appeared in Zhengzhou's suburbs in 1991; within a few years, every township had established one. As the farmland surrounding Zhengzhou was contracted out to private entrepreneurs (including those disguised as collectives) for industrial development, the city periphery prospered, and the RCFs grew in scale. In mid-1996 their average capitalization in Zhengzhou's suburbs was 40 to 50 million *yuan*.

Understandably, the PBOC became wary of the continued growth of RCFs (and ordered their closure in 1999). Aside from the political and financial competition that they posed for state banks, they were virtually unregulated, which meant that the collapse of a large-scale RCF would ultimately reflect upon the PBOC's incapacity to maintain the economy's financial health. The Agricultural Office was generally supportive but experienced political pressure to be proactive in monitoring RCFs. Concretely, this entailed issuing policy documents (with official red-inked rubber stamps, or "chops") that proclaim the importance of upholding the spirit of red-chopped policy documents previously issued by the State Council, People's Bank of China, and Ministry of Agriculture. In an impressive show of respect for official regulations governing RCFs, the Agricultural Office had compiled all the central-level and Henan provincial policy documents concerning RCFs that had been issued since the State Council first sanctioned them in 1983—and published them in 1995 as a book for internal reference.[56] The volume includes policy document No. 7, issued by the Ministry of Agriculture in April 1995, concerning the need to ensure that

---

55. The Gongyi City government manages only 1 million of the total RCFs' capital.

56. Henansheng nongye ting (Henan Provincial Agricultural Office), *Nongcun hezuo jijinhui zhengce fagui huibian* (Compilation of policy, laws, and regulations on RCFs) (Zhengzhou: Henansheng nongye ting, 1995).

RCFs are registered properly with the county-level Agricultural Office.[57] The document even pointed out problems that governmental agencies should look out for—including the fact that some organizations called themselves RCFs when they were not registered as such—and reiterated the societal objective: RCFs were meant to serve rural shareholders and not intended to be high-interest, profitmaking businesses. The Ministry of Agriculture (MOA) carbon-copied document No. 7 to the PBOC, the central-level People's Court, and the central Tax Bureau.

The book also includes document No. 8, a policy statement issued jointly by the Henan provincial Agricultural Office, the PBOC, Economic System Reform Committee, Tax Bureau, and Civil Affairs Office.[58] It echoes the MOA's concern about the proper management of RCFs and makes eleven points that reveal the regulatory problems involved:

1. Although RCFs fall under the jurisdiction of the MOA, they should comply with PBOC's regulations.
2. RCFs should be registered with county-level organs or higher.
3. RCFs are meant to provide collectives, cooperative stock enterprises, and TVEs with short-term working capital. RCF capital should not be invested in nonagricultural businesses, construction and real estate projects, or used to invest in the stock market or the stocks of unlisted private joint-stock enterprises.
4. The paid-in capital of shareholders cannot be touched for at least one year, and it should not be used as interest-bearing savings.
5. Savings deposits should be kept in local state banks rather than on the RCF's premises.
6. RCFs should be democratically managed. No high-level Party members may serve as chair of the board of directors (except for those that are named as honorary members).
7. RCFs must have proper credit, financial, and human resource management systems in place and issue regular financial reports to the appropriate administrative authorities.
8. RCF staff cannot use RCF capital to run their own businesses.
9. RCFs are not "financial institutions" (*jinrong jigou*). They should

---

57. Ibid., Nongyebu wenjian (Ministry of Agriculture document [no. 7]), "Guanyu fazhan nongcun jijinhui dengji gongzuo de tongzhi" (A notice regarding the registration of developing RCFs), April 20, 1995.

58. Henansheng nongye ting, Zhongguo renmin yinhang Henansheng fenhang, Henansheng jingji tizhi gaige weiyuanhui, Henansheng difang shuiwuju, Henansheng minzheng ting (Henan Agricultural Office, Henan branch PBOC, Henan Economic System Reform Committee, Henan Tax Bureau), "Guanyu jiaqiang wosheng nongcun hezuo jijinhui guifanhua guanli de yijian" (An opinion on strengthening the standardization of the management of our province's RCFs), document no. 8, October 11, 1995.

retain a social nature and serve their members, rather than mobilize savings deposits as a business end in itself.

10. RCFs do not belong to the realm of officials. Officials cannot be held responsible for the RCFs' financial risk. RCFs need an internal system to protect against financial loss.

11. All levels of the Agricultural Office should adhere to the regulations stipulated by the MOA and PBOC. RCFs should permit the PBOC, Civil Affairs Office, Economic System Reform office, and other bureaucratic agencies to inspect their performance.

These normative-legal statements imply that in fact RCFs were not being managed in a standardized manner; if they were, the points would not be worth restating in red-chopped policy documents. Interviews with managers of RCFs confirm that villagers indeed tended to rely on them more for savings deposits than for agriculture-related working-capital loans. Managers also acknowledge that as in other nonbanking financial institutions, the interest rates at RCFs tended to be substantially higher than the official limit imposed by the PBOC. A small RCF on the rural outskirts of Kaifeng, for example, offered 15.6 percent per annum in interest on savings deposits and charged 25.2 percent annually on loans; its staff admitted, however, that in actuality both the savings and lending rates were higher. In general, the RCFs operated with a fair degree of flexibility and did not conduct particularly formalized assessments of credit risk, since they were so localized. The village committee, for instance, ran the RCF cited above. The director was a former employee of a Rural Credit Cooperative,[59] but the RCF itself had no connection with the Agricultural Bank of China. The smallest loan extended is 200 *yuan*, and the shortest duration for a loan was two days. No identification was necessary at the "teller window" (thin wooden strips about three feet high) since the village is so small. Physically, the RCFs were quite modest in appearance. One of the RCFs I visited in Kaifeng looked like a small abandoned schoolhouse, even though it had been in operation for only one year at the time. Three girls were eating watermelon on bamboo mats when we entered. Two turned out to be employees of the RCF: the older one, barely nineteen, was the accountant, and the younger one, fifteen, served as the cashier. Two other employees, the director and the credit officer (both men), were out collecting loan repayments by bike.

Private Societies and Mutual Assistance Associations

Although village committees or township governments generally managed RCFs, other forms of nonbanking financial institutions run by private

---

59. Incidentally, the director is also the village Party secretary.

entrepreneurs are appearing all over urban and peri-urban areas in Henan. They have not attempted to operate private banks as openly as those in Wenzhou, but a number of nongovernmental financial institutions have appeared in the legal form of nonprofit financial "societies" or "social groups" (*shehui tuanti*). These societies are similar in structure to credit cooperatives. According to 1993 policy document No. 34, issued by the Henan Economic System Reform Committee and the PBOC, however, their registration status as societies comes with the condition that they aim to "assist the poor and supply private businesses with capital . . . [thereby] promoting the values of material and spiritual civilization."[60] A cursory look at their lending portfolios revealed that most, if not all, their debtors are private entrepreneurs who have substantial savings deposits with the societies.[61] The commercial nature of their operations is further evidenced by the fact that the PBOC is responsible for some of them. Technically, the PBOC possesses authority over all financial institutions, but many financial societies are simply managed by the Civil Affairs Bureau. The Cooperative Suburban Savings Foundation in Kaifeng (*Kaifengshi jiaoqu hezuo chu jijin-hui*) is one such example. Although its charter indicates that it is a poverty alleviation society whose objectives are: "to support the poor, help disaster areas, and supply enterprises with capital," it is the last activity, along with savings mobilization (at 15.6 percent interest annually) that dominates their day-to-day work. The point is that registering as a "society" provides private financial entrepreneurs with a more politically acceptable guise for engaging in their de facto for-profit financial activities.

Some disguises are particularly ingenious. Consider, for example, the creative entrepreneurialism of Mr. Zhang Shaohong, who left his desk job at the People's Bank of China in 1985 to open a magazine reading club in Zhengzhou.[62] He reasoned that people would be willing to pay a nominal amount to come and explore his private collection of magazines from all over China and a handful from abroad. The only condition for membership would be a monthly deposit of five *yuan*, which would be refundable at the end of the year—with a bonus. The operation was tremendously successful. Within the first year, the Henan Reading Here and Reading There Society" (*Henansheng dulai duqu dushushe*) had several hundred members, thereby generating sufficient deposit money for Mr. Zhang to start trading futures and offering members a higher rate of return than standard rates in state banks.

When I visited the reading club in the summer of 1996, half of the first

60. Henansheng jingji tizhi gaige weiyuan hui; remin yinhang (Henan provincial economic system reform committee and PBOC), policy document no. 34, 1993.

61. This is also the case in other urban areas of Henan Province. Interviews with managers and staff of specialized banks, credit cooperatives, societies, and other financial institutions. Interview Nos. 94, 101, 104, 105, 107, 108, 109, 111, 184.

62. Interview No. 100.

floor had wide reading tables flanked by displays of magazines from around the world. Large red banners hung from the ceiling with politico-inspirational slogans such as "Serve the People by Fostering Literacy" and "Promote Spiritual Civilization by Investing in Our Reading Club." In the other half of the room were rows of bank teller–type windows where people were lined up to make deposits. The juxtaposition of a library setting next to that of a retail bank was disconcerting. A uniformed security guard stood watch along the back side of the room that lead to a stairway. As he led us upstairs, Mr. Zhang explained that members now had the option of investing in increments of 10, 20, and even 1,000 *yuan*; 1,000-*yuan* investors were generally rewarded with a 15 to 20 percent "reading bonus" (*jiangdujin*). The second floor of the reading club was expansive. There was a cafeteria for the fifty employees, a banquet hall complete with a high-tech karaoke center for entertaining officials, and, most impressively, a room with row after row of computers hooked up to Bloomberg, UPI, Reuters, and other on-line information services essential for trading futures. When asked if he had ever experienced official interference in his unusual operation, Mr. Zhang said, "Of course not. My business promotes the spiritual civilization of the country, so the highest officials of the Henan provincial government support it. . . . In fact, a number of cadres are members of the club as well." As if to prove his point, he handed us a glossy brochure and a press kit full of newspaper articles extolling the reading club.

According to the survey, the reading club earns a net income of approximately 100 million *yuan* per month and has an aggregate of 200 million *yuan* in debt outstanding with all the state banks except for the Bank of China and the China Construction Bank. Mr. Zhang said that he applied for a loan from the Small Enterprise Development division of the World Bank, but they rejected his application because of the perceived "political risk" of investing in China.

Besides registering as nonprofit "societies," another legally sanctioned institutional disguise for privately run banks takes the form of "people-run enterprises capital mutual assistance associations" (*minying qiye zijin huzhuhui*).[63] CMAs too are registered as "societies" and provide private businesses in Henan with short-term commercial loans, but they are actually overseen by the Industrial and Commercial Management Bureau rather than the PBOC. This means that they possess more operational leeway than societies because the CMAs are legally permitted to operate as for-profit businesses—even if the business happens to be retail savings and loans. In essence, the CMAs are similar to the private money houses (*qianzhuang*) in Wenzhou. They operate as private banks that serve the local market of

---

63. Zhengzhou City ICMB policy document no. 40, 1995.

private entrepreneurs and do not make much of an effort to disguise their private-sector-oriented, for-profit mission.

Unlike the more socially conscious societies, the CMAs base their legitimacy upon a provincial policy document that specifically sanctions the establishment of capital mutual assistance associations. The first page in every CMA's charter explains that the financial institution was created in accordance with the Henan People's Provincial Government's policy document No. 40, issued in 1995, which encourages the growth of CMAs to supply private enterprises with working capital. As indicated on the brochure of the Zhengzhou City People-Run Enterprises Capital Mutual Assistance Association (*Zhengzhoushi minying qiye zijin huzhuhui*)—a one-page summary of objectives and operating principles printed on bright pink tissue paper—its purpose is to provide private entrepreneurs with "small loans in a highly efficient and timely manner" (*xiaoe, gaoxiao, kuaisu*).[64] In ownership structure, CMAs are similar to credit cooperatives. Private enterprises become members and therefore shareholders by contributing at least 50,000 *yuan*; individuals are required to deposit 10,000 *yuan*. Membership brings a host of rights and responsibilities, including the right to vote on the management of the association and how the profits are invested, the right to receive credit as long as collateral requirements are met, the right to share in dividend distributions, and the right to quit the association. Members' basic responsibilities entail observing the country's laws and ensuring that the loan portfolio maintains low risk and high liquidity.

Given the CMAs' striking resemblance to UCCs, it is not surprising that the PBOC does not approve of their operations and applies public pressure on them to abide by its regulations. Nonetheless, CMA managers do not express concern that the PBOC will attempt to colonize them, since they are administratively independent from the PBOC. We stumbled upon an example of the battle of wills between the PBOC and CMAs in Kaifeng. On the day that the opening of the Kaifeng People-Run Mutual Assistance Association was proudly announced on the front page of the *Kaifeng ribao* (Kaifeng Daily), an editorial style "Public Announcement Strictly Forbidding (Nonbanking) Financial Institutions from Accepting Savings Deposits from the Public," signed by the Kaifeng PBOC, appeared on the lower half of the front page.[65] It started by listing the recent proliferation

64. The Zhengzhou People-run Enterprises CMA was established on April 23, 1996: *Zhengzhou wanbao* (Zhengzhou evening news), April 25, 1996. As of July 1996 it already had ten branches throughout Zhengzhou: Interview No. 184.

65. Chao Yuanchang, "Shi fazhan minying jingji zijin huzhuhui chengli" (The city has established a capital mutual assistance asssociation [that promotes] economic development), *Kaifeng ribao* (Kaifeng daily), July 8, 1996, 1; Zhongguo renmin yinhang Kaifeng fenhang (PBOC, Kaifeng branch), "Guanyu yanjin fei jinrong jigou xishou gongzhong cunkuan de

of nonbanking financial institutions such as, "rural and urban cooperative foundations, savings associations, capital mutual assistance associations, supply and marketing stock capital service bureaus," which it charged with illegally spreading propaganda about the propriety of their operations. In fact, the Kaifeng PBOC's leaders pointed out, the PRC State Council allows only a limited set of financial institutions to accept savings deposits from the general public; any others are operating illegally.[66] The public announcement concluded by threatening the offending institutions and warning the public not to defy central-government policy by engaging in financial transactions with non-PBOC-approved institutions.

The front-page PBOC admonishment was clearly targeted at the opening of the Kaifeng CMA, but the CMA was not intimidated.[67] Aside from the fact that it was registered as a "society" and thus safe from the direct grasp of the PBOC, we were told that the mayor of Kaifeng City masterminded the CMA's creation. The staff felt confident that the mayor would prevail over the PBOC, despite the latter's access to the local media.

CMAs versus RCFs

Even though RCFs appeared to be privately run (and in most cases their management could be traced to a discrete group of individuals in the township or village committee), their mandate was fundamentally different from that of the people-run mutual assistance associations. In theory (and sometimes practice), RCFs existed to serve the broader business concerns of local community, regardless of whether they happened to be "collective" or "private" ones. Mutual assistance associations, on the other hand, target the local private sector; they do not possess any institutional obligation to extend credit to state-owned or collective enterprises. The business implications of the contrast can be seen in Chengguan Township, Yanshi City, a rural coal-mining district to the east of Luoyang.

On February 27, 1993, the Chengguan Township Yanshi City Cooperative Foundation (*Yanshishi Chengguanzhen hezuo jijinhui*) was established for the purpose of providing credit to local collective enterprises. Its charter states that it was formed in accordance with policy documents issued by the Ministry of Agriculture (No. 8) and the Luoyang People's Government

---

gonggao" (A public announcement strictly forbidding [nonbanking] financial institutions from accepting savings deposits from the public), *Kaifeng ribao* (Kaifeng daily), July 8, 1996, 1.

66. Institutions in Kaifeng City legally permitted by the Kaifeng PBOC to accept savings deposits from the public include "Industrial and Commercial Bank, Agricultural Bank, Bank of China, Construction Bank and Rural Credit Cooperatives, Urban Credit Cooperatives, Trust and Investment Companies, Post Offices, etc.": *Kaifeng ribao* (Kaifeng daily), July 8, 1996, 1.

67. Interview No. 108.

(No. 103) in 1993; therefore it aims primarily to promote rural development in a socially beneficial way, rather than to maximize its own profit.[68]
As of August 1996 the majority of its business volume derived from savings
rather than lending (100 million *yuan* in savings versus 80 million *yuan* in
loans outstanding). Like other RCFs, the one in Chengguan offered higher
interest rates on savings deposits and charged higher interest rates on loans
than those mandated by the PBOC. For example, its monthly call deposit
rate was 4.2 percent, whereas the official PBOC monthly rate was 2.4
percent. Although the bulk of the RCF's business was with the thirty-four
large TVEs in Chengguan, it also accepted savings deposits from private
individuals. The manager explained that because the collective sector
had not been performing well in the preceding year (1995–96), the
RCF decided to extend its business into the private sector by permitting
depositors to borrow up to 70 percent of their fixed savings.[69] Once the
new lending policy was implemented, private entrepreneurs, who were
savers, became thirty percent of the borrowers.

In contrast to the Chengguan Township RCF, the Chengguan Township
Yanshi City Private Enterprise Economic Mutual Assistance Association
(*Yanshishi chengguanzhen minying qiye jingji huzhuhui*) had been thriving
since it started business in October 16, 1995. The association justified its
existence by appealing to provincial (1995, No. 40) and Yanshi City (1995,
No. 56) policy documents, which encouraged the growth of financial institutions to alleviate the credit constraints of private entrepreneurs.[70] Sure
enough, 90 percent of the CMA's clients were private entrepreneurs. By
August 1996, the cooperative already had one hundred borrowers and
nearly three hundred depositors. Its capitalization, started with only "a few
10,000s" of *yuan*, had increased to over 6 million *yuan* within the first nine
months of its operation. The director of the cooperative (who was the
former director of the Yanshi Agricultural Bank of China)[71] reported that
about 5 million was used for lending and the remaining million maintained
as fixed collateral; he expected that the total volume of transactions for
1996 would reach 100 million *yuan*. The credit requirements were much
stricter and the interest rates higher than those of either the PBOC or the

68. Chengguanzhen nongcun hezuo jijinhui huiyuan daibiao dahui (Members of Congress
of the Chengguan Township RCF), "Yanshi chengguanzhen nongcun hezuo jijinhui
zhangcheng" (Constitution of the RCF in Chengguan Township, Yanshi), December 27, 1993.

69. Interview No. 111.

70. "Yanshishi chengguanzhen minying qiye jingji huzhuhui zhangcheng" (Constitution of
the Chengguan Township, Yanshi City People-run Enterprises Mutual Economic Assistance
Association), October 16, 1995.

71. The director said that he ran into "political problems" during his tenure as head of
the Yanshi Agricultural Bank of China. As punishment, he was supposed to be sent to the
countryside, but he resisted and was instead assigned to serve as head of the Capital Mutual
Assistance Association.

Cold drinks anyone? Yanshi, Henan, July 1996.

RCF. The cooperative offered an annual interest rate of 16.8 percent on savings deposits and charged 21 percent on loans. When asked if such high rates might elicit interference from the PBOC, the director answered in the negative without hesitation. He explained that the cooperative had been established in accordance with the (1995) No. 40 and (1995) No. 56 Henan provincial government policy documents. Moreover, the cooperative clearly fell under the jurisdiction of the ICMB, with which it was registered. In fact, it was also physically housed in the ICMB's former office space.

CMAs are typically run by private individuals and therefore are more committed to serving private entrepreneurs than RCFs or state banks. A growing number of CMAs, however, have been established through the auspices of the United Society of Industry and Commerce (USIC, *gongshang lianhe she*), a mass organization comprising lower-level ICMBs.[72] The purpose of such CMAs is to relieve the credit constraints of the private busi-

72. Ma Yuefeng, "Zhichi minying jingji fazhan de xin tujing" (Support new channels for the development of the people-run economy), *Henan gongshang jie* (World of commerce in Henan) 6 (1996): 37.

nesses that are members of the USIC. Like the RCFs, they are supposed to extend credit only to official members of the association. "Enterprise" members (*qiye huiyuan*) may join if they contribute 10,000 *yuan* in "mutual assistance capital" (*huzhujin*); individuals are required to invest 2,000 *yuan*. In 1994 the USIC in Jiyuan City was the first one in Henan to create a "Commercial Association Capital Mutual Assistance Association" (*shanghui zijin huzhuhui*). After two years of operation, the staff of seven had extended 124 loans to enterprises (totaling 6.83 million *yuan*) and 78 loans to individuals (totaling 1.75 million *yuan*). Apparently, the association keeps long hours and takes servicing its members quite seriously; it is open for business on Sundays, makes loan deliveries to factories, and goes to stores to collect loan repayments. According to the Jiyuan USIC-CMA's director, both the Jiyuan City government and Jiyuan PBOC support its operations; and judging by a magazine article it published, the provincial ICMB also feels that USIC-sponsored CMAs play a valuable role in meeting the financial needs of private entrepreneurs.[73] Because I did not interview any USIC-CMA managers directly, it is difficult to say whether these CMAs are indeed sanctioned by the PBOC. It is certainly credible that lower-level PBOCs might have a more lenient attitude toward their provision of credit to the local private sector, but it would be more consistent with the PBOC's general notion of administrative territoriality to be critical of the USIC-CMA's financial practices. I would wager that the USIC-CMAs probably offer and charge interest rates that are already higher than the official PBOC level and that the PBOC would attempt to interfere with their operations should they reach a more substantial scale.

Government-Supported Microfinance Programs

Not all government-sanctioned "nonprofit" financial institutions are used to disguise for-profit operations. In the mid-1990s the provincial government itself started implementing microfinance programs in officially designated impoverished counties. Providing increased access to credit is only one of the policy instruments being employed as part of the central government's "8-7 Poverty Alleviation Plan."[74] While the credit programs vary widely in terms of administration and target group, they share the

73. Ibid.
74. Inaugurated in 1993, the 8-7 plan aimed to raise the living standards of 80 million impoverished people in seven years (i.e., by the year 2000). As of 1996 the PRC government estimated that 65 million Chinese people were still living in poverty; the World Bank, however, estimated 350 million, based on a threshold level for defining poverty in China at one dollar per day per person (using purchasing power parity exchange rates). See World Bank, *Poverty Reduction and the World Bank: Progress and Challenges in the 1990s* (Washington, D.C.: International Bank for Reconstruction and Development/World Bank, 1996).

basic characteristic of extending small, low-interest loans to rural house-holds in impoverished counties for the purpose of financing private income-generating activities. Since its establishment in 1994, the Agricultural Development Bank (ADB) has been assigned to handle the poverty alleviation credits earmarked by the State Council. Operationally though, most of the programs are directed by the provincial Poverty Alleviation Bureau and implemented by its county-level branches in collaboration with township and village governments. Meanwhile, a number of internationally sponsored microfinance projects have also appeared since the mid-1990s, but even they are implemented in collaboration with local governmental agencies because the central government is uneasy about permitting international NGOs to operate without supervision. In this respect, the experience of academics affiliated with the Chinese Academy of Social Sciences in implementing Grameen Bank replications in rural China is noteworthy.

Professor Du Xiaoshan, an economist with the Rural Development Institute (RDI), Chinese Academy of Social Sciences first heard about the Grameen Bank (GB) at the 1984–85 Asia Pacific Development Center Conference in Malaysia. He was intrigued by its model of peer group savings and lending and wanted to try it in the Chinese setting, but not until financial liberalization began to accelerate after 1990 did he think the PRC government would permit such a scheme. In 1993 he visited the GB headquarters in Dhakah, Bangladesh, and discussed his proposal to introduce the Grameen model to China. Professor Muhummad Yunus, the founder of GB, agreed to lend the project US$5,000 at 2 percent annual interest. The Ford Foundation in Beijing then provided a US$110,000 grant, and the Canada Fund contributed US$6,000 for implementation. After a year of operation, Grameen Trust extended a US$50,000 loan for the original project site in Yixian County, Hebei, and subsequently another US$350,000 as the project developed in other localities.

The Funding the Poor (Fu Pin) Cooperative (FPC, *fupinshe*) was formally established in May 1994 in collaboration with the local Civil Affairs Office and the Poverty Assistance Bureau (which provides the office space). As a member of CASHPOR: Network for the Hard-Core Poor in Asia-Pacific, Du has participated in its Financial Management Workshop and Credit Discipline Workshop. When asked why he did not work through the local Women's Federation, Du explained that he thought their power too limited to approve such a program.

As of 2001, RDI was managing three GB replications, in Yixian County (Hebei), Yucheng County (Henan), and Nanzhao County (Henan) respectively; see Table 5.1 for selected performance indicators. Each of the FPCs is registered as a nongovernmental "society" and managed by the Management Committee of the Farmer's Development Fund. The Management

Table 5.1 Selected Performance Indicators of RDI's Funding the Poor (FPC) Grameen Bank Replications in China

FPC Branch	Yixian County, Hebei	Yucheng County, Henan	Nanzhao County, Henan
Date established	May 1994	August 1995	November 1995
Date of statistics below	December 2000	December 2000	December 2000
Cum. no. members	4,568	3,822	5,218
Cum. no. borrowers	4,476	3,822	5,134
% Women borrowers	95	100	100
Repayment rate	99%	95%	99.8%
No. Full-time staff	28	26	23
% Female staff	63	62	67

Source: Yixian FPC; Yucheng FPC; Nanzhao FPC.

Committee, established by RDI as an administrative shell to oversee the GB replications, now has its own funding and staff, though the RDI staff remains actively involved.

The three FPC branches share certain characteristics operationally. As in other GB replications elsewhere, five members are organized into a group, and five or six groups constitute a center. The target client base is low-income women with income-generating ability, though men may be permitted to participate if they are single or widowers. The economic eligibility criteria employed for identifying impoverished households are consistent with those of the PRC government: annual per capita income of less than 500 *yuan* and total value of assets less than 8,000 *yuan*.[75] Small loans are disbursed sequentially according to a 2:2:1 pattern: the first two members must start to repay their loans (starting in the third week) before the second two members can receive their loans; in turn, the fifth member receives hers only after the third and fourth members start their repayments. Peer pressure and mutual support within the small groups thus reinforce loan repayment. The maximum size of the first loan is 1,000 *yuan* (US$123); the second, 1,500; and the third, 2,000. Second loans cannot be disbursed before full repayment of the first. The effective annual interest rate is 16 percent, substantially higher than the 2.88 percent charged for government-sponsored poverty alleviation loans and roughly comparable to the official commercial bank rate, but lower than necessary for operational self-sufficiency.[76] As a condition for participation, members must save one *yuan* per week. Savings are deposited in a local bank (typically, the

75. In U.S. dollars these represent a per capita income of less than $62 and total assets less than $988 using the conversion rate of US$1 = 8.1 RMB.

76. During an October 1996 Workshop on Chinese Microfinance, held in Beijing, Professor Liu Wenpu of RDI/FPC indicated that 31 percent would be a more appropriate rate. As of 2002, however, such a high rate was still not feasible politically.

ABOC or are RCC), where they earn interest at the call deposit (*huoqi*) rate. At the end of the year, members are permitted to withdraw their savings if they wish to do so.

In practice, there are some deviations from the GB model. For example, in the Yucheng centers, some households receive second loans before the first loan was fully repaid.[77] The reason for this departure from GB methodology is the need to extend seasonal loans for agricultural production. Relatedly, during the harvest period (*nongmang*), meetings are not always held on a weekly basis because the centers are often quite a distance from the members' homes.[78] There are also deviations in the target clientele: although FPC Yucheng reports that 100 percent of its borrowers are women, some loans are being used for income-generating activities undertaken by men. Moreover, some of the member households appear to fall into the lower-middle income bracket in the officially designated impoverished county.

Tailoring the GB model to local conditions is not necessarily problematic. The state's level of involvement or interference, however, may be cause for greater concern. For one thing, the central government believes that "poverty alleviation loans" should be extended at subsidized interest rates rather than rates that would enable the cooperative to cover its administrative costs, and thus achieve operational self-sufficiency; charging market interest rates, the state reasons, would exploit the poor.[79] For another, the FPC branches (and other internationally supported microfinance programs) work in areas where the local Poverty Alleviation Bureau also runs

77. FPC Yucheng was the branch that hosted a study tour by seventy participants of the Workshop on Chinese Microfinance in October 1996. The Yucheng County and Dianji Township governments' pride that such a large delegation of international and domestic visitors had come to observe a local organization made it difficult for us to get a natural perspective of the branch's everyday operations; the center meetings were orchestrated to coincide with our arrival, and the households that we were encouraged to interview had been prepared to expect visitors. Even so, certain problems were apparent, which have been well summarized in Henry Jackelen and Mi Xianfeng, "UNDP Microfinance Assessment Report: China," prepared as a component of the MicroStart Feasibility Mission, United Nations Capital Development Fund, New York, October 1997.

78. Group members who sometimes skipped meetings or sent their husbands in their place explained that it was too time-consuming to walk nearly three hours, round trip, to make loan repayments every week—especially when they had to care for young children and work in the fields.

79. Although the central government has welcomed in principle the introduction of international microfinance programs to China, the issue of allowing financial NGOs (e.g., FPCs) to charge interest rates that would cover the costs of running the programs remains a highly sensitive issue. The argument that several decades of accumulated experience in international microfinance demonstrates the importance of fostering local financial self-sustainability generally falls on deaf ears. The economists at RDI are a notable exception to this mentality. See esp. Du Xiaoshan and Li Jing, "Dui fupin she de sikao" (Reflections on the poverty alleviation experiment)," *Zhongguo nongcun jingji* (Chinese rural economy) 6 (1998): 44–49.

its own credit programs. Not only do the state-sponsored programs offer substantially lower interest rates than those of the FPCs, but they also tend to operate with a quota-driven mentality. In other words, emphasis tends to be placed on the aggregate number of loans disbursed rather than the quality of the loan portfolio or whether the loan recipient adequately meets the profile of the intended client base. There is also reason to believe that some loan decisions are influenced by patronage (*guanxi*) considerations—but of course the FPCs are not immune to this tendency either.[80]

Urban Credit Cooperatives

Urban credit cooperatives are often owned and managed by a discrete group of individuals, but because the People's Bank of China is officially responsible for them, they face more official interference than the financial societies or people-run capital mutual assistance associations. "Official interference" ranges from periodic in-house audits (in addition to the standard reporting requirements) to demands that loans be extended to specific state or collective enterprises. My interview with Mr. Qian revealed some political challenges associated with running a UCC.

In 1996, Mr. Qian was a forty-seven-year-old director of a UCC in Zhengzhou, a real estate investor, a high-ranking Communist Party member, and a millionaire with a "revolutionary past."[81] He has been called a "red capitalist" (*hong zibenjia*). Although Mr. Qian's father was branded with the landlord class label and his family's land in Hebei was confiscated during the revolution, his father joined the CCP in 1937 during the Anti-Japanese War. Over the years Mr. Qian slowly climbed up the Party ranks and became the president of a prestigious university in Henan. He also served as the chief economist at a high-profile think tank.

On the eve of double-digit inflation in 1988, Mr. Qian established a UCC with about 150,000 *yuan*. The registration process with the PBOC required substantial networking and bribing: as of July 1996 he was paying a total of 20,000 *yuan* a month to sixty people in the Provincial Party Committee, as well as 200 *yuan* a month to cadres in the Political Research Division for "protection." When asked what sort of protection is required to run a credit

---

80. Aside from the local government and RDI, a number of multilateral and bilateral donor organizations have initiated microfinance programs based upon the GB model of peer group guarantees. Various microfinance programs are discussed in Liu Wenpu with Du Xiaoshan, Zhang Baomin, and Sun Ruomei, eds., *Zhongguo nongcun xiaoe xindai fupin de lilun yu shijian: 1996 zhongguo xiaoe xindai fupin guoji yantao huilun wenjian* (Theory and practice of poverty alleviation using microcredit in rural China: collected works of the 1996 international conference on microcredit and poverty alleviation in China) (Beijing: Zhongguo jingji chubanshe, 1997); and Albert Park and Changqing Ren, "Microfinance with Chinese Characteristics," *World Development* 29, 1 (2001): 39–62.

81. Interview No. 101.

cooperative, he responded, "Merchants must collaborate with the government to avoid problems," such as Financial Inspection officials accusing
him of violating procedures by, for example, setting high interest rates. He
could in fact be harassed by any of the three levels of the judicial system:
the Inspection Division (*jiancha yuan*) could sue him; the Public Security
Bureau (*gongan ju*) could arrest him; the People's Court (*renmin fayuan*)
could sentence him. Thus, Mr. Qian pays off all three levels. He admits that
his UCC's interest rates exceed the limit stipulated by the PBOC, but after
all, he reasons, "interest rate differentials are how financial institutions in
liberalized capital markets make money"—that is, by they maximizing the
spread between the lending and savings rates. The official one-year spread
is supposed to lie within 3.6 percentage points; his spread is 10 percentage
points. Thanks to his contributions to government salaries, however, his
cooperative is generally left alone.

Still, Mr. Qian sometimes receives memos from officials requesting that
he grant a large loan to an inefficient state-owned enterprise. He generally
refuses, knowing that the loan will never be repaid. (Most UCCs lack the
financial clout to avoid such demands, so their loan portfolios remain bur-
dened by late repayments and defaults.) The major exception to Mr. Qian's
profit-driven modus operandi occurs when the request comes from a judge,
since he spends much time in court suing delinquent clients and typically
has thirty to forty cases on the docket at any given point in time. Once a
judge in Zhengzhou asked him to extend a loan of approximately 150,000
yuan to the judge's relative, an aspiring private entrepreneur. Mr. Qian
agreed, and the judge ruled in his favor for the case under consideration.
The loan was never repaid.

Because of his experience in finance and willingness to share information, I also asked Mr. Qian if he knew of other strategies that private entrepreneurs employ to get access to credit.[82] He went into colorful detail about
popular ways to bribe credit officers and managers of state banks, such as
giving exorbitant gifts: cars, furnished apartment villas, "girlfriends," and
even trips to Macau, which might include accompanying the bank director
to a casino and giving him cash that he (they are almost always male) can
either gamble away or keep. Mr. Qian claimed that hundreds of millions
of *yuan* in loans are disbursed through such procedures. Why would people
spend so much money on bribery to secure a bank loan? Apparently, the
pampered director of a state bank will ensure that no one hassles the gift
giver for loan repayments.

---

82. This interviewee may have been willing to speak in this apparently uncensored way for
two reasons. First, he told me repeatedly that he was well protected by the relevant branches
of government, so he had no fear that my research could harm him in any way. Second, at
the end of the interview he revealed his impression that I could help him get in contact with
influential people in the United States. I made the limits of my contacts clear.

Sometimes UCCs are clearly established to serve a distinct *danwei* or group of government-affiliated people. A research institute, for example, ran a credit cooperative in Zhengzhou in the mid-1990s, supposedly for members of the institute, but it also attempted to mobilize savings from nonaffiliated depositors in order to bolster the institute's ailing finances. After a few years the credit cooperative was struggling because the academics running it lacked experience in financial and credit management—and unlike state banks, their UCC faced a hard budget constraint. Before it went bankrupt, however, a local woman entrepreneur bought it out. The Jingu (Women's) UCC provides a more politically complex example of how some UCCs come about.

The Jingu Urban Credit Cooperative was established on August 8, 1995—not coincidentally, shortly before the UN's Fourth World Conference on Women was held in Beijing. According to its director, when the UN named China as the site of the conference, each province was instructed by the Women's Federation in Beijing to make a lasting contribution that would enhance the status of women.[83] She and a group of her colleagues thought that it would be more productive to establish a financial institution for women than to launch yet another "women's health" (i.e., family planning) campaign. But even though leaders of the WF at the provincial, municipal, and city levels unanimously supported the idea of establishing a credit cooperative specifically for women, they encountered substantial administrative difficulties in securing approval for it.

First, with the nominal support of the Henan Development Bureau, a group of WF cadres approached the provincial People's Bank of China. "The People's Bank was really condescending to us," the director recounted. "They told us to go run a nursery school, flower shop, or clothing store and said that women should not get in involved in something as complex as finance." The WF cadres reported that encounter to the WF director in Henan, who sent them to the general secretary of the Zhengzhou City government. He signed his name on the WF's petition and wrote a memo to the city-level PBOC reiterating his support for a women's credit cooperative. Upon receipt of the memo, the director of the city-level PBOC added his endorsement and in turn wrote a letter to the director of the provincial PBOC. The latter responded that the provincial PBOC had recently adopted a policy of limiting the number of new UCCs and could not sanction the project. Fortunately for the WF, the intransigent provincial PBOC director retired within days, and his protégé, the vice director, was immediately transferred (demoted) to the provincial Agricultural Bank

83. Interview No. 94. The director, formerly a teacher in the Women's Cadre School, studied economic management for a few years and was then appointed director of the credit cooperative by the Women's Federation.

of China. Meanwhile, the WF cadres approached the director of Education, Scientific Research, and Women's Affairs and wrestled an endorsement out of him after a few visits: "He was embarrassed at being confronted by four strong women," the UCC director suspected. When a new director was installed at the provincial PBOC, the WF cadres approached him as well. In March 1995, eighteen months after they had first proposed the project, the provincial PBOC finally approved it.

The building for the UCC was constructed in three months. The staff was trained in July, and the Jingu UCC opened its doors to the public a month later.[84] Twenty-five percent of the UCC's shares are held by the WF, and the other stockholders are staff of the UCC and members of the Women's Cadre School. The starting capitalization was 2 million *yuan*; a year later, it had increased to 60 million *yuan*. As of July 1996 it had 1,293 individual depositors, 75 percent of whom were women, and eighty-two institutional (*danwei*) depositors. The UCC lends primarily to state units (thirteen of them), though it also has seven individual borrowers. It focuses on short-term loans (up to six months) and the smallest loan that it extends is 10,000 *yuan* and the largest thus far is 100,000 *yuan*. Their credit assessment procedures are relatively strict; they require collateral in the form of real estate, state bonds, savings deposits, or institutional guarantors. Apparently, its repayment rate has been exemplary.[85] Exceptions to standard loan disbursement procedures are made for the WF, however: because the WF holds so many shares, the UCC makes special donations to its activities, such as Children's Day (June 1), Women's Day (March 3), and the Communist Party's Birthday (July 1). In addition to assisting the WF, the UCC extends credit to women-related operations. When the *Oriental Family Weekly*, for example, was denied financial support from the WF, even though it focuses on women's issues, the UCC extended the magazine a 60,000-*yuan* loan at a low interest rate. But some of the UCC's clients are simply for-profit businesses that have been referred by people in the WF or Women's Cadre School, and if someone "important" has an urgent need for a loan, the UCC's in-house messenger will deliver the cash immediately. In short, the UCC has strayed to a certain extent from its original mission—to serve women entrepreneurs.

As in other major cities, by the mid-1990s the Zhengzhou PBOC was trying to centralize the regulation of UCCs by requiring them all to become members of an umbrella organization. The Zhengzhou United Society of Urban Credit Cooperatives (*Zhengzhoushi chengshi xinyongshe lianheshe*) was

84. The staff consists of one director, four savings tellers, four credit officers, four accountants, two cash disbursement tellers, one messenger, and one driver who also serves as security guard. All are women except for the messenger and the driver.
85. *Zhengzhou wanbao* (Zhengzhou evening news), December 2, 1995.

Table 5.2 Aggregate Savings Deposits and Loans in Zhengzhou's UCCs, 1990 vs. 1995 (in 100 million *yuan*)

	1990	1995	Increase
Savings deposits	6.2	57.7	9.3 x
Loans	4.4	37.6	8.5 x

Source: Zhengzhou chengshi xinyongshe lianheshe (Zhengzhou City United Society of Urban Credit Cooperatives), 1996.

established on August 18, 1995.[86] In 1996, it had forty-eight UCC members. Although they remain responsible for their own profits and losses, membership in the United Society means that they are subject to PBOC standards of operation in terms of loan loss reserve requirements, interest rate differentials, and calculation of late repayments and defaults. All the member UCCs are being computerized and connected to the central United Society so that the latter can track their aggregate performance on a daily basis. A United Society brochure printed in 1996 indicates that during the five-year period between 1990 and 1995 the volume of savings deposits in UCCs had increased by a multiple of 9.3 times; the volume of loans, 8.5 times (see Table 5.2).

Rural Credit Cooperatives

Just as urban cooperatives are being converted into commercial financial institutions and urban finance is increasingly subject to standardized regulation by the PBOC, a similar trend is occurring in rural finance. In mid-1994 the ABOC spun off its development-oriented "policy lending" (*zhengce daikuan*) operations into a new entity, the Agricultural Development Bank (ADB) so that the ABOC and other specialized banks could operate as commercial banks without the burden of development-oriented lending. Following the commercializing trend, two years later the management of RCCs was transferred from the ABOC to the PBOC.[87] The transition of RCCs and ABOCs into genuine commercial banks is more complicated than that of the UCCs, however. In areas where there are no ADBs, the ABOC will have to continue extending policy loans.[88] Moreover,

86. The first United Society of Urban Cooperatives was established in Zhengzhou on January 22, 1991, but not until five years later were all UCCs required to join it and become subject to its oversight.

87. "Henan Holds Conference on Rural Banking System Reform," *HNRB*, September 17, 1996, 1, reported in FBIS-CHI-96-195.

88. "Guowuyuan zhaokai nongcun jinrong tizhi gaige huiyi: Zhu Rongji yaoqiu jiji wentuo tuijin nongcun jinrong tizhi gaige" (The State Council commences a conference on the

the RCCs are not entirely immune from governmental requests to grant policy loans, though the PBOC's effort to consolidate them into Rural Cooperative Banks (*nongcun hezuo yinhang*) may enable them to shed the nonperforming loans from their lending portfolios.

Hard Hats and Hard Times

Rationalizing the operation of UCCs in Zhengzhou under a United Society was only the first step toward converting them into quasi-state-owned commercial banks. As in other large cities and municipalities, a portion of the UCC shares (typically around 30 percent) was transferred to local governments, and a number of UCCs were forced to merge into Urban Cooperative Commercial Banks (UCBs; *hezuo shangye yinhang*).[89] These reforms represented a compromise between the PBOC and local governments in sharing the administrative oversight and fiscal revenues of the new entity.[90] By mid-1996, there were already fifty-nine UCBs in twenty-three cities in Henan.[91]

The takeover of the UCCs in Zhengzhou reflected the PBOC's growing concern about the ability of the formal financial system to keep up with the ambitious economic reform strategy set forth by Jiang Zemin and Zhu Rongji at the Fifteenth National Party Congress in late 1997, coupled with an attempt to avoid China's slipping into the Asian financial crisis. Given the dual pressures of reforming the state sector and rationalizing the financial sector, Henan's nonbanking financial institutions became the target of investigations by the PBOC.

The first target of the crackdown on illicit financial businesses was the Sanxing ("Three Star") Holding Company (*Sanxing jituan gongsi*), an industrial conglomerate founded in 1992 by a former farmer from the suburbs of Zhengzhou.[92] When the business ran into financial difficulties in 1995,

---

reform of rural finance: Zhu Rongji demands energetic yet safe reform of the rural financial system), *Xinhua meiri dianxun* (Xinhua daily newswire), July 16, 1996.

89. UCBs were first established in 1995 in Shenzhen and had spread to Shanghai, Beijing, Nanjing, Shijiazhuang, and Jinan by the beginning of 1996. By the end of 1996 the State Council planned to have UCBs in an additional thirty-five large and medium-sized cities: "Cooperative Banks," *China Daily*, June 25, 1996, 5. By 1998 there were seventy-nine UCBs: "China Enjoys Thriving Urban Cooperative Banks," *Xinhua News Agency*, April 12, 1998 reported in FBIS-CHI-98-102; Liu Qingfen, "Qiantan chengshi hezuo yinhang fazhan celue" (An elementary introduction to the developing strategy of urban cooperative banks), *Zhengzhou wanbao* (Zhengzhou evening news), June 21, 1996, 6.

90. Phone interview with Mr. Jiansheng Wong of the International Finance Corporation, World Bank Group, November 13, 1997.

91. Interview No. 112.

92. This was initially brought to my attention in written correspondence dated July 7, 1998, from Interviewee No. 87.

the owner started a "flexi-sales" scheme to "honorary employees" who would invest in the company and sell products from home on consignment. By promising a 20 to 30 percent return on its shares to "gold card" and "silver card" member employees, who contributed 20,000 and 10,000 *yuan*, respectively, the company managed to attract 899 million *yuan* (US$109.6 million) in deposits.[93] When the PBOC and the ICMB conducted a joint investigation into its operations in March 1998, the investors and depositors got nervous and made a run on Three Star to withdraw their money. Two months later the city government forced it to close down, and a large portion of its 30,000 depositors took to the streets in protest. They were enraged that a small, private financial institution had been investigated, while larger state banks continued to make bad loans on the scale of 4 to 5 billion *yuan*. The Henan provincial government issued an emergency notice to all state units (*danwei*), instructing them to keep their workers from protesting in the streets. At the same time, Three Star's depositors were asked to register with the government so that partial compensation on the lost savings could be arranged. Manual workers and retired cadres would receive 6 percent of their cash assets, and depositors of over 100,000 *yuan* were required to explain the source of their savings. That requirement reduced the ranks of protesters substantially, and it became apparent that many of the depositors had accumulated their funds through illegal means.[94]

Shortly after the Three Star incident the owners of another private financial institution posing as an industrial conglomerate, the Baihua ("White Flower") Industrial Company (*Baihua gongsi*), suddenly closed the operation down and fled to the United States with 15 million *yuan* of their depositors' money, but not before burning the company's financial records.[95] White Flower's closure triggered a citywide bank run, and all sixteen of the privately owned finance companies in Zhengzhou became insolvent.

Meanwhile, people began making a run on the newly established UCBs (formerly UCCs). As of July 1998 the forty-six UCBs were operating under emergency conditions: they had not been shut down, since the government feared additional public displays of the local financial distress in the streets, but had capped the maximum daily withdrawal at 40,000 *yuan*, and only

93. The official account of the event is chronicled in Wang Fashen, "'San Xing' shenhua de jiejue—Li Guofa feifa yinshou gongzhong cunkuan zuian zhenpo jishi" (The myth of 'San Xing' is over—A record of how the criminal case of Li Guofa illegally accepting savings deposits from the public was resolved), *Dahebao* (Big river news), September 6, 1998, 4–5.

94. People suspected that substantial bribe money was tied up in the large accounts.

95. In March 2001 the Intermediate People's Court of Zhengzhou found that between May 1996 and May 1998, Baihua had illegally mobilized 336 million *yuan* (US$40.6 million) and US$120,000 in deposits from 12,295 individuals. The former general manager, Li Jian, was sentenced to death, and six of his accomplices to prison terms ranging from eighteen months to fifteen years: "Man Sentenced to Death for Financial Fraud," *RMRB*, March 31, 2001.

20,000 *yuan* in a single bank visit. When this policy was first announced, depositors expressed anger at their individual UCBs but were soon lining up there every morning and bringing small gifts to curry favor with the bank staff. Nonetheless, sporadic protests by depositors at the provincial government and Party buildings, in the commercial center of Zhengzhou, and even the along the Beijing-Guangzhou railway line continued through September and November 1998.[96]

In some ways, the financial mayhem in Zhengzhou was evocative of the turbulence in Wenzhou's financial markets during the mid-1980s. The life savings of average citizens were lost, and the local government tried desperately to contain the damage. A defining difference, however, was the proximate cause of the financial turmoil. In Wenzhou, people were caught up in complex networks of pyramidal investment schemes (similar to those in Albania in 1997), whereas the bank runs in Zhengzhou were triggered by official investigations into high-interest-yielding private financial companies—including one that turned out to be the largest pyramid scheme since the 1993 Wuxi scandal that led to former Beijing Party Secretary Chen Xitong's downfall.[97] Residents of a provincial capital such as Zhengzhou have always been more attuned to shifts in state policy (whether at the national, provincial, or city level), since they tend to witness its implementation in a more immediate manner than, say, farmers in remote rural areas do. Consequently, the closure of a single finance company was sufficient to trigger a crisis of confidence in the viability of the city's private financial institutions. A related contrast between Wenzhou and Zhengzhou is that private-sector development occurred much earlier in the former; the latter has been more constrained by its SOEs and associated Maoist suspicion toward capitalist profit. In light of these structural differences, it is striking that Zhengzhou's entrepreneurs have gone as far as they have in finding creative ways to engage in private finance. The recent crackdown on these very institutions was certainly unexpected, but to those who came of age before the reform era, it was not surprising.

Summary of Financial Institutions in Henan

Henan's diverse financial institutions are summarized in Table 5.3: their policy justification, responsible agency, intended versus actual mission (i.e.,

96. "500 Shareholders in Zhengzhou Protest Investment Losses after Firms Go Bust," *Pingguo ribau* (Apple daily), September 2, 1998, A23, reported in FBIS-CHI-98-245; Chan Yee Hon, "Investors Take to Streets over Billion-Dollar Scams," *South China Morning Post* (SCMP), September 27, 1998; "Three Star Payouts Begin," *SCMP*, October 26, 1998; and David Rennie, "Street Protests as Chinese are Bled of Their Savings; Banks Face a Run as Deposits Vanish into the Black Hole of State-run Enterprises," *Daily Telegraph*, November 19, 1998.

97. Kai Peter Yu, "Facts behind Pyramid Firm Fraud Emerge," *SCMP*, September 22, 1998.

Table 5.3. Summary of Nonbanking Financial Institutions in Henan

Name	Policy Doc. Justification	Responsible Bureaucratic Agency	Intended Mission	Actual Mission	Annual Interest Rates	
					Savings	Loans
Rural cooperative foundations (RCFs) (*nongcun hezuo jijinhui*)	State Council (1983) no. 1; (1984) no. 1; (1985) no. 1; Henan (1991) no. 9; (1992) no. 5; (1992) no. 32; (1992) no. 12; (1994) no. 1; (1994) no. 4	Ministry of Agriculture; managed by townships and village committees; closed by PBOC since 1999	promote rural development and serve RCF members and farmers; not supposed to focus on profit; should not accept savings deposits from nonmembers	popular means of savings mobilization in rural areas; provide credit to collective enterprises and some private ones	15.6%	25.2%
Peri-urban cooperative savings foundations (*jiaoqu hezuochu jijinhui*)	Henan Econ. Sys. Reform Committee (1993) no. 134	Civil Affairs Bureau	assist the poor and provide credit to private businesses; promote material and spiritual civilization	savings mobilization; provide credit to private enterprises	15.6%	—
People-run enterprises capital mutual assistance associations (CMAs) (*minying qiye zijin huzhuhui*)	Henan (1995) no. 40	ICMB	provide member private entrepreneurs with credit	provide member private entrepreneurs with credit; savings mobilization	9–16.8%	21%
Urban credit cooperatives (UCCs) (*chengshi xinyongshe*)	Henan (1979); PBOC (1989) no. 346; State Council (1995) no. 25	United Society of UCCs; PBOC	provide co-op members with financial services	provide credit to co-op members and government recommended businesses	6.0%	18–35%
Rural credit cooperatives (RCCs) (*nongcun xinyongshe*)	State Council (1977) no. 154	formerly, ABOC; since 1996, PBOC	provide co-op members in rural areas with financial services	provide credit to co-op members and government recommended businesses	—	18%
Funding the poor cooperatives (FPCs) (*fupin she*)	State Council (1993)	CASS; Poverty Alleviation Bureau; county governments	provide small, low-interest loans to impoverished rural household (some target women)	provide small, low-interest loans to households in poor counties	—	16%

target clientele), and interest rates. None of the field research sites in Henan possesses the full range of these nonbanking financial institutions, but the particular mix of institutions in any given area has had implications for the competitive (or noncompetitive) dynamics between them and the formal financial sector, as well as among themselves. And as suggested in several of the foregoing cases, bribery often plays a central role in the establishment and survivability of a given institution. Most interviewees describe corruption as an operational reality: it is troublesome and illegal, but necessary to expediting transactions and avoiding official interference.

It is worth noting that the central government recognizes its pervasiveness and engages in periodic campaigns to punish offending officials.[98] Bureaucrats in Henan have not been spared. The manager of a state-owned textile factory in Anyang City, for example, was sentenced to death for "embezzling 600,000 *yuan* in public money, 100,000 *yuan* of company investment funds and accepting more than a million *yuan* in bribes." During the investigation the manager implicated the mayor of Anyang City, who was subsequently found guilty of attempting to hide over 165,000 *yuan* in bribes and sentenced to a ten-year prison term. At the provincial level too, Henan has been attempting since 1984 to crack down on dishonest officials through mass campaigns in the media.[99] Such front-page-style exposés, however, have not deterred others from partaking in graft.[100]

A wealth of nonbanking financial institutions exists in Henan, even though it is a province that most observers do not associate with rapid

98. "10 Years' Jail for Mayor who Tried to Hide Bribes," *SCMP*, July 15, 1998, originally reported in *China Youth Daily*, July 14, 1998.

99. Jieh-min Wu, "Local Property Rights Regime in Socialist Reform: A Case Study of China's Informal Privatization" (Ph.D. diss., Columbia University, 1998), chap. 5, p. 4. For a discussion of provincial efforts in combatting corruption since Jiang Zemin's anticorruption speech in August 1993 at the Second Plenary Session of the Central Discipline Inspection Committee, in which he compared corruption to a virus, see Ma Hongtu, Wu Hua, and Yu Ji, "Eliminate the Impure from the Pure and Rectify Party Style," *HNRB* (Henan daily), 1, 3, reported in FBIS-CHI-97-270; and Wu Ye, "Henan Reviews 1996 Anti-Corruption Work," *HNRB*, 1, reported in FBIS-CHI-97-021. The articles delineate some of the most egregious offenses in recent years, many involving state bankers. One large case of bank fraud involved assistant managers in the Bank of China's branch in Xinyang City, Henan, who apparently were underreporting the deposits and pocketing the difference. They collectively skimmed 510 million *yuan* (US$62 million) from the savers' accounts, left town, and were chased by a special task force of Henan and Zhengzhou Public Security investigators all over China. After nineteen months they were captured in the United States and "persuaded" to return to China: Vivien Pik-kwan Chan, "Five Held in 'Crazy' HK$477M Bank Scam," *SCMP*, August 23, 1998, 1.

100. Note that nongovernmental efforts to monitor progress in alleviating corruption were not yet permitted as of 1998. In October 1998 the Civil Affairs Ministry rejected the application by a private individual, An Jun, to register an NGO called "Corruption Watch," which according to the Associated Foreign Press had eighty members in ten provinces: "Henan Corruption Watch Group Banned," *Hong Kong AFP*, October 31, 1998, reported in FBIS-CHI-98 304.

private-sector development in the reform era. Undeniably, there is regional variation between the coastal south and northern interior in the timing, pace, and content of commercial development, but the broader dynamic of "capitalist" innovation is evident in both regions. Despite the dual burdens of over-industrialization in certain districts and underdevelopment in neglected rural areas, Henan clearly possesses its share of private entrepreneurs willing to undertake the risk inherent in leaving the countryside and especially the state sector. Often, they have had no choice but to resort to self-employment to maintain their livelihood, yet many entrepreneurs also admit to having nakedly capitalistic motivations. In a transitional economy where state employment no longer offers the taken-for-granted security of the Mao era, even the "reddest" members of society are showing their true colors, so to speak. The pursuit of private profit through basic commodity exchange has expanded into the trickier realm of finance, where individuals manage de facto private financial institutions under the guise of policy-sanctioned objectives.

Until the PBOC or specialized state banks can enforce administrative authority over them, the nongovernmental financial "associations" and "societies" will assert the right to operate as legitimate organizations which are protected, albeit at a price, by the ICMB in Henan and elsewhere. As the associations grow in volume and scale, the ICMB's incursion into PBOC administrative territory can be expected to generate political conflict, as seen in Wenzhou and most vividly on the streets of Zhengzhou. In the interim, innovative attempts to practice the business of finance will continue to evolve. The people-run financial associations and societies in Henan exhibited an ability to cultivate political ties that not only enabled them to continue operating until the 1998 crisis but also enlisted highly publicized support among the highest officials. Other creative institutional forms of private financing will undoubtedly continue to emerge as both the central and local governments place increasing emphasis on private-sector development as a means to facilitate the consolidation of the ailing state sector. But the question remains of how long such commercial financial institutions will be able to operate without facing the supervisory fiat of the PBOC. The existing range of nonbanking financial institutions poses a serious challenge to financial regulators. As a harbinger of the PBOC's crackdown on informal finance, in a February 1998 conference on finance, Henan's Vice Governor Li Yucheng instructed local governments to increase their efforts at rectifying financial institutions in their territories:

> Governments at all levels should support and instruct pertinent departments to rectify and standardize all foundations, mutual aid groups, reserve groups, and stock capital service centers that engage in financial businesses in viola-

tion of laws and to strictly investigate and punish the behavior of raising funds through illegal means and raising funds through raising interest rates in disguised forms, with a view to ensuring the financial order of localities.[101]

PBOC regulators in Henan obviously had no idea that their very efforts at financial rectification would backfire so badly.

101. "Henan Holds Financial Conference," *HNRB*, Feburary 8, 1998, reported in FBIS-CHI-98-051.

6

Curb Markets in Comparative Context

> Small-scale enterprise is new to this country, to the banks,
> implementing agencies and the beneficiaries alike. So we are all
> still learning and hope there will come a time when
> entrepreneurs can walk into a bank on their own and ask for a
> loan without coming to us.
>
> —Joyce Mapoma, Chair, Village Industry Service, Zambia

> We are trying to bridge a gap where people cannot reach their
> leaders and the leaders cannot reach the people. We are trying to
> do or get done what the government does not do, cannot do, will
> not do or should not do.
>
> —Chandra de Fonseka, Founder, Uvagram,
> a financial NGO in Sri Lanka

> Introducing political power into economic affairs initiates a
> dialectical process of adjustments and counteradjustments. In
> what resembles reflex action, markets rechannel regulatory power
> as regulatees short-circuit regulators' intentions both by finding
> and exploiting loopholes and by the simpler expedient of
> disobeying the law. . . . The dialectical can resolve itself in
> numerous ways, but seldom before the nation has experienced a
> wasteful cycle of political and economic reactions.
>
> —Edward J. Kane, *Journal of Money, Credit, and Banking*, 1977

The narratives that ground explanations for variation in the supply of informal finance among localities in China and in private entrepreneurs' use of financing mechanisms (Chapters 3, 4, 5) reveal a wide range of interactive dynamics between the demand and supply of informal finance, formal and informal financial institutions, and, most generally, public and private actors. Ultimately, none of these dyadic interactions are zero-sum relationships. They are mutually constitutive rather than mutually exclusive. Informal finance does not necessarily come at the expense of formal finance, and state co-optation of informal financial intermediaries does not necessarily mean that informal finance is doomed. But the fact that they coexist does mean that they influence each other—and therefore cannot be ignored by the state. The state will have a proclivity to regulate, ban, or incorporate various curb market institutions, although sometimes its interventionist impulse may prove ineffectual or even self-defeating.

Similar dynamics may be observed in other countries.[1] How does their developmental experience with novel forms of financial intermediation compare with the political economic logic of informal finance in China? Revisiting the arguments presented thus far and considering how they relate to one another will establish an analytic basis for such a comparison.

Connecting the Subthemes

Broadly speaking, this book is about the efforts of local political and economic actors to create institutions that provide a service formerly monopolized by the socialist state: the supply and allocation of credit in the economy. To elucidate the dynamics of this process, I posed two separate questions. First, why do some areas harbor a wide range of informal financing mechanisms, while others have barely any at all? Second, why do private entrepreneurs use different types of financing mechanisms? In reality, the two issues have mutually reinforcing effects.

At the most basic level, it is apparent that the financing choices of private entrepreneurs are limited by the options available in their particular locality. For example, a male business owner who has strong political ties and has resided in a particular locality his entire life might be expected to use more highly institutionalized forms of finance than a female migrant who has no political ties. But if the well-connected man happens to live in an area where the local government is not supportive of the private sector, chances are that highly institutionalized sources of private credit do not even exist there. In short, the supply of informal finance in any given locality defines the choice set for private entrepreneurs in raising capital.

Yet the supply of financial institutions itself is not static. In Changle County, for example, the local government was initially more interested in developing the collective sector. But as the locality started to receive more foreign capital, and private businesses developed a stronger presence, the

---

1. See Ibrahima Bakhoum et al., *Banking the Unbankable: Bringing Credit to the Poor* (London: Panos Publications, 1989).

government became more accommodating toward private enterprise and finance. Without necessarily intending to do so, then, private entrepreneurs may change the political and economic incentives that local governments have in defining their local development strategy.

By the end of the 1990s there were increasing indications that even areas known for following the Sunan model of collective-sector rural industrial development were experiencing changes in development orientation. First, it began to appear that the TVEs' impressive growth rates might not be sustainable over time. Aside from the standard challenges of scaling up and coping with increasing domestic and international competition after the initial stage of growth, the very factors that accounted for their early growth were becoming obstacles to efficient operation. Just as certain local governments identified their economic welfare with that of TVEs and provided favorable conditions for their development, the political viability of these same governments also depended on maintaining adequate employment for their populations, even if that meant keeping TVE payrolls when they were not needed. Second and relatedly, certain TVEs have experienced explicit privatization.[2] It has long been recognized that many "collective" enterprises were in fact privately owned, that they were merely wearing red hats, but some are starting to shed their disguises. Given that the primary sources of institutional financing for TVEs have been urban credit cooperatives, rural credit cooperatives, and rural cooperative foundations, it is conceivable that the privatized TVEs are continuing to receive credit from these sources. From anecdotal evidence, however, it is apparent that some are also "raising capital from the public" by issuing non-publicly-traded shares in their businesses.[3] This latter practice is not technically legal in all parts of China and should be considered another form of informal finance.[4] The conversion of TVEs into shareholding cooperatives (*gufen hezuo qiye*) has also taken various forms in the ways that shares are actually distributed and held.[5] In some areas, shareholding cooperatives have not

2. "A Quarter of Township Enterprises in Jiangsu Privately Owned," *China Business Information Network*; and "Privately Owned Rural Enterprises Increasing," *Xinhua News Agency*, December 30, 1998. Cf. Jean C. Oi, *Rural China Takes Off: Institutional Foundations of Economic Reform* (Berkeley: University of California Press, 1999); and Susan H. Whiting, *Power and Wealth in Rural China: The Political Economy of Institutional Change* (New York: Cambridge University Press, 2001).

3. This is not the same as registering legally as a joint-stock enterprise.

4. In official statistics, the "other funds" category for sources of financing for TVEs increased from 2.9 percent of the GDP during the 1985–88 period to 4.7 percent in 1992–96. Wing Thye Woo treats "other funds" as a proxy for informal credit: "Improving Access to Credit in Rural China," in Baizhu Chen, J. Kimball Dietrich, and Yi Feng, eds., *Financial Market Reform in China: Progress, Problems, and Prospects* (Boulder, Colo.: Westview Press, 2000), 321–45.

5. Eduard B. Vermeer, "Shareholding Cooperatives: A Property Rights Analysis," in Jean C. Oi and Andrew G. Walder, eds., *Property Rights and Economic Reform in China* (Stanford, Calif.: Stanford University Press, 1999).

fundamentally changed the collective structure of enterprise ownership. In others, shareholding cooperatives have presented local elites with an opportunity to appropriate collective assets for their own benefit.[6] In places such as Wenzhou, however, shareholding cooperatives are essentially privately owned.[7] My research suggests that to the extent that TVEs become genuinely privatized in a given area, the orientation of the local government toward the private sector would be expected to become more favorable.[8] And by extension, local financial institutions (but not necessarily state banks) would be expected to engage in more lending to private businesses, and additional forms of private finance would be expected to evolve.

In addition to the observation that the developmental orientation of local governments may change over time, another complicating factor is that *the local government is not a unified entity*. As shown in the case of Wenzhou, local state banks may be expected eventually to oppose private banks and other illegal forms of financial intermediation, largely because they are pressured from higher levels of the PBOC to do so. At the same time, however, the local Industrial and Commercial Management Bureau lacks such higher-level pressure. The ICMB's mandate is to register, monitor, and collect fees from private businesses. If some registered private businesses also happen to be engaged in lucrative financial intermediation, the ICMB will not go out of its way to chastise them for violating the PBOC's regulations. By the same token, the local Agricultural Office is assigned to promote favorable conditions for agricultural development, not to enforce PBOC-defined laws. In urban areas, all *danwei* are technically part of the state, but the majority are not affiliated with the banking bureaucracy. When the local government is as complex and differentiated as in China, the possibility always exists that one of its branches will overlook or even sanction illicit financial activities. In this sense, the bureaucratic organization of the Chinese state is structurally prone to subvert its own policies—or at least to encounter coordination challenges in policy implementation.

Just as the local government in fact consists of multiple agencies with different interests, *local credit markets are also segmented*. Small-scale private entrepreneurs as a group may share a basic need for financial services, but different identities and networks affect their ability to tap certain types of

6. Sally Sargeson and Jian Zhang, "Reassessing the Role of the Local State: A Case Study of Local Government Interventions in Property Rights Reform in a Hangzhou District," *China Journal* 42 (July 1999): 77–99.

7. On the comparison of shareholding cooperatives in Shanghai versus Wenzhou, see Susan H. Whiting, "The Regional Evolution of Ownership Forms: Shareholding Cooperatives and Rural Industry in Shanghai and Wenzhou," in Oi and Walder, *Property Rights*, 171–200.

8. This is consistent with Oi, *Rural China Takes Off*, and Whiting, *Power and Wealth*.

credit. Part of the rationale for this segmentation stems from the socially rooted nature of local economic transactions. Because credit transactions inherently carry an element of risk for the lender, personal knowledge of the borrower serves as a form of insurance against default, so it should not be surprising to find that discrete private financial transactions cluster around entrepreneurs with similar gender and residential origin. In addition to the social and economic logic of market segmentation, however, the political connections of local entrepreneurs also influence the types of financial intermediaries that they may access or operate. Strong political ties may also provide a certain degree of insulation from bureaucratic interference—depending, of course, on the nature of the political ties and the broader policy environment at any given time. In sum, the reality of market segmentation in informal finance means that a diversity of financing mechanisms may flourish within a single locality, since they serve different sections of the population. A related implication is that no single type of institution is likely to dominate the entire credit market; therefore, governmental efforts to curb informal finance will not be effective if they target only the most obvious culprits of regulatory violations.

The combination of the three complicating factors outlined above—the potential for local governmental preferences to change, the fragmented nature of policy implementation, and the segmentation of credit markets—suggests that informal finance will remain an important part of the Chinese economy for years to come. To be sure, the state banking system is making efforts to rationalize the management of nonbanking financial institutions and to encourage the legal institutions to extend loans to small and medium-sized enterprises. Moreover, financial reformers would like to reduce the proportion of bad loans on the balance sheets of state banks and ensure that new loans are disbursed on the basis of creditworthiness rather than political pressure. But the state sector continues to require subsidization, and it is difficult to force state banks to act like commercial banks after their decades of behaving more like instruments of state policy. China is not alone in grappling with such challenges. Studies of informal finance in other countries show that most of the political economic issues discussed in this book are not unique to China. Indeed, financial regulators there could learn from both positive and negative examples of how other developing countries have coped with large informal financial sectors. The argument that the development of curb market institutions is driven not only by economic need but by political considerations can be illustrated by a discussion of four themes as they relate to various countries:

- Informal finance is not necessarily microfinance, and what appears to be microfinance may have macro-level effects,

- Attempts at regulating or banning informal finance can backfire,
- State-subsidized poverty alleviation loans generally fail to reach the targeted population, and
- The informal and formal financial sectors may complement one another and do not have to be mutually exclusive.

The Macro Effects of Informal Finance

Informal finance may have macro-level effects in three basic ways; these are also the reasons why political scientists should pay attention to a phenomenon so seemingly apolitical. First, as shown in my case studies, informal finance is not necessarily *micro*finance. Even private businesses with fewer than eight employees may have substantial start-up and working capital requirements. To the extent that large portions of the economically active population rely on informal finance, their transactions may infringe upon state control over the supply of credit in the economy. Second, precisely because the curb market can expand to large proportions, informal finance may actually assist in achieving the state's developmental goals. This may seem counterintuitive, since curb markets are technically illegal; they may nonetheless serve important niches ignored by the formal financial system. Third, and in contrast to the second point, the self-regulating nature of informal finance may translate into a greater propensity for financial crises at the grassroots level. This is to say not that institutions subject to the state's prudential supervision are perfectly insulated from financial malfeasance or poor management of risk but that the warning signs of impending financial collapse may not be as readily evident in the realm of informal finance.

Comparative Scale of Informal Finance

Most countries harbor an informal financial sector, and developing or transitional economies tend to have financially repressed environments that are especially conducive to the emergence of curb markets. Although measuring the relative scope of informal finance is notoriously difficult, Table 6.1 presents statistics from studies that have attempted to estimate informal credit as a percentage of formal borrowing in various national economies, as well as the percentage of the population participating in curb market activities. (See Appendix E for the use of rotating credit associations around the world.)

These percentages provide only a rough snapshot of the prevalence of informal borrowing in developing countries. They do not reflect the fluctuations of informal finance over time as a result of exogenous shocks such as extreme weather conditions, natural disasters, and shifts in the

Table 6.1. Informal Finance in Comparative Perspective

Country	Informal Credit as % of Total Formal Borrowings	% of Population Participating in Informal Finance	Source[a]	Date of Survey/ Estimate
Bangladesh (rural)	63	36.5	Germidis, Kessler, and Meghir (1991)	
Bolivia (urban)	49.4	>33	Berthoud and Milligan (1995); Adams and Canavesi (1989)	1987
Cameroon	27	70	Schrieder and Cuevas (1992)	1988
China (rural)	25	20	Shi (1996) Huang (1996), IFC (2000)	1994
Dominican Republic	20	—	Christen (1992)	1980s
India (rural)	39	—	Ghate et al. (1992): AIDIS national sample	1981–82
Indonesia	>80	—	Robinson (1994)	
Gambia	c. 67	—	Aryeetey (1994)	
Ghana	60	—	Dadson (1996)	
Guinea	>200[b]	—	Walker (1996)	
Korea (rural)	50	—	Ghate et al. (1992): Yearbook of Agric and Forestry	1986
Laos	46.5	38	UNDP/UNCDF (1997)	1996
Malawi	>100	>19	Chipeta and Mkandawire (1991)	1988
Malaysia (rural)	62	—	Van Nieuwkoop (1992)	1986
Mexico (rural)	50–55	—	Germidis, Kessler, and Meghir (1991)	
Niger (rural)	45	—	Graham (1992)	1985–86
Nigeria (Kaduna State)	65	85	Udry (1990)	1987–88
Nepal (rural)	57.1	—	Ghate et al. (1992): Nepal Rashtra Bank	1982
Pakistan (rural)	69	33	Van der Harst (1974); Ghate et al. (1992): PRCS	1985
Philippines (rural)	59–70	33	Ghate et al. (1992): Social Weather Survey	1987
Sri Lanka	45	—	Ghate et al. (1992): Central Bank of Ceylon	1976
Taiwan	24–40	>50	Shea (1994) Smith (1999)	1964–90 pre-1995
Thailand	21–50	—	Vongpradhip (1985); Siamwalla et al. (1990)	
West Bank and Gaza Strip	—	38.6	Hamed (1998)	MAS, 6/1996
Zambia	84	—	Germidis, Kessler, and Meghir (1991)	
Zimbabwe	87	—	Germidis, Kessler, and Meghir (1991)	

Note: Where multiple estimates were available for the same country, the lower figure was chosen.

[a] For complete references, see the list of sources following Appendix E.

[b] The volume of capital flows in Guinea's informal financial sector has been estimated to be twice that in the formal financial sector: Walker, "Guinea" (1996).

political or macroeconomic environment. In the Philippines, for example, a large number of rural banks closed down during the economic crisis of 1983–85, dramatically restricting the official supply of rural credit; during this period, informal moneylenders gained a substantial share of the credit market, but their popularity declined as formal credit sources reemerged.[9] By the same token, macroeconomic crises may expose and exacerbate weaknesses in informal financing mechanisms, thereby curbing their use. For instance, Israel's anti-inflationary policies in 1985 stimulated a debt crisis in the entire cooperative agriculture sector and revealed a systemic weakness in the cooperative credit system—a tendency for overborrowing through mutual liability arrangements.[10] This revelation led to the discrediting of cooperative credit, such that neither commercial banks nor private lenders were willing to extend additional credit to the cooperatives; and most regional cooperatives collapsed. In short, even though events may mediate trends in the informal financial sector, to the extent that formal sources of credit are limited—and they are, in most developing countries—the scale of informal finance may be quite substantial. Large sums of money may be circulating beyond the purview of the state's banking and fiscal authorities.

Potential Developmental Contribution of Informal Finance

Whatever its oppositional stance vis-à-vis the official supply of credit, informal finance may also affect the broader political economy through its developmental impact. The functional spectrum of informal finance ranges from the low end of the economy, where it represents a self-help strategy for mere survival, to the higher end, where it represents a self-help financing strategy for private businesses that may be quite profitable.[11] In the middle of the spectrum, informal finance may facilitate household accumulation of consumer durables or the building and purchase of residential housing.[12]

9. Meliza Agabin, "A Review of Policies Impinging on the Informal Credit Markets in the Philippines," Working Paper Series No. 88–12, Philippine Institute for Development Studies, Quezon City, cited in Prabhu Ghate et al., *Informal Finance: Some Findings from Asia* (Hong Kong: Oxford University Press for Asia Development Bank, 1992), 12.

10. Yaov Kislev, Zvi Lerman, and Pinhas Zusman, "Cooperative Credit in Agriculture—The Israeli Experience," in Karla Hoff, Avishay Braverman, and Joseph E. Stiglitz, eds., *The Economics of Rural Organization: Theory, Practice, and Policy* (New York: Oxford University Press, 1993), 214–27.

11. In socialist Hungary, Szelenyi described private entrepreneurship in the second economy as a "strategy of resistance" against state control, but the broader applicability of this conceptualization hinges upon the political economy of the country under consideration. Ivan Szelenyi, *Socialist Entrepreneurs: Embourgeoisement in Rural Hungary* (Madison: University of Wisconsin Press, 1988).

12. See, e.g., Timothy Besley and Alec R. Levenson, "The Role of Informal Finance in Household Capital Accumulation: Evidence from Taiwan," *Economic Journal* 106 (1996): 39–59.

Informal finance may serve the entire spectrum of functions in countries that have suffered ongoing hardships and in which the vast majority of the population is employed in the second economy. The ubiquity of informal finance in Chad, the fifth largest country in Africa, provides one such example. Between droughts, civil wars, and a sharp drop in the world price of its primary commodity, cotton, private farmers and traders have had little relief from extreme conditions since the late 1970s. Moreover, micro-entrepreneurs are completely excluded from the formal financial system, which allocates most of its credit to Cotonchad, the largest SOE in Chad. Therefore, like their counterparts in other parts of Africa, both entrepreneurs and consumers in Chad rely on curb market practices such as rotating credit associations called *tontines*.[13]

Despite the range of developmental functions that curb markets may serve, governments usually view the formal rather than the informal financial system as a policy tool for achieving their growth objectives. By definition, the informal sector comprises economic activities that lie beyond the scope of the regulatory state, so one would not expect the state to regard it as readily subject to instrumental manipulation. Yet studies of industrial development more generally are beginning to note states' implicit recognition of curb market finance as a complement to their developmental strategies. More salient examples come from two of the newly industrialized countries (NICs) in East Asia, Taiwan, and South Korea, which experienced rapid economic growth under financially repressed conditions for decades.

It is well known that Taiwan's export-promoting growth trajectory during the 1960s and 1970s relied on a combination of state-directed investment in large public enterprises and tens of thousands of small private firms engaged in labor-intensive light manufacturing. The latter accounted for approximately 40 percent of manufactured output during this miraculous phase of double-digit growth.[14] Yet family-owned businesses had limited access to credit from state banks, relying instead on curb market sources such as moneylenders, pawnbrokers, ROSCAs, credit unions, underground investment companies, and extensive use of the post-dated check.[15] During

---

13. Ousa Sananikone, "Chad," in Leila Webster and Peter Fidler, eds., *The Informal Sector and Microfinance Institutions in West Africa* (Washington, D.C.: World Bank, 1996), 105–13. Rotating credit associations are also called *paris, esusus, susus,* or *osusus* in West Africa.

14. Robert Wade, *Governing the Market: Economic Theory and the Role of Government in East Asian Industrialization* (Princeton: Princeton University Press, 1990), 110.

15. Overviews include Sheng-yi Lee, *Money and Finance in the Economic Development of Taiwan* (London: Macmillan, 1990); Jia-Dong Shea, "Taiwan: Development and Structural Change of the Financial System," in Hugh Patrick and Yung Chul Park, eds., *The Financial Development of Japan, Korea, and Taiwan: Growth, Repression, and Liberalization* (New York: Oxford University Press, 1994), 222–87; and Shui-Yan Tang, "Informal Credit Markets and Economic Development in Taiwan," *World Development* 23, 5 (1995): 845–56.

the 1970s the volume of curb market financing was estimated at 30 percent as much as all formal sector lending.[16] Given the curb market's economic significance, the Central Bank of Taiwan has tracked its interest rates on a monthly basis since the late 1950s and even maintains three separate statistical categories for rates of loans against post-dated checks, unsecured loans, and deposits with firms, respectively.[17] The reason for monitoring curb market rates so closely is that they reveal valuable information about fluctuations in the real cost of capital in the economy, which in turn enables the central bank to adjust its monetary policy.[18] In sum, by financing small enterprises the curb market may be seen as supporting much of Taiwan's export-oriented growth, while providing the central bank with a fairly reliable gauge of price conditions in the economy.[19] The curb market has also been a source of financial turmoil, but on balance, Taiwanese politicians and bankers alike recognize its contribution to adjusting allocational inefficiencies in the formal financial system.

Although Korea's industrial structure consists of larger corporate groups than those in Taiwan, there too the curb market has played a key role in financial intermediation, especially during critical periods of economic adjustment.[20] In Korea's first postwar financial crisis (1969–1971), for example, the International Monetary Fund (with U.S. pressure) forced the country to adopt extreme stabilization policies, including the elimination of export subsidies and import restrictions, temporary limits on foreign borrowing, and, most painfully, devaluation of the *won*. Given that Korea's industrial enterprises were highly leveraged with foreign capital, the devaluation severely limited their ability to service this debt. Since state banks were saddled with nonperforming loans and thus not in a position to extend additional credit, even the largest firms found themselves borrowing from private financial intermediaries. Thus the curb market ballooned: in 1969 informal financial flows accounted for approximately

16. Wade, *Governing the Market*, 161.

17. In official documents, the curb market is referred to as the "unorganized money market." See Central Bank of China, *Financial Statistics Monthly* (Taipei, Taiwan District, Republic of China), various issues.

18. Nicholas H. Reigg, "The Role of Fiscal and Monetary Policies in Taiwan's Economic Development" (Ph.D. diss., University of Connecticut, 1979), 253, cited in Wade, *Governing the Market*, 161.

19. During the 1980s, small and medium enterprises accounted for "60 percent of employment, 45 percent of production, and 60 percent of exports in manufacturing": Tein-Chen Chou, "Taiwan," in Stephan Haggard and Chung H. Lee, eds., *Financial Systems and Economic Policy in Developing Countries* (Ithaca: Cornell University Press, 1995).

20. Overviews of Korean industrialization include Alice A. Amsden, *Asia's Next Giant: South Korea and Late Industrialization* (New York: Oxford University Press, 1989); David Cole and Yung Chul Park, *Financial Development in Korea, 1974–1978* (Cambridge: Harvard University Press, 1983); Wade, *Governing the Market*; and Jung-en Woo, *Race to the Swift: State and Finance in Korean Industrialization* (New York: Columbia University Press, 1991).

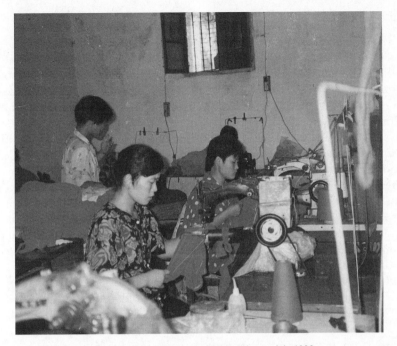

Sweating far away from home. Kaifeng, Henan, July 1996.

82 percent of the money supply and about 30 percent of all bank loans outstanding.[21]

Before long, however, businesses were not able to meet their financial obligations to the curb market either. On the eve of regime change in 1971, the Federation of Korean Industrialists demanded on behalf of large corporations that the government declare a moratorium on all curb market debt. And after some political haggling, it did. All creditors and debtors were required to register with the government, and a three-year freeze on payments was imposed, after which the debts would be converted into five-year loans with an interest ceiling of 18 percent. Of the 209,896 creditors who registered, 70 percent turned out to be small-scale lenders (with assets less than US$2,889), and most did not even realize that their informal savings had been channeled into the corporate sector by curb market intermediaries. To put it crudely, the curb market bailed out big business and then when the latter exerted political pressure on the fragile government, informal creditors suffered the consequences. Still, this picture of the developmental role of informal finance does demonstrate the potential political utility of the curb market.

21. This discussion draws from Woo, *Race to the Swift*, 109–15.

Curb Market Crises

The third way in which informal finance may become a formal political issue for the state occurs when the normally low-profile workings of informal finance run into difficulties and affect substantial portions of the local population. Crises in the informal financial sector are not always triggered by top-down policy changes such as structural adjustment programs. Grassroots financing mechanisms themselves may be sources of instability. As in Quanzhou and Wenzhou, even rotating-credit associations (*hui*) may cause serious local political turmoil if they become large-scale operations and then collapse all at once. Similar incidents occurred with *hui* in Vietnam during the 1990s. When such crises occur, mass participation in curb market activities may be self-limiting in the short term. Losing money or seeing other people lose money provides a powerful negative demonstration. Nevertheless, if alternative sources of financial intermediation do not develop, there is reason to believe that credit-strapped businesses will return to the curb market. Despite Taiwan's disastrous experiences with *hui* and other curb market mechanisms during 1983–85, participation in *hui* bounced back to a large extent in 1986 and by 1991 had recovered to 1977 levels (20 to 30 percent of all households).[22]

When the scope of curb market crises encompasses enough of the local population, government intervention may be required to organize emergency compensatory programs, perhaps issue stringent financial regulations, or undertake more fundamental financial reforms.[23] Prior to the massive *hui* collapses in Wenzhou and Quanzhou, local authorities had not paid much attention to "popular" (*minjian*) financing activities, for the latter seemed to be fueling growth in the local private economy. But as the scale of the incidents became too large to ignore, the local governments were forced by the victims to perform crisis management and punish the offending *hui* organizers in a public manner. In the end, neither the *hui* victims nor local governmental officials were fully satisfied with the outcome, since people could not be fully compensated for their losses.

Regulation as a Double-Edged Sword

Sometimes, when informal finance creates problems for the otherwise complacent staff of the state, proposed regulatory solutions may backfire.

22. Alec R. Levenson and Timothy Besley, "The Anatomy of an Informal Financial Market: Rosca Participation in Taiwan," *Journal of Development Economics* 51, 1 (1996): 45–68; see esp. 58 for a graph that tracks levels of *hui* participation, 1977–91.

23. The pyramidal schemes that collapsed in Albania in 1997 affected an estimated 75 percent of the population and resulted in extreme civil unrest, but the political outrage stemmed from the fact that the government sponsored the schemes, through which an esti-

Most states face the fundamental dilemma of striking the proper balance between allowing financial markets to operate on their own and regulating them. For prudential reasons, there has been a bias toward the regulatory end of the spectrum. Formal financial institutions are subject to licensing requirements, capital adequacy ratios, standardized reporting procedures, and portfolio diversification—regulations intended to minimize financial risk in the economy. In developing and transitional economies, not only has financial liberalization been one of the last areas to experience the relaxation of state control (e.g., after abandoning price controls of commodities), but the very process of liberalization has typically been accompanied by the proliferation of additional regulations. Adding to the complexity of this process is the more basic challenge of how to enforce financial regulations without triggering unwanted responses from curb market participants—responses ranging from financial panic to the less destructive but nonetheless problematic outcome of continued or additional regulatory subversion.

To Panic or Not to Panic

The way that banking authorities attempted to discipline illicit financial institutions in Zhengzhou in 1998 offers a local-level example of an unwanted response. Many private financial institutions were promising returns that were not sustainable over time, so on their own they probably would have triggered a small-scale panic as each one went bankrupt and discrete networks of depositors lost their savings or principal investments. But the high-profile manner in which financial regulators went about rectifying the institutions triggered panic among the city's depositors at large. Even state-sanctioned NBFIs experienced runs, and they were not even the ones under immediate investigation.

A similar chain of events transpired on an even larger scale in the Indian state of Kerala. As migration to the Persian Gulf increased in the 1970s, the demand for informal finance expanded, and its supply took the form of finance companies. By the time of the mass collapses there were approximately 12,000 finance companies engaged in the business of mobilizing high-interest-bearing deposits and providing credit or investment equity to assorted business concerns. The triggering event of the crash occurred in March 1987 when the Monopolies and Restrictive Practices Commission declared that one particular finance company, the Oriental Finance and Exchange Company, did not have an investment portfolio capable of yield-

mated US$1 billion (about one-third of the country's GNP) was lost: Sharon Johnson-Cramer and Uliana Kociu, "End of a Nation? Why Albania Fell Apart," *Christian Science Monitor*, March 20, 1997, 7.

ing the 28 to 35 percent returns promised to investors. Depositors rushed to withdraw their savings not only from Oriental Finance but from most of the others as well. In the end, about 56 percent of the total deposits in these finance companies was lost.[24]

In contrast, when gray-market financial institutions in Taiwan ran into liquidity problems during the early to middle 1980s, the government forestalled rather than inspired further public panic—although ultimately, the Nationalist government had to discipline its own officials. Upon learning that the best-known debtor of the Tenth Credit Cooperative Association, the Cathay Group (Taiwan's largest investment and trust company at the time), had run into financial difficulties in 1985, TCCA depositors crowded outside the cooperative's gates to claim their savings. The government urgently summoned the Cooperative Bank of Taiwan for assistance. The CBT immediately paid off all the TCCA's debts, absorbed the entire cooperative, and calmed down the depositors (who had already withdrawn a total of US$150 million in two days).[25] Potential panics involving three other informal financial institutions were similarly resolved.[26] The TCCA incident eventually exposed more than the financial risk inherent in nonbanking financial institutions, however. The Cathay Group itself became the focus of a series of high-profile investigations, which revealed not only speculative real estate investments but also corruption at the highest levels of the Kuomingtang (KMT) government to cover it up.[27] The exposés resulted in resignations on the part of the minister of Economic Affairs, officials in the Ministry of Finance, and the general secretary of the KMT.

Regulatory Avoidance

Short of generating anxiety among curb market depositors, financial regulations may simply inspire the more mundane response of regulatory avoidance. As Anand Chandavarkar observes, "Attempts to regulate the informal sector are liable to fail because its very rationale derives from its informality and immunity from official regulation. Regulation is more likely to be counterproductive since it may lead to evasion of laws without providing for adequate institutional substitutes."[28] A few examples of finan-

24. This example is discussed in Ghate et al., *Informal Finance*, 75–76.

25. "A Taiwanese Bank, Tenth Credit Cooperative, Suffered a US$150M Run on February 11 and 12 1985," *Asian Wall Street Journal*, February 14, 1985, 5; "The Taiwanese Government Has Taken Over Tenth Credit Cooperative at the Request of the Bank's Depositors," *Asian Wall Street Journal*, February 19, 1985, 3.

26. Ya-Hwei Yang, "Taiwan: Development and Structural Change of the Banking System," in Patrick and Park, *The Financial Development of Japan, Korea, and Taiwan*, 314–15.

27. Wade, *Governing the Market*, 293.

28. Anand G. Chandavarkar, "The Informal Financial Sector in Developing Countries: Analysis, Evidence, and Policy Implications," IMF Working Paper, Washington, D.C., 1985.

cial regulations that have failed to achieve their intended objective will demonstrate that efforts to "formalize" specific curb market arrangements may have the perverse effect of creating alternative forms of informal finance.

An archetypal example may be seen in India's continual efforts to eliminate the informal financial sector ever since the first decennial All-India Rural Credit Survey in 1951 revealed that 93 percent of rural households relied on informal sources of credit at the time.[29] Official consternation, rooted in normative concerns over the apparent ubiquity and monopolistic position of the usurious village moneylender, has led various Indian governments to pass reams of regulations aimed at enforcing interest-rate ceilings and wiping out what legislators perceive to be exploitive financial practices. Yet informal finance continues to thrive.[30] One reason for the ineffectiveness of even well-intentioned anti-usury laws is their failure to address the underlying source of high interest rates: that demand for rural credit continues to exceed the availability and distribution of its official supply.[31]

The Kerala Chitties Act of 1975, for instance, sought to regulate rotating credit associations (called *chit* funds or *chitties*) by requiring them to register with the state.[32] Instead of bringing chit funds under state supervision, however, the act dramatically curtailed their use, for members did not want to subject their community-based activities to official monitoring. Shortly thereafter, former chitty organizers devised a new way to conduct the business of finance. They formed private "partnership firms" that were registered through the Indian Partnership Act (a corporate law) and obtained special moneylending licenses requiring them to keep their capitalization below 100,000 *rupees* and to comply with the Kerala Money Lenders Act, which limited annual interest rates to 12 percent: these two conditions enabled private financial institutions to evade supervision by the Reserve Bank of India. The firms' activities proved to be extremely popular,

29. F. J. A. Bouman, with René Bastiaansen, Han Van Den Bogaard, Henny Gerner, Otto Hospes, and Joost Groot Kormelink, *Small, Short, and Unsecured: Informal Rural Finance in India* (New York: Oxford University Press, 1989), 12–14.

30. Although the All-India Debt and Investment Survey of 1981–82 indicates that the percentage of all households (urban and rural) borrowing from the informal sector has declined to 38.8 percent, most analysts believe that that the figure vastly underestimates the true scope of informal finance. See, e.g., Clive Bell, "Interactions between Institutional and Informal Credit Agencies in Rural India," in Hoff, Braverman, and Stiglitz, 186–213; and Ghate et al., *Informal Finance*, 58–60.

31. A succinct discussion is Robert C. Vogel and Robert Weiland, "Regulatory Avoidance in Informal Financial Markets," in Dale W. Adams and Delbert A. Fitchett, eds., *Informal Finance in Low-Income Countries*, (Boulder, Colo.: Westview Press, 1992), 293–302.

32. The impact of the Kerala Chitties Act of 1975 on the informal financial sector in Trichur, Kerala, is analyzed in B. A. Prakash, "Private Financing Firms in Kerala: A Study," *Economic and Political Weekly* 19 (1984), cited and critiqued in Bouman et al., *Small, Short, and Unsecured*, 117–120.

profitable—and illegal. They provided traders and small businesses with short-term loans at 30 to 40 percent annual interest, offered depositors 24 percent interest annually, and kept two sets of books. In short, the attempt to regulate chit funds only led to even more sophisticated and institutionalized forms of private finance. Neither interest-rate ceilings nor chitty registration was achieved, and small businesses continued to rely on informal finance. As F. J. A. Bouman observes, "Unrealistic legislation and policies seem to nourish their own culture of discontent, stimulating evasive tactics and manipulative routines."[33]

Regulatory Denial

Not all informal financial intermediaries are intrinsically determined to circumvent state regulation and taxation. Formal registration offers certain advantages that come with third-party enforcement, such as internal operational discipline and the projection of legitimacy to the public, qualities whose absence can lead to financial mismanagement and localized crises. Nonetheless, there are instances when the state chooses not to regulate certain informal financial institutions, preferring instead to outlaw them altogether. For example, in Wenzhou (Chapter 4), when the local PBOC saw firsthand the economic utility of private money houses in the 1980s and lobbied the central PBOC to legalize them and subject their operations to People's Bank regulations, the PBOC instead banned private money houses. Their operators thus faced the choice of either going underground or converting themselves into UCCs. The former option obviously meant operating illegally, whereas the local interpretation of requirements for operating as a UCC offered sufficient flexibility for evading national banking laws, just as the partnership firms did in Kerala. (The consolidation of UCCs into UCBs has since circumscribed the scope of this gray area, however.)

The rapid rise and fall of private finance companies in Pakistan during the late 1970s provides an even more remarkable illustration of how counterproductive regulatory denial can be.[34] With the influx of remittances from the Middle East during 1977–79, private finance companies proliferated in Pakistan. They mobilized deposits from villages where nationalized banks did not operate and invested the funds in real estate, commerce, transportation concerns, and other profitable sectors. Apart from the convenience of handing their savings to local community members–sons of powerful village families–who were employed by the finance companies,

33. Bouman et al., *Small, Short, and Unsecured*, 118, 120–21.

34. Naved Hamid and Ijaz Nabi, "Private Finance Companies in LDCs: Lessons from an Experiment," *World Development* 17, 8 (1989): 1289–97.

Islamic villagers also appreciated the religious propriety of "sharing invest-ment returns" on their deposits, as opposed to "earning interest."[35] As more and more companies emerged, however, some began using the deposits for conspicuous consumption rather than investing them properly. Meanwhile, it became increasingly difficult for depositors to distinguish the well-managed companies from the fraudulent ones.

At the peak of their popularity in mid-1979, therefore, a group of the more reputable finance companies petitioned the state to regulate their activities via licensing, auditing, staffing, depository insurance, and other requirements. The petitioners reasoned that subjecting themselves to pru-dential supervision and official registration would restore public confi-dence. The Banking Council not only refused the request but prohibited finance companies from keeping deposits in the nationalized banks. Osten-tatious investigations into a handful of the less scrupulous companies further alarmed depositors; as might be expected, the finance companies experienced depository flight and began to collapse. The government out-lawed all private financial institutions shortly thereafter.

At the time of their destruction, finance companies had mobilized over 5 percent of Pakistan's total savings from grassroots depositors who were excluded from official banks. Thus, ordinary people paid the cost of state efforts to reclaim a monopoly on savings mobilization, and the irony is that official banks lacked the administrative reach to mobilize the same pool of savings after eliminating the finance companies. By turning down the opportunity to regulate private finance companies and forcing them to withdraw their funds from nationalized banks, the state self-destructively cut itself off from a valuable source of deposits.

The impact of regulatory intervention (or lack thereof) on informal finance, then, cannot be diagramed in unidirectional terms. For pruden-tial security, the state needs to demonstrate its willingness to enforce its financial regulations; yet rashly publicized efforts at exposing fraudulence in curb market institutions may provoke the worse short-term evil of public panic. By the same token, legislative efforts to protect the public from high interest rates may push regulatory-avoidant moneylenders into even less supervised spheres of operation or illegality. And if the underlying reason for regulatory hostility toward the curb market is that the state seeks to monopolize savings deposits, then regulatory denial may simply shut the state out from those very deposits. Seemingly straightforward solutions have feedback effects.

---

35. On banking in Islamic contexts, see, e.g., Elias G. Kazarian, *Islamic versus Traditional Banking: Financial Innovation in Egypt* (Boulder, Colo.: Westview Press, 1993); and Abdulla Saeed, *Islamic Banking and Interest: A Study of the Prohibition of Riba and Its Contemporary Inter-pretation* (New York: E. J. Brill, 1976).

Subsidized Poverty Alleviation Loans As Band-Aids

To a certain extent, informal finance may be seen as a reactive phenomenon to gaps between the official supply and demand for financial services.[36] Governments have not been oblivious to the fact that large portions of the population (typically but not exclusively rural) may be excluded from the formal financial system; hence, most developing countries have established specialized banks, credit cooperatives, or other institutions intended to fulfill welfare or distributional objectives rather than to meet the broader market demand for commercial credit per se. The subsidization of interest rates in these credit programs underscores their developmental orientation; they are not meant to profit from the poor.

Be that as it may, low-interest microfinance schemes sponsored by the government are best described as Band-Aids: they are cheap;[37] they cover up obvious wounds; and they either fall off once the adhesive wears thin or stick stubbornly to the affected area even after they are no longer needed. The metaphor is hardly controversial in light of decades of development experience with failed subsidized microfinance projects. Both scholarly and policy impact studies have argued that subsidized credit programs share certain weaknesses: the loans typically benefit local elites and people who are already relatively well off rather than the intended lower-income population; the programs have higher default rates than programs that charge market interest rates and fees; and they are not sustainable tools for development because their low-interest rates discourage savings mobilization and fail to cover their operating expenses.[38]

The logic underlying these three weaknesses may seem counterintuitive. Why would low-interest rates inhibit the achievement of developmental goals when the whole point of specialized credit programs is to enhance the economic welfare of disadvantaged populations? Moreover, how could poor people possibly benefit from paying market interest rates on loans? To explain these apparent paradoxes, we return to a familiar refrain: local political and social factors fundamentally mediate the allocation of credit at the ground level. Although the cases of financial institutional creation considered in this book developed from below, the political and social logic

36. On the distinction between "reactive" and "autonomous" financial institutions, see Anand G. Chandavarkar, "The Premium for Risk as a Determinant of Interest Rates in Underdeveloped Rural Areas: Comment," *Quarterly Journal of Economics* 79, 2 (1965): 322–25.

37. Actually, such programs are expensive to maintain, but the loans themselves are cheap to the borrower.

38. The classic critique of subsidized credit schemes is compiled in Dale W. Adams, Douglas H. Graham, and J. D. Von Pischke, eds., *Undermining Rural Development with Cheap Credit* (Boulder, Colo.: Westview Press, 1984). A contrarian view is Jonathan Morduch, "The Microfinance Schism," Development Discussion Paper No. 626, Harvard Institute for International Development, February 1998.

may be extended to the distribution of subsidized government credit emanating from higher bureaucratic organs. More concretely, the mediating effects of this logic can explain why informal finance continues to flourish even in areas that have substantial flows of subsidized credit. A purely economic logic would expect an increase in the official supply of credit to limit the demand for informal finance.[39] Yet such a result has not been borne out empirically.

The government of Thailand, for example, has experimented with various ways to increase the availability of credit to farmers since 1916. Political pressure for redistributive policies that would benefit rural areas became particularly intense after the downfall of the military government in 1973. Banks were subsequently required to lend to a specialized agricultural bank, the Bank of Agriculture and Agricultural Cooperatives (BAAC), which in turn was instructed to increase its lending to rural credit cooperatives and individual households. Despite a tremendous increase in the supply of agricultural credit, poorer villagers have continued to rely primarily on high-interest sources of informal credit. The formal credit cooperatives prefer to disburse larger loans to landed farmers, whereas village moneylenders and traders are willing to work with poorer householders whom official institutions regard as a high-risk client base but who are willing to pay high interest rates in exchange for loans. Yet the local credit market is not bifurcated strictly along economic lines. As Amman Siamwalla and his colleagues observe, even farmers who are able to secure credit from the credit cooperatives find themselves borrowing from moneylenders to repay debts to credit cooperatives, since the latter are not willing to roll over working capital loans.[40] Siamwalla's work reveals additional dimensions of social complexity, but the main point here is that because of the political and social segmentation of local credit markets, merely increasing the official supply of credit may not have a substitution effect for informal finance.

The Thai rural credit case is somewhat unusual, however, in that the credit cooperatives have not experienced the high arrears and defaults that most subsidized programs have. A 1984 World Bank study of agricultural credit projects in Africa, Asia, and Latin America revealed an average arrears rate of 39.4 percent, and default rates from 50 to 95 percent have

39. This is the "supply-leading" view of finance. Classic articulations include Harvey Leibenstein, *Economic Backwardness and Economic Growth* (New York: Wiley, 1957); W. A. Lewis, *The Theory of Economic Growth* (Homewood, Ill.: Irwin, 1955); and Hugh T. Patrick, "Financial Development and Economic Growth in Developing Countries," *Economic and Cultural Change* 14, 2 (1966): 174–89.

40. Ammar Siamwalla, Chirmsak Pinthong, Nipon Poapongsakorn, Ploenpit Satsanguam, Prayong Nettayarak, Wanrak Mingmaneenakin, and Yuavares Yubpun, "The Thai Rural Credit System and Elements of a Theory: Public Subsidies, Private Information, and Segmented Markets," in Hoff, Braverman, and Stiglitz, 154–85.

been reported in similar programs.[41] Apart from production-related factors for the incapacity of borrowers to repay loans on time (e.g., weather effects on crop yields in a particular year), two noneconomic reasons for the poor developmental performance of these programs have been identified. First, as suggested previously, official credit programs are frequently captured by local elites and deployed for their own political and economic ends. Subsidized credit from above has difficulty making it through the filter of local political hierarchies.[42] Second and relatedly, governments have given the impression that these programs do not face hard budget constraints, meaning that defaulters will not be punished and the credit programs will simply continue to receive infusions of subsidized credit.[43] In some cases, governments have forgiven the debts of a particular sector of the population for political reasons.[44] Similarly, governments have overtly used subsidized credit as a political side payment. For example, Bolivia's General Hugo Banzar rose to power in 1971 via a military coup supported by a coalition that included farmers from the lowlands of Santa Cruz. During the course of Banzar's rule from 1971 to 1978, Santa Cruz received a disproportionate amount of agricultural credit, which went into the pockets of rural elites at the expense of farmers in Bolivia's highlands.[45]

Instead of disbursing soft loans through government agencies, critics of "traditional" credit programs thus advocate building independent, local financial institutions that extend loans to micro-entrepreneurs in a financially self-sustainable manner.[46] These institutions may take the form of

41. World Bank, "Agriculture Credit: Sector Policy Paper," 2d ed., 1984, cited Marguerite S. Robinson, "Financial Intermediation at the Local Level: Lessons from Indonesia, Part Two, A Theoretical Perspective," Development Discussion Paper No. 482, Harvard Institute for International Development (March 1994), 38; Nimal Sanderatne, "An Analytical Approach to Loan Defaults by Small Farmers," *Savings and Development* 2, 4 (1978): 290–304, excerpted in J. D. Von Piscke, Dale W. Adams, and Gordon Donald, eds., *Rural Financial Markets in Developing Countries: Their Use and Abuse* (Baltimore: Johns Hopkins University Press, 1983), 184.

42. See, e.g., Bruce L. Robert Jr., "Agricultural Credit Cooperatives, Rural Development and Agrarian Politics in Madras, 1837–1937," *Indian Economic and Social History Review* 16, 2 (1979): 163–64, adapted in Piscke, Adams, and Donald, *Rural Financial Markets*, 354–364.

43. Sandaratne, "Analytical Approach," 88–89. This is practically conventional wisdom among microfinance practitioners.

44. India is cited as an example in Jacob Yaron, McDonald P. Benjamin Jr., and Gerda L. Piprek, *Rural Finance: Issues, Design, and Best Practices*, Environmentally and Socially Sustainable Development Studies and Monographs Series 13 (Washington, D.C.: World Bank, 1997), 102, cited in Joanna Ledgerwood, *Microfinance Handbook: An Institutional and Financial Perspective* Sustainable Banking with the Poor Series (Washington, D.C.: World Bank, 1999); Box 1.3, 15.

45. Farmers in the highlands ended up receiving assistance from USAID: Jerry R. Ladman and Ronald L. Tinnermeier, "The Political Economy of Agricultural Credit: The Case of Bolivia," *American Journal of Agricultural Economics* 63, 1 (1981): 66–72.

46. This view is advanced in Malcolm Harper, *Profit for the Poor: Cases in Micro-Finance* (London: Intermediate Technology Publications, 1998); Jan Pieter Krahnen and Reinhard H. Schmidt, *Development Finance as Institution Building: A New Approach to Poverty-Oriented Banking*

financial NGOs (e.g., BRAC in Bangladesh, K-REP in Kenya), finance companies (e.g., Finansol in Colombia), peer solidarity lending groups (e.g., Grameen Bank), credit unions, village banks (e.g., BRI in Indonesia, FINCA in Mexico and Costa Rica), or even full-fledged commercial banks (e.g., BRI and Bank Dagang Bali in Indonesia, BancoSol in Bolivia, Caja Social in Colombia, Hatton National Bank in Sri Lanka).[47] Regardless of their corporate status, they are all encouraged to charge interest rates that cover the operating and financial costs of extending small loans to economically active members of community and, often in particular, to women micro-entrepreneurs.

Among financial intermediaries that specialize in extending financial services to women, the cumulative experience of microfinance practitioners throughout the world suggests that women are more likely than men to repay their loans, and more likely to invest their earnings in developmental uses such as education, health care, and food.[48] Men of comparable socioeconomic status are more likely to default on loans and to spend their disposable income on personal consumption of cigarettes, alcohol, and entertainment.[49] In fact, one of the most popular microfinance models, Grameen Bank, did not have a gender focus when its programs first started in Bangladesh; over time, though, women proved to be better credit risks and came to dominate Grameen's group-lending programs, which are now replicated all over the world.[50] In this respect, charging higher interest rates may serve as a screening mechanism for reaching the intended population. Those who are engaged in productive ventures and expect to generate income are more likely to take on high-interest

(Boulder, Colo.: Westview Press, 1994); Ledgerwood, *Microfinance Handbook*; and Maria Otero and Elisabeth Rhyne, eds., *The New World of Microenterprise Finance* (West Hartford, Conn.: Kumarian Press, 1994); and practitioner-oriented publications by members of CGAP and the International Coalition on Women and Credit.

47. Banco Solidario, SA (BancoSol) is a derivative of a financial NGO, PRODEM, which serves micro-entrepreneurs; see Amy J. Glosser, "The Creation of BancoSol in Bolivia," in Otero and Rhyne, *New World of Microenterprise Finance*, 229–50; The Hatton National Bank in 1989 started a microfinance program called the Gami Pubuduwa Program; see "Scaling to Microfinance: The Hatton National Bank," *CGAP Newsletter* 3 (January 1997).

48. See Marguerite Berger and Mayra Buvunic, eds., *Women Ventures: Assistance to the Informal Sector in Latin America* (Hartford, Conn.: Kumarian Press, 1989); publications by Women's World Banking; and Daisy Dwyer and Judith Bruce, eds., *A Home Divided: Women and Income in the Third World* (Stanford, Calif.: Stanford University Press, 1988), which cites earlier studies (5).

49. Many of my informants echoed this view of a gendered pattern in investment versus consumption behavior, including, Interviewee Nos. 23, 27, 34, 38, 72, 76, 97.

50. David Bornstein, *The Price of a Dream: The Story of the Grameen Bank* (Chicago: University of Chicago, 1997); Susan Holcombe, *Managing to Empower: The Grameen Bank Experience of Poverty Alleviation* (London: Zed Books, 1995); and Shanhidur R. Khandker, Baqui Khaliliy, and Zahed Khan, *Grameen Bank: Performance and Sustainability*, World Bank Discussion Paper, no. 306 (Washington, D.C.: World Bank, 1995).

Repaying a micro-loan in a Grameen Bank replication. Yang Shigou Village, Henan, October 1996.

loans.[51] As evidenced by the persistence of the moneylender, people who really need credit for income generation are willing (and able) to pay for it; hence, the reasoning goes, microfinance institutions should charge financially sustainable rates to weed out the lemons and stay in business themselves. That is how low-income producers can benefit from unsubsidized rates.

Despite the high-profile international consensus on the negative impact of subsidized credit programs,[52] and warnings from experienced donors and practitioners, China's current poverty alleviation strategy is retracing the well-worn steps that dozens of developing countries have traveled; by August 1998 the government had spent 600 million *yuan* (US$72.6 million)

51. Karla Hoff and Joseph E. Stiglitz, "Imperfect Information and Rural Credit Markets: Puzzles and Policy Perspectives," in Hoff, Braverman, and Stiglitz, *Economics of Rural Organization*, 33–52.

52. The most outspoken proponents of unsubsidized microfinance institutions include CGAP, a consortium of donors led by the World Bank; and international network NGOs such as Women's World Banking, ACCION, and FINCA.

in *subsidized* microfinance programs.[53] The interest rates are capped at 2.9 percent annually, which is over 10 percent below PBOC commercial rates and, of course, even lower than curb market rates. Some of the government's microfinance loans are even interest-free.[54] The reasons for pursuing this outmoded style of microfinance are political. The distribution of such funds entails an element of state-building (and perhaps party rejuvenation) in that campaign-style mobilization tactics are used to implement these quota-driven programs.[55] Moreover, all the internationally funded microfinance programs have had to work through the local Poverty Alleviation Bureau, Civil Affairs Office, Agricultural Office, or Women's Federation, even though most of the donors would prefer to support or create local NGOs directly.[56] Taking an active and direct role in distributing subsidized loans allows the state to receive the credit, so to speak, for its poverty alleviation efforts.

At the same time, the center realizes that these efforts have encountered difficulties in execution, difficulties symptomatic of the broader challenges of policy implementation in China. Local governments may have ideas of their own, as acknowledged in the official publication *Qiu Shi* (Seeking truth from facts):

> From time to time some localities and cadres fail to implement policies resolutely and conscientiously, and sometimes even go their own ways, adopting countermeasures to circumvent policies issued by superior bodies. . . . *Some localities . . . divert or retain procurement funds, agricultural support funds, and poverty alleviation funds, thus hindering peasants from obtaining due benefits. A*

53. This figure was supplied by the Office of the Leading Group for Economic Development in Poor Areas, cited in Albert Park and Changqing Ren, "Microfinance with Chinese Characteristics," *World Development* 29, 1 (2001): 39–62.

54. E.g., in 1997 Yunnan reported extending over 6 million yuan in interest-free loans to 7,000 households in 25 impoverished townships: "China Distributes Anti-Poverty Loans to Households," *Xinhua News Agency*, December 10, 1997.

55. Official statements in the media claim that increasing numbers of people have been lifted out of poverty each year: a 1998 report said 7 million in 1996, 8 million in 1997, and the goal for 1998 was 10 million; a report in early 1999 said 8 million in 1998, and the goal for 1999 was an additional 10 million: "Yang Yongzhe on Ability of PRC To Eliminate Poverty," *Xinhua News Agency*, reported in FBIS-CHI-98-071, March 29, 1998; and "PRC to Increase Poverty Alleviation Budget in 1999," *Xinhua News Agency*, reported in FBIS-CHI-99-028, January 29, 1999. By 2001, a total of 220 million people was claimed, bringing the impoverished population down to 30 million people, about 8 percent of the rural population: "Jiang Hails China's Poverty-Relief Success," *Beijing Xinhua*, May 25, 2001, reported in FBIS-CHI-2001-0525; and "China Declares Success of Key Poverty-Relief Program," *Beijing Xinhua*, May 24, 2001, reported in FBIS-CHI-2001-0524.

56. In some cases, governmental poverty alleviation lending programs coexist with and dwarf international credit programs. For example, the FPC (Grameen Bank) operation in Daifeng County, Shaanxi, was squeezed out by the official government program, which was also modeled along GB lines.

failure to resolve such problems will dampen peasants' enthusiasm, damage the relationship between the Party and the masses and between cadres and the masses, and affect rural development and stability.[57]

Indeed, an official investigation carried out between 1997 and 1999 found that local officials had illegally diverted 20.4 percent (equivalent to 4.3 billion *yuan*, or US$519 million) of government funds earmarked for poverty alleviation to other purposes, including balancing budgets in several provinces, financing "unscheduled projects," purchasing property and cars, and forging invoices to cover up embezzlement.[58]

Returning to the Band-Aid metaphor, sometimes subsidized credit projects do not even cover up the obvious wounds. Worse yet, they may instigate new ones as the application of Band-Aids itself becomes a source of local contestation and resentment. This not to deny that the government's poverty alleviation programs have benefited millions of people in the countryside, or to trivialize the developmental challenges that China faces; rather, it is to reinforce the point that central mandates may diverge from local outcomes.

(State) Building on Grassroots Banking

Can the central-local dynamic be juxtaposed against the formal-informal finance relationship in a more developmentally productive manner? My rather grim sampling of state interventions in the informal financial sector has shown that prudential supervision can backfire and that directed credit seems to benefit local elites rather than more disadvantaged households. One may wonder if there is any way for the state to play a more effective role in increasing access to formalized sources of credit at the local level. Perhaps the state is doomed to reproduce hackneyed mistakes by virtue of political realities and regulatory ineptitude. Perhaps the state has no business in dealing with grassroots finance. The examples of the Syndicate Bank in India and the Bank Raykayat Indonesia, however, offer evidence to the contrary. Despite the fact that both countries continue to face various financial-sector challenges at the macro-level, the relative success of these state-owned banks in serving micro-entrepreneurs offers a glimmer of emulatory hope.

57. Yu Yunyao, deputy head of the Organizational Department of the CCP Central Committee, "Strengthen and Improve the Party's Leadership over Rural Work," *Qiushi* (Seeking truth from facts), no. 1 (January, 1 1999): 9–12, reported in FBIS Translated Text (emphasis added).

58. "Corruption in China Absorbs One Fifth of Poverty Fund," *Hong Kong AFP*, July 15, 2000, reported in FBIS-CHI-2000-0718.

Syndicate Bank in India

Until 1969, India's large urban banks generally did not work with small and medium enterprises in the farm and nonfarm sectors, largely because the perceived transaction costs of doing so seemed prohibitively high. Yet a rural bank established in a remote area in 1925 did ultimately succeed in devising cost-effective means to work with small and medium-sized businesses—and, of particular interest, it succeeded in enlisting central-bank support for its practices after the 1969 nationalization of the major banks.[59] In many ways, the work of the Syndicate Bank and its branches was inspired by developmental objectives as evidenced by their provision of technical assistance to farmers and small industrialists, establishment of village-level educational institutions to train existing and potential banking staff, and savings mobilization. Yet this development-oriented approach did not interfere with the bank's profitability. For instance, in 1928 a savings deposit scheme called the Pigmy Deposit was initially viewed as a profitable commercial service: with banking agents sent directly to the doorsteps of vendors and rural households to collect deposits at set intervals, people were more inclined to save money and keep it in an interest-earning account.[60] Most farmers and shopkeepers could afford to save money, but few were willing to travel to the bank to make deposits. In 1960 about 21 percent of the bank's total deposits came from Pigmy Deposits. Their share declined after that, with the growth of alternative savings options and competition from new banks who copied the Syndicate Bank's services. Nonetheless, in the 1997–98 fiscal year Pigmy Deposits still accounted for 15.6 percent of the bank's total domestic deposits (or 5.6 percent of its global deposits), and plans to expand the number of branches from 1,632 to 2,000 were under way.[61]

The broader import of this example is that new banks entered the market niche of serving rural households because the Syndicate Bank seemed to be profiting from it.[62] Furthermore, the policy attitude toward

59. V. V. Bhatt, "On Financial Innovations and Credit Market Evolution," *World Development* 16, 2 (1988): 281–92. Unless otherwise noted, the empirical information in this section relies primarily on Bhatt's article.

60. The risk of embezzlement on the part of agents was minimized by the requirement that they keep a security deposit with the bank equivalent to 10 percent of their commissions.

61. "India: Syndicate Bank Aims at 2,000 Branches," *Hindu Business Line*, November 26, 1998; "India: Syndicate Bank Balance Sheet Fudged," *Business Standard*, March 11, 1997; "India's Syndicate Bank Records $6.1 Bln Business," *Asia Pulse*, June 1, 1998. According to its web page at (⟨http://www.syndicatebank.com/frame-network.html⟩), as of June 14, 2001, it had 1,733 branches, including one in London.

62. The Syndicate Bank has had its share of rough moments—e.g., it suffered losses in the early 1990s, and the Reserve Bank of India discovered an attempt at covering up losses on its 1995–96 balance sheet—but by the late 1990s it was reporting profits again. See "India: Syndicate Bank Needs Tough Steps," *Economic Times*, November 18, 1993, 12; Dilip Maitra, "Syndicate Bank Takes the High Road," *Business Today*, June 7, 2000.

grassroots banking changed: before the nationalization of India's major banks, the Reserve Bank of India criticized the Syndicate Bank's unconventional practices, but since then it has encouraged banks to widen and deepen their services by setting up branches in rural areas and working with small businesses.

Bank Rakyat Indonesia

The Bank Raykyat Indonesia (BRI), one of five state commercial banks in Indonesia, provides a larger-scale illustration of how a state-owned bank succeeded in tapping an apparently unprofitable market in a commercially viable manner. Its "unit desa" or village banking system is a leading example of a state-led credit and savings program that evolved into one of the country's largest and most respected commercial banks. Aid donors, academics, and development practitioners have studied BRI in part because it succeeded in mainstreaming its operations on such a large scale. Its key contribution is its demonstration effect. As Marguerite Robinson argues, "In a path-breaking shift from government-subsidized credit delivery to profitable financial intermediation at the local level, BRI demonstrated for the first time on a large scale that the massive demand for microfinance in developing countries can be supplied by sustainable institutions providing financial services commercially, and that these services can have important effects on social and economic developments."[63]

But BRI's unit desa system was not always a success story. As part of the national strategy called BIMAS (*Bimbigan Massal*, or Mass Guidance) to promote self-sufficiency in rice production, the unit desas were established experimentally in 1969 to provide subsidized credit to farmers. The basic idea was that each unit, consisting of four employees, would be responsible for conducting fieldwork to identify potential clients and to ensure timely loan repayments. The latter proved difficult, yet despite ongoing operating losses, the unit desa network expanded rapidly throughout the 1970s.[64] As village representatives of local banks (*cabang*), the units were essentially subsidized by the Ministry of Finance. When the BIMAS

63. Marguerite S. Robinson, "Leading the World in Sustainable Microfinance: The 25th Anniversary of PRI's Unit Desa System," Harvard Institute for International Development (manuscript, November 1995), 2. The following discussion also draws from Robinson, "Financial Intermediation."

64. BRI, itself derived from an 1895 bank, was formally established in 1968 as a state-owned commercial bank specializing in rural credit. In 1970 there were 470 unit desas nationwide; the number had expanded to 3,626 by 1984, though their physical expansion was not accompanied by commensurate growth in lending. See Richard H. Patten and Jay K. Rosengard, *Progress with Profits: The Development of Rural Banking in Indonesia* (San Francisco, CA: ICS Press with International Center for Economic Growth and Harvard Institute for International Development, 1991), 57–58, 62–65.

program was phased out at the end of 1983, however, BRI faced potential bankruptcy. With the losses of its 3,600 village units totaling US$28 million that year, the bank considered abandoning the system.[65]

It is important to note the political economic conditions under which the government subsidies dried up. Because the Suharto regime was concerned about the potential drop in oil revenues during the early 1980s—and the World Bank and IMF recommended financial liberalization—a series of fiscal and financial reforms were implemented to enhance the productive capacity of Indonesia's non-oil exports. More significantly, having achieved national self-sufficiency in rice production, the government deemed increasing private-sector savings and investment a priority; this developmental strategy was accompanied by the attempt to reform state banks into genuine commercial banks. Therefore, rather than dismantling BRI's vast network of grassroots units, the government attempted to commercialize them. The unit desa system was redefined as an independent cost center or "strategic business unit" within BRI; interest rates on both loans and deposits were liberalized; and after a two-year transitional period, BRI started to make profits in 1986. The financial reason for its success was simple: the unit desas set the interest rate spread between lending and savings rates at a level that would cover the unit's operating costs.[66] Furthermore, the field staff was given economic incentives to take a personal interest in mobilizing deposits, extending loans, and collecting payments; under a profit-sharing system implemented in 1984, the staff would receive 10 percent of the annual profit as a bonus, and individual salaries were also performance based.

By the 1990s the spectacular performance of BRI's unit desa system in providing financial services to small businesses was widely acknowledged in the international development community. The system was serving over 10 percent of Indonesia's population by 1996. Moreover, it held about 30 percent of the total number of savings accounts in Indonesia; it extended an average of over 160,000 loans per month with a total value of US$159 million; and its banking operation was completely self-sustaining with a savings-to-loan ratio of over 170 percent.[67] Although the Grameen Bank's solidarity group-lending model has dominated the Western press as one of the most innovative (and perhaps successful) microfinance programs, BRI's unit desa system is actually larger in scale (compare GB's 25,000 new members per month with BRI's 160,000-plus loans per month) and mobi-

65. Robinson, "Financial Intermediation," 19.

66. In the mid-1980s the deposit rate was set at 15 percent, and the lending rate was 32 percent: Ibid., 66–82.

67. The average loan size in 1996 was US$1,007: Stephanie Charitonenko, Richard H. Patten, and Jacob Yaron, "Indonesia: Bank Rakayat Indonesia Unit Desa 1970–1996," *World Bank Case Studies in Microfinance* (June 1998): 5–6, 12.

lizes more savings as a portion of its lending (GB, 45 percent; BRI, 170 percent). And as BRI's supporters pointout, the unit desas no longer rely on subsidies.[68]

One might expect the financial crisis that swept Southeast Asia in the late 1990s to have left a sobering imprint on BRI's success story. After all, Indonesia was ultimately the hardest hit in the region by currency devaluation, spiraling inflation and interest rates, economic contraction (approximately 10 percent in 1998), and political upheaval. Yet the BRI unit desas actually grew stronger during the crisis. The number of depositors, says Paul McGuire, "increased sharply from 16.99 million in June 1997 to 19.13 million in March 1998, apparently reflecting a 'flight to quality.'" The number of borrowers also increased, though less dramatically, from 2.55 to 2.61 million. Most remarkably, the unit desas maintained their high repayment rates through the peak of the financial crisis: 97.82 percent in June 1997; 97.8 percent in March 1998. By May 2001, BRI unit desas had 26.7 million savings accounts and a repayment rate of 99.2 percent.[69] Apparently, the crisis mainly affected the rural banks and specialized MFIs.

The cases of the Syndicate Bank in India and the Bank Raykyat Indonesia show that state-owned banks are not by necessity ineffectual in providing financial services to grassroots populations. And though these banks are unusual, they are not alone. Other noteworthy examples of state banks that engage in microfinance in a relatively profitable manner include the Banque Nationale de Devéloppement Agricole (BNDA) in Mali and the BAAC in Thailand.[70] Given that they are state banks, it may seem redundant to point out that the broader policy environment has fundamentally affected the degree to which they have been able to operate without governmental interference (e.g., staff appointments, interest rate ceilings, quotas). The Syndicate Bank persisted in its Pigmy Deposits and provision of technical assistance programs when it was not in official favor, but once a major policy shift occurred—the nationalization of banks—its practices were "mainstreamed." BRI's success may also be traced to specific policy changes, though in a different way from the Syndicate Bank's. BRI's ability

68. Ibid. Note, however, that the Grameen Bank's members tend to be lower-income than BRI's clients: Morduch, "Microfinance Schism," 5.

69. Paul B. McGuire, "The Asian Financial Crisis—Some Implications for Microfinance," *Microbanking Bulletin* 2 (July 1998): 9–10; correspondence with Jay Rosengard, June 22, 2001. For more background detail, see Richard H. Patten, Jay K. Rosengard, and Don E. Johnston Jr., "Microfinance Success amidst Macroeconomic Failure: The Experience of Bank Rakayat Indonesia during the East Asian Crisis," *World Development* 29, 6 (2001): 1057–69.

70. Siamwalla et al., "Thai Rural Credit System," focuses on the shortcomings of BAAC, but it has also been held up as an example of a bank that has extensive reach, serving about 1 million borrowers and 3.6 million depositors: Joyita Mukherjee, "Strengthening Asian MFIs," *CGAP Newsletter* 5 (January 1998). Michael Montesano's field work in 1988 further reinforces BAAC's positive impact at the grassroots level (correspondence with author, March 28, 1999).

to develop such a vast (even though money-losing) network of unit desas was a direct function of the government's rice self-sufficiency program, BIMAS, and the state played a similarly instrumental role in its transformation into a commercial bank.[71] State policies toward the financial sector do not have to be pathologically inept.

That said, it is important to point out that these examples should not be regarded as ready-made models of financial intermediation that can be transplanted unmodified in other countries, including China. As Elinor Ostrom emphasizes and several decades of international development experience have confirmed, mere importation of institutional solutions is problematic.[72] Observers point out that a particular combination of political, economic, and social conditions have contributed to the effectiveness thus far of BRI's unit desa system.[73] First, as mentioned above, the government facilitated the establishment and later the commercialization of the village units. Systematic political support for its programs was vital. Second, BRI matured during a period of relative macroeconomic stability. Attempting to establish a village banking system during the hyperinflationary environment of the mid-1960s would have been a formidable task. Third, the spatial and social organization of the local economy has been conducive to efficient financial intermediation. The unit desa system has flourished in Java and Bali, densely populated islands with relative social cohesion and homogeneity;[74] hence, unit desa staff are able to draw upon preexisting social networks (including their own) to identify and screen potential clients. Whereas the staff of the Syndicate Bank may have to travel great distances to reach the clients, the unit desa staff already live there.

Of these conditions for BRI's success—political support, economic stability, and social embeddedness—it is apparent that China lacks a critical one: political support for independent, commercially viable financial institutions at the grassroots level. China already has a network of rural institutions that offer the potential for greater outreach and commercialization

71. Cecile Lapenu, "Indonesia's Rural Financial System: The Role of the State and Financial Institutions," *World Bank Microfinance Case Studies* (Washington, D.C.: World Bank, Sustainable Banking for the Poor, May 1998); March 1999.

72. Elinor Ostrom, *Governing the Commons: The Evolution of Institutions for Collective Action* (New York: Cambridge University Press, 1990). Cf. Timothy W. Guinnane, "A Failed Institutional Transplant: Raiffeisen's Credit Cooperatives in Ireland, 1894–1914," *Explorations in Economic History* 31 (1994): 38–91.

73. See Patten and Rosengard, *Progress with Profits*, 91–103; and Robinson, "Financial Intermediation," 19–23.

74. This is of course a vast oversimplification of their similarities. On the basis of field work conducted in the 1950s, Clifford Geertz observed that Java had a Chinese merchant population and an individualistic economic tradition of interacting with itinerant traders, whereas Balinese society was more group oriented and the economy more derivative of traditional political hierarchies: *Peddlers and Princes: Social Change and Economic Modernization in Two Indonesian Towns* (Chicago: University of Chicago Press, 1963).

—the rural credit cooperatives and rural cooperative foundations.[75] As of 1998 there were approximately 50,000 RCC units (accounting for 12.7 percent of total deposits and 10 percent of total loans in the formal financial system).[76] RCFs (numbered more than 18,000, serving over five million depositors), but the PBOC never recognized the RCFs as legitimate financial institutions because the Ministry of Agriculture established them and they we are run by townships and villages.[77] As part of broader national efforts to rectify the financial system, in March 1999 the Central Bank announced a 15 billion *yuan* (US$1.8 billion) infusion to RCCs to increase lending to farmers at concessional rates.[78] Contemporaneously, however, the State Council announced the closure of poorly performing RCCs and RCFs, and the takeover of better performing ones by RCCs, actions that triggered farmers' protests in at least six provinces and cities, including Sichuan, Hubei, Hunan, Henan, Guangxi, and Chongqing.[79] Rather than subjecting RCFs to better prudential supervision, the center chose regulatory denial and outright abolishment, thereby (unintentionally) fomenting additional discontent in the countryside.

All these complicating realities add breadth to the story. Although a local institutional supply of finance defines the range of options available to private entrepreneurs, that supply itself changes over time, as does the orientation of the local government toward the private sector. Adding to the fluidity of institutional supply and local developmental strategies is the reality that no local government possesses a unified stance toward private finance. Various branches of the state may trespass on the territory of the banking bureaucracy, leaving a trail of mismatched footprints.

Why should political science care about mismatched footprints on the state's financial terrain? I have argued that informal finance matters politically, in and beyond China, for three reasons. First, large portions of the economically active population may be engaged in financial activities that

75. On how China may learn from BRI with a focus on the reform of RCCs to serve TVEs better, see Woo, "Improving Access to Credit in Rural China."

76. "Bank Official Praises Role of Rural Credit Cooperatives," *China Business Information Network,* January 14, 1999.

77. For a partial provincial breakdown of RCF activity, see Carsten A. Holz, "China's Monetary Reform: The Counterrevolution from the Countryside," *Journal of Contemporary China* 20, 27 (2001): 189–217.

78. "Central Bank Gives Farmers $1.8B Spending Boost," *FP*, March 22, 1999; and correspondence with Stephen McGurk, Program Officer, Ford Foundation–Beijing, March 28, 1999.

79. "Central Bank Official Interviewed on Risk Management in Banking and Finance Sector," *Zhongguo dangzheng ganbu luntan* (Forum for China's party cadres), No. 2 (February 6, 1999): 4–7; reported in BBC Summary of World Broadcasts, March 19, 1999; "China Closes Credit Coops," *Associated Press*, March 22, 1999; "Over 1,000 Investors Protest Closure of Credit Cooperative in Hubei," *FP*, March 23, 1999.

compromise the state's control over the allocation of credit. Second, informal finance may actually complement the state's developmental goals. Third, informal finance may be destabilizing and command state intervention. The combination of these three reasons means that the state continually finds itself either exercising its regulatory powers in a proactive policy-driven manner, or reacting to curb market developments. Simply banning informal finance rarely works for long. The developmental dynamics of informal finance relies on more than a simple supply-versus-demand economic logic; it also has a political and social logic, which is why seemingly straightforward economic policies may yield unexpected political and economic consequences.

7

The Local Logics of Economic Possibility

> The mountains are high and the Emperor is far away. (*Shangao huangdi yuan.*)
>
> —Ancient Chinese proverb

> If the local grassroots level organizations are firm and forceful, we can appropriately implement the principles and policies of the central government and the work planned by the higher levels in connection with local reality, arouse the enthusiasm of the masses, and guide, protect, and lead the masses to common prosperity. . . . The political power at the grassroots level directly faces the masses so it is extremely important to strengthen the building of the basic level cadres and ensure proper distribution of them.
>
> —Li Lanqing, Vice Premier, PRC State Council, 2000

Most countries have their share of underground financiers who fill the market gaps created by the formal banking system, and most of these gray-area financial actors go about their everyday business relatively unnoticed—that is, until the high drama of a full-fledged financial crisis commands official attention. The operators of rotating credit associations, pawnshops, and back-alley money houses generally avoid politically charged publicity; it's bad for business. But in countries with imperfect markets and fuzzy property rights, financial entrepreneurs must also be political entrepreneurs. By the same token, private enterprises—the primary clients of financial entrepreneurs—need to be as politically and socially adroit as neighborhood loan sharks to survive.

The stunning growth of China's non-state sector suggests that in the aggregate, private economic actors have apparently succeeded in striking the political bargains that are required to conduct business. Neon-lit retailers have moved into the once dank concrete factories in which Soviet-inspired machinery formerly operated, and flashy department stores and discos have sprung up in the middle of thousand-year-old rice fields. Behind these visible expressions of prosperity, however, are peddlers pawning assets for short-term liquidity, quasi-private banks registering as social charities, and other curb market coping mechanisms. These stories, taken together, challenge conventional ideas about the political economy of development.

First, the notion of an enlightened *developmental state*, which derived from the success of newly industrialized countries (NICs) in East Asia, cannot explain China's impressive economic performance convincingly. The fact that private entrepreneurs have managed to establish elaborate, wide-ranging financing mechanisms suggests limits on the central state's capacity. Informal finance violates a host of regulatory institutions and national banking laws. Furthermore, the finding that some localities have more developed curb markets than others points to the importance of local governments in shaping economic outcomes at the ground level. During the first two decades of reform, localities evolved along different developmental trajectories, which are reflected in the orientation of the local government toward the private sector and their financing mechanisms. Moreover, even in areas dominated by the private sector, local governments have not treated entrepreneurs in a uniformly "developmental" manner. By definition, a developmental state should not engage in predatory behavior. Disciplined bureaucrats should not pillage produce markets. Nor should they abuse their authority to permit, at considerable personal profit, informal financiers to wear outrageous hats.

Second, China's economic miracle challenges *new institutional economics*, which emphasizes the importance of property rights in advanced industrialized countries in the West. A country with poorly defined property rights should not inspire private-sector development at a double-digit pace. Curb market transactions should not appear, much less thrive, in the absence of clear legal codes about the rights and responsibilities of debtors and creditors. Relatedly, if private entrepreneurs really are single-mindedly motivated by profit, they should not lend to illiterate friends without assets.

Rather than declare that China and Chinese entrepreneurs are therefore "illogical," a valid conclusion if one respects the integrity of those two popular theories, one must embrace the country's multiple realities to articulate a different narrative for economic growth. Ultimately, the locus of private-sector growth and informal finance relies on what I call the local logics of economic possibility. The production of informal finance involves mobilizing political and social resources in ways that transcend limitations defined by the central state and create possibilities for economic survival, if not wealth, from the raw materials of day-to-day existence.

A Developmental State?

During the 1980s the concept of the developmental state emerged as an alternative to neoclassical economic explanations of growth in East Asia. Detailed studies of Japan, Korea, and Taiwan revealed that the state played productive roles in their respective postwar economies through a combination of industrial policy (i.e., "picking winners"), directed credit programs, and repression of labor.[1] Carefully managed state intervention in these economies promoted rather than thwarted growth, as neoclassical economists would expect.[2] Given that the experience of socialist command economies around the world has yielded suboptimal if not devastating results, the developmental state argument was controversial in contending that under certain circumstances, state bureaucracies may be capable of Weberian-style efficiency and restraint.[3] In the East Asian NICs these special conditions included a meritocratic civil service, a collaborative or "embedded" relationship between the state and big business, a well-educated and motivated workforce, and, at least in the early decades, an authoritarian or state corporatist regime.[4] Coupled with strategic state intervention in the economy, the net result was rapid economic growth for decades.

The PRC state has also played an active role in liberalizing the economy since the late 1970s, and overall, there has been substantial growth. Therefore, it is understandable that some scholars view China as a developmental state, or at least one evolving toward a similar pattern of state-directed capitalist development.[5] During the Deng era, to be sure, bureaucratic recruitment become more meritocratic and less political or ideological. Specialized agencies were set up to regulate collective and private enterprises; special economic zones were established; educational institutions were revitalized after atrophying for a decade; input prices remained subsidized in key sectors; state banks engaged in "policy lending" to large enterprises in strategic industries; and overall, the state became more tech-

---

1. See citations in Chapter 1, note 17; and Frederic C. Deyo, *Beneath the Miracle: Labor Subordination in the New Asian Industrialism* (Berkeley: University of California Press, 1989).

2. Bela A. Balassa, *The Newly Industrializing Countries in the World Economy* (New York: Pergamon Press, 1981). A number of economic theories, however, do pay attention the potentially productive role of the state in economic development; see Juhana Vartiainen, "The Economics of Successful State Intervention in Industrial Transformation," in Meredith Woo-Cumings, ed., *The Developmental State* (Ithaca: Cornell University Press, 1999), 200–234.

3. The exposure of corruption scandals in Japan and Korea has shown, however, that the developmental state in practice was never as virtuous as initially implied.

4. Peter Evans, *Embedded Autonomy: States and Industrial Transformation* (Princeton: Princeton University Press, 1995); cf. Andrew MacIntyre, ed., *Business and Government in Industrializing Asia* (Ithaca: Cornell University Press, 1994).

5. See the citations in Chapter 1, note 12. On the failure of the "Maoist developmental state," see Gordon White, *Riding the Tiger: The Politics of Economic Reform in Post-Mao China* (London: Macmillan, 1993).

nocratic in orientation. With the major exception of propping up inefficient SOEs with bank loans, those are all indications that PRC state intervention in the economy may be productive.

The most interesting (if not entirely persuasive) reason for thinking of China as a developmental state, however, is that it seeks to become one. Prior to the crisis of 1989, intellectuals employed in research institutes sponsored by then CCP General Secretary Zhao Ziyang actively debated the pros and cons of China emulating the East Asian NIC model.[6] Dubbed "neo-authoritarianism" (*xin quanwei zhuyi*) by its advocates, the idea was that China needed to go through a transitional stage of having a so-called hard government with a soft economy before it could contemplate greater political liberalization.[7] Ironically, the political repression following the upheaval of 1989 effectively suppressed public debate over neo-authoritarianism. Nonetheless, ruling elites in the Jiang regime assume that authoritarianism is necessary for economic growth at this stage of China's development.[8] In public discourse the central state defines itself as an aspiring developmental state and uses the promise of stability and prosperity to justify restrictions on political activity.

Reform-era China nevertheless lacks a number of the attributes of its developmental neighbors, including a consensus among the ruling elite, the resulting policy coherence over the course of economic reform, and the partially privatized economies that preceded state-led development in the East Asian NICs.[9] Yet I would argue that the primary limitation on conceptualizing China as a developmental state is that "the state" does not act as a unified whole in practice. The central state headquartered in Beijing has presided over two decades of impressive economic growth, but at the subnational level its actual staff exercise considerable leeway in interpreting central mandates. Tremendous subnational variation in political economic conditions reflects, in part, the deviance of local governments from the will of the central government. Although the balance and texture of central-local relations have fluctuated over time, localities possess

6. Joseph Fewsmith, *Dilemmas of Reform in China: Political Conflict and Economic Debate* (Armonk, N.Y.: M. E. Sharpe, 1994); cf. Merle Goldman, *Sowing the Seeds of Democracy in China: Political Reform in the Deng Xiaoping Era* (Cambridge: Harvard University Press, 1994).

7. Stanley Rosen and Gary Zou, eds., "The Chinese Debate on the New Authoritarianism," *Chinese Sociology and Anthropology*, winter 1990–91, spring–summer 1991; Barry Sautman, "Sirens of the Strongman: Neo-Authoritarianism in Recent Chinese Political Theory," *China Quarterly* (March 1992): 72–102. Note that a number of intellectuals referred specifically to Samuel P. Hungtington's *Political Order in Changing Societies* (New Haven: Yale University Press, 1968), which was translated into various Chinese editions in 1987.

8. On how Jiang Zemin seeks to transform China from a Leninist party-state to a "developmental dictatorship," see Bruce Gilley, *Tiger on the Brink: Jiang Zemin and China's New Elite* (Berkeley: University of California Press, 1998).

9. Shaun G. Breslin, "China: Developmental State or Dysfunctional Development?" *Third World Quarterly* 17, 4 (1996): 689–706.

different resources, face different incentives, and implement state policies differently.

One way to salvage the application of the developmental state to China is to propose that geographical variations exist in the expression of developmentalism. Perhaps there are hierarchical levels: Ming Xia contends that China actually has a "dual developmental state," whereby local developmental states are nested within the central one.[10] And even though China has a unitary rather than a federal political system, China scholars have indeed identified local developmental states. First, a number of sector-specific studies have attributed the developmental success of local industrial sectors—including feather and leather goods, automobiles, and high-technology enterprises—to local government policies that "picked winners" and then gave them tax breaks and preferential access to credit.[11] Second, local governments that had strong commune and brigade institutions in the Mao era seemed to promote TVEs in the 1980s and deal with privatization in the 1990s in a developmental manner.[12] Third, even though studies of the Wenzhou model of early private-sector growth have not defined it as developmental, local governments in such areas have certainly promoted private enterprise, as evidenced by their willingness to extend red hats in the 1980s and allow unusual financing practices.

The foregoing examples could provide a basis for accepting the concept of the local developmental state in the lexicon of economic growth explanations. That said, however, I generally refer to the orientation of the "local government" toward the private sector, not the orientation of the "local state," because the latter lumps different types of agencies into a monolithic complex. The Industrial and Commercial Management Bureau may conflict with the People's Bank of China, which may conflict with the Agricultural Office, which may conflict with the Women's Federation, and so forth. Reifying the local state would obscure such realms of potential disagreement. Yet they are the crevices in which informal finance has flourished.

In addition to the analytic limits of the term, labeling local "states" as "developmental" is problematic. First, well before the term was applied to

10. Ming Xia, *The Dual Developmental State: Development Strategy and Institutional Arrangements for China's Transition* (Brookfield, Vermont: Ashgate, 2000).

11. Marc Blecher and Vivienne Shue, "Into Leather: State-led Development and the Private Sector in Xinji," *China Quarterly* 167 (June 2001); and Eric Thun, "Changing Lanes in China: Industrial Development in a Transitional Economy, 1999" (Ph.D. diss., Harvard University, 1999). Cf. Adam Segal and Eric Thun, "Thinking Globally, Acting Locally: Local Governments, Industrial Sectors, and Development in China," *Politics and Society* 29, 4 (2001): 557–88.

12. Jean Oi calls this model "local state corporatism" because in it township and village governments act like the board of directors of a single corporation: "Fiscal Reform and the Economic Foundations of Local State Corporatism," *World Politics* 45, 1 (1992): 99–126.

China, the developmental state tended to be defined by its positive economic outcomes. Late-developing countries with impressive economic growth rates were praised for being developmental (while that growth lasted), and laggards were diagnosed as being "weak," "predatory," "prebendal," "patrimonial," "inverted," or pathological in other ways.[13] Only developmental states and mature capitalist states in advanced industrialized countries could be associated with prosperity, because the pejorative labels were derived inductively for countries with troubled economies—even if certain rapidly growing countries had patrimonial or other nonrational legal qualities.

Besides the tautological application of the developmental state framework, a deeper shortcoming is that the concept obscures dynamics that may become increasingly problematic or unsustainable over time. During the Asian financial crisis, prudent developmentalism was, virtually overnight, reinterpreted as crony capitalism. Yet most of the scholars who applied the concept to their country of expertise would agree that in practice, the East Asian developmental states were never as virtuous as they may have appeared to observers of the more slowly developing countries. Rapid growth was associated with the human cost of limited political freedom and depressed wages. Even Chalmers Johnson, whose work inspired the entire research agenda, acknowledges the mixed implications of industrial policy: "The state *can* structure market incentives to achieve developmental goals, as the Japanese case clearly illustrates, but it can also structure them to enrich itself and its friends at the expense of consumers."[14] By the same token, channeling preferential credit to chosen industrial winners became increasingly problematic over time.[15]

The developmental state may be a transitional phenomenon. As suggested by the Korean experience, the successful developmental state might dig its own grave because of increased labor militancy, the reduced dependence of industrial capital on the state, and perhaps requests from within the societally infiltrated bureaucracy to reduce state intervention.[16] Or—a more general observation from state-centric theorists—"whether originally

13. Evans, *Embedded Autonomy*; Joshua Forrest, "State Inversion and Nonstate Politics," in Leonardo A. Villalon and Phillip A. Huxtable, eds., *The African State at a Critical Juncture* (Boulder, Colo.: Lynne Reinner, 1998), 45–56; Richard Joseph, "Class, State, and Prebendal Politics in Nigeria," *Journal of Commonwealth and Comparative Politics* 221, 3 (1983): 21–38; and Joel Migdal, *Strong Societies, Weak States: State-Society Relations and State Capabilities in the Third World* (Princeton: Princeton University Press, 1988).

14. Chalmers Johnson, "The Developmental State: Odyssey of a Concept," in Woo-Cumings, *The Developmental State*, 48.

15. David Kang, "Bad Loans to Good Friends: Money Politics and the Developmental State in Korea," *International Organization* 56, 1 (2002): 179–209.

16. Evans, *Embedded Autonomy*, 229.

autonomous or not, state interventions in socioeconomic life can, over time, lead to a diminution of state autonomy and to a reduction of any capacities the state may have for coherent action."[17]

I would argue that precisely because the concept of the developmental state encompasses paradoxical phenomena, applying it to reform-era China would not be analytically productive. Tempting as it is to claim that the Sunan or Wenzhou models are developmental because local governments have promoted the non-state sector, different branches of the local government in those areas have acted in a distinctly *non*developmental manner. In several of my potentially developmental research sites, for example, street-level bureaucrats harass and levy arbitrary fines on private vendors.[18] If apparently developmental local states may have predatory agents, then the term developmental is misleading. Furthermore, even localities known for close government-business relationships may not be truly developmental. In areas that followed the Sunan model of collective-sector dominance, it became increasingly apparent during the 1990s that local authorities did not always pursue policies that promoted the local economy. Some local governments have actively thwarted private sector development to retain a controlling stake in collective enterprises; in other areas, political elites have used the conversion of collective enterprises into shareholding cooperatives as an excuse to appropriate collective assets for personal enrichment.[19] Such behavior resonates more with what Peter Evans calls "klepto-patrimonialism" or, more simply, predation.[20]

The difficulties with calling China a developmental state are also apparent from other studies that have identified hybrid forms of local states. Between the extremes of developmental and predatory states, China scholars have come up with a host of classificatory labels for the local state—"entrepreneurial," "market-facilitating," "clientelistic" and "managerial corporatist," "paralyzed"[21]—and more significantly, some point out,

17. Peter B. Evans, Dietrich Reuschemeyer, and Theda Skocpol, eds., *Bringing the State Back In* (New York: Cambridge University Press, 1985), 354.

18. On how low-level employees in social service agencies face considerable pressure and discretion, see Michael Levitsky, *Street-Level Bureaucracy* (New York: Russell Sage Foundation, 1983).

19. Sally Sargeson and Jian Zhang, "Reassessing the Role of the Local State: A Case Study of Local Government Interventions in Property Rights Reform in a Hangzhou District," *China Journal* 42 (July 1999): 77–99; and Susan H. Whiting, *Power and Wealth in Rural China: The Political Economy of Institutional Change* (New York: Cambridge University Press, 2001).

20. Peter Evans, "Predatory, Developmental, and Other Apparatuses: A Comparative Political Economy Perspective on the Third World State," *Sociological Forum* 4, 4 (1989): 561–87.

21. Respectively, see Marc Blecher, "Developmental State, Entrepreneurial State: The Political Economy of Social Reform in Xinji Municipality and Guanghan County," in Gordon White, ed. *The Chinese State in the Era of Economic Reform* (Armonk, N.Y.: M. E. Sharpe, 1991), and Jane Duckett, *The Entrepreneurial State in China: Real Estate and Commerce Departments in Reform Era Tianjin* (London: Routledge, 1998), 273; Jude Howell, *China Opens Its Doors: The*

Is business any better across the street? Huian, Fujian, November 1996.

they are not mutually exclusive. For example, a developmental state may also be entrepreneurial; some local governments perform their regulatory functions quite well but also run profitable businesses on the side.[22] According to other scholars, the combination of entrepreneurial and developmental attributes yields a "market-facilitating" state.[23] But the combination of entrepreneurial and patrimonial qualities yields a "booty socialist" state, meaning a corrupt one.[24] Rather than reconciling the growing variety of

---

Politics of Economic Transition (Boulder, Colo.: Lynne Reinner, 1993); Gregory A. Ruf, "Collective Enterprise and Property Rights in a Sichuan Village: The Rise and Decline of Managerial Corporatism," in Jean C. Oi and Andrew G. Walder, eds., *Property Rights and Economic Reform in China* (Stanford, Calif.: Stanford University Press, 1999), 27–48; and Kevin J. O'Brien, "Implementing Political Reform in China's Villages," *Australian Journal of Chinese Studies* 32 (July 1994): 33–60.

22. As Duckett explains, "Since state entrepreneurialism refers to only one dimension of state activity, it may exist within developmental local governments. Governments may co-ordinate the promotion of developmental and infrastructural projects while still allowing individual departments to run businesses": *Entrepreneurial State*, 173.

23. Howell, *China Opens Its Doors*; and Shu-Yun Ma, "The State, Foreign Capital, and Privatization in China," *Journal of Communist Studies and Transition Politics* 15, 3 (1999): 54–79.

24. Xiaobo Lü, "Booty Socialism, Bureau-preneurs, and the State in Transition: Organiza-

classificatory labels for the PRC state and local state,[25] or privileging a single interpretation, I find it more fruitful to acknowledge that multiple political economic modes coexist at the local level, and to focus on how such diversity has emerged.

Path-Dependent Diversity in Local Development

Within the eighteen localities discussed in this book, certain path-dependent developmental patterns may be identified. "Path dependence" means that preexisting resources and institutions influence the relative salience and convenience of options that actors face at any given point in time.[26] Rather than a deterministic exercise, my use of the term is consistent with that of David Stark and László Bruszt, who see that "the past can provide institutional resources for change in the present," in contrast to the involutionist approach to path dependence, which sees "in the present the dead weight of the past."[27] Indeed, all the localities that I studied changed substantially in the first two decades of reform, and even over the course of my field research between 1994 and 2001. Some changes reflect major shifts in central state policy, including the initiation of urban enterprise reform in 1984, the legal recognition of larger private enterprises (*siying qiye*) in 1988, the political crisis in 1989, Deng's southern tour in 1992, fiscal reform in 1994, commercial bank reform in 1995, state-sector reform in 1997, and the closure of rural cooperative foundations in 1999, coupled in that same year with a constitutional amendment that extended stronger legal protection to the private sector.

Yet in dealing with informal finance for private businesses, officials and entrepreneurs have responded quite differently to these central policies across localities. Even within a particular province, the scope and scale of the curb market varies substantially. These differences may be traced to political and economic conditions during the Mao era, which left different resources and possibilities.[28] Just as the former Soviet-bloc countries started

---

tional Corruption in China," *Comparative Politics* 32, 3 (2000): 273–94. Cf. Paul D. Hutchcroft, *Booty Capitalism: The Politics of Banking in the Philippines* (Ithaca: Cornell Universty Press, 1998).

25. For a typological effort at differentiating entrepreneurial, clientelist, predatory, and developmental states, see Richard Baum and Alexei Shevchenko, "The 'State of the State,'" in Merle Goldman and Roderick MacFarquar, eds., *The Paradox of China's Post-Mao Reforms*, Harvard Contemporary China Series 12, (Cambridge: Harvard University Press, 1999), 334–60.

26. In this case, "actors" refers to local governments and local branches of their agencies, as well as private entrepreneurs.

27. David Stark and László Bruszt, *Postsocialist Pathways: Transforming Politics and Property in East Central Europe* (New York: Cambridge University Press, 1998), 7.

28. A path-dependent argument about variation in reform-era property rights arrangements is Whiting, *Power and Wealth*.

with varying degrees of industrialization, which have influenced the course of their political and economic development since 1989–90, the same can be said of subnational units in China.[29] At the outset of reform, some localities were readily able to build their non-state sectors with the rural surplus labor unleashed by decollectivization. Such governments have been relatively supportive of private-sector development in the sense that local officials may overlook the infractions of national laws by private entrepreneurs or even actively devise legal loopholes to facilitate novel business practices. These governments tend to be in areas where some commerce existed before 1949 but which then suffered neglect under Communism because of their geostrategic or political sensitivity. Although they differ in many ways, Wenzhou and Quanzhou exemplify this developmental trajectory of relative commercial prominence, followed by decay under Communism and then private-sector development.

In contrast, local governments that inherited an immense concentration of SOEs have been willing to foster economic growth through any means possible but are simultaneously restrained by the challenge of maintaining state-sector payrolls and, since the mid-1990s, dealing with disgruntled workers. The governmental stance toward private-sector development in these industrialized areas has been ambivalent. Because the developmental preferences of local officials are constrained by the hands that they were dealt, private entrepreneurs sometimes pay a high fiscal price for existing alongside fledgling SOEs. Nonetheless, as can be seen in the industrial centers of Henan, various branches of the local governments are eager to reap the benefits of developing the non-state sector and supporting their unusual financing mechanisms.

The third attitude that local governments may have toward the private sector is best characterized as nonsupportive. At least two paths led to this attitude. First, some localities developed strong communal and brigade structures during the Mao era, which meant that when communes were converted into township governments, and production brigades into villages, many of the power relations and institutions from the communal period continued to shape local modes of economic production and popular mobilization. Hence, at the outset of reform these local governments preferred to develop the collective sector, which entailed a close if not clientelistic relationship between business and local government. The second path associated with lack of support for the private sector was followed in those areas that were impoverished and ecologically disadvantaged during the Mao era and thereafter either remained stagnant or

29. David Stark, "Path Dependence and Privatization Strategies in East Central Europe," in Vedat Milor, ed., *Changing Political Economies: Privatization in Post-Communist and Reforming Communist States* (Boulder, Colo.: Lynne Reinner, 1994), 115–46.

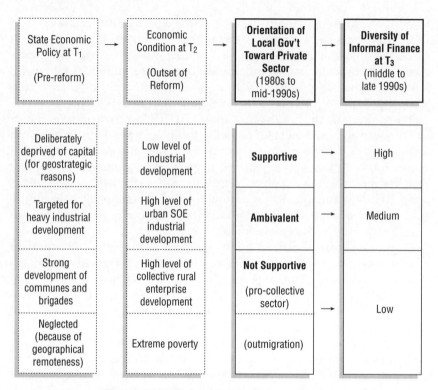

Figure 7.1 Paths to Local Variation in Informal Finance

further deteriorated. In such areas the government may have a permissive attitude toward private income-generating activities, but both the local cadres and inhabitants tend to view permanent outmigration as the most expedient means to escape poverty.

Additional developmental paths with finer levels of detail could be identified. For example, the relative availability of overseas Chinese or foreign capital, the structure of social relations at the grassroots level (e.g., kinship dynamics in single-surname villages), the ethnic composition of the locality (Han-dominated versus ethnic diversity), and critical historical experiences all mediate contemporary economic dynamics at the local level. The developmental paths summarized in Figure 7.1, however, capture the basic range of variation in informal finance that I observed in my field sites.

I would not use those observations and paths to classify local states as being inherently developmental, predatory, entrepreneurial, clientelist, or some hyphenated combination of those terms. When we met with local officials or large private enterprises in a prosperous locality, the local state seemed developmental. When we spoke with farmers and peddlers in dire straits, the local state seemed predatory. When we saw a government think tank running a credit cooperative, the local state looked entrepreneurial. When we found the ICMB extending a business license to an ambitious moneylender, the local state appeared developmental or clientelist— although if that business license ended up costing a lot more than others, then the local state looked predatory. My classification of local governmental attitudes toward the private sector serves only as a proxy for the overall environment conditioning the creation and survival of informal finance. The simplifying, descriptive categories of supportive, ambivalent, and nonsupportive refer to their preexisting biases toward the private economy and, by extension, informal finance.

By the end of the first two decades of reform the overwhelming majority of China's private entrepreneurs still relied, though to varying degrees around the country, on self-financing.[30] Macroeconomic statistics give the impression that China as a whole is privatizing under Communist rule, but in reality, vast portions of the state and collective sectors are being privatized only in the sense that local elites are implementing enterprise reform in name without actually relinquishing their personal stakes in the local economy. In such areas, the real private enterprises operate at a disadvantage. A legal-rational developmental state in Beijing has not nourished private-sector growth through directed credits. Instead, while state banks have attempted to salvage the state sector, certain local governments manipulate local resources and national laws to allow alternative modes of financing. Despite ongoing central-state efforts at dictating regulatory homogeneity, no overarching, national developmental trajectory exists in practice. Laws promulgated in Beijing have vastly different meanings and implications by the time they reach ground level. The particular expressions of financial cooperation among entrepreneurs and local governmental complicity in crafting elaborate masks for private finance are highly contingent upon preexisting local resources and developmental biases.

The Local Logics of Economic Growth

If we accept that the engine for China's private-sector development resides at the subnational level, then the issue remains of how this has occurred without secure property rights. The crux of the argument that a

30. In 1999 the International Finance Commission and the State Economic and Trade Commission conducted a survey of private entrepreneurs (*siying qiye*) in Beijing, Chengdu, Shunde, and Wenzhou (*n* = 628) and found that 90.5 percent relied on self-financing: This is consistent with the findings in my own survey. International Finance Corporation, *China's Emerging Private Enterprises: Prospects for the New Century* (Washington, D.C.: International Finance Corporation, 2000).

well-defined system of property rights is necessary for national prosperity is that economic actors—including entrepreneurs, investors, and consumers—need to be sure their economic exchanges are protected by the rule of law; otherwise, the risk of acquiring, using, and transferring assets would be prohibitively high. As Douglass North and Robert Thomas explain, "Individuals must be lured by incentives to undertake the socially desirable activities. . . . If the private costs exceed the private benefits, individuals ordinarily will not be willing to undertake the activity."[31] According to this perspective, property rights reduce the transaction costs of gathering information; minimize shirking by opportunistic actors; and enable everyday people to make credible economic commitments to one another.[32] In well-functioning market economies, the state serves as the ultimate third-party enforcer of contracts so that all the parties involved believe that breaching contracts carries a real threat of expensive penal consequences. The system is geared toward reducing the uncertainty of risk-averse yet profit-maximizing individuals.

How, then, could a country with poorly defined property rights grow so rapidly? Scholars have generally examined the issue from the perspective of how township and village enterprises, the basis of rural industrialization throughout the 1980s, could have occurred without explicit privatization.[33] Others view the first two decades of high growth rates as making up for lost time, catching up, by mobilizing underemployed agricultural labor; they argue that China's growth is bound to slow down because of the distortions created by the gradualist approach to reform (versus the free-market shock therapy undertaken in Poland and Russia).[34] The question my research has raised, however, is how the private sector itself could have expanded to the point of producing one-third of China's GDP by the end of the 1990s without access to formal sources of credit. If a large part of the answer is informal finance, as I am suggesting, the deeper analytical issue is how informal finance could persist when in most cases it lacks the juridical right to exist. Entrepreneurs have been operating in an awkward situation in

31. Harold Demsetz, "Towards a Theory of Property Rights," *American Economic Review* 57, 2 (1967): 347–57; Douglass North and Robert Thomas, *The Rise of the Western World: A New Economic History* (New York: Cambridge University Press, 1973), 2–3.

32. Ronald H. Coase, "The Problem of Social Cost," *Journal of Law and Economics* 3 (October 1960): 1–44; Oliver E. Williamson, *The Economic Institutions of Capitalism* (New York: Free Press, 1985).

33. Oi and Walder, *Property Rights* (3–4, nn. 9–13, cite other explanations).

34. Jeffrey D. Sachs and Wing Thye Woo, "Structural Factors in the Economic Reforms of China, Eastern Europe, and the Former Soviet Union," *Economic Policy* 18 (1994): 102–45; cf. Chong-En Bai, David D. Li, and Yijiang Wang, "Thriving on a Tilted Playing Field: China's Non-State Enterprises in the Reform Era," Center for Research on Economic Development and Policy Reform, Working Paper, No. 856, Stanford University, March 2001.

which private businesses are legal, but most private sources of finance are not.

This book offers two complementary propositions to explain the emergence and persistence of informal finance in the PRC. First, *informal finance derives from local initiative.* Business owners have not waited for the state to legalize private property or clarify ownership rights. They have not waited for state banks to clean up their books and extend loans to a newly emerging, potentially creditworthy market. Instead, entrepreneurs have gone ahead and pieced together a variety of financing mechanisms based on practical need and opportunism. They do it in the normal course of purchasing raw materials, building inventories, and investing in fixed assets.

Second, *informal finance relies on local political protection and social enforcement.* Informal finance generally works because it derives from rules of the game that are locally defined and locally enforced. Private banks wear different disguises throughout the country because local governmental agencies are willing to tolerate different camouflaging techniques. Any private financial institution that wants to operate openly still has to register as some form of business or social organization. Displaying a registration certificate signifies that some branch of the local government has approved it. More often than not, however, the "rules" are not written in contractual terms or even systematically articulated. They evolve and are reinforced in the course of everyday transactions. They become habits, however practical or impractical.[35] In addition to the motivating factors of need and opportunism, many curb market transactions work because of a sense of social obligation—not the certainty that reneging on a debt or refusing to extend a loan will have punitive legal consequences. Since most forms of informal finance are illegal to begin with, a moneylender who collects exorbitant interest payments is already violating state laws, so pursuing official recourse could be a self-revealing, self-destructive option. To the debtor, however, the possibility that defecting from a curb market transaction could carry long-lasting *personal* consequences is powerful motivation for complying with the terms of the agreement.

In this respect, the local logic of informal finance adds another counterintuitive dimension to new institutional economics, because neither the incentive nor the enforcement mechanisms are purely economic. Entrepreneurs face a financial need for credit, and tapping the curb market entails lower transaction costs than attempting to secure a loan from a state bank, yet some entrepreneurs participate in informal financing arrangements in the absence of obvious material benefits. Curb market transac-

35. This resonates with Pierre Bourdieu's notion of *habitus*: *The Logic of Practice* (Stanford, Calif.: Stanford University Press, 1980).

Muslim woman who can sew, though she never attended school. Zhengzhou, Henan, August 1996.

tions are rooted in a richer web of interpersonal and social norms than the rationalist model of the profit-maximizing economic actor would accept. Sometimes people participate in rotating credit associations simply because they have been invited to join one by a relative, a neighbor, a friend, or a friend of a friend.

This often-social basis for curb market arrangements is precisely why they typically function reasonably well in the absence of legal recognition and official third-party enforcement. They are self-governing because they rest on norms of reciprocity, trust, or other social conventions.[36] In many cases, local networks and shared identities exercise stronger disciplinary author-

36. Elinor Ostrom, *Governing the Commons: The Evolution of Institutions for Collective Action* (New York: Cambridge University Press, 1990).

ity over curb market creditors and debtors than sternly worded regulations issued in Beijing and parroted in provincial capitals. Financial debtors can be social creditors when it comes to "face," but no one would ever put that in writing. Arguably, codifying its motivating essence would diminish its practical power. Commanding collective welfare has failed radically around the world. Informal social institutions, not formal political institutions, regulate grassroots financing; taken-for-granted norms and habits condition transactions as if they were protected under an explicit system of property rights. They generate the hope, if not certainty, that entrepreneurs need to run and finance their businesses. Indeed, entrepreneurs themselves participate in designing and redesigning these normative scripts through their daily interactions.[37] Paradoxically, entrepreneurs and local officials draw on the uncertainty of formal political and economic institutions to create informal financial institutions that bear the potential for enhancing local prosperity. To aspiring entrepreneurs, the inverse of uncertainty is flexibility and, more optimistically, *possibility*.

None of this means that informal finance is always efficient, reliable, or associated with other positive outcomes. Informal finance generally works when it is used for productive—as opposed to speculative—income-generating purposes. And as demonstrated in previous chapters, exogenous shocks such as a change in the regulatory environment (political campaigns to wipe out illicit financial institutions, for example) interfere with curb market stability.

A Transitional Phenomenon?

Given that China is still in the process of "growing out of the plan,"[38] the argument could be made that the colorful range of informal financial institutions presented here is merely a transitional phenomenon. Perhaps certain areas have a particularly wide variety of financial institutions because they are still going through a formative period of competition in the local curb market. Perhaps continued competition will foster organizational conformity and reduce the range of institutional forms over time. Organizational sociologists have argued that

in the heat of competition, organizations adopt efficient structures and practices or risk failure to relatively better-adapted rivals. Institutional environ-

37. Ethnomethodologists are particularly attuned to how everyday interactions constitute social order. See Harold Garfinkel, *Studies in Ethnomethodology* (Englewood Cliffs, N.J.: Prentice-Hall, 1967).

38. Barry Naughton, *Growing Out of the Plan: Chinese Economic Reform, 1978–1993* (New York: Cambridge University Press, 1996).

ments shape organizations through social pressure and result in *institutional isomorphism*. Organizations in a common institutional environment begin to look like each other as they respond to similar regulatory and normative pressures, or as they copy structures adopted by successful organizations under conditions of uncertainty.[39]

In other words, the Darwinian logic of competition may squeeze out inefficient organizations under archetypal laissez-faire conditions. I would argue, however, that the presence of a nonmarket actor such as the regulatory state changes the terms of the playing field. If institutional isomorphism in fact emerged in China's banking system, it would not necessarily stem from the eliminative logic of competition, but rather, because the financial institutions operating above ground would be subject to state regulation. The convergence in institutional form would be imposed by juridical fiat, not feral competition.

Within the sphere of informal finance, however, there is no compelling reason why institutions that remain underground would become alike. In fact, it is plausible that financial institutional diversity will persist as long as structurally induced competition exists in the broader political environment. This dynamic is not peculiar to the Chinese case. Walter Powell observes in the U.S. context, "Multiple levels of government—federal, state, and local—and different kinds of government agencies compete for control and provide dissimilar kinds of regulation as well as inducements. Contradictory pressures and overlapping jurisdictions create organizational heterogeneity and complexity."[40] Rather than delimiting the range of possible organizational forms, interbureaucratic and central-local competitive dynamics may actually spawn greater institutional diversity.

A separate concern about the potentially transitional nature of informal finance in China is that rationalization of the banking system will eventually obviate the need for curb market financing. This is partially an empirical question of how exclusionary the formal financial system remains over time. To the extent that an economically active portion of the population (small businesses, or enterprises run by minorities or women) is structurally restricted from access to official sources of credit, informal finance is likely to continue. Even though comparative evidence from other countries shows that informal finance is not as widespread among economic actors who have unimpeded access to officially sanctioned financial institutions, it is also apparent that the mere availability of credit does not translate

---

39. Marco Orrù, Nicole Woolsey Biggart, and Gary H. Hamilton, "Organizational Isomorphism in East Asia," in Powell and Paul J. DiMaggio, eds., *The New Institutionalism in Organizational Analysis* (Chicago: University of Chicago Press, 1991), 361–62.

40. Walter W. Powell, "Explaining the Scope of Institutional Analysis," in Powell and DiMaggio, *New Institutionalism*, 196.

neatly into decreased reliance on the curb market.[41] The substitution effect between formal and informal sources of finance is imperfect because they are not functionally equivalent. In financially repressed environments, formal bank credit may offer borrowers lower interest rates than the curb, but commercial bank loans generally entail complex application procedures, collateral or legal guarantees, and fixed repayment schedules. These conditions are usually more relaxed among informal creditors at the price of higher interest rates—or none at all. To potential savers and indirect creditors, the economic trade-off is typically between lower returns but greater security in formal financial institutions versus higher returns but higher risk in the curb market. Regardless of purely monetary considerations, however, sometimes informal finance is simply more convenient in locally and personally defined terms.

The stubborn persistence of informal finance may also be traced to the segmentation of local credit markets. Increasing the official supply of (subsidized) credit at the grassroots level may not crowd out the curb market because entrepreneurs are motivated by more than economic considerations. To be sure, private business owners are profit-seeking actors, but they are not a monolithic group that shares and pursues identical interests. Some are rural migrants; others are underemployed state workers; and a number serve as agents of the party-state. They all face capital constraints, but their ways of addressing this economic need depend on their specific political and social location. Business owners' competing political and social identities filter the range of financing options available to them. Because of these socially constructed identities, entrepreneurs who appear equal in strictly material terms are unequal in their everyday lives. One cannot assume that two vendors selling the same products in the same marketplace pays the same amount in taxes and fees, or relies on the same types of financing mechanisms. Entrepreneurs have varying backgrounds, social and kinship networks, and interests.

Entrepreneurial Possibilities

One quality that entrepreneurs do share is the willingness to undertake the risk of profit or loss. Regardless of how well- or vaguely defined private property rights may be in a particular country, all entrepreneurs put themselves in a position of potential economic vulnerability. In the early years of reform, Chinese entrepreneurs also faced serious political risks. Yet tens

41. Even bank employees may prefer to participate in rotating credit associations rather than deal with their own bank, given the flexibility associated with informal finance. See Mayada M. Baydas, Zakaria Bahloul, and Dale W. Adams, "Informal Finance in Egypt: 'Banks' within Banks," *World Development* 23, 4 (1995): 651–61.

of millions of individuals and families have entered the private sector as investors, owners, workers, and uncounted supporters. They have done so for different reasons. Some have also left the private sector for different reasons. But the larger point is that all the individual and group actors involved in the production of informal finance are entrepreneurial to some extent. They all assume risks, though not necessarily strictly economic ones. Financial entrepreneurs have landed in prison and on death row. So have the CCP officials who protected them. Organizers of rotating credit associations lose lifelong friends when they collapse. Unregistered peddlers have their products confiscated, get beaten up, yet return the next day. Such potentially negative consequences of entrepreneurship are well known and frequently reported in the state media for deterrence purposes.

Nonetheless, private enterprise and private finance have flourished. To understand these paradoxes, scholars need to shelve their own implicit impressions about tolerable levels of risk and acknowledge that however irrational the foregoing observations appear, they have their own local logic. This methodological caveat is not limited to China, even though the country offers seemingly endless local logics. Ultimately, this book is about the multiple rationalities through which an entire economic sector has developed without ready legal access to its fuel, finance. Sometimes unwittingly, sometimes intentionally, entrepreneurs in villages, factories, and government agencies collaborate to allow the possibility of marginal if not major improvements in their lives. It is the local logic of what seems possible—just possible; not probable, but not impossible—that explains apparent economic paradoxes, including the tremendous variation in private-sector development and informal finance. The very idea of possibility requires suspension of certainty. What some economists might dismiss as incredible commitments are credible when viewed through the lens of local possibilities.

That is why one cannot simply look to Beijing, which is committed to building "market socialism," and presume that China is evolving into a developmental capitalist state where private capital sacrifices political power for the broader protection of its material interests. Nor is China necessarily becoming a crudely capitalist state captured by big business, or even a (post-) socialist welfare state where the private sector is heavily taxed for extensive provision of public goods. All these trends and many more are discernible at the local level. Rather than an irrepressible rolling or convergence toward a familiar model of market capitalism, China's reform era has seen divergence in the political economic strategies of localities, divergence in local logics, and the emergence of unanticipated forms of economic organization. It is within this context of developmental diversity and possibility that private entrepreneurs have conducted their banking—behind the state, with the state, and despite the state. Neither loyal bureaucrats nor perfect private property rights could orchestrate such local miracles and tragedies. Entrepreneurs create credit—not only out of greed but also out of gratitude, guilt, and gullibility. They deserve credit for daring to do so.

Appendix A

Research Methodology

> Informal sector statistics are especially needed in developing
> countries, where the informal sector usually plays a significant
> role in total employment and income-generation. . . . It was often
> stated in the past that data collection on the informal sector is
> virtually impossible, because the units involved and their activities
> are "unmeasureable." However, . . . it is possible to obtain
> statistical data on the informal sector through various types of
> surveys, provided that the survey design and operations are
> adapted to the particular characteristics of the informal sector.
>
> —Bohuslav Herman, *Unveiling the Informal Sector*, 1996

Indicators Measured by the Survey

This study has two dependent variables at two levels of analysis: (DVa)
financial institutional supply in particular localities and (DVb) *individual choice
of financing mechanisms.* The first explanatory objective entailed conducting
extensive interviews with government officials, state bankers, and private
financiers in eighteen localities in Henan, Fujian, and Zhejiang. Survey
methodology was used to ascertain the individual-level characteristics of
private entrepreneurs.[1] Conducted from 1996 to 1997, the surveys collected the following information from private business owners:

1. Basic business and personal indicators (business type, number of
   employees, years in operation, types of fixed and nonfixed assets, age,
   education level, marital status, sex, employment history, class background, living conditions, migratory patterns).
2. Sources of income from private income-generating activities and their
   percentage of total household income.

1. A copy of the actual survey is available on-line at the author's webpage:
⟨http://jhunix.hcf.jhu.edu/~ktsai⟩.

Table A.1. Regional Distribution of Surveys

Region	Urban	Peri-Urban	Rural	Subtotal
North (Henan)	80	20	no surveys; just interviews	100
South (Fujian and Zhejiang)	185	73	16 [plus interviews]	274
Subtotal	265	93	16	Total: 374 surveys

Table A.2. Age Distribution of Surveyed Entrepreneurs

Age	n	% of Total	Cum. %
<19	7	1.9	1.9
19–24	58	15.5	17.4
25–29	75	20.0	37.4
30–34	71	18.9	56.4
35–39	43	11.5	67.9
40–44	51	13.6	81.6
45–49	22	5.9	87.4
50–54	26	7.0	94.4
55–59	10	2.7	97.1
60–69	7	1.9	98.9
>70	4	1.1	100.0
Total	374	100.0	100.0

3. Whether the individual has interacted with formal financial institutions for savings or credit purposes. If so, how was the transaction arranged (direct or brokered) and what were the terms (interest rate, amount, length, collateral, repayment)? If not, why not?

4. Savings and borrowing experiences with nonformal financial institutions and arrangements (e.g., friends, relatives, colleagues, neighbors, loan sharks, pawnshops, rotating credit associations).

5. Strategies employed for enhancing access to all types of credit (e.g., registering as a cooperative, cultivating relationships with officials or peers).

6. Payment of taxes, licensing fees, and other charges.

7. Sexual division of labor and decision-making power in the household and business.

8. Degree of satisfaction with current occupation as a private entrepreneur (in such areas as compensation, social status, self-fulfillment).

Tables A.1–A.10 present descriptive statistics, including the regional distribution of the surveys (Table A.1), and basic socioeconomic indicators (age and education, Tables A.2 and A.3), that were not explicitly used for

Table A.3. Education Level of Surveyed Entrepreneurs

Education	n	% of Total	Cum. %
Some elementary	34	9.1	9.1
Elementary	68	18.3	27.4
Junior high	120	32.3	59.7
Senior high	88	23.7	83.4
Junior technical	18	4.8	88.2
Senior technical	26	7.0	95.2
College	17	4.6	99.8
Graduate school	1	0.3	100.0
Total	372	100.0	100.0

Table A.4. Private Entrepreneurs' Income Level (GROSSY)

Self-Reported Gross Monthly Income (RMB)[a]	n	%
1,000 or less	64	18.2
1,001 to 5,000	173	49.1
More than 5,000	115	32.7
Total	352	100.0

[a] Minimum RMB reported: 0; maximum: 812,270; median: 2,565; mean: 9,301.

hypothesis testing. A numbered list of the individual surveys is presented in Appendix C, and the business codes in Appendix D.

The Economic Hypothesis

Private entrepreneurs' self-reported monthly income was used to test the economic hypothesis that associates the institutionalization of their financing arrangements with their economic resources. It was coded in the data set as a continuous variable (GROSSY).[2] See Table A.4.

Experience in Business

The length of time that an entrepreneur had been in business was correlated with the institutionalization of the financing mechanisms they used. An ordinal scale was created to determine how "established" private businesses were by running basic descriptive statistics on the number of years that vendors had been in business. On an interval basis, the mean number

2. The manuscript refers to coded variables by their code name in all caps to distinguish them from words that are not meant in a statistical sense.

Table A.5. Private Entrepreneurs' Length of Time in Business

Time in Business	No. of Businesses	Percent of Total
Less established businesses (<3 years)	151	40.5
Established businesses (3 to 5 years)	105	28.1
Well-established businesses (>5 years)	117	31.4
Total	373	100

of years was 4.89, median was 3 years, and 2 years represented the lowest of multiple modes. Given the relative youth of China's private sector in the post-Mao era, it was decided that "less-established businesses" would be those with two or fewer years of experience; "established businesses," those in operation for three to five years; "well-established," those with more than five years of experience (Table A.5). The resulting variable BUSTIME was coded ordinally: less-established business (1), established business (2), and well-established business (3). A dichotomous variable BUSTIMED is also available and uses five years in business as the dividing line between less-established business (0) and more-established business (1). (In case the categorization obscured the continuous effect of time in business, the raw scores in the field labeled YEARS were maintained so that the variable could also be analyzed on an interval basis.)

Strength of Political Ties

It was hypothesized that entrepreneurs with stronger political ties would use more institutionalized financing mechanisms than those with weaker ones. The survey explicitly asked whether the business owner or his/her spouse had ever worked in a governmental administrative unit, as a cadre, or as a cadre in a governmental administrative unit (Table A.6).

The problem with relying on the self-reported responses, however, is that as of 1996–97 government officials and party members were not legally permitted to engage in private enterprise, which means that interviewees may have denied their political connections. It was therefore decided that "relative tax burden" (percentage of gross income paid in taxes and assorted fees) would serve as a better proxy for the "strength of political ties," since some businesses literally pay no taxes or fees, whereas others may pay well over half of their gross income in fees. There are inherent reliability problems with relying on private entrepreneurs' self-reported income and taxes since most people do not feel comfortable disclosing financial issues to strangers. As discussed at the end of this Appendix, however, the survey process was structured such that responses to financial questions could be cross-checked in a variety of ways.

Table A.6. Private Entrepreneurs' Self-Reported Political
Background

Employment History	%[a]	n
No political work experience	85.3	162
Worked in government administration	14.2	28
Worked as a cadre	6.3	12
Worked as a cadre in government	3.7	7

[a] The sum of these percentages exceed 100 due to overlapping
responses.

Table A.7. Official and Actual Tax Rates

Gross Monthly Income	Official Tax Rate[a] (%)	Actual Rate Paid		
		(%)	(min/max)	n
Less than 5,000 *yuan*	5	20.4	0/100	243
5,000 to 10,000 *yuan*	10	18.0	1.8/100	69
10,000 to 30,000 *yuan*	20	18.3	0.9/76.8	42
30,000 to 50,000 *yuan*	30	7.0	2.1/12.5	4
More than 50,000 *yuan*	35	17.5	0/84.4	16

[a] See Zhonghua renmin gongheguo caizhengbu shuizhengju (Taxation Agency, Ministry of Public Finance,
People's Republic of China), in *Zhongguo shuishou zhidu 1996 nianban* (China's tax system, 1996 edition)
(Beijing: Qiye guanli chubanshe, 1996), 111.

As shown in Table A.7, the official tax code is graduated by income-level
such that businesses earning 5,000 *yuan* or less on a monthly basis are
expected to pay only 5 percent of their gross income in taxes, while those
earning over 50,000 *yuan* are taxed at 35 percent. A quick glance at the
table reveals substantial gaps between the official tax rate and actual taxes
paid. The logic of this variable rests on the premise that paying less than
the required amount by reported income level is a plausible indication that
political strings have been pulled for tax relief; by the same token, private
entrepreneurs who pay substantially higher rates of taxes probably lack
strong political ties.[3] Other studies of private entrepreneurs in China offer
support for the validity of the working assumption that the tax payments
of private business owners are a better reflection of their political connections than is their actual tax bracket.[4]

3. Of course, paying below the official tax level may also indicate independent success at
tax evasion. One way to control for the impact of tax evasion without relying on political ties
is to eliminate all the mobile outdoor vendors who could pack up and run away (or ride away
by bike) when tax collectors made their daily, weekly, or monthly rounds through particular
markets.
4. See for example, Dorothy J. Solinger, "Urban Entrepreneurs and the State: The Merger
of State and Society," in *China's Transition from Socialism: Statist Legacies and Market Reforms,*

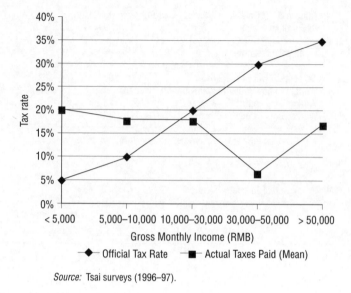

Source: Tsai surveys (1996–97).

Figure A.1 Official versus Actual Taxes Paid by Private Entrepreneurs

Table A.8. Operationalizing Private Entrepreneurs' Strength of Political Ties by Relative Tax Burden (POLTIES and POLTIESD)

POLTIES	POLTIESD	$T_p - T_d$	%[a]	n
None (0)	0	≥50%	5.3	20
Low (1)	0	10 to 49%	35.3	132
Medium (2)	1	9% to –9%	43.0	161
High (3)	1	≤–10%	8.3	31

[a] Represents percentage of a total of 344 valid responses.

Based on the data in Table A.7, Figure A.1 illustrates the divergence between the official tax rate and the average taxes actually paid by private entrepreneurs at different income levels. Since income level is not a perfect indicator of either undue tax burden or successful tax evasion, a field was created to measure the difference between the actual taxes paid (T_p) and taxes due (T_d). A normal curve of the distribution of actual tax rates was then used to construct the scale shown in the third column of Table A.8.

1980–1990 (Armonk: M.E. Sharpe, 1993); and David L. Wank, "Bureaucratic Patronage and Private Business: Changing Networks of Power in Urban China," in Andrew G. Walder, ed. *The Waning of the Communist State: Economic Origins of Political Change in China and Hungary* (Berkeley: University of California Press, 1995), 153–183.

Table A.9. Residential Origin of Private Entrepreneurs

Residential Origin (HOME)	n	Percent of Total
Local (0)	250	67.6
Within province (1)	80	21.6
Outside of province (2)	40	10.8
Total	370	100

Table A.10. Gender of Private Entrepreneurs

GENDER	n	Percent
Women	207	55.4
Men	167	44.6
Total	374	100

To increase the diversity of testing options, the resulting variable is coded two ways. POLTIES was coded ordinally: none (0), low (1), medium (2), high (3), POLTIESD was coded as a dummy variable where 0 indicates the absence of strong political ties and 1 indicates its presence.

Residential Origin

It was hypothesized that private entrepreneurs indigenous to a particular area were more likely to employ highly institutionalized financing practices, migrants more likely to use less institutionalized financing practices, ceteris paribus. The variable was measured on the survey and coded as a categorical variable labeled HOME (see Table A.9): local (0), from within the province (1), and from outside of the province (2). A dummy variable (HOMED) was also created for statistical purposes (where local is coded as 0 and outsider is coded as 1).

Gender

It was hypothesized that women entrepreneurs were more likely than men to employ financing mechanisms with low to medium degrees of institutionalization, men more likely to employ financing mechanisms with high degrees of institutionalization, ceteris paribus (see Table A.10).

Limitations and Potential Bias in the Data

Sampling Bias

Although the sampling technique was "random" in the sense that I would identify not only official markets but undesignated trading areas (down alleyways, in side streets, behind factories, night markets, etc.), systematic bias may have occurred both in the choice of those we approached and in the types of entrepreneurs who were willing to participate in the survey. On the sampling side, i.e., how we determined which vendors to approach and when to administer the survey, we generally planned our survey sessions during times that business was less active. For example, it would have been counterproductive to visit wholesale vegetable and produce markets before nine in the morning, their peak period for selling. By the same token, restaurant owners would have been too busy to answer questions during mealtimes, and central retail shopping districts were typically crowded on weekends. In short, rainy days tended to be especially productive for surveying businesses because they experienced less commercial traffic.

Aside from avoiding vendors during busy times of the day or week, and those who had their hands full with customers, our choice of potential respondent was also influenced by the appearance of the storekeeper. We wanted to survey only business owners, not their employees. Sometimes it was obvious that the only person in the store was not the owner (e.g., a very young child). In such cases, our standard operating practice was to inquire if the owner was available or, if not, when he or she was expected to return.

A more serious source of bias in our selection may have been unconscious. Generally speaking, my research assistant and I attempted to capture a typical cross-section of the vendors in a particular marketplace. If, for example, we were surveying a garment district, which is typically dominated by women, we would end up surveying more women than men. In markets that sold a variety of goods, we would attempt to survey a mix of businesses rather than only dried foods stands or only music stores.[5] Whenever I was not accompanied by a research assistant (about one-third of the time), I may have unintentionally solicited survey participation from vendors who looked as if they could speak Mandarin Chinese rather than only a local dialect. Language was usually not a problem in urban and peri-urban areas, and in the rural sites I rarely attempted to administer surveys alone. Moreover, if the language issue did bias the sample toward better-

---

5. By the same token, we avoided "quota sampling" of vendors, i.e., we did not interview each particular type of vendor if the business type was atypical.

educated respondents, the only independent variable that this might have affected was gender, since the average educational level of women is lower than that of men. In other words, women may have been underrepresented in the sample.

In addition to the potential biases in our sampling procedure, reliance on voluntary participants introduced a number of self-selection biases. We were not pushy about insisting that vendors participate; hence, those who were willing to answer survey questions may have been more confident, better educated, and less busy than those who refused. To be sure, illiterate peddlers and owners of heavily trafficked stores were less enthusiastic about answering survey questions.

As far as I could tell, potential respondents did not "de-select" me because of my age or gender; young entrepreneurs seemed as willing as elderly ones to speak with us; and men did not seem any more likely than women to decline participation in the survey.[6] It is possible, however, that certain types of vendors were more likely to refuse our request on the basis of my nonlocal appearance and accent. Most entrepreneurs could tell that I was not a local, and many made a point of inquiring about my hometown or "native place." People in the north thought I was from the south and vice versa.[7] Still, the extent to which respondents answered less truthfully because I was not a local may have been ameliorated by the presence of local research assistants; they performed much of the initial solicitation in the local dialect or accent. After the respondent had agreed to participate in the survey, we would switch to Mandarin, or if the respondent did not speak Mandarin, my assistant would ask the survey questions, and I would intervene when it seemed that a response required clarification or elaboration.

Remedy: None of these potential sampling biases have serious implications for the arguments made in this book. The survey data are not treated as representing China as a whole. Instead, each empirical chapter discusses the findings with reference to local idiosyncrasies that affect the particular expression of the relevant variables. Furthermore, most of my empirical claims do not depend solely on strict tests of statistical significance but draw on material from the survey encounters which could be considered "informant" information rather than "respondent data" per se.

---

6. A number of older respondents (both male and female) did ask my age and marital status and recommend that I get married. They seemed concerned that I was spending key childbearing years administering surveys. Two young single men jokingly proposed marriage for green card purposes.

7. When I explained that I was an academic from the United States, many respondents did not seem to believe me. In Changle, Quanzhou, and Wenzhou—places where many people have relatives living abroad—people were less surprised about my citizenship.

Omitted-Variable Bias

Virtually all research designs run the risk of overlooking variables that possess explanatory power, which means that the hypothesized strength between the independent and dependent variables may be spurious. This survey, for example, did not collect data on many indicators that may in fact have an important impact on the direction of the dependent variable. The local policy environment is one such variable. Certain sites did not have well-developed regimes for regulating and taxing private entrepreneurs; others appeared hyperextractive in comparison. Because the survey was supplemented by formal interviews, document research, and the personal experience of living in the locality, I can identify a variable such as the policy environment as likely to have had a systematic, as opposed to unsystematic or random, impact on entrepreneurs' attitudes toward the degree of official intervention in their activities.[8]

Similarly, the fact that entrepreneurs in the southern coastal sites were more likely to have relatives living abroad, or to benefit from overseas Chinese or Taiwanese investment, is of interest to my research, but not explicitly captured by the survey.[9] The omission of other systematic factors, however, such as the number of black chickens in a village dependent upon the export of black chickens, may not cause bias if the number of black chickens does not correlate with another hypothesized independent variable (i.e., endogeneity is ruled out), or if it has no impact on the dependent variable.[10]

Questionable Reliability of Responses

People lie, forget, and misunderstand. Given the perceived arbitrary habits of tax or fee collectors, vendors tended to underestimate their profitability and net worth. This may be considered a systematic bias to the extent that all or most respondents underestimated their net incomes. Even though few vendors mistook me for a collector ("they demand payment immediately and don't bother to chat with us first the way you did"), many did not believe that I was an "objective" academic whose only motive was to understand their work. In cases where interviewees insisted

8. Gary King, Robert Keohane, and Sidney Verba, *Designing Social Inquiry* (Princeton: Princeton University Press, 1994), 61–63.

9. Intraprovincial variation in the extent of ties to Chinese in other countries is also evident. Changle County and City, for example, represent the primary port of exit for Fujianese immigrants; hence, the local economy is very much structured around the trade of illegal emigration to the United States and elsewhere, and cash remittances back to Changle from the emigrants are a key source of capital. In southern coastal Fujian, however, the source of overseas capital tends to come from Taiwanese investment.

10. King, Keohane, and Verba, *Designing Social Inquiry*, 168–76.

on believing that I was a journalist from Beijing, their complaints about the burden of local state extraction and reliance on coercive tactics may have been exaggerated, for they hoped that I would report their accounts of local corruption. In four of the six markets where entrepreneurs complained about the use of extreme violence in tax collection, however, I directly witnessed the events that elicited such complaints against state staff, since my surveying schedule unintentionally shadowed that of the tax collectors in those sites.

Remedy: Fieldwork requires judgment calls. I did not always take responses at face value, and I took the liberty of evaluating the living condition of interviewees through direct observation. For example, if a vendor claimed that the household did not own a motorcycle (one of the standard-of-living indicators on the survey), and then I saw the respondent's spouse ride off on one that had been parked inside the courtyard, I would ask about it and probably record on the survey that the family had access to a motorcycle. In other cases, bystanders and neighboring vendors challenged the responses of the interviewee on the basis of their own experiences and perceptions. The point is that the survey process was accompanied by regular conversations with the business owners to get a better sense of their attitudes toward a variety of subjects, thereby complementing and sometimes correcting responses to the formally structured survey questions. Unfortunately, I do not have a statistical record of how many answers were revised in light of obvious discrepancies.

As for the reliability of responses to direct questions about income and tax payment, the survey was organized such that questions about the payment of assorted taxes preceded those about gross income. Specifically, I would first ask casually, "In some of the other places that I've been, there are various monthly fees like the Industrial and Commercial Management Bureau Fee and Sanitation Fee. Do vendors around here have to pay such charges?" Respondents generally jumped at the opportunity to complain about their tax burden. A typical answer: "Not only do we have those fees, but we also have to pay X, Y, and Z fees." Entrepreneurs who were able to obtain special tax breaks tended to speak about their political connections with pride: for example, "Most people have to pay the X fee, but I have a friend in the X bureau, so I pay less than other vendors in the area." In speaking about fees and taxes, the issue of income would often arise. For instance, after delineating all the taxes, fees, and bribes that had to be paid to stay in business, one restaurant owner said, "I pay 70 percent of my profits in these fees, so you do the calculation."[11] He added that a 30 percent profit still yielded a take-home income ten times his old factory

11. Survey No. 225.

salary. Suspecting that I might be mathematically challenged, he said point-edly, "I net about 5,000 *yuan* a month."

When respondents were not as forthcoming about earnings or I suspected that they might not have provided truthful answers, four other questions gave me an opportunity to identify discrepancies and probe for a more accurate assessment of their income. The first cross-check question asked about current business performance relative to the previous year.[12] If, for example, a restaurant owner said that she earned only 400 *yuan* per month, but she had said that business was better this year than last, I might comment that most restaurants in the area seemed to be making at least 800 *yuan* a month. The second cross-check question concerned seasonal fluctuations in earnings. Since most consumer-oriented businesses reported higher earnings around Spring Festival and slower periods during the summer and fall months, vendors were asked about the high and low ends of their income over the course of the year. These extremes could be compared with the reported current income, and the respondent would be asked to explain if there had been unusual business circumstances that had skewed income level in one direction or another. The third cross-check question asked if his or her spouse earned more or less than the respondent. If husband and wife were running the business together full time and did not have *danwei* employment on the side, then the question would not do much to clarify the profitability of the business. But if one spouse had a nonbusiness source of income, this question provided another opportunity for me to see whether the numbers made sense. The fourth cross-check question was less subtle than the first three. It asked about the total household income from all sources and included a subcomponent asking the respondent to distinguish between business income and nonbusiness income.

12. The survey question is phrased as follows: "Is your current business performance (1) better than last year, (2) worse than last year, (3) about the same as last year, or (4) hard to say?"

Appendix B

List of Non-Survey Field Interviews, 1994–2001

	Date	Place	Admin. Level	Province	Country	Position	Institution Name	Type
1	5/20/94	Shatin	NA	NT	HK	assistant director	CUHK—University Service Centre	research
2	5/27/94	Changle	county	FJ	PRC	department director	Econ. Sys. Reform Committee	government
3	5/27/94	Changle	county	FJ	PRC	secretary	FAO—Changle People's Government	government
4	5/27/94	Changle	county	FJ	PRC	director	WF	mass org.
5	5/27/94	Changle	county	FJ	PRC	director	ABOC	financial
6	5/28/94	Fuzhou	provincial	FJ	PRC	researcher	FASS	research
7	5/28/94	Fuzhou	provincial	FJ	PRC	director FAO	FASS	research
8	5/28/94	Fuzhou	provincial	FJ	PRC	associate professor	FASS	research
9	5/28/94	Fuzhou	provincial	FJ	PRC	administrator	FASS	research
10	5/28/94	Fuzhou	provincial	FJ	PRC	director	China Maritime Silk Route Studies Centre	research
11	5/30/94	Fuzhou	provincial	FJ	PRC	vice director	WF	mass org.
12	5/30/94	Fuzhou	provincial	FJ	PRC	chief, propaganda secretary	WF	mass org.
13	5/31/94	Fuzhou	provincial	FJ	PRC	vice deputy director	ABOC	financial
14	5/31/94	Hong Shan	township	FJ	PRC	vice director	RCC	financial
15	5/31/94	Hong Shan	village	FJ	PRC	committee member	village committee	government
16	6/2/94	Quanzhou	municipal	FJ	PRC	administrator	FAO	government
17	6/2/94	Quanzhou	municipal	FJ	PRC	director	ABOC	financial

	Date	Place	Admin. Level	Province	Country	Position	Institution Name	Type
18	6/2/94	Quanzhou	municipal	FJ	PRC	credit officer	ABOC	financial
19	6/2/94	Quanzhou	municipal	FJ	PRC	manager	UCC	financial
20	6/2/94	Quanzhou	municipal	FJ	PRC	director	China Maritime Silk Route Studies Centre	research
21	6/3/94	Huian	county	FJ	PRC	director	FAO	government
22	6/3/94	Huian	county	FJ	PRC	director	ABOC	financial
23	6/3/94	Huian	county	FJ	PRC	director	WF	mass org.
24	6/3/94	Huian	county	FJ	PRC	vice director	FAO	government
25	6/3/94	Huian	county	FJ	PRC	president	Friendship Associate of Capable Women	NGO
26	6/3/94	Huian	county	FJ	PRC	vice chair	CPPCC	government
27	6/4/94	Quanzhou	municipal	FJ	PRC	vice director	WF	mass org.
28	6/4/94	Quanzhou	municipal	FJ	PRC	chair	WF	mass org.
29	6/4/94	Quanzhou	municipal	FJ	PRC	vice chair	WF	mass org.
30	6/7/94	Fuzhou	provincial	FJ	PRC	researcher	FASS	research
31	6/7/94	Fuzhou	provincial	FJ	PRC	researcher	FASS—International Cultural Economical Center	research
32	6/7/94	Fuzhou	provincial	FJ	PRC	manager	ABOC	financial
33	6/7/94	Fuzhou	township	FJ	PRC	director	RCC	financial
34	6/8/94	Fuzhou	provincial	FJ	PRC	vice chair	WF	mass org.
35	6/8/94	Li Ming	village	FJ	PRC	vice chair	WF	mass org.
36	6/8/94	Li Ming	village	FJ	PRC	manager	TVE	enterprise
37	6/15/94	Beijing	central	BJ	PRC	director of propaganda	All-China WF	mass org.
38	6/15/94	Beijing	municipal	BJ	PRC	cultural editor	*China Features*	news
39	6/15/94	Beijing	municipal	BJ	PRC	staff writer	*China Features*	news
40	6/29/94	Beijing	NA	BJ	PRC	consultant	Ford	IO
41	7/6/94	Beijing	NA	BJ	PRC	consultant	UNDP	IO
42	7/22/94	Beijing	NA	BJ	PRC	pop. & rural dev. adviser	FAO/UNFPA	IO
43	8/6/94	Beijing	municipal	BJ	PRC	associate professor	Women's National Managerial College	research

	Date	Place	Admin. Level	Province	Country	Position	Institution Name	Type
44	8/8/94	Beijing	municipal	BJ	PRC	lecturer	Beijing Univ.	research
45	8/9/94	Beijing	municipal	BJ	PRC	researcher	CASS—RDI	research
46	3/25/96	Shatin	NA	NT	HK	researcher	CUHK—University Service Center	research
47	3/26/96	Shatin	NA	NT	HK	professor	CUHK—Anthropology	research
48	3/28/96	Shatin	NA	NT	HK	graduate student	CUHK—Anthropology	research
49	3/27/96	Shatin	NA	NT	HK	assistant professor, economist	City University of Hong Kong	research
50	3/28/96	Shatin	NA	NT	HK	associate professor, government	CUHK	research
51	3/27/96	Shatin	NA	NT	HK	researcher	French Center for Research on Contemporary China	research
52	4/19/96	Liancheng	county	FJ	PRC	administrator	Cultural Affairs Bureau	government
53	4/21/96	Fuzhou	provincial	FJ	PRC	credit officer	CCB	financial
54	4/21/96	Fuzhou	provincial	FJ	PRC	manager	CCB	financial
55	4/5/96	Fuzhou	provincial	FJ	PRC	vice director	People's Government	government
56	4/18/96	Fuzhou	provincial	FJ	PRC	economist	PBOC	financial
57	4/18/96	Fuzhou	provincial	FJ	PRC	manager	PBOC	financial
58	4/26/96	Fuzhou	provincial	FJ	PRC	vice director	WF	mass org.
59	5/9/96	Hongshan	village	FJ	PRC	director	RCC	financial
60	5/9/96	Hongshan	village	FJ	PRC	vice director	RCC	financial
61	6/7/96	Fuzhou	provincial	FJ	PRC	researcher	FASS	research
62	6/10/96	Fuzhou	provincial	FJ	PRC	entrepreneur	NA	enterprise
63	6/12/96	Changle	city	FJ	PRC	vice director	FAO	government
64	6/12/96	Changle	city	FJ	PRC	secretary	FAO	government
65	6/12/96	Changle	city	FJ	PRC	director	ICB	financial
66	6/12/96	Changle	city	FJ	PRC	director	ABOC	financial
67	6/12/96	Changle	city	FJ	PRC	director	ILA	government
68	6/12/96	Changle	city	FJ	PRC	manager	RCF	financial
69	6/13/96	Changle	city	FJ	PRC	entrepreneur	NA	enterprise
70	7/10/95	Beijing	municipal	BJ	PRC	professor, director	People's University, Women Research Centre	research
71	7/10/95	Beijing	municipal	BJ	PRC	researcher	Labor & Personnel College, Women Study	research
72	6/14/96	Changle	city	FJ	PRC	director	WF	mass org.

	Date	Place	Admin. Level	Province	Country	Position	Institution Name	Institution Type
73	6/14/96	Changle	city	FJ	PRC	staff	WF	mass org.
74	6/14/96	Changle	city	FJ	PRC	staff	WF	mass org.
75	6/14/96	Changle	city	FJ	PRC	staff	WF	mass org.
76	6/17/96	Changle	city	FJ	PRC	administrator	ILA	mass org.
77	6/18/96	Changle	city	FJ	PRC	entrepreneur	dance hall	enterprise
78	6/20/96	Yingqian	township	FJ	PRC	manager	TVE	enterprise
79	6/20/96	Haixing	village	FJ	PRC	director	village committee/CCP	government
80	6/20/96	Yingqian	township	FJ	PRC	owner	Sixiang peanut oil factory	enterprise
81	6/20/96	Yingqian	township	FJ	PRC	director	TVE	government
82	6/21/96	Shiyan	village	FJ	PRC	villagers	household	household
83	6/21/96	Shiping	village	FJ	PRC	villagers	household	household
84	6/21/96	Gao Hutang	village	FJ	PRC	farmer	household	household
85	6/21/96	Yan Yang	village	FJ	PRC	villagers	household	household
86	7/3/96	Fuzhou	provincial	FJ	PRC	director	China Maritime Silk Route Studies Centre	research
87	7/5/96	Zhengzhou	provincial	HN	PRC	researcher	HASS	research
88	7/8/96	Zhengzhou	provincial	HN	PRC	chair	Provincial CPPCC; ICMB union	government
89	7/8/96	Zhengzhou	provincial	HN	PRC	manager	Hongshan hotel	enterprise
90	7/9/96	Jinshui	district	HN	PRC	director	family planning	government
91	7/10/96	Zhengzhou	provincial	HN	PRC	director	WF	mass org.
92	7/10/96	Zhengzhou	provincial	HN	PRC	economist	HASS	research
93	7/9/96	Zhengzhou	provincial	HN	PRC	manager	ICMB	government
94	7/15/96	Zhengzhou	provincial	HN	PRC	director	Jingu UCC	financial
95	7/12/96	Zhengzhou	provincial	HN	PRC	economist	HASS	research
96	7/12/96	Zhengzhou	provincial	HN	PRC	director	HASS	research
97	7/15/96	Zhengzhou	provincial	HN	PRC	vice director	Oriental Family Weekly	news
98	7/15/96	Zhengzhou	provincial	HN	PRC	vice president	Women's Life Monthly	news
99	7/16/96	ZZ Suburb	township	HN	PRC	entrepreneur	Plastics factory	enterprise
100	7/15/96	Zhengzhou	provincial	HN	PRC	entrepreneur	Three D's Reading Club	enterprise
101	7/18/96	Zhengzhou	provincial	HN	PRC	director	UCC	financial
102	7/23/96	Kaifeng	city	HN	PRC	professor	Henan University	research
103	7/21/96	Kaifeng	city	HN	PRC	director	coal factory	research

	Date	Place	Admin. Level	Province	Country	Position	Institution Name	Type
104	7/21/96	Kaifeng	village	HN	PRC	cashier	RCF	financial
105	7/21/96	Kaifeng	village	HN	PRC	accountant	RCF	financial
106	7/21/96	Kaifeng	village	HN	PRC	entrepreneurs	nursing home	enterprise
107	7/22/96	Kaifeng	city	HN	PRC	staff	suburban cooperative foundation	financial
108	7/22/96	Kaifeng	city	HN	PRC	staff	KF CMA	financial
109	7/23/96	Kaifeng	district	HN	PRC	staff	Huanbing UCC	financial
110	7/25/96	Kaifeng	city	HN	PRC	director	dance hall; investment companies, etc.	enterprise
111	8/6/96	Chengguan	township	HN	PRC	staff	Chengguan RCF	financial
112	8/16/96	Luoyang	city	HN	PRC	researcher	HASS	research
113	8/18/96	Shamen	village	HN	PRC	farmers	NA	household
114	9/4/96	New York	NA	NA	US	professor	University of California–Riverside	research
115	9/24/96	Shatin	NA	NT	HK	professor	CUHK—Anthropology	research
116	9/26/96	Shatin	NA	NT	HK	assistant director	CUHK—USC	research
117	9/27/96	Beijing	NA	BJ	PRC	program officer	Ford Foundation	IO
118	10/14/96	Beijing	NA	NA	United States	researcher	World Bank—CGAP	IO
119	10/14/96	Beijing	NA	NA	Bangladesh	practitioner	Grameen Bank	financial
120	10/14/96	Beijing	NA	NA	United States	director, private sector development	UNDP	IO
121	10/14/96	Beijing	NA	NA	Australia	Qinghai community development	AusAid	IO
122	10/15/96	Chengdu	provincial	SC	PRC	director	Sichuan Academy of Social Sciences	research
123	10/15/96	Beijing	municipal	BJ	PRC	director	CASS—RDI	research
124	10/15/96	Beijing	NA	NA	Germany	senior adviser	German Technical Cooperation	IO
125	10/18/96	Dianji	county	HN	PRC	farmer	household	household
126	10/18/96	Dingzhuang	village	HN	PRC	farmer	household	household
127	10/22/96	Beijing	municipal	BJ	PRC	deputy secretary general	ICCIC	NGO
128	10/24/96	Beijing	municipal	BJ	PRC	vice director	ICCIC	NGO
129	10/24/96	Beijing	municipal	BJ	PRC	staff	ICCIC	NGO
130	10/24/96	Beijing	municipal	BJ	PRC	researcher	Women's College	research
131	10/25/96	Beijing	NA	BJ	PRC	assistant resident representative	UNDP	IO

Friendship Association

Date	Place	Admin. Level	Province	Country	Position	Institution Name	Type
132	10/18/96	Shangqiu	prefecture	HN	PRC	vice commissioner & president	administration office; Friendship Association	government
133	10/18/96	Shangqiu	prefecture	HN	PRC	section chief	FAO	government
134	10/18/96	Yucheng	county	HN	PRC	vice mayor	county government	government
135	10/18/96	Shangqiu	prefecture	HN	PRC	editor	*Henan Economic Daily*	news
136	10/24/96	Beijing	NA	BJ	PRC	program officer	UN—FAO	IO
137	11/11/96	Anxi	county	FJ	PRC	vice director	FAO	government
138	11/11/96	Anxi	county	FJ	PRC	staff	FAO	government
139	11/11/96	Anxi	county	FJ	PRC	office director	county government	government
140	11/11/96	Anxi	county	FJ	PRC	director	FAO	government
141	11/11/96	Anxi	county	FJ	PRC	chair	WF	mass org.
142	11/11/96	Anxi	county	FJ	PRC	vice chair	WF	mass org.
143	11/11/96	Anxi	county	FJ	PRC	staff	WF	mass org.
144	11/12/96	Anxi	county	FJ	PRC	director	PBOC	financial
145	11/12/96	Anxi	county	FJ	PRC	director	ABOC	financial
146	11/12/96	Anxi	county	FJ	PRC	director	RCC	financial
147	11/13/96	Anxi	county	FJ	PRC	admin.	ICMB	government
148	11/13/96	Anxi	county	FJ	PRC	admin.	ILA	mass org.
149	11/14/96	Hutou	township	FJ	PRC	farmers	NA	household
150	11/16/96	Quanzhou	city	FJ	PRC	curator	QZ Maritime Museum	research
151	11/17/96	Quanzhou	city	FJ	PRC	assistant researcher	QZ Maritime museum	research
152	11/17/96	Quanzhou	city	FJ	PRC	vice director	WF	mass org.
153	11/17/96	Li Cheng	district	FJ	PRC	staff	ICMB	government
154	11/17/96	Quanzhou	city	FJ	PRC	staff	ILA	mass org.
155	3/11/97	Wenzhou	city	ZJ	PRC	staff	FAO	government
156	3/12/97	Wenzhou	city	ZJ	PRC	chair	WF	mass org.
157	3/12/97	Wenzhou	city	ZJ	PRC	vice chair	WF	mass org.
158	3/13/97	Wenzhou	city	ZJ	PRC	director	Popular Culture Research Institution	NGO
159	3/13/97	Wenzhou	city	ZJ	PRC	assistant director	Popular Culture Research Institution	NGO

	Date	Place	Admin. Level	Province	Country	Position	Institution Name	Type
160	3/13/97	Wenzhou	city	ZJ	PRC	director	Econ System Reform Committee	government
161	3/17/97	Wenzhou	city	ZJ	PRC	staff	ILA	mass org.
162	3/17/97	Wenzhou	city	ZJ	PRC	director	PEA	mass org.
163	3/17/97	Wenzhou	city	ZJ	PRC	staff	ICMB	government
164	3/18/97	Wenzhou	city	ZJ	PRC	consultant	contracting company	enterprise
165	3/19/97	Qiaotou	county	ZJ	PRC	director	ICMB	government
166	4/17/97	Fuzhou	provincial	FJ	PRC	vice director	ICMB	government
167	4/17/97	Fuzhou	provincial	FJ	PRC	vice director	ICMB	government
168	4/17/97	Fuzhou	provincial	FJ	PRC	director	ILA/PEA	mass org.
169	4/17/97	Fuzhou	provincial	FJ	PRC	director	ICMB	government
170	5/19/97	Beijing	NA	BJ	PRC	program officer	UNDP	IO
171	5/20/97	Beijing	municipal	BJ	PRC	researcher	CASS—RDI	research
172	5/20/97	Beijing	municipal	BJ	PRC	director	CASS—RDI	research
173	5/20/97	Beijing	NA	NA	Bangladesh	sr. principal officer	Grameen Bank	financial
174	5/21/97	Yixian	county	HB	PRC	director	FPC—Yixian	NGO
175	5/21/97	Yixian	county	HB	PRC	accountant	FPC—Yixian	NGO
176	5/21/97	Taipingyu	village	HB	PRC	center leader	FPC—Yixian	NGO
177	5/22/97	Beijing	municipal	BJ	PRC	president	ICCIC	NGO
178	5/25/97	Nanzhao	county	HN	PRC	director	FPC—Nanzhao	NGO
179	5/26/97	Nanzhao	county	HN	PRC	vice director	FPC—Nanzhao	NGO
180	5/26/97	Yang Shigou	village	HN	PRC	farmer	household	household
181	5/26/97	Nanzhao	county	HN	PRC	entrepreneur	Nanyang Huifeng Arts & Crafts	enterprise
182	6/13/97	Fuzhou	city	FJ	PRC	director	Fuzhou UCB	financial
183	6/13/97	Fuzhou	city	FJ	PRC	driver	Fuzhou UCB	financial
184	1/15/2001	Yongzhong	township	ZJ	PRC	entrepreneur	leather factory	enterprise
185	1/15/2001	Ouhai	county	ZJ	PRC	entrepreneur	electrical components factory	enterprise
186	1/19/2001	Wenzhou	city	ZJ	PRC	senior economist	ABOC—Wenzhou	financial

Appendix C

List of Surveys, 1996–97

	Date	Site	Province	Bus. Type[a]		Date	Site	Province	Bus. Type[a]
1	4/7/96	Fuzhou	Fujian	B5	40	4/12/96	Fuzhou	Fujian	A3
2	4/10/96	Fuzhou	Fujian	B5	41	4/14/96	Fuzhou	Fujian	A11
3	4/10/96	Fuzhou	Fujian	A7	42	4/14/96	Fuzhou	Fujian	C6
4	4/11/96	Fuzhou	Fujian	B5	43	4/13/96	Fuzhou	Fujian	C2
5	4/11/96	Fuzhou	Fujian	C8	44	4/14/96	Fuzhou	Fujian	C5
6	4/11/96	Fuzhou	Fujian	A1	45	4/14/96	Fuzhou	Fujian	A9
7	4/11/96	Fuzhou	Fujian	B1	46	4/14/96	Fuzhou	Fujian	B5
8	4/11/96	Fuzhou	Fujian	A1	47	4/12/96	Fuzhou	Fujian	C13
9	4/11/96	Fuzhou	Fujian	C2	48	4/12/96	Fuzhou	Fujian	A10
10	4/11/96	Fuzhou	Fujian	A1	49	4/14/96	Fuzhou	Fujian	C17
11	4/11/96	Fuzhou	Fujian	B5	50	4/14/96	Fuzhou	Fujian	B4
12	4/11/96	Fuzhou	Fujian	A7	51	4/14/96	Fuzhou	Fujian	C15
13	4/11/96	Fuzhou	Fujian	A1	52	4/14/96	Fuzhou	Fujian	C3
14	4/11/96	Fuzhou	Fujian	A7	53	4/14/96	Fuzhou	Fujian	B5
15	4/11/96	Fuzhou	Fujian	B5	54	4/12/96	Fuzhou	Fujian	A0
16	4/11/96	Fuzhou	Fujian	A8	55	4/12/96	Fuzhou	Fujian	C4
17	4/11/96	Fuzhou	Fujian	A1	56	4/12/96	Fuzhou	Fujian	CX
18	4/11/96	Fuzhou	Fujian	B3	57	4/12/96	Fuzhou	Fujian	A11
19	4/12/96	Fuzhou	Fujian	A11	58	4/12/96	Fuzhou	Fujian	CX
20	4/12/96	Fuzhou	Fujian	C2	59	4/12/96	Fuzhou	Fujian	B5
21	4/13/96	Fuzhou	Fujian	A16	60	4/12/96	Fuzhou	Fujian	A8
22	4/13/96	Fuzhou	Fujian	C5	61	4/11/96	Fuzhou	Fujian	C8
23	4/13/96	Fuzhou	Fujian	A7	62	4/12/96	Fuzhou	Fujian	C13
24	4/13/96	Fuzhou	Fujian	C16	63	4/11/96	Fuzhou	Fujian	CX
25	4/13/96	Fuzhou	Fujian	B5	64	4/11/96	Fuzhou	Fujian	B5
26	4/13/96	Fuzhou	Fujian	C5	65	4/12/96	Fuzhou	Fujian	C5
27	4/13/96	Fuzhou	Fujian	BX	66	4/13/96	Fuzhou	Fujian	B4
28	4/13/96	Fuzhou	Fujian	C8	67	4/14/96	Fuzhou	Fujian	A19
29	4/15/96	Fuzhou	Fujian	A3	68	4/13/96	Fuzhou	Fujian	C11
30	4/13/96	Fuzhou	Fujian	A3	69	5/4/96	Fuzhou	Fujian	B1
31	4/13/96	Fuzhou	Fujian	A18	70	5/4/96	Fuzhou	Fujian	B2
32	4/12/96	Fuzhou	Fujian	C7	71	5/4/96	Fuzhou	Fujian	B7
33	4/12/96	Fuzhou	Fujian	A3	72	5/4/96	Fuzhou	Fujian	C5
34	4/12/96	Fuzhou	Fujian	A3	73	5/4/96	Fuzhou	Fujian	B1
35	4/12/96	Fuzhou	Fujian	C17	74	5/4/96	Fuzhou	Fujian	A1
36	4/12/96	Fuzhou	Fujian	A6	76	5/3/96	Fuzhou	Fujian	A3
37	4/12/96	Fuzhou	Fujian	A6	77	5/3/96	Fuzhou	Fujian	A3
38	4/12/96	Fuzhou	Fujian	A3	78	5/3/96	Fuzhou	Fujian	A1
39	4/12/96	Fuzhou	Fujian	C5	79	5/3/96	Fuzhou	Fujian	A1

	Date	Site	Province	Bus. Type[a]		Date	Site	Province	Bus. Type[a]
80	5/3/96	Fuzhou	Fujian	B5	130	4/10/96	Fuzhou	Fujian	A1
81	4/12/96	Fuzhou	Fujian	A3	131	4/13/96	Fuzhou	Fujian	A1
82	4/12/96	Fuzhou	Fujian	A20	132	4/13/96	Fuzhou	Fujian	A11
83	4/19/96	Fuzhou	Fujian	A3	133	4/13/96	Fuzhou	Fujian	A19
84	4/19/96	Fuzhou	Fujian	A3	134	4/14/96	Fuzhou	Fujian	B4
85	4/19/96	Fuzhou	Fujian	A3	135	4/13/96	Fuzhou	Fujian	B4
86	5/3/96	Fuzhou	Fujian	A1	136	4/13/96	Fuzhou	Fujian	B1
87	4/19/96	Fuzhou	Fujian	A3	137	4/13/96	Fuzhou	Fujian	B3
88	4/19/96	Fuzhou	Fujian	A3	138	4/13/96	Fuzhou	Fujian	A7
89	4/19/96	Fuzhou	Fujian	A3	139	4/12/96	Fuzhou	Fujian	A1
90	4/19/96	Fuzhou	Fujian	A3	140	5/3/96	Fuzhou	Fujian	A1
91	4/19/96	Fuzhou	Fujian	A3	141	5/3/96	Fuzhou	Fujian	B1
92	4/19/96	Fuzhou	Fujian	A3	142	5/3/96	Fuzhou	Fujian	A1
93	4/19/96	Fuzhou	Fujian	A3	143	5/3/96	Fuzhou	Fujian	B1
94	4/19/96	Fuzhou	Fujian	A3	144	5/3/96	Fuzhou	Fujian	A1
95	4/19/96	Fuzhou	Fujian	A3	145	4/11/96	Fuzhou	Fujian	B5
96	4/19/96	Fuzhou	Fujian	A3	145	6/13/96	Changle	Fujian	A4
97	4/19/96	Fuzhou	Fujian	A3	146	6/13/96	Changle	Fujian	A16
98	4/19/96	Fuzhou	Fujian	B2	147	6/13/96	Changle	Fujian	A11
99	4/19/96	Fuzhou	Fujian	B2	148	6/13/96	Changle	Fujian	A14
100	4/19/96	Fuzhou	Fujian	B2	149	6/13/96	Changle	Fujian	BX
101	4/19/96	Fuzhou	Fujian	B2	150	6/15/96	Changle	Fujian	B5
102	4/19/96	Fuzhou	Fujian	A5	151	6/15/96	Changle	Fujian	A11
103	4/19/96	Fuzhou	Fujian	A5	152	6/16/96	Changle	Fujian	A4
104	4/19/96	Fuzhou	Fujian	A5	153	6/16/96	Changle	Fujian	A10
105	4/19/96	Fuzhou	Fujian	A5	154	6/16/96	Changle	Fujian	C11
106	4/19/96	Fuzhou	Fujian	B3	155	6/16/96	Changle	Fujian	A4
107	4/19/96	Fuzhou	Fujian	B3	156	6/16/96	Changle	Fujian	A4
108	4/19/96	Fuzhou	Fujian	B3	157	6/16/96	Changle	Fujian	A8
109	4/19/96	Fuzhou	Fujian	B3	158	6/16/96	Changle	Fujian	B8
110	4/19/96	Fuzhou	Fujian	B3	159	6/17/96	Changle	Fujian	A2
111	4/19/96	Fuzhou	Fujian	B7	160	6/17/96	Changle	Fujian	A1
112	4/19/96	Fuzhou	Fujian	B3	161	6/17/96	Changle	Fujian	B1
113	4/19/96	Fuzhou	Fujian	B1	162	6/17/96	Changle	Fujian	B2
114	4/19/96	Fuzhou	Fujian	B1	163	6/17/96	Changle	Fujian	B8
115	4/19/96	Fuzhou	Fujian	B3	164	6/17/96	Changle	Fujian	B1
116	4/19/96	Fuzhou	Fujian	B3	165	6/17/96	Changle	Fujian	B1
117	4/19/96	Fuzhou	Fujian	B3	166	6/17/96	Changle	Fujian	B1
118	4/19/96	Fuzhou	Fujian	B3	167	6/17/96	Changle	Fujian	A6
119	4/19/96	Fuzhou	Fujian	B3	168	6/17/96	Changle	Fujian	A1
120	4/19/96	Fuzhou	Fujian	B3	169	6/17/96	Changle	Fujian	B5
121	4/19/96	Fuzhou	Fujian	B3	170	6/17/96	Changle	Fujian	B5
122	4/19/96	Fuzhou	Fujian	B2	171	6/18/96	Changle	Fujian	A15
123	4/19/96	Fuzhou	Fujian	B2	172	6/18/96	Changle	Fujian	A15
124	4/19/96	Fuzhou	Fujian	B2	173	6/18/96	Changle	Fujian	A11
125	4/19/96	Fuzhou	Fujian	A6	174	6/18/96	Changle	Fujian	A15
126	4/19/96	Fuzhou	Fujian	A6	175	6/18/96	Changle	Fujian	A15
127	4/19/96	Fuzhou	Fujian	A6	176	6/18/96	Changle	Fujian	A5
128	4/19/96	Fuzhou	Fujian	A10	177	6/18/96	Changle	Fujian	A14
129	4/19/96	Fuzhou	Fujian	A4	178	6/18/96	Changle	Fujian	B5

	Date	Site	Province	Bus. Type[a]		Date	Site	Province	Bus. Type[a]
179	6/19/96	Changle	Fujian	A4	230	7/25/96	Kaifeng	Henan	BX
180	6/19/96	Changle	Fujian	A16	231	7/25/96	Kaifeng	Henan	C5
181	6/19/96	Changle	Fujian	A4	232	7/25/96	Kaifeng	Henan	C15
182	6/19/96	Changle	Fujian	A8	233	7/27/96	Zhengzhou	Henan	A4
183	6/19/96	Changle	Fujian	A5	234	7/27/96	Zhengzhou	Henan	A4
184	6/19/96	Changle	Fujian	A8	235	7/27/96	Zhengzhou	Henan	A4
185	6/19/96	Changle	Fujian	A4	236	7/27/96	Zhengzhou	Henan	A4
186	6/19/96	Changle	Fujian	A11	237	7/28/96	Zhengzhou	Henan	B5
187	6/19/96	Changle	Fujian	A4	238	7/28/96	Zhengzhou	Henan	A6
188	6/20/96	Changle	Fujian	BX	239	7/28/96	Zhengzhou	Henan	A6
189	6/20/96	Changle	Fujian	B2	240	7/28/96	Zhengzhou	Henan	B1
190	6/21/96	Changle	Fujian	A1	241	7/28/96	Zhengzhou	Henan	C10
191	7/4/96	Fuzhou	Fujian	AX	242	7/29/96	Zhengzhou	Henan	B5
192	7/7/96	Zhengzhou	Henan	B2	243	7/29/96	Zhengzhou	Henan	A16
193	7/7/96	Zhengzhou	Henan	A1	244	7/29/96	Zhengzhou	Henan	A11
194	7/9/96	Zhengzhou	Henan	C5	245	7/29/96	Zhengzhou	Henan	A17
195	7/13/96	Zhengzhou	Henan	A10	246	7/29/96	Zhengzhou	Henan	B5
196	7/13/96	Zhengzhou	Henan	A16	247	7/30/96	Zhengzhou	Henan	B1
197	7/13/96	Zhengzhou	Henan	A5	248	7/30/96	Zhengzhou	Henan	B7
198	7/13/96	Zhengzhou	Henan	B4	249	7/30/96	Zhengzhou	Henan	BX
199	7/14/96	Zhengzhou	Henan	A5	250	7/30/96	Zhengzhou	Henan	A3
200	7/14/96	Zhengzhou	Henan	A2	251	7/31/96	Zhengzhou	Henan	A16
201	7/14/96	Zhengzhou	Henan	A5	252	7/31/96	Zhengzhou	Henan	A13
202	7/14/96	Zhengzhou	Henan	A9	253	7/31/96	Zhengzhou	Henan	B7
203	7/15/96	Zhengzhou	Henan	A3	254	7/31/96	Zhengzhou	Henan	A16
204	7/15/96	Zhengzhou	Henan	B3	255	7/31/96	Zhengzhou	Henan	AX
205	7/16/96	Zhengzhou	Henan	AX	256	8/1/96	Zhengzhou	Henan	CX
206	7/16/96	Zhengzhou	Henan	A8	257	8/1/96	Zhengzhou	Henan	A4
207	7/18/96	Zhengzhou	Henan	A4	258	8/1/96	Zhengzhou	Henan	A4
208	7/18/96	Zhengzhou	Henan	A14	259	8/1/96	Zhengzhou	Henan	A4
209	7/18/96	Zhengzhou	Henan	A4	260	8/1/96	Zhengzhou	Henan	A14
210	7/18/96	Zhengzhou	Henan	A4	261	8/2/96	Zhengzhou	Henan	A4
211	7/18/96	Zhengzhou	Henan	A4	262	8/2/96	Zhengzhou	Henan	A11
212	7/18/96	Zhengzhou	Henan	CX	263	8/7/96	Luoyang	Henan	A3
213	7/21/96	Kaifeng	Henan	AX	264	8/7/96	Luoyang	Henan	A3
214	7/22/96	Kaifeng	Henan	A4	265	8/7/96	Luoyang	Henan	A8
215	7/22/96	Kaifeng	Henan	A4	266	8/7/96	Luoyang	Henan	A3
216	7/22/96	Kaifeng	Henan	B3	267	8/7/96	Luoyang	Henan	AX
217	7/22/96	Kaifeng	Henan	B7	268	8/7/96	Luoyang	Henan	B7
218	7/22/96	Kaifeng	Henan	B1	269	8/8/96	Luoyang	Henan	A16
219	7/22/96	Kaifeng	Henan	A19	270	8/8/96	Luoyang	Henan	A16
220	7/23/96	Kaifeng	Henan	A1	271	8/11/96	Zhengzhou	Henan	BX
221	7/23/96	Kaifeng	Henan	B8	272	8/11/96	Zhengzhou	Henan	A1
222	7/23/96	Kaifeng	Henan	A4	273	8/11/96	Zhengzhou	Henan	B2
223	7/23/96	Kaifeng	Henan	C1	274	8/11/96	Zhengzhou	Henan	A4
224	7/23/96	Kaifeng	Henan	B1	275	8/11/96	Zhengzhou	Henan	B5
225	7/23/96	Kaifeng	Henan	B5	276	8/13/96	Zhengzhou	Henan	B3
226	7/24/96	Kaifeng	Henan	A1	277	8/13/96	Zhengzhou	Henan	B3
227	7/24/96	Kaifeng	Henan	B5	278	8/13/96	Zhengzhou	Henan	B3
228	7/25/96	Kaifeng	Henan	B1	279	8/14/96	Zhengzhou	Henan	B1
229	7/25/96	Kaifeng	Henan	BX	280	8/14/96	Zhengzhou	Henan	B1

	Date	Site	Province	Bus. Type[a]		Date	Site	Province	Bus. Type[a]
281	8/14/96	Zhengzhou	Henan	AX	328	11/25/96	Huian	Fujian	A19
282	8/15/96	Zhengzhou	Henan	BX	329	11/25/96	Huian	Fujian	AX
283	8/15/96	Zhengzhou	Henan	B1	330	11/25/96	Huian	Fujian	B1
284	8/15/96	Zhengzhou	Henan	A1	331	11/26/96	Huian	Fujian	A16
285	8/15/96	Zhengzhou	Henan	B3	332	11/26/96	Huian	Fujian	B7
286	8/17/96	Zhengzhou	Henan	A12	333	11/26/96	Huian	Fujian	A16
287	8/17/96	Zhengzhou	Henan	B7	334	11/26/96	Huian	Fujian	A4
288	8/17/96	Zhengzhou	Henan	AX	335	11/26/96	Huian	Fujian	A15
289	8/17/96	Zhengzhou	Henan	B1	336	11/26/96	Huian	Fujian	C2
290	8/17/96	Zhengzhou	Henan	B1	337	11/26/96	Huian	Fujian	BX
291	8/20/96	Zhengzhou	Henan	A6	338	11/26/96	Huian	Fujian	B1
292	11/12/96	Anxi	Fujian	A2	339	11/27/96	Huian	Fujian	B5
293	11/12/96	Anxi	Fujian	C11	340	11/27/96	Huian	Fujian	C13
294	11/12/96	Anxi	Fujian	A12	341	11/27/96	Huian	Fujian	A4
295	11/13/96	Anxi	Fujian	A1	342	11/27/96	Huian	Fujian	C5
296	11/13/96	Anxi	Fujian	A13	343	11/27/96	Huian	Fujian	B5
297	11/14/96	Anxi	Fujian	B5	344	11/28/96	Huian	Fujian	C14
298	11/14/96	Anxi	Fujian	A11	345	11/28/96	Huian	Fujian	B1
299	11/14/96	Anxi	Fujian	BX	346	11/28/96	Huian	Fujian	A4
300	11/14/96	Anxi	Fujian	A4	347	11/28/96	Huian	Fujian	A6
301	11/14/96	Anxi	Fujian	A16	348	11/28/96	Huian	Fujian	B1
302	11/15/96	Anxi	Fujian	A1	349	3/12/97	Wenzhou	Zhejiang	A1
303	11/15/96	Anxi	Fujian	A6	350	3/14/97	Wenzhou	Zhejiang	A11
304	11/15/96	Anxi	Fujian	A4	351	3/14/97	Wenzhou	Zhejiang	B5
305	11/15/96	Anxi	Fujian	A1	352	3/14/97	Wenzhou	Zhejiang	B3
306	11/18/96	Quanzhou	Fujian	C5	353	3/14/97	Wenzhou	Zhejiang	A6
307	11/18/96	Quanzhou	Fujian	A4	354	3/14/97	Wenzhou	Zhejiang	A11
308	11/19/96	Quanzhou	Fujian	B3	355	3/15/97	Wenzhou	Zhejiang	A5
309	11/19/96	Quanzhou	Fujian	AX	356	3/15/97	Wenzhou	Zhejiang	AX
310	11/19/96	Quanzhou	Fujian	BX	357	3/15/97	Wenzhou	Zhejiang	AX
311	11/19/96	Quanzhou	Fujian	A4	358	3/15/97	Wenzhou	Zhejiang	A4
312	11/19/96	Quanzhou	Fujian	A10	359	3/15/97	Wenzhou	Zhejiang	AX
313	11/20/96	Jinjiang	Fujian	AX	360	3/16/97	Wenzhou	Zhejiang	AX
314	11/20/96	Jinjiang	Fujian	A6	361	3/16/97	Wenzhou	Zhejiang	AX
315	11/20/96	Jinjiang	Fujian	A1	362	3/16/97	Wenzhou	Zhejiang	AX
316	11/20/96	Jinjiang	Fujian	A1	363	3/16/97	Wenzhou	Zhejiang	AX
317	11/21/96	Quanzhou	Fujian	A4	364	3/16/97	Wenzhou	Zhejiang	AX
318	11/21/96	Quanzhou	Fujian	A1	365	3/17/97	Wenzhou	Zhejiang	A13
319	11/21/96	Quanzhou	Fujian	B1	366	3/18/97	Wenzhou	Zhejiang	B5
320	11/21/96	Quanzhou	Fujian	A1	367	3/19/97	Wenzhou	Zhejiang	A13
321	11/22/96	Quanzhou	Fujian	A2	368	3/19/97	Wenzhou	Zhejiang	A15
322	11/22/96	Quanzhou	Fujian	B2	369	3/19/97	Wenzhou	Zhejiang	AX
323	11/23/96	Quanzhou	Fujian	B5	370	3/19/97	Wenzhou	Zhejiang	AX
324	11/25/96	Huian	Fujian	A1	371	3/19/97	Wenzhou	Zhejiang	AX
325	11/25/96	Huian	Fujian	A6	372	3/20/97	Wenzhou	Zhejiang	A17
326	11/25/96	Huian	Fujian	B5	373	3/20/97	Wenzhou	Zhejiang	A19
327	11/25/96	Huian	Fujian	C3	374	3/20/97	Wenzhou	Zhejiang	A5

[a] See Appendix D.

Appendix D

Coding for Business Types

The business codes to the surveys I assigned indicated whether the business was an "indoor" or "outdoor" operation (1 or 2), the broad category of products, foods, or services (A, B, or C), and the specific type of business. For example, "2C14" would indicate an outdoor fortune-telling business. In Appendix C, however, the "Bus. Type" column lists only the latter two designations.

A	Products	B	Food	C	Services
0	department store	1	fruits and/or	1	bicycle repair
1	everyday sundries		vegetables	2	shoe repair
2	low budget	2	meat and/or	3	tailor
	household goods		seafood	4	laundry
3	higher-end household	3	biscuits and/or	5	hairdresser
	products		dried fruits	6	typing/word-
4	outer clothing	4	fast food stand		processing
5	underwear	5	sit-down restaurant	7	lodging (hotel)
6	shoes	6	livestock	8	photocopying
7	newspapers and	7	bottled, canned, or	9	electronics repair
	magazines		paper carton drinks	10	key copying
8	books	8	tea	11	film developing
9	stationery and office	X	other	12	cleaning
	supplies			13	transportation
10	electronics				(e.g., cab, bike)
11	music (tapes, CDs)			14	fortune-telling
12	bicycles			15	KTV or disco
13	jewelry			16	billiard hall
14	handbags, wallets			17	video arcade
15	hair accessories			X	other
16	gifts				
17	cosmetics				
18	eyeglasses				
19	flowers				
20	sporting goods				
X	other				

Appendix E

Comparative Summary of Rotating Savings and Credit Associations

Country	Region/Area	Ethnicity, Gender	Name(s)	Lending Method	Use of Funds	Sources[a]
Bolivia	Urban		*pasanakkus*	pre-set, need-based	agricultural production; emergencies	Adams and Canavesi (1992)
Cameroon	rural	women	*djanggis njanjis tontines*	pre-set, need-based	living expenses (rent, school fees, kitchen equipment)	Rowlands (1995); Schreider and Cuevas (1992)
China	Fujian—FZ, CL, QZ Jiangxi Guangdong Zhejiang—WZ, Ningbo	Han, women	*biaohui, huzhuhui yaohui chenghui, juhui, lunhui, zhuanhui, maihui, ganhui yahui*	auction, need-based, rolling dice	business, savings, housing (weddings), migration	Tsai field work (1994–97); Cui (1996); Pairault (1990); Ma (1995); Xu and Li (1988); Zhang and Mao (1993)
Congo	urban	Mbochi, Teke, women	*likilimba, otabaka, kiteme, etion*		religion, funerals	Seibel and Marx (1987)

Country	Region/Area	Ethnicity, Gender	Name(s)	Lending Method	Use of Funds	Sources[a]
Egypt	urban and rural	women	*gam'iyas*	lottery or ad hoc	mutual aid, savings	Baydas, Bahloul, and Adams (1995)
Gambia	urban and rural	men and women	*osusu (kafos)*	pre-set or lottery	small business	Shipton (1992); Esim (1996)
Ghana	south, marketplaces	women	*susu*	need, balloting	business, savings	Bortei-Doku and Aryeetey (1995)
Guinea-Bissau	marketplaces	similar age, gender, ethnicity	*abotas*		business, farming (seasonal), emergencies, equipment purchasing	Esim (1996)
Guyana		Yoruban roots, women	*boxi money, throwing a box*	pre-set by head	business, farming, weddings	Besson (1995)
India	Kerala, south India	women	*chit funds*	mostly auction	business, savings	Nayar (1973)
Indonesia	central Java, west coast of Sumatra	urban women; rural, some Chinese	*arisan, arisan call (julu-julu in Sumatra)*	lots, auction (in urban areas)	purchasing household utensils & furniture (women); roofing, piping materials (men)	Geertz (1962); Dewey (1964); Penny (1968)
Ivory Coast	rural areas	Kru Akan Mande	*akpole wule, susu, aposumbo n'detie, m'bhlisika monu, mone*		agricultural production	Seibel and Marx (1987)
Japan	rural areas until mid-1900s; 1st documented in 1275 A.D.	farmers, samurais, women	*kou, kō, tanomoshi-kou, mukin-kou*	lottery, auction	farming, business, savings, local fiscal expenditures	Izumida (1992); Miyanaga (1995)

Country	Region/Area	Ethnicity, Gender	Name(s)	Lending Method	Use of Funds	Sources[a]
Kenya	squatter area of Nairobi	Gikuyu, women	*itega*	pre-set	savings, school fees, investments	Nelson (1995)
Korea	rural	women	*kye*	lottery, pre-set, need	farming, business, charity	Janelli and Yim (1988)
Malawi		[lower-income]	*chiryelano, chiperigani*	"negotiation"	consumption, savings, education, farming	Chipeta and Mkandawire (1992)
Mexico	urban	[prisoners]	*tanda (or ronda, quincela)*	pre-set, need, bidding	consumption, savings (marijuana in prisons)	Kurtz and Showman (1978); Vélez-Ibañez (1983)
Nepal	Himalayas—rural (Lo region of Mustang)	Loba (Tibetan)	*dhikuri*	lottery	business, savings	Chhetri (1995)
	Pokhara, Kathmandu—urban	Nepali	*dhikuri*	lottery	business, savings, investment	Messerschmidt (1978)
	Pokhara—urban	Thakali	*sihku dhikuri*	lottery	adaptation after migration	Vinding (1984); Chhetri (1995)
Niger	urban and rural	popular in general; women	*tontines*	need-based	business, farming	Graham (1992); Colleye (1996)
Nigeria	western	Yoruba, Igala	*ojo* *isusu*	rotating or need-based	savings, insurance, farming	Siebel and Marx (1987)
Pakistan	eastern		*bisi committees*		low-income housing	Van der Harst (1974)
Papua New Guinea	Rabaul (German New Guinea) ⇒ Port Moresby	Han Chinese from Guangdong with wives from Hong Kong; teachers	*piu-wui (biao hui)*	auction	business, savings, consumption	Wu (1974); Fernando (1992)

Country	Region/Area	Ethnicity, Gender	Name(s)	Lending Method	Use of Funds	Sources[a]
Philippines	Sapang Palay markets; Dasmarinas Resettlement Area (near Manila)	female fish vendors, families	*paluwagan*		housing, savings for consumption, appliances, children's education, business	Keyes (1983); Lamberte and Bunda (1988)
Senegal	urban areas; some rural	women	*natt, teck, piye, pari*		production, consumption	Chidzero (1996)
Sierra Leone	rural	relatives, ethnic groups	*esusus*	seniority in membership; some ad hoc	farming, consumption, emergency	Hadjimichael (1996)
South Africa	urban	women (esp. single mothers)	*stokvel, gooi-gooi*	pre-set	savings, consumption, burials	Burman and Lembete (1995)
Sri Lanka			*cheetus*	lottery, auction or pre-set	funerals, cultivation	Sanderatne (1992)
Taiwan	[esp. public sector employees]	households with women	*biao hui*	auction	consumption, business	Levenson and Besley (1996)
Tanzania	urban	women	*upatu, mchezo*	cash	business, consumption	Malkamäki (1991)
Thailand	squatter settlements; Bangkok	women	*chaer or pia huey*	auction	business	Rozental (1967); Angel and Sevilla (1978); Vongpradhip (1985)
Togo		Ewe, women Kotokoli	*sodyokyo aboo*	rotating	business	Seibel and Marx (1987)

Country	Region/Area	Ethnicity, Gender	Name(s)	Lending Method	Use of Funds	Sources[a]
Trinidad		Yoruban (west African) roots	*susu*	determined by organizer	consumption, housing	Herskovits and Herskovits (1947)
Turkey	(Turkish Republic of) Northern Cyprus	housewives, government employees, teachers	*altn günü, gümüs günü*	rotating	savings (in the form of gold)	Khatib-Chahidi (1995)
United Kingdom	London	Northern Somali, women	*hagbad*	need	utility bills, medicine	Summerfield (1995)
	Oxford	Eritrean, women	*iqqubs*	pre-set	consumption	Almedom (1995)
United States	urban centers with immigrants	Mexicans Koreans Chinese	*cundina kye san yi hui*	pre-set, need, bidding	consumption, business, savings, weddings, funerals, gambling	Kurtz (1973); Vélez-Ibañez (1983); Light (1972)
Vietnam	Ho Chi Minh City	Chinese, women	*ho, whoo-ie, hui*	pre-set, bidding	business, savings	Leshkowich (2000)
West Bank/ Gaza Strip	urban; refugee camps	white collar employees		lottery, pre-set, or need		Hamed (1998)

Note: This is by no means a comprehensive listing of ROSCAs around the world.
[a] For complete references, see the source list that follows.

Sources Cited in Table 6.1 and Appendix E

Adams, Dale W., and Marie L. Canavesi. "Rotating Savings and Credit Associations in Bolivia." *Savings and Development* 13 (1989): 219–36.

——. "Rotating Savings and Credit Associations in Bolivia." In Adams and Fitchett (1992), 313–23.

Adams, Dale W., and Delbert A. Fitchett, eds. *Informal Finance in Low-Income Countries.* Boulder, Colo.: Westview Press, 1992.

Almedom, Astier M. "A Note on ROSCAs among Ethiopian Women in Addis Ababa and Eritrean Women in Oxford." In Ardener and Burman (1995), 71–76.

Angel, Shlomo, J. H. de Goede, and Ramon Sevilla. "Sharing the Risk of Being Poor: Communal Savings Games in Bangkok." *Journal of the Siam Society* 66, 2 (1978): 123–45.

Ardener, Shirley, and Sandra Burman, eds. *Money-Go-Rounds: The Importance of Rotating Savings and Credit Associations for Women.* Oxford: Berg, 1995.

Aryeetey, Ernest. "Private Investment under Uncertainty in Ghana." *World Development* 22, 8 (1994): 1211–21.

Baydas, Mayada M., Zakarea Bahloul, and Dale W. Adams. "Informal Finance in Egypt: 'Banks' within Banks." *World Development* 23, 4 (1995): 651–61.

Berthoud, Olivier, and Walter Milligan. *Sector Informal Urbano y crédito.* La Paz, Bolivia: Dirección de la Cooperación Técnica Suiza, 1995.

Besson, Jean. "Women's Use of ROSCAs in the Caribbean: Reassessing the Literature." In Ardener and Burman, 263–88.

Bortei-Doku, Ellen, and Ernest Aryeetey. "Mobilizing Cash for Business: Women in Rotating *Susu* Clubs in Ghana." In Ardener and Burman (1995), 77–94.

Burman, Sandra, and Nozipho Lembete. "Building New Realities: Women and ROSCAs in Urban South Africa." In Ardener and Burman (1995), 23–48.

Chhetri, Ram B. "Rotating Credit Associations in Nepal: *Dhikuri* as Capital, Credit, Saving, and Investment." *Human Organization* 54, 4 (1995): 449–53.

Chidzero, Anne-Marie. "Senegal." In Webster and Fidler (1992), 195–202.

Chipeta, Chinyamata, and Mjedo L. C. Mkandawire. "The Informal Financial Sector in Malawi." *African Review of Finance, Money, and Banking* 2 (1992).

Christen, Robert P. "Formal Credit for Informal Borrowers: Lessons from Informal Lenders." In Adams and Fitchett (1992), 281–92.

Colleye, Pierre-Olivier. "Niger." In Webster and Fidler (1996), 177–84.

Cui, Liukang. "Dui fazhan nongcun hezuo jijinhui jige wenti de bianxi" (On the problems and differential analysis of rural cooperative foundations). *Nongye jingji wenti* (Problems of agricultural economy) 5 (1996): 15–18.

Dadson, Christine. "Non-Bank Financial Institutions in Ghana." In *Establishing a Microfinance Industry: Proceedings of the 4th Microfinance Network. Annual Conference,* Establishing a Microfinance Industry, 1996, in Niagara-on-the-Lake Canada, Washington D.C.: Microfinance Network, 1997.

Dewey, Alice. "Capital, Credit, and Saving in Javanese Market." In Raymond Firth and B. S. Yamey, eds., *Capital, Savings, and Credit in Peasant Societies: Studies from Asia, Oceania, the Caribbean, and Middle America.* (London: George Allen & Unwin, 1964), 230–55.

Esim, Simel. "The Gambia." In Webster and Fidler (1996), 115–26.

———. "Guinea-Bissau." In Webster and Fidler (1996), 139–51.

Fernando, Nimal A. "Informal Finance in Papua New Guinea." In Adams and Fitchett (1992), 119–31.

Geertz, Clifford. "The Rotating Credit Association: A 'Middle Rung' in Development." *Economic Development and Cultural Change* 4 (1962): 241–63.

Germidis, Dimitri, Dennis Kessler, and Rachel Meghir. *Financial Systems and Development: What Role for the Formal and Informal Financial Sectors?* Paris: Organisation for Economic Co-operation and Development, Development Center Studies, 1991.

Ghate, Prabhu, Arindam Das-Gupta, Mario Lamberte, Nipon Poapongsakorn, Dibyo Prabowo, Atiq Rahman, and T. N. Srinivasan. *Informal Finance: Some Findings from Asia.* Hong Kong: Oxford University Press for Asia Development Bank, 1992.

Graham, Douglas H. "Informal Rural Finance in Niger: Lessons for Building Formal Institutions." In Adams and Fitchett (1992), 71–83.

Hadjimichael, Bita. "Sierra Leone." In Webster and Fidler (1996), 203–13.

Hamed, Osama, with Samia Al-Botmeh and Fause Ersheid. "Informal Finance and Lending NGOs in the West Bank and Gaza Strip." Working Paper, Palestine Economic Policy Research Institute (MAS), Jerusalem and Ramallah, August 1998.

Herskovits, Melville J., and Frances S. Herskovits. *Trinidad Village.* New York: Knopf, 1947.

Huang, Weiting. *Zhongguo de yinxing jingji* (China's hidden economy). Beijing: Zhongguo shangye chubanshe, 1996.

IFC (International Finance Corporation). *China's Emerging Private Enterprises: Prospects for the New Century.* Washington, D.C.: IFC, 2000.

Izumida, Yoichi. "The *Kou* in Japan: A Precursor of Modern Finance." In Adams and Fitchett (1992), 165–80.

Janelli, Roger L., and Dawnhee Yim. "Interest Rates and Rationality: Rotating Credit Associations among Seoul Women." *Journal of Korean Studies* 6 (1988): 159–85.

Keyes, William J. "Freedom to Build—Philippines: Experience with the Freedom to Build Project at Dasmarinas, 1976–1982." Research Report no. 3, Division of Human Settlements Development, Asian Institute of Technology, Bangkok, 1983.

Khatib-Chahidi, Jane. "Gold Coins and Coffee ROSCAs: Coping with Inflation the Turkish Way in Northern Cyprus." In Ardener and Burman (1995), 241–61.

Kurtz, Donald V. "The Rotating Credit Association: An Adaptation to Poverty." *Human Organization* 32 (1973): 49–58.

Kurtz, Donald V., and Margaret Showman. "The *Tanda*: A RCA in Mexico." *Ethnology* 17 (1978): 65–74.

Lamberte, Mario B., and Ma. Theresa Bunda. "The Financial Markets in Low-Income Urban Communities: The Case of Sapang Palay." Working Paper, Series 88-05, Philippine Institute for Development Studies, Manila, March 1988.

Leshkovich, Ann Marie. "Tightly Woven Threads: Gender, Kinship, and 'Secret Agency' among Cloth and Clothing Traders, in Ho Chi Minh City's Ben Thanh Market." Ph.D. diss., Harvard University, 2000.

Levenson, Alec R., and Timothy Besley. "The Anatomy of an Informal Financial Market: Rosca Participation in Taiwan." *Journal of Development Economics* 51, 1 (1996): 45–68.

Light, Ivan H. *Ethnic Enterprise in America: Business and Welfare among Chinese, Japanese, and Blacks.* Berkeley: University of California Press, 1972.

Ma, Jinlong. "Wenzhou jinrong shichang" (Wenzhou's financial market). In Zhang Xu and Zheng Dajiong, eds., *Wenzhou shichang* (Wenzhou's market). Beijing: Zhonggong dangshi chubanshe, 1995.

Malkamäki, Marrku, et al. *Banking the Poor: Informal and Semi-formal Financial Systems Serving the Microenterprises.* Helsinki: Institute of Development Studies, University of Helsinki, 1991.

Messerschmidt, Donald A. *Dhikuris: Rotating Credit Associations in Nepal.* The Hague: Mouton, 1978.

Miyanaga, Kuniko. "Economic *Kou* (ROSCAs) in Japan: A Review." In Ardener and Burman (1995), 149–62.

Nayar, C. P. Smananthan. *Chit Finance: An Exploratory Study of Chit Funds.* Bombay: Vora, 1973.

Nelson, Niki. "The Kiambu Group: A Successful Women's ROSCA in Mathare Valley, Nairobi (1971–1990)." In Ardener and Burman (1995), 49–70.

Pairault, Thierry. "Approches Tontinières: Formes et Mécanismes Tontiniers" (Tontine Approaches: Typology and operation of tontines), pts 1–2. *Etudes Chinoises* 9, 1–2 (1990).

Penny, D. H. "Farm Credit Policy in the Early Stages of Agricultural Development." *Australian Journal of Agricultural Economics* 12, 1 (1968): 32–45.

Robinson, Richard, ed. *Indonesia Assessment 1994: Finance as a Key Sector in Indonesia's Development.* Singapore: Institute of Southeast Asian Studies and Australian National University, 1994.

Rowlands, Michael. "Looking at Financial Landscapes: A Contextual Analysis of ROSCAs in Cameroon." In Ardener and Burman (1995), 111–24.

Rozental, Alek A. "Unorganized Financial Markets and Developmental Strategy." *Journal of Developing Areas* 1, 4 (1967): 453–60.

Sanderatne, Nimal. "Informal Finance in Sri Lanka." In Adams and Fitchett (1992), 85–101.

Schrieder, Gertrud, and Carlos E. Cuevas. "Informal Financial Groups in Cameroon." In Adams and Fitchett (1992), 43–56.

Seibel, Hans Dieter, and Michael T. Marx. *Dual Financial Markets in Africa.* Saarbrücken: Verlag Breitenbach, 1987.

Shea, Jia-Dong. "Taiwan: Development and Structural Change of the Financial System." In Hugh T. Patrick and Yung Chul Park, eds. *The Financial Development of Japan, Korea, and Taiwan.* New York: Oxford University Press, 1994.

Shi, Jiliang. "Guanyu nongcun xinyongshe gaige he fazhan de jige wenti" (Issues relating to the reform and development of rural credit cooperatives). *Nongcun jingji wengao* (Rural economic essay draft), 1996.

Shipton, Parker. "The Rope and the Box: Group Savings in Gambia." In Adams and Fitchett (1992), 25–41.

Siamwalla, A., et al. "The Thai Rural Credit System: Public Subsidies, Private Information, and Segmented Markets." *World Bank Economic Review* 4, 3 (1990): 271–95.

Smith, Heather. "The State, Banking, and Corporate Relationships: Korea and Taiwan." Paper presented to International Conference on Reform and Recovery in East Asia: The Role of the State and Economic Enterprise, Australian National University, Canberra, September 21–22, 1999.

Summerfield, Hazel. "A Note on ROSCAs among Northern Somali Women in the United Kingdom." In Ardener and Burman (1995), 209–15.

Udry, Christopher. "Credit Markets in Northern Nigeria: Credit as Insurance in a Rural Economy." *World Bank Economic Review* 4, 3 (1990): 251–70.

UNDP and UNCDF (United Nations Development Programme and United Nations

Capital Development Fund). *Microfinance in Rural Lao PDR: A National Profile.* Vientiane, Laos: UNDP/UNCDF, 1997.

Van der Harst, J. "Factors Affecting Housing Improvement in Low-Income Communities, Karachi, Pakistan." *Ekistics* 39, 235 (1974).

Van Nieuwkoop, Marien. "Rural Informal Credit in Peninsular Malaysia." Bank Pertanian Malaysia, December 1986. In Ghate et al. (1992).

Vélez-Ibañez, Carlos G. *Bonds of Mutual Trust: The Cultural Systems of RCAs among Urban Mexicans and Chicanos.* New Brunswick, N.J.: Rutgers University Press, 1983.

Vinding, Michael. "Making a Living in the Nepal Himalayas: The Case of the Thakalis of Mustang District." *Contributions to Nepalese Studies* 12, 1 (1984): 51–105.

Vongpradhip, Duangmanee. "Urban Unorganized Money Markets in Thailand." Paper presented to SEACEN Seminar, Yogyakarta, Indonesia, November 1985. In Ghate et al. (1992).

Walker, Angela. "Guinea." In Webster and Fidler (1996), 127–37.

Webster, Leila, and Peter Fidler, eds. *The Informal Sector and Microfinance Institutions in West Africa.* Washington, D.C.: World Bank, 1996.

Wu, David Y. H. "To Kill Three Birds with One Stone: The Rotating Credit Associations of the Papua New Guinea Chinese." *American Ethnologist* 1 (1974): 565–84.

Xu, Guangyue, and Li Tao. *Guai Tai* (Strange fetus). Zhejiang: Zhongguo qingnian chubanshe, 1988.

Zhang, Zhenning, and Mao Chunhua. *Wenzhou jinrong xianxiang toushi* (Perspectives on the phenomenon of finance in Wenzhou). Hangzhou: Zhejiang daxue chubanshe, 1993.

Glossary of Chinese Terms

Pinyin	Chinese	English
Technical Terms		
anminpu	安民鋪	Huian women
baoxian gongsi	保險公司	insurance company
bendiren	本地人	native or local resident
biaohui	標會	"bidding" association
changzhu niangjia	長住娘家	delayed-transferred marriage
chengshi hezuo yinhang	城市合作銀行	urban cooperative bank
chengshi shangye yinhang	城市商業銀行	urban commercial bank
chengshi xinyongshe lianheshe	城市信用社聯合社	United Society of Urban Credit Cooperatives
chengshi xinyongshe	城市信用社	urban credit cooperative
dangpu	當鋪	pawnshop
danwan hui	單萬會	"single 10,000" credit association
danwei	單位	work unit
dai hongmaozi	帶紅帽子	wearing a red hat
daiguanjin	貸管金	capital managed by another person (euphemism for savings deposit)
diandangye	典當業	pawn brokering
duihui	隊會	rotating credit associations in work units
fenkou	分口	"separate sources" (fiscal system)
fupinshe	扶貧社	funding the poor cooperative
geti laodongzhe xiehui	個體勞動者協會	Individual Laborers' Association
getihu	個體戶	individual entrepreneur (<8 employees)
gewuting	歌舞廳	singing and dance halls
gongan ju	公安局	Public Security Bureau
gonggong xiaojie	公共小姐	public relations misses
gongshang guanliju	工商管理局	Industrial and Commercial Management Bureau

Pinyin	Chinese	English
gongshang lianhe she	工商聯合社	United Society of Industry and Commerce
guahu qiye	挂戶企業	hang-on enterprise
guanxi	關系	relationship, connection
gufen hezuo gongsi	股份合作公司	shareholding cooperative company
gufen hezuo qiye	股份合作企業	shareholding cooperative enterprise
gufenzhi qiye	股份制企業	shareholding enterprise
guxi	股息	distribute dividends
hangye xinyong	行業信用	trade credit
hehui	合會	rotating credit association
hehuo hu	合伙戶	partnership household
hongtou wenjian	紅頭文件	official red-sealed policy document
hong zibenjia	紅資本家	red capitalist
Huiannü	惠安女	Huian women
huitou	會頭	organizer of rotating credit association
huoqi	活期	call deposit
huzhuhui	互助會	mutual assistance (financing) associations
huzhujin	互助金	mutual assistance capital
huzhu xingshi	互助形勢	mutual assistance in nature
jiancha yuan	檢查院	Inspection Division
jiehebu	結合部	united bureau
jiaoqu hezuo chu jijinhui	郊區合作儲基金會	peri-urban cooperative savings foundation
jiangdujin	獎讀金	reading bonus
jieshaoren	介紹人	introducers
jizi	集資	raising capital collectively
jinrong jigou	金融機構	financial institutions
jiuming hui	救命會	"life-saving" credit association
juhui	舉會	rotating credit association
laowu shichang	勞務市場	labor market
lianhe hu	聯合戶	joint household enterprises
lixi	利息	interest
liudong tanr	流動攤兒	floating street vendors
lunhui	輪會	rotating credit association
luohou	落後	backward (in economic development)
mianbao che	面包車	"bread loaf" mini-vans
minjian	民間	popular, folk, of the people

Pinyin	Chinese	English
minjian jiedai	民間借貸	interpersonal lending
minjian zijin	民間資金	popular/informal capital funds
min'nan hua	閩南話	min'nan dialect
minsheng qiye jingji fuwubu	民生企業經濟服務部	people's livelihood service bureaus
minsheng qiye jingji youxian gongsi	民生企業經濟有限公司	people's livelihood enterprise economy limited liability companies
mingxing qiye	明星企業	bright star enterprise
minying qiye	民營企業	people-run enterprises
minying qiye zijin huzhuhui	民營企業資金互助會	people-run enterprises capital mutual assistance association
minying qiye zijin huzhushe	民營企業資金互助社	people-run enterprises capital mutual assistance society
neibuchuli	內部處理	internal resolution (of problem)
neibujin	內部金	internal funds of state units
nongcun hezuo jijinhui	農村合作基金會	rural cooperative foundation
nongcun hezuo yinhang	農村合作銀行	rural cooperative banks
nongcun jinrong fuwushe	農村金融服務社	rural financial service society
nongcun xinyongshe	農村信用社	rural credit cooperative
nongmang	農忙	harvest season
paihui	排會	escalating association
pibao shang	皮包商	briefcase merchant
pinkun xian	貧困懸	impoverished county
rugu	入股	issuing shares
sanxian jianshe	三線建設	third tier construction
sanzi qiye	三資企業	partially or wholly owned foreign enterprises
shanghui	商會	trade association
shanghui zijinhuzhuhui	商會資金互助會	Commercial Association Capital Mutual Assistance Association
shetou	蛇頭	snake head (smuggler of humans)
shehui tuanti	社會團體	societies, social organizations
sheng nongye ting	省農業廳	provincial agricultural office
shidian diqu	試點地區	experimental district (for reform)
shuangwan hui	雙萬會	"double 10,000" credit association
siren chengbao	私人承包	leased by a private individual
siying jinrong qiye	私營金融企業	private financial enterprises
siying qiye	私營企業	private enterprise (>8 employees)
taihui	抬會	escalating association
toudu	偷渡	illegal migration

Pinyin	Chinese	English
toufangjin	投放金	invested money (euphemism for savings deposit)
qianpu	錢鋪	money-changing shops
qianzhuang	錢庄	(private) money house
qinghui bangongshi	清會辦公室	office to eradicate rotating-credit associations
qiye huiyuan	企業會員	enterprise members
renmin fayuan	人民法院	People's Court
xiahai	下海	jumping into the sea of business
xiang shehui chouzi	向社會籌資	raising capital from the public
xintuo gongsi	信托公司	trust and investment company
xin quanwei zhuyi	新權威主義	neo-authoritarianism
xitong	系統	vertical bureacracy
yinbei	銀背	moneylenders, middlemen
yihang liangzhi	一行兩制	one bank, two systems
yaohui	搖會	"dice-shaking" association
youdian paichusuo	郵電派出所	postal savings office
zhengce daikuan	政策貸款	policy loans
zhuanye pifa shichang	專業批發市場	specialized wholesale markets
zijin tiaoji feilü	資金條級費率	adjusted capital fee (euphemism for interest on savings)
zijin zhanyong feilü	資金占用費率	capital use fee (euphemism for interest on savings)
zuotai xiaojie	坐態小姐	young female sitting companions

Places

Fujian Province

Anxi xian	安溪縣	Anxi County
Yanyang cun	燕洋村	Yanyang Village
Cangshan qu	倉山區	Cangshan District
Changle xian	長樂縣	Changle County
Chendai zhen	陳埭鎮	Chendai Township
Chongwu zhen	崇武鎮	Chongwu Township
Cizao zhen	磁灶鎮	Cizao Township
Dongshi zhen	東石鎮	Dongshi Township
Gulou qu	故樓區	Gulou District
Haixing cun	海星村	Sea Star Village
Hongshan zhen	洪山鎮	Hongshan Township
Huian xian	惠安縣	Huian County
Jinan qu	晉安區	Jinan District

Pinyin	Chinese	English
Jinjiang xian	晉江縣	Jinjiang County
Fuzhou shi	福州市	Fuzhou Municipality
Gaohu cun	高湖村	Gaohu Village
Lianjiang xian	連江縣	Lianjiang County
Luncang zhen	倉蒼鎮	Luncang Township
Mawei qu	馬尾區	Mawei District
Qingyang zhen	青陽鎮	Qingyang Township
Shiping cun	石屏村	Shiping Village
Shishi zhen	石師鎮	Shishi Township
Shiyan cun	石燕村	Shiyan Village
Taijiang qu	臺江區	Taijiang District
Quanzhou shi	泉州市	Quanzhou Municipality
Xiamen	廈門	Xiamen

Zhejiang Province

Cangnan xian	蒼南縣	Cangnan County
Dongtou xian	洞頭縣	Dongtou County
Jin xiang	金鄉	Jin Township
Lishui xian	麗水縣	Lishui County
Ouhai xian	甌海縣	Ouhai County
Pingyang xian	平陽縣	Pingyang County
Qianku zhen	錢庫鎮	Qianku Township
Taizhou xian	臺州縣	Taizhou County
Wenzhou shi	溫州市	Wenzhou Municipality
Yiwu xian	義烏縣	Yiwu County
Yongjia xian	永嘉縣	Yongjia County
Yueqing xian	樂清縣	Yueqing County

Henan Province

Chengguan zhen	城關鎮	Chengguan Township
Gongyi qu	鞏義區	Gongyi District
Jiyuan City	濟愿市	Jiyuan City
Kaifeng shi	關封市	Kaifeng City
Luoyang shi	洛陽市	Luoyang City
Nanzhao xian	南召縣	Nanzhao County
Wangshan qu	亡山區	Wangshan District
Xinmi qu	新密區	Xinmi District
Yanshi shi	偃師市	Yanshi City
Yucheng xian	虞城縣	Yucheng County
Zhengzhou shi	鄭州市	Zhengzhou City

Localities in Other Provinces

Hebei sheng Yixian xian	河北省易縣縣	Yixian County, Hebei Province
Shaanxi sheng Danfeng xian	陝西省丹風懸	Danfeng County, Shaanxi Province

Phrases

dang fandui douneng zhuanqian	党反對都能賺錢	Whatever the Chinese Communist Party opposes must be profitable.
nan zhu wai nü zhu nei	男住外女住內	Men reside outside; women reside inside.
shangao huangdi yuan	山高皇帝遠	The mountains are high and the Emperor is far away.
shangyou zhengce xiayou duice	上有政策下有對策	Whenever there are policies from the top, the bottom produces counterstrategies.
tingxin liuzhi	停薪留職	Taking a leave of absence from state employment.
wuben wanli	無本萬利	Earning 10,000 in interest without a principal investment.
xiaoe, gaoxiao, kuaisu	小額，高校，快速	Small (loans) in a highly efficient and timely manner.

Index

A *t*, *f*, or *n* following a page number indicates the reference may be found in a table, figure, or note respectively.

Agricultural Bank of China (ABOC), 29, 93, 99, 142
  interest rates of, 162
  loan application process, 69–70
  loans to collective enterprises, 75, 100
  loans to private entrepreneurs, 163, 184
  and RCCs/RCFs, 152–54
  reform of, 100, 207–8
Agricultural Development Bank (ADB)
  microfinance programs of, 200
  policy loans, 100, 207–8
  poverty alleviation loans, 100
  and RCCs, 207
  separation from ABOC, 207–8
Agriculture
  credit facilities (*see* Agricultural Bank of China; Rural Credit Cooperatives; Rural Cooperative Foundations)
  decollectivization of, 13n, 16, 44, 114, 173, 186, 255
  See also Ministry of Agriculture
Anxi County, 99–101
  banking in, 100
  collective sector in, 61, 99–100, 119
  employment in, 41t, 102f
  foreign investment in, 99
  and gender, 101

  governmental attitude toward private sector, 103t
  lack of informal finance in, 107
  and poverty alleviation loans, 100–101
  private sector in, 101–3f
  RCCs and RCFs in, 100
  sexual division of labor in, 101
Asian financial crisis, 21, 208, 242

Bangladesh
  BRAC, 235
  informal finance in, 221t
  See also Grameen Bank
Bank Raykyat Indonesia (BRI). *See* Indonesia
Banking system. *See* Financial system
Banque Nationale de Devéloppement Agricole of Mali (BNDA), 242
Blecher, Marc, 9n, 12n, 250n, 252n
Bolivia
  BancoSol, 235
  embezzlement of poverty alleviation loans in, 234
  informal finance in, 221t
Bourdieu, Pierre, 20n, 36n, 259n
Brokering, 39, 127, 155t
  legality of, 35, 37t
  See also Moneylenders

307